Palgrave Politics of Identity and Citizenship Series

Series Editors: **Varun Uberoi,** Brunel University, UK; Nasar Meer, University of Northumbria, UK and Tariq Modood, University of Bristol, UK

The politics of identity and citizenship has assumed increasing importance as our polities have become significantly more culturally, ethnically and religiously diverse. Different types of scholars, including philosophers, sociologists, political scientists and historians make contributions to this field and this series showcases a variety of innovative contributions to it. Focusing on a range of different countries, and utilizing the insights of different disciplines, the series helps to illuminate an increasingly controversial area of research and titles in it will be of interest to a number of audiences including scholars, students and other interested individuals.

Titles include:

Tariq Modood and John Salt (*editors*)
GLOBAL MIGRATION, ETHNICITY AND BRITISHNESS

Nasar Meer
CITIZENSHIP, IDENTITY AND THE POLITICS OF MULTICULTURALISM
The Rise of Muslim Consciousness

Ganesh Nathan
SOCIAL FREEDOM IN A MULTICULTURAL STATE
Towards a Theory of Intercultural Justice

Therese O'Toole and Richard Gale
POLITICAL ENGAGEMENT AMONGST ETHNIC MINORITY YOUNG PEOPLE
Making a Difference

Momin Rahman
HOMOSEXUALITIES, MUSLIM CULTURES AND IDENTITIES

Michel Seymour (*editor*)
THE PLURAL STATES OF RECOGNITION

Katherine Smith
FAIRNESS, CLASS AND BELONGING IN CONTEMPORARY ENGLAND

Paul Thomas
YOUTH, MULTICULTURALISM AND COMMUNITY COHESION

Milton Vickerman
THE PROBLEM OF POST-RACIALISM

Eve Hepburn and Ricard Zapata-Barrero
THE POLITICS OF IMMIGRATION IN MULTI-LEVEL STATES
Governance and Political Parties

Palgrave Politics of Identity and Citizenship Series
Series Standing Order ISBN 978–0–230–24901–1 (Hardback)

(*outside North America only*)

You can receive future titles in this series as they are published by placing a standing order. Please contact your bookseller or, in case of difficulty, write to us at the address below with your name and address, the title of the series and the ISBN quoted above.

Customer Services Department, Macmillan Distribution Ltd, Houndmills, Basingstoke, Hampshire RG21 6XS, England

The Politics of Immigration in Multi-Level States

Governance and Political Parties

Edited by

Eve Hepburn
School of Social and Political Sciences, University of Edinburgh, UK

and

Ricard Zapata-Barrero
Department of Political Sciences, Pompeu Fabra University, Spain

First published 2014 by
PALGRAVE MACMILLAN

Palgrave Macmillan in the UK is an imprint of Macmillan Publishers Limited, registered in England, company number 785998, of Houndmills, Basingstoke, Hampshire RG21 6XS.

Palgrave Macmillan in the US is a division of St Martin's Press LLC, 175 Fifth Avenue, New York, NY 10010.

Palgrave Macmillan is the global academic imprint of the above companies and has companies and representatives throughout the world.

Palgrave® and Macmillan® are registered trademarks in the United States, the United Kingdom, Europe and other countries

ISBN: 978–1–137–35852–3

This book is printed on paper suitable for recycling and made from fully managed and sustained forest sources. Logging, pulping and manufacturing processes are expected to conform to the environmental regulations of the country of origin.

A catalogue record for this book is available from the British Library.

A catalog record for this book is available from the Library of Congress.

Contents

List of Figures

List of Tables

Preface and Acknowledgements

This edited volume was originally conceived in April 2010 when we were invited to a workshop organized by Alain-G. Gagnon and Michael Keating at the Universidad Carlos III in Madrid, Spain, titled 'Autonomy: Imagining Democratic Alternatives in Complex Settings'. From the beginning, we realized that we had common research concerns on multi-level states, but our disciplinary backgrounds were quite diverse. While Hepburn's specialization was in comparative territorial politics, with a book then in press (*New Challenges for Stateless Nationalist and Regionalist Parties*, 2011), Zapata-Barrero pursued a trajectory on immigration research, shortly to result in his book *Immigration and Self-Government of Minority Nations* (2012). Yet this was to be one of the strengths of the project: by bringing together our perspectives in an interdisciplinary effort, we hoped in this way we could add value to the current debates on immigration and territorial politics in multilevel states.

Thanks to the economic support of the Institut Ramon Llull of the Catalan Government, Zapata-Barrero was able to travel to the Institute of Governance at the University of Edinburgh in June 2010 to meet with Hepburn to sculpt a research project from something akin to an untarnished rock. This was the initial driving force of this book. In Edinburgh, we drew up an initial structure and strategy for the research, which has been carried through to the present volume. The original idea was always to develop a book with two different but complementary parts: one on Governance and another on Political Parties, in order to bring together the 'structure' and 'agency' aspects of the dynamics of immigration politics in multilevel states. To meet this goal, we developed proposals for two workshops – one on each theme – to which we invited leading scholars from around the world working on these issues, and we also envisaged a third conference that would gather all of the selected contributors for a final discussion of our research findings.

The first panel entitled 'Immigration and Multilevel Governance: politics and society' was held at the International Conference of the Council for European Studies on 20–22 June 2011 in Barcelona (Catalonia, Spain). The second one entitled 'Immigration and Multilevel Party Politics' was held at the European Consortium for Political Research (ECPR) General Conference on 25–27 August 2011 in Reykjavik, Iceland. At this stage, we and the contributors worked on revising the papers in anticipation of collecting all of our findings at a fully funded conference entitled 'The New European Agenda: Regions, Multilevel Governance and Immigrant Integration' which was held at the University of Edinburgh in June 2012. This meeting was generously funded by the Jean Monnet Centre for Excellence at the Europa Institute, University of Edinburgh. The conference brought together all of the participants in the project, where they presented revised versions of their papers and received feedback and comments from the group, with a view to developing the final book. With good fortune smiling on us, in attendance at this conference was Nasar Meer, Co-Editor of the *Politics of Identity and Citizenship* series at Palgrave Macmillan, who gave us the initial necessary motivation to submit the book project. We are very grateful to him and his colleagues at Palgrave for allowing us to reach a happy conclusion to this research journey. The final stages of the book were aided by a grant from the Carnegie Trust for the Universities of Scotland, which enabled Hepburn to work on the final manuscript while undertaking research at the European University Institute in Florence.

Of course this journey has its own long list of anecdotes. Seeing the path of this book project in hindsight, nothing can compete with the dire consequences of the volcanic eruption of the unpronounceable Eyjafjallajökull in Iceland, whose ashes caused enormous disruption to air travel across western and northern Europe during one week in April 2010 when Hepburn and Zapata-Barrero first met in Madrid. Three months pregnant, Hepburn was one of the lucky Britons 'rescued' from Spain by a naval battleship sent by the UK government to assist its patriots stranded abroad. She spent three days on board the gunboat with 200 civilians and 600 sailors and soldiers just returned from Afghanistan – an experience she will never forget. Zapata-Barrero meanwhile still remembers pursuing the pregnant Hepburn through the European geography to reach his home from Montreal, Canada, where he travelled just after Madrid to attend the Seventeenth International Conference of Europeanists, Council for European Studies (April 15–17, 2010), and where he was also marooned for several days. Thankfully we both made it home and were able to take up this project with renewed vigour, enervated by the volcanic energy blessing the conception of this book project.

Eve Hepburn and Ricard Zapata-Barrero

Notes on Contributors

Ilke Adam is a senior researcher at the Institute for European Studies, Vrije Universiteit Brussel, Belgium.

Jean-Thomas Arrighi de Casanova is a postdoctoral researcher at the European University Institute, Florence, Italy.

Fiona Barker is Lecturer in the School of History Philosophy Political Science and International Relations, Victoria University, Wellington, New Zealand.

Francesca Campomori is a research fellow in the Department of Philosophy, Università Ca' Foscari, Venezia, Italy.

Tiziana Caponio is a research fellow in the Department of Political Studies, Università di Torino, Italy.

Régis Dandoy is a researcher at Cevipol (Centre for the Study of Politics), Université Libre de Bruxelles, Belgium.

Jan Erk is Associate Professor in Comparative Politics, Faculty of Social Science, Universiteit Leiden, The Netherlands.

Núria Franco-Guillén is a doctoral researcher in the Department of Political and Social Sciences, Universitat Pompeu Fabra (Barcelona, Catalonia, Spain) and GRITIM-UPF (Interdisciplinary Research Group on Immigration)

Eve Hepburn is Senior Lecturer in Politics and Depute Director of the Academy of Government, School of Social and Political Science, University of Edinburgh, UK.

Raffaele Iacovino is Assistant Professor in the Department of Political Science, Carleton University, Ottawa, Canada.

Dirk Jacobs is Professor in Sociology and Political Science at the Institute of Sociology, Université Libre de Bruxelles, Belgium.

Michael Rosie is Senior Lecturer in Sociology, School of Social and Political Science, University of Edinburgh, UK.

Oliver Schmidtke is Professor in the Departments of History and Political Science and a Jean Monnet Chair in European History and Politics, University of Victoria, Canada.

Peter Scholten is Associate Professor of Public Policy & Politics at the Erasmus Universiteit Rotterdam, The Netherlands.

Ricard Zapata-Barrero is Professor of Political Science at Universitat Pompeu Fabra (Barcelona, Catalonia, Spain), and Director of GRITIM-UPF (Interdisciplinary Research Group on Immigration)

Andrej Zaslove is Assistant Professor of Comparative Politics, Political Science, Radboud Universiteit Nijmegen, The Netherlands.

List of Abbreviations

ADQ	Action Démocratique du Québec (Democratic Action of Quebec)
AN	Alleanza Nazionale (National Alliance)
BBC	British Broadcasting Corporation
BNP	British National Party
CDH	Centre Démocratie Humaniste (Humanist Democratic Centre)
CDU	Christlich Demokratische Union (Christian Democratic Union)
CD&V	Christen-Democratisch & Vlaams (Christian Democratic & Flemish)
CEE	Central and Eastern Europe
CEOOR	Centre for Equal Opportunities and Opposition to Racism
CiU	Convergència i Unió (Convergence and Union)
CMP	Comparative Manifesto Project
COSLA	Convention of Scottish Local Authorities
CSU	Christlich-Soziale Union (Christian Social Union)
CVOA	Canadian Visa Officers Abroad
DC	Democrazia Cristiana (Christian Democracy)
DP	Democratic Party
EC	European Community
E-R	Emilia-Romagna
ERC	Esquerra Republicana de Catalunya (Republican Left of Catalonia)
EREC	Enfield Racial Equality Council
EU	European Union
FCC	French Community Commission of the Brussels-Capital Region
FDF	Fédéralistes Démocrates Francophones (Francophone Democratic Federalists)
FDP	Freie Demokratische Partei (Free Democratic Party)
FI	Forza Italia
FN	Front National (National Front)
FPTP	first-past-the-post
FTwiss	Fresh Talent: Working in Scotland Scheme

GLA	Greater London Authority
ICV	Iniciativa per Catalunya Verds (Initiative for Catalonia Greens)
LN	Lega Nord (Northern League)
MAC	Migration Advisory Committee
MIPEX	Migration Policy Index
MLG	multilevel governance
MP	member of parliament
MPG	Migration Policy Group
MSP	Member of the Scottish Parliament
MV	Mouvement Réformateur (Reformist Movement)
NGO	nongovernmental organization
NRW	North Rhine Westphalia
NV-A	Nieuw-Vlaamse Alliantie (New Flemish Alliance)
OECD	Organisation for Economic Cooperation and Development
PDL	People of Freedom
PLQ	Parti libéral du Québec (Quebec Liberal Party)
PM	prime minister
PNI	National Pact for Immigration
PNP	Provincial Nominees Program
PP	Partido Popular (Spain) (People's Party)
PP	Parti Populaire (Belgium) (People's Party)
PQ	Parti Québécois (Quebec's Party)
PR	proportional
PS	Parti Socialiste (Socialist Party)
PSC	Partit dels Socialistes del Catalunya (Catalan Socialist Party)
PT	provincial territory
REP	Republikaner (Republicans)
RW	Rassemblement Wallon (Walloon Rally)
SME	small and medium-sized enterprise
SNP	Scottish National Party
SNRP	stateless nationalist and regionalist party
SOC	Employment Services of Catalonia
SP.A	Socialistische Partij Anders (Flemish Socialist Party)
SPD	Sozialdemokratische Partei Deutschlands (German Social Democratic Party)
SPF	Social Policy Fund
UK	United Kingdom
UKBA	United Kingdom Border Agency
UKIP	United Kingdom Independence Party

USA   United States of America
VB   Vlaams Blok/Belang (Flemish Block/Interest)
VLD   Vlaamse Liberalen en Democraten (Flemish Liberals and
       Democrats)
VU   Volksunie (People's Union)

Part I
Conceptual Framework

1
Introduction: Immigration Policies in Multilevel States

Eve Hepburn and Ricard Zapata-Barrero

The context and academic debate

Immigration has become one of the most contested issues in advanced democracies. Blamed for threatening national cultures and disrupting social cohesion, immigration has also been identified as the only way to mitigate the pending demographic crises of Western states. Yet despite these demographic arguments, there are few issues that have aroused the concern of electorates more than the prospect of rapid social change resulting from migration. This issue has become increasingly apparent in light of the Arab Spring, which has prompted new population movements. A survey on public attitudes towards migration in six European states revealed that a significant share of citizens is apprehensive about immigration, often perceiving it as a threat to employment, public order, and safety (Diamanti and Bordignon, 2005). We also believe that there are difficulties in tracing a clear dividing line between the social and political rhetoric of these perceptions (Zapata-Barrero and Díez-Nicolas, 2012). This edited book corroborates a number of studies highlighting the potentially destabilizing effects of immigration on the politics and societies of host states (Messina, 2002).

Immigration-related issues have risen to the top of the public policy agenda of the European Union (EU) and its member states (Messina and Thouez, 2002), resulting in a widespread tightening of illegal immigration controls (Coleman, 2002: 47). In response to such concerns, many countries have seen a public and media backlash against increasing immigration, the emergence of grassroots anti-immigrant protests (Della Porta, 1996; Gómez-Reino, 2002: 132; Tyler and Marciniak, 2013), the rise of radical-right anti-immigrant parties in statewide elections (Zaslove, 2004; Mudde, 2007), and the need to build a new

European discourse on tolerance (Zapata-Barrero and Triandafyllidou, 2012).

However, in federal and devolved multilevel systems, immigration is not only an important issue at the *state* level; it has also become a key concern for *sub-state* political units (Zapata-Barrero, 2009; Joppke and Seidle, 2012). With the decentralization of powers to sub-state levels of government, regional assemblies have been empowered with control over large sections of social and economic policy, including health, education, housing, culture, the environment, planning, and economic development (Keating, 2001; Marks et al, 2008). And although immigration policy generally falls under the rubric of central-state control, being governed by the state's citizenship rules and requirements, certain aspects of migration policy have devolved to the sub-state level[1] – most notably, migrant integration policies but also in some cases control over admissions/selection, such as in Quebec. The primary reason why regions have been steadily gaining powers over migration is because many sub-state policy areas 'overlap' with issues of migration, which affects regional demographic growth, the labour market, economic development, and the delivery of public services (such as schooling, health and social care, and housing). As such, some sub-state territories are seeking, and being granted, more control over migration issues (Joppke and Seidle, 2012). The decentralization of such a key policy area is also indicative of a general trend towards the 'decentralization' of states in Europe, which acknowledges that sub-state territories are important political, social, and economic communities for citizens – including migrants (Keating, 2001; Hepburn, 2010a).

Furthermore, the impact of immigration on sub-state societies, public services, and economies has necessitated a response from sub-state political actors. And, as in other policy areas, sub-state governments and parties may adopt quite distinctive policies on migration, which may diverge from, or even contradict, those of the state. While some sub-state territories may seek to distinguish themselves from a 'restrictive' state by proposing a more progressive approach to migration, others may criticize the state for advocating an open-door policy of migration by proposing more restrictive measures at the sub-state regional level (Hepburn, 2011). This may become an especially contentious issue in cases where sub-state territories are seeking to pursue greater autonomy and must identify what is 'distinct' about their culture, and demarcate who belongs to the sub-state community (and equally, who does not) (Banting and Soroka, 2012; Barker, 2012). Often, these sub-state political approaches to immigration conflict directly with central-state (national) models, resulting in tensions over policy coordination and the framing of immigration in different parts of a country.

As immigration has become 'rescaled' across several levels of multi-level states, there is an urgent need to develop a deeper understanding of how immigration is governed and framed by political actors across different territorial levels, and to explore the degree of cooperation and contestation between these levels. Immigration has rarely been examined from a multilevel perspective, including the sub-state/devolved view. The vast majority of works on immigration focus on the state level, and more recently on the European level. Yet, it is precisely at this sub-state territorial level that migrants seek full participation in the social, economic, and cultural life of a host community. Sub-state territories now hold substantial power over the rights of citizenship – social, cultural, economic, and political – and control over institutions that provide access to participation and belonging. This has important implications for migrant integration. As a representative of the EU Committee of the Regions (CoR) recently argued, 'regional authorities play a decisive role in creating the right conditions for third-country nationals to access a whole range of public services, including above all education, healthcare, employment and housing. Cities and regions are the linchpins that enables immigrants to develop a strong and constructive connection with the host society, developing a climate of trust and maintaining social cohesion' (CoR Press Release, 15 February 2012). The importance of sub-state territorial policy on migration is therefore becoming increasingly recognized.

Yet scholarship on the territorial rescaling of immigration politics and policy across federal and devolved states is hampered by the fact that multilevel politics tend to be understood as an exclusively EU-state relationship. Certainly, the multilevel governance approach evolved from the study of governmental interaction in the European Union. Gary Marks (1993) was one of the first scholars to describe the interactions of governments in the EU context as resulting in multilevel governance. Marks and Hooghe (2001) furthermore presented different types of multilevel governance at the EU level and focused their analysis on the EU-state relationship. But since this elaboration of multilevel governance, there have been far fewer examinations of this multilevel perspective at the state/sub-state political level (for some exceptions, see Hepburn, 2010a; Detterbeck, 2012) nor has it ever been examined with regard to the specific area of immigration, which is clearly a cross-cutting policy issue that affects both levels (see the seminal comparative work by Joppke and Seidle, 2012).

The purposes of the book

The aim of this edited book is therefore to tackle the topical issue of immigration from a widely neglected multilevel perspective that incorporates the analysis of state/sub-state approaches to, and coordination of, immigration policy and politics. The book addresses the complex politics of immigration in states of a federal or devolved nature where immigration, and especially migrant integration, have become 'overlapping' policies between central-state and sub-state levels. It also considers the effects and consequences of the 'territorial rescaling' of immigration in multilevel political frameworks, seeking to identify the challenges and opportunities for the emergence of different immigration approaches following decentralization. These challenges and opportunities include issues of how migrant integration policy diverges across different regions of a state; intergovernmental relations and coordination between states and sub-state territories on immigration policy; the regionally differentiated economic dimensions of the multilevel integration of immigrants; and the possible tensions arising from migration to a region that considers itself a stateless nation or linguistic minority group.

In order to understand the differences between state and sub-state approaches to immigration, an important part of this analysis is to examine immigration through the prism of 'territorial interests' that dominate the regional level. These territorial interests may be cultural, economic, or political in nature; and immigration affects them all.

With regard to cultural territorial interests, there is a rich body of literature detailing the distinctiveness of regional identities, cultures, and languages within states. For instance, within the EU's 27 member states, there are 74 sub-state territories with legislative powers and over 100 more regions with administrative powers (AER, 2009). These sub-state territories provide important spaces for social and political attitudes, behaviour, cultures, and identities (Keating, 1996; Henderson, 2010; Hepburn, 2010b). Many of these sub-state territories make claim to a distinctive local culture and traditions that have evolved separately from state-building processes. These include, for instance, the 'Celtic' traditions of Galicia in Spain and the 'Alpine' traditions of Bavaria in Germany. Sub-state territories also often boast a particular religious concentration, such as the predominance of Catholicism in North-Rhein Westphalia or Presbyterianism in Scotland. Finally, some sub-state territories also speak their own language instead of the central-state language. In addition to the 23 official languages of the EU, there are over 65 more that are spoken at the sub-state level; some of which have been included in the European Charter for Regional and Minority Languages (CoE, 1992) and many others that have no official recognition at all (Hornsby and Agarin, 2012). These languages provide an important lens through which citizens understand and make sense of the world, and many efforts have been made to prevent their extinction. These culturally distinctive characteristics of regions mean that migrants are often presented with a challenge when moving to a particular sub-state territory: integrating into the culture and learning the language is often more important for their participation in social, political, and economic life than adopting the culture/language of the state. In particular, some sub-state languages may be perceived as more 'difficult' to learn than state languages (i.e., Basque and Welsh) while other sub-state territories place an emphasis on learning an accent or dialect as a sign of belonging.

Yet one of the greatest fears of sub-state territories with a strong linguistic identity is the possibility that immigration erodes that linguistic identity (Erk, 2003). As Zapata-Barrero (2007: 12) argues, 'if the minority community does not have sufficient competencies in the matter, the tendency of the immigrants who settle in the national territory is to integrate into the dominant culture...if immigrants become integrated into the dominant culture, then the minority nation may become a minority within its own territory'. So immigration raises concerns for the protection of minority languages in sub-state regions and nations, as immigrants often adopt the language of the majority as the best route for social mobility, which subsequently reduces the sub-state population speaking a minority language. As a result, sub-state political actors may view immigration as a threat to their identity, language, customs, traditions, or ways of life. In some cases this has directly led to the rise of anti-immigrant nationalist parties in sub-state territories that have won a large share of the vote (on the Belgian case, see Adam and Jacobs, Erk, and Dandoy in this volume; and for the Spanish case, see the contribution by Franco-Guillén and Zapata-Barrero).

Second, with regard to economic territorial interests, a wealth of scholarly studies has emerged on the issues of regional economic development and regional economic policy (see Storper, 1995; Piore and Sabel, 1984). Sub-state territories are not only viewed as distinctive economic systems and labour markets; they are also seen as autonomous economic actors with devolved economic powers. Economic regionalization means that immigrants must be attuned to the needs of the sub-state economy and labour market when they arrive in their host community (on the German and Italian cases in particular, see Schmidtke and Zaslove's contribution in this volume). For instance, some sub-state economies are dominated by the tourism industry, others by the services industry, and others by high-tech manufacturing, which may be different from other parts of the country (Storper, 1995). And while some sub-state territories may be performing better in economic terms than the state average, others may be doing poorly (for an examination of regional economic inequality and immigration in the Italian case, see Campomori and Caponio's chapter). In response, sub-state governments and parties may seek to protect traditional modes of economic development within the sub-state territory (such as an emphasis on small and medium-sized businesses), demanding that the territory requires certain labour-market skills from immigrants in order to maintain the specific territorial mode of economic development (on how this has been encouraged at the local municipal/city level, see Scholten's analysis of the United Kingdom and the Netherlands).

Third, with regard to political territorial interests, there may exist demands for autonomy and/or independence within the regional and/ or statewide party system, which are affected by immigration. Recent studies show that party systems and party competition at the regional level are becoming increasingly distinctive from the state level, whereby statewide parties must operate in a peculiarly regional context and compete on regional issues (Hough and Jeffery, 2006). In response to decentralization, political parties in federal and devolved states have strengthened their sub-state organizational structures and programmes (Detterbeck and Hepburn, 2010). The decentralization of political parties has enabled party branches operating at the sub-state level to diverge in their policy agendas from their statewide 'parent' parties. This 'sub-state dimension' acquires particular salience in cases where stateless nationalist and regionalist parties (SNRPs) exist whose constitutional goals have won formidable electoral support (Hepburn, 2009b). If immigration becomes a key concern of SNRPs in their development of a nation-building project, then it must also become a concern of sub-state branches of statewide parties in order to represent regional interests. This dynamic means that party competition over issues such as immigration at the sub-state level may be entirely distinctive from party competition at the statewide level. For instance, party competition may be highly polarized on immigration if it is seen to threaten the culture or language of the region (see Erk's chapter on the situation in Flanders). Yet party competition may also be consensually in favour of immigration if this is seen as a way to bolster the region's demography and economic growth (see the chapters by Hepburn and Rosie on Scotland; and Franco-Guillén and Zapata-Barrero on Catalonia).

Immigration therefore affects the autonomy/independence of sub-state territories in several ways. Demographically, the sub-state territory in question may be experiencing low demographic growth, and increasing the population through immigration may make the territory more 'viable' as a self-determined political unit (see Arrighi de Casanova's contribution on Scotland). Conversely, demands for self-determination may be based on the existence of a distinct history, culture or language, and immigration may be perceived as threatening this claim (unless immigrants are fully integrated into the culture/language of the region – see Iacovino's chapter on the Quebec case). As Bauböck (2001: 333) maintains, 'if a national linguistic minority were to become a minority in its own province through intermarriage, the immigration of other groups, or the emigration of its own members, this demographic shift would undermine its power to claim regional autonomy and special representation at the federal level.' Clearly, there are several ways in which immigration may intersect with the 'territorial' dimension of party competition in multilevel states.

Themed issues: *Governance and Political Parties*

In order to tackle the ways in which territorial interests intersect with immigration in multilevel states, this book addresses two principle themes. The first theme focuses on the *governance of immigration* in multilevel states, especially in countries with a federal, devolved, or multinational character. Following the framework of R. Dahl's *Who Governs?* (1961), we assume that there are unresolved tensions between 'who does' (implementation) and 'who decides' (decision-making process) in immigration governance. This tension invites us to follow a conflict-oriented perspective (for example, between administrations or how each administration resolves conflicts related to immigration). This perspective connects the dimensions of social dynamics, policy responses, and legal frameworks. This discussion revolves around external and internal dimensions of governance institutions – an analytical distinction that is made from the perspective of the sub-state unit (be it a region, state-less nation, or other form of sub-state administrative unit). To elaborate, the 'external dimension' addresses the main issues arising from the relationship between the sub-state units and the central-state. The 'internal dimension', on the other hand, addresses issues that arise from the relationship between the national units and societal culture. These dimensions are explored from three perspectives: (1) (policy) competencies, (2) power relationships and intergovernmental relationships, and

(3) effects of the management of diversity. The 'Governance' section of the book therefore focuses on the impact of multilevel governance on immigration policies, and vice versa, the impact of immigration policies on multilevel governance more broadly.

A second, equally important, theme of the book is to understand the response of political parties to the question of immigration, especially at the overlooked sub-state level. This level has so far been almost absent in the field of immigration studies, which has tended to focus on the nation-state or supranational level. However, this level is crucial in understanding immigration, because sub-state territories have become increasingly responsible for designing policies of migrant integration. At this sub-state territorial level, quite distinct party systems can often be detected, which do not follow the logic of statewide politics (Hough and Jeffery, 2006). In particular, in sub-state territories with claims to a distinct identity (be it cultural, historical, economic, or linguistic) party competition is often influenced by a territorial or linguistic cleavage that is often absent from competition at the state level (Keating, 1996; Hepburn, 2009b). This territorial/linguistic cleavage interacts with the issue of immigration in peculiar ways. While some parties may perceive immigration as threatening the identity or language of their own territory, others may view immigration as a way to boost the membership vis-à-vis the state in their claims for self-determination (Erk, 2003; Bauböck, 2001; Kymlicka and Patten, 2003; Hepburn, 2009a). In any case, immigration has become an important focus of political parties at the sub-state level – including stateless nationalist and regionalist parties (SNRPs) and regional branches of statewide parties – whose responses have been informed by strong 'territorial interests', as described above.

The distinctive approach to immigration evident in sub-state territories is further exacerbated if the unit in question also considers itself to form a 'nation' with a claim to special treatment. In this case, sub-state elites may be preoccupied with promoting a distinctive nation-building project and conception of citizenship that diverges from the state. Sub-state political actors may prefer to set their own terms for territorial membership and migrant integration within the contours of the nation-building project, whose terms may be more open *or* more restrictive than those decreed at the state level, and which may cause tensions with central statewide party offices. For SNRPs in particular, this may lead to demands to wrest control over immigration policy from the central government in order to develop a distinct approach that reflects the specific needs and interests of the sub-state territorial community.

This twofold approach to studying both the governance and the party politics of immigration allows us to examine not only how, and by whom, immigration policy is decided and implemented at multiple territorial levels, but also how it has become an important dimension of party competition in multilevel states. The analysis of state/sub-state coordination and conflict over immigration has become increasingly important due to the growing responsibilities that sub-state territories have been given in the field of immigration (especially integration policies). But until now, scholarship on state/sub-state immigration has been very much lacking in this area. As Zaslove (2006) argues, immigration is a cross-cleavage issue in left-right terms, posing challenges for traditional parties. Yet in multilevel states, regional-level parties often pursue quite divergent approaches to immigration compared to national parties.

Overview of different contributions

The book is organized thematically. It begins with two 'conceptual' chapters, which together provide a theoretical framework for understanding the governance and party competition dimensions of immigration in multilevel states. The first of these, by Ricard Zapata-Barrero and Fiona Barker, proposes an interpretative framework that can help to map the nexus between multilevel governance and immigration policy. This model has two main dimensions – Structure and Policy. The dimension of 'structure' addresses how powers are organized in terms of the relationship between central and sub-state levels. Zapata-Barrero and Barker introduce three main analytical distinctions: two driving forces (efficiency and national identity), two principles (coordination and coherence), and three scenarios (centralist, cooperative, asymmetric) which are later employed by contributors in the Governance section of the book. Along the policy dimension, they map out tensions that can arise between levels of government with reference to concrete elements of immigration policies, such as admissions, reception, and citizenship. In doing so, they acknowledge the impact that language, as a common marker of national identity, can have in multinational states.

The second conceptual paper, written by Eve Hepburn, develops an analytical framework for the Political Parties section of the book. She explores the dynamics of party competition on the issue of immigration, especially at the sub-state regional level. Immigration has become an important focus of regional political parties which have responded in diverse ways to the challenges and opportunities associated with immigration. The impact of territorial interests – political, economic, and cultural – on the immigration strategies of regional parties encourages them to take distinctive positions from national-level parties. To account for this, Hepburn develops an explanatory framework for understanding the positioning of both sub-state regional *and* statewide political parties on immigration. She presents several hypotheses to account for the immigration stances of regional and statewide parties, and the divergence between the two, by drawing on variables relating to demographics, economics, language, ideology, the electoral system, policy control, and party polarization. These hypotheses are then employed by contributors seeking to empirically examine party positioning on immigration in the Political Parties section of the book.

The book then proceeds in the following manner. The section on Governance comprises five chapters focusing on the institutional aspects of governing immigration in federal, devolved, and multinational states. It focuses on the question 'Who does what', and how the related questions of 'Who decides' and 'Who does' are managed from a theoretical and conflict-based approach. This section includes a mix of case studies (Belgium, Canada, Italy, Spain, the UK and the Netherlands) and different methodological perspectives on multilevel governance. It also considers broader governance themes including the impact of European integration on migration policy; obstacles in the management of diversity and societal integration; the link between citizenship and integration; and the relationship between security and migration.

The first chapter in the Governance section, written by Ilke Adam and Dirk Jacobs, explores immigration and migrant integration policy-making in the centrifugal multilevel context of Belgium. The authors show that while immigration and citizenship policy is still a prerogative of the central-state, legislative *and* executive power over migrant integration have been devolved to the sub-state regions since 1980. Moreover, immigration politics and policy-making at the central-state level must be situated in the context of a regionalized party system and the absence of statewide parties. In their findings, the authors show that regional policy responses on migrant integration, as well as Flemish and Francophone political party positioning on the central-state's immigration and citizenship policy, largely diverge. The authors explain these differences by pointing at divergent party dynamics and sub-state nation-building processes in Flanders and Francophone Belgium.

The next chapter by Raffaele Iacovino focuses on Canada. It examines how immigration policy has shaped two nation-building projects – the Québécois and the Canadian – which compete in their affirmation as primary host societies and national identities. This competition, which is also marked by interdependence, has led Quebec and the federal government to carve out a shared governance framework that that has remained in place for around 20 years. Yet, in recent years Canada has introduced a considerable degree of decentralization in both admissions and reception policy to other parts of the country, incrementally extending and signing a patchwork of bilateral agreements with all of the other provinces/territories. As such, Canada's immigration regime can be characterized as one of variable decentralization grounded on two primary justificatory schemes (efficiencies/functional vs. national identity/autonomy). While these separate and sometimes conflicting logics operate simultaneously, the nature and scope of asymmetry emerges in the variance associated with the federal government's capacity as a steering agent vis-à-vis the provinces, which is much more circumscribed in Quebec.

Examining two other cases of multinational states, Jean-Thomas Arrighi de Casanova explores the relationship between minority nationalism and migration in Spain and the UK. Addressing the question of 'who governs', he compares how the Catalan and Scottish governments have sought to gain greater control over the regulation of aliens' entry into their own jurisdictions between 1999 and 2011. His findings show that their demands have remained largely unfulfilled as the UK and Spanish central administrations have proved equally reluctant to share their prerogatives in a matter that they view as closely associated with their sovereignty. However, while the sub-state governments may have failed to gain administrative or legislative control over admissions policy, their success in criticizing the central-state's immigration regime could also be interpreted as a political victory.

Francesca Campomori and Tiziana Caponio then focus our attention on migrant integration in the highly regionally diverse system of multi-level governance in Italy. They compare migrant integration policies in sub-state regions that represent the so-called three (political and social) 'Italies' – Veneto in the North, Emilia-Romagna in the Centre-North, and Calabria in the South – which are differentiated by two cleavages: the North/South cleavage and the Red/White political culture cleavage. In order to understand what policy control the regions actually exert, Campomori and Caponio consider two dimensions: the framing of immigrants and immigration and the implementation structures. From their analysis, the authors reveal a fascinating and complex patchwork of centre-periphery/state-society relations, characterized by high levels of fragmentation and divergence in regional policies, which clearly contradicts the principle of coherence that is supposed to inspire the multilevel governance of immigration in multilevel settings.

Peter Scholten brings up the rear of the Governance section by examining multilevel governance as a relevant phenomenon also in unitary states. As he argues, local governments, especially large cities, often do much more than implement national policies in a top-down manner in unitary states. Instead, they often play a key role in the formulation of their own policies while also influencing national policies. Scholten tests this hypothesis in two (decentralized) unitary states – the Netherlands and the UK – examining cases of migrant integration policies in four cities within these states: Amsterdam and Rotterdam in the Netherlands and London and Glasgow in the UK. The diverse approaches to integration found at the local level provide significant challenges in terms of the effective multilevel governance of migrant integration and for adopting effective policy strategies.

In the next section on Political Parties, the focus turns from structure to the 'agents' of immigration policy. In other words, the role of political actors in framing and mobilizing immigration issues in multilevel states, and the distinct dynamics of party competition on issues of immigration at different territorial levels. The five chapters in this section offer several case studies on the party politics of immigration in multilevel states (Belgium, Canada, Germany, Italy, Spain, and the UK respectively). The authors explore several themes relating to the politics of immigration, including the impact of the electoral system on substate party competition over immigration, ideological convergence and the 'ownership' of immigration policies, and the influence of regional political cultures on party positioning.

Opening the Political Parties section, Oliver Schmidtke and Andrej Zaslove argue that migration and integration are at the centre of competitive party politics in Europe. But while this development is predominantly described in terms of national contexts, it is not yet clear whether regional party politics are vulnerable to similar dynamics that exist at the national (state) level, in particular with respect to the exploitation of anti-immigrant sentiments. In response to this, Schmidtke and Zaslove examine whether there is a different logic at play in politicizing migration-related issues at the national-state and sub-state regional levels. They focus on four regions in Germany and Italy that are characterized by opposing traditional political identities: North Rhine Westphalia and Emilia-Romagna, which both share a legacy of social-democratic or communist rule, and Bavaria and Lombardy with a tradition of conservative dominance. Here they explore how the socioeconomic position and political culture of the region shapes political party responses to immigration.

Régis Dandoy then shifts our focus to regionalism and party competition on immigration in the federal state of Belgium. He argues that scholars of the Belgian case often perceive extreme-right (anti-immigrant) parties as the only 'owners' of the immigration issue. However, with the help of a quantitative and qualitative analysis of party manifestos since 1977, Dandoy demonstrates how the ownership of extreme-right parties on immigration is not as clear-cut as expected. His findings show that regionalist and liberal parties also significantly emphasize immigration. In particular, the position of the regionalist parties on immigration is more a question of ideology than the consequence of party competition (that is, the effects of extreme-right parties on their own positions) and that the issue of immigration is often combined with the parties' main policy interests, that is, decentralization and the linguistic conflict between Flemish and French-speaking parties.

Jan Erk also focuses on Belgium as a multination democracy with a strong sub-state nationalist movement, in a detailed comparison with Canada. He argues that Québec and Flanders are both facing growing immigration, but while the goal of self-rule/independence unites the agendas of the main nationalist parties, there is a clear difference in terms of their positions on immigration. *Parti Québécois* actively courts the immigrant vote and has placed immigrant inclusion at the centre of its party programme, while opposition to immigration is a core part of the programme of *Vlaams Blok/Vlaams Belang*. Erk examines whether the electoral system can explain these different positions, whereby the first-past-the-post system may pressure the Parti Québécois to cast a wide political net to bring in as many immigrant votes as possible, while the proportional electoral system presents no similar political incentives to appeal to the immigrant vote in Flanders.

Eve Hepburn and Michael Rosie then examine the intersection of immigration and nationalism in Scotland. They present a puzzle: while UK parties link immigration to insecurity, crime, and a threat to British national culture, Scottish parties focus on its economic, demographic and social benefits and embrace the discourse of multiculturalism and inclusion. The authors employ four hypotheses to explain this divergence: the demographic needs of low-population Scotland, the perceived low barriers to becoming a member of the Scottish nation, the lack of Scottish control over immigration policy, and the lack of party polarization in a system characterized by a broad liberal consensus on immigration. However, as the authors warn, if Scotland gains control over immigration policy following the independence referendum of 2014, then we may see a rather different, and more polarized, dynamic.

In the final Political Parties chapter, Núria Franco-Guillén and Ricard Zapata-Barrero explore the interaction between minority nationalism and immigration through the examination of SNRP discourses in Catalonia. They develop an analytical framework to explain how elements of nationalism appear in the construction of a discourse on immigration. The framework, which includes a system of categories related to identity (belonging, values and function of language) that is partly based on the distinction between civic and ethnic nationalisms, has the novelty of proposing the transversal inclusion of language across the civic/ethnic distinction. In an analysis of the immigration discourses of the two most relevant SNRPs in Catalonia (Convergència i Unió – CiU and Esquerra Republicana per Catalunya – ERC), the authors argue that a party's stance (positive/negative) towards immigration determines the shape of the nationalist discourse.

In the concluding chapter, Ricard Zapata-Barrero and Eve Hepburn summarize the key issues pertaining to the governance and party politics of immigration in multilevel states. They reflect on the diverse findings of the chapters, and compare and contrast trends in the governance mechanisms and party competition dynamics in the multilevel states analysed. Finally, they develop the first contours of an exploratory theory of the politics of immigration in multilevel states based on the general patterns detected in the book and suggest some pathways for future research.

Note

1. As concepts are not cut in stone, there are different ways to refer to sub-state level in the multilevel governance and comparative territorial politics literature. We have given contributors the freedom to express this conceptual reference without trying to recommend just one 'undisputable' concept, thereby acknowledging that there are different concepts that refer to the same empirical fact, i.e. region, province, autonomous community, sub-state nation, stateless nation. However, in this Introduction we have decided to use the term 'sub-state territory' or 'sub-state level' as the most descriptive (and possibly most neutral) concept.

References

AER (2009) 'Tabula Regionum Europae' (Strasbourg: Assembly of European Regions).

K. Banting and S. Soroka (2012) 'Minority Nationalism and Immigrant Integration in Canada', *Nations and Nationalism*, 18: 156–176.

F. Barker (2012) *Immigration and Contested Nation Building: Explaining the Political Salience of Immigration in Multi-National Societies*. GRITIM Working Paper. Barcelona: Universitat Pompeu Fabra.

R. Bauböck (2001) 'Cultural Citizenship, Minority Rights and Self-Government' in A. Aleinikoff and Doug Klusmeyer (eds) *Citizenship Today: Global Perspectives and Practices*. (Washington, DC: Carnegie Endowment).

CoE (1992) *European Charter for Regional or Minority Languages*. (Strasbourg: Council of Europe).

D. Coleman (2002) 'Mass Migration to Europe: Demographic Salvation or Unwanted Foreigners?' in A. Messina (ed.) *West European Immigration and Immigrant Policy in the New Century*. (Westport CT: Praeger).

R. Dahl (1961) *Who Governs? Democracy and Power in an American City*. (New Haven: Yale University Press).

D. Della Porta (1996) 'Immigration and Protest: New Challenges for Italian Democracy', *South European Society & Politics*, 5(3): 108–132.

K. Detterbeck (2012) *Multi-level Party Politics in Western Europe*. (Basingstoke: Palgrave).

K. Detterbeck and E. Hepburn (2010) 'Party Politics in Multi-level Systems: Party Responses to New Challenges in European Democracies' in W. Swenden and J. Erk (eds) *Exploring New Avenues of Comparative Federalism Research*. (London: Routledge).

A. Diamanti and F. Bordignon (2005) *Immigrazione e cittadinanza in Europe. Orientamenti e attagiamenti dei cittadini europei*. (Urbino: Fondazione Nord-Est).

J. Erk (2003) '"Wat We Zelf Doen, Doen We Beter": Belgian Substate Nationalisms, Congruence and Public Policy', *Journal of Public Policy*, 23(2): 201–224.

M. Gómez-Reino Cachafeiro (2002), *Ethnicity and Nationalism in Italian Politics*. (Aldershot: Ashgate).

A. Henderson (2010) 'Why Regions Matter: Sub-State Polities in Comparative Perspective', *Regional and Federal Studies*, 20(4/5): 441–447.

E. Hepburn (2009a) 'Regionalist Party Mobilisation on Immigration', *West European Politics*, 32(3): 514–535.

E. Hepburn (ed.) (2009b) *New Challenges for Stateless Nationalist and Regionalist Parties*, Special Issue of Regional & Federal Studies, 19(4/5): 477–650.

E. Hepburn (2010a) *Using Europe. Territorial Party Strategies in a Multi-level System*. (Manchester: Manchester University Press).

E. Hepburn (2010b) 'Small Worlds in Canada and Europe', *Regional & Federal Studies*, 20(4/5): 527–544.

E. Hepburn (2011) '"Citizens of the Region": Party Conceptions of Regional Citizenship and Immigrant Integration', *European Journal of Political Research*, 50(4):504–529.

M. Hornsby and T. Agarin (2012) 'The End of Minority Languages? Europe's Regional Languages in Perspective', *Journal on Ethnopolitics and Minority Issues in Europe*, 11(1): 88–116.

D. Hough and C. Jeffery (2006) *Devolution and Electoral Politics: A Comparative Evaluation*. (Manchester: Manchester University Press).

C. Joppke and F.L. Seidle (eds) (2012) *Immigration Integration in Federal Countries*. (Montreal: McGill-Queen's University Press).

M. Keating (1996) *Nations Against the State: The New Politics of Nationalism in Quebec, Catalonia and Scotland*. (London: Macmillan).

M. Keating (2001) *Plurinational Democracy. Stateless Nations in a Post-Sovereignty Era*. (Oxford: Oxford University Press).

W. Kymlicka and A. Patten (2003) *Language Rights and Political Theory*. (Oxford: Oxford University Press).

G. Marks (1993) 'Structural Policy and Multilevel Governance' in A. Cafruny and G. Rosenthal (eds) *The State of the European Community*. (Harlow: Longman).

G. Marks and L. Hooghe (2001) *Multi-Level Governance and European Integration*. (Boulder, CO: Rowman & Littlefield).

G. Marks, L. Hooghe and A. Schakel (eds) (2008) 'Regional Authority in 42 Countries, 1950–2006: A Measure and Five Hypotheses', *Regional & Federal Studies*, 18(2/3): 111–302.

A. Messina (2002) 'Introduction' in A. Messina (ed.) *West European Immigration and Immigrant Policy in the New Century*. (Westport CT: Praeger).

A. Messina and C. Thouez (2002) 'The Logics and Politics of a European Immigration Regime' in A. Messina (ed.) *West European Immigration and Immigrant Policy in the New Century*. (Westport CT: Praeger).

C. Mudde (2007) *Populist Radical Right Parties in Europe*. (Cambridge: Cambridge University Press).

M. Piore and C. Sabel (1984) *The Second Industrial Divide: Possibilities for Prosperity*. (New York: Basic Books Inc).

M. Storper (1995) 'The Resurgence of Regional Economies, 10 Years Later', *European Urban and Regional Studies*, 2(3): 191–221.

I. Tyler and K. Marciniak (eds) (2013) 'Immigrant Protests', special issue in *Citizenship Studies*, 17(2): 143–292.

R. Zapata-Barrero (2007) 'Setting a Research Agenda on the Interaction between Cultural Demands of Immigrants and Minority Nations', *Journal of Immigrant & Refugee Studies*, 5(4): 1–25.

R. Zapata-Barrero (ed.) (2009) *Immigration and Self-government of Minority Nations*. (Brussels: Peter Lang).

R. Zapata-Barrero and J. Díez-Nicolas (2012) 'Islamophobia in Spain?: Political Rhetoric Rather than a Social Fact' in M. Helbling (ed.) *Islamophobia in Western Europe and North America*. (London: Routledge).

R. Zapata-Barrero and A. Triandafyllidou (eds) (2012) *Addressing Tolerance and Diversity Discourses in Europe. A Comparative Overview of 16 European Countries* Barcelona: Fundació CIDOB [Download: http://www.upf.edu/gritim/actualitat/accept_libro.html #.UZDsTbXZZ2A]

A. Zaslove (2004) 'Closing the Door? The Ideology and Impact of Radical Right Populism on Immigration Policy in Austria and Italy', *Journal of Political Ideologies*, 9(1): 99–118.

A. Zaslove (2006) 'The Politics of Immigration: A New Electoral Dilemma for the Right and the Left?', *Review of European and Russian Affairs*, 2(3): 10–36.

2
Multilevel Governance of Immigration in Multinational States: 'Who Governs?' Reconsidered

Ricard Zapata-Barrero and Fiona Barker

Introduction

This chapter constructs a theoretical framework for approaching both the impact of multilevel governance on immigration policies and the impact of immigration policies on multilevel governance. While the question could be applied to almost all federal regimes, we focus on multinational states. Within the emerging debate connecting multilevel governance and immigration policies, we propose a heuristic model; that is, an interpretative framework containing a set of concepts and categories that can help to map the nexus between multilevel governance and immigration policy. This mapping task aims to suggest a research programme that is theoretically grounded and empirically viable. To accomplish its interpretative function, this heuristic model has to meet three main methodological conditions: first, it must be comprehensive enough to encompass the variety of perspectives within this nexus; second, it must be integrative in the sense that it takes into account all of the steps in the governance and policy processes; and third, it should provide a toolkit for empirical comparison.

We take as our starting point the premise of Robert A. Dahl's (1961) *Who Governs?* that there can be a tension in governance between who decides and who does. Dahl's configuration seems to imply a standard view of policy whereby central government decides and then a sub-state unit of government implements. This picture is obviously more complex in a multilevel system where the sub-state unit may equally be involved in deciding, and where the interests (and so the policy preferences) of the sub-state unit and central state may conflict, especially in relation to concepts of national identity, membership, or particular linguistic, cultural or economic interests.

Given this framework of analysis, we address some key foundational questions related to the distribution of competencies, power/intergovernmental relationships, and the management of diversity. How do multilevel systems resolve the question of 'who decides' and 'who does' in the area of immigration, and how much does this vary across multilevel polities? Might we expect immigration policy to function differently in a multilevel governance situation, both in terms of process and outcome? If so, how and why? When there is no clear division of competencies for particular immigration-related policy areas, what are the implications for policy coherence between the levels of government?

Focusing specifically on the case of multinational states, we can further ask: which features distinguish federal states with and without multinational character? How are 'multiple diversities' (Zapata-Barrero, 2013) accommodated; that is, situations where historical national diversity and more recent, immigration-driven diversity coexist? What struggles exist (or could exist) between the central-state and sub-state units in relation to the distribution of power governing immigration, and the resulting policy?

Our heuristic model has two main component dimensions – Structure and Policy – and along each we identify potential tensions in the relationship between sub-state units and central states regarding immigration and integration policies. The dimension of 'structure' addresses how powers are organized in terms of the relationship between central and sub-state levels and the character of governance in multilevel and multinational systems. We cover structural governance issues, and introduce three main analytical distinctions: two driving forces (efficiency and national identity), two principles (coordination and coherence), and three scenarios (centralist, cooperative, asymmetric). Along the second dimension of 'policy', we identify and map out tensions that can arise between levels of government due to the distinctive features of immigration and integration policies, with reference to concrete elements of immigration policies, such as admissions, reception, and citizenship. In doing so, we acknowledge the particular impact that language, as a common marker of national identity, can have on multinational states. The conclusion summarizes the heuristic model and deals with democratic issues both in structure and policy.

Governance structure: mapping a framework of analysis

To map a framework of analysis of the structure of Governance in multilevel and multinational systems, three main questions are identified which follow logically. First, we need to ask how the dynamics of decentralization/centralization function in immigration governance.[1] For instance, not all multilevel and multinational systems have the same allocation of power and responsibilities in immigration issues. It is important to distinguish analytically the different criteria and models followed by different systems.[2] Here we identify two driving forces: efficiency and national identity. Then, there follows a second key question concerned with identifying the factors moderating these driving forces: which principles help fuel these two driving forces? We will identify two main principles, according to two main dimensions: the principle of cooperation (procedural dimension) and the principle of coherence (normative dimension). Building on these two steps we will then identify three potential scenarios for the structure of immigration governance: the centralist, the cooperative, and the asymmetric scenarios.[3] Schematically, the map of the structure of immigration governance that we will follow is represented in Figure 2.1 below.

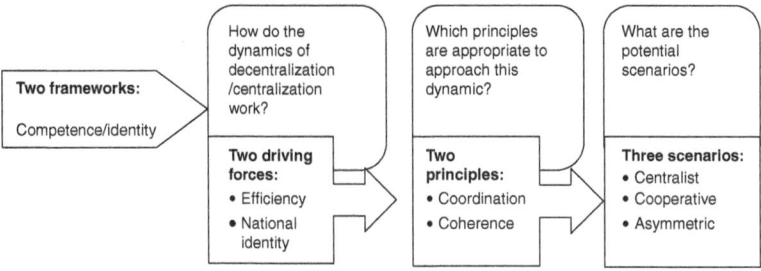

Figure 2.1   Structure of immigration governance in multilevel and multinational systems

The dynamics of centralization and decentralization in immigration governance

One of the main features distinguishing multinational states and federal states without a multinational character is that, apart from issues of competency in understanding how powers are territorialized, there are also identity considerations that mostly involve ethnic, religious, or language-based markers of difference.[4]

The first feature of the heuristic model we propose is grounded in the system of competence needed at each level of government to manage all of the stages in the process of immigration (from admission, reception, and integration to the acquisition of citizenship, as the next section discusses). It concerns how powers related to immigration governance are allocated, and what the limits are in a given territory.[5] The second feature is grounded in the fact that behind each government decision an identity argument may be present, since immigration policies are at least in part identity policies (Zapata-Barrero, 2009).

These two frameworks generate two main criteria that play a driving role in multilevel systems with regard to immigrant governance: efficiency (based mainly on the subsidiarity principle)[6] and national identity (based mainly on self-governance for some subunits).[7] Efficiency and national identity concerns can push in the direction of both decentralization and centralization. They can, for instance, be the basis of an argument for greater centralization based on security and maintenance of the multilevel structure of governance and national sustainability.[8] For those endorsing centralization, state and territorial-based national sustainability will be invoked. However, national sustainability arguments can also be adopted by sub-state units in a multinational state when they argue in favour of decentralization. This accords with the linguistic hypothesis of Erk and Koning (2010) who conclude that decentralization is likely to be more pronounced in heterogeneous linguistic settings than in homogeneous ones. For the purposes of our model, national sustainability arguments underpin the centralization/decentralization logic of governance and immigration policies, although they can be used for different purposes.

We now move to the second step of the framework, which considers which principles feed the driving forces of efficiency and national identity.

Principles underlying decentralization

Two principles arising out of the literature on federalism and multi-level systems are important to consider when examining the particular case of immigration governance – the principle of cooperation and the principle of coherence.[9] To understand the role we need to focus on multilevel relations, both vertical (among different levels of governments, for instance, between the regional and central government), and horizontal (between different governments but at the same level of power, say, between local authorities). Both principles share the fact that there is a common framework for working among units, including a common constitutional framework and minimum rule of law. Without this minimum common framework, multilevel relations could not be possible, and the units could simply be independent. However, as there are different driving forces pushing towards centralization or decentralization, we need to know which principles fuel these forces. This 'working together' means that the different levels of government can work with the same criteria or with different criteria to develop their own policies in different areas of immigration management, according to how they interpret the driving forces of efficiency and national identity.

The first principle – coordination – is procedural in character and emphasizes the fact that some issues related to immigration management are of common interest, such as employment or health services. The second principle – coherence – is normative in character and points to the fact that in the field of immigration different levels of government have different interests as to the kind of linguistic, reception, or education policies they wish to pursue. Different interests might be grounded in identity concerns, but this is not necessarily the case. For instance, given the uneven geographic distribution of immigrants, units may develop different criteria and thus distinct policies in response to their experience of immigration flows.

Coordination means that, as the different units of government have to work together, they must try not to have negative effects among them. The 'golden rule' of this principle is to avoid negative effects of one unit's decisions on others at the same level (horizontal) or at another level (vertical) of government. For instance, sometimes one unit can make a decision to manage integration issues that affects other levels of government, given that immigrants can move from one territorial unit to another. This lack of coordination can be one ground for claiming more self-government – that is, arguing that one level of government directly affects other units of government. Another example can be the claim that immigrant admissions policy is generally managed centrally and the criteria followed to admit or reject immigrants directly affects other levels of government, without there being a structure of participation to make decisions together.

The principle of coherence targets another potential feature of the multilevel governance of immigration. This principle is grounded in the fact that some units of government can work separately because they have exclusive competences in a particular policy area (for example, education). The principle emphasizes that, as all units share a framework of collaboration, they have to try not to contradict each other. The 'golden rule' in this case is that a decision made at one level of government cannot contradict others, since there may be conflicting interests and approaches at different governmental levels (both vertical and horizontal relationships). This principle can play a determining role in, for instance, issues related to religious management in education or on the regulation of the wearing of the *niqab* or *burka* in public spaces. Thus, one level of government having competence in education or public spaces should not follow the *laïcité* principle while other units follow the principle of allowing religious education in schools. In other words, from a multilevel perspective, there should not be contradictions between levels of government both horizontally and vertically.

Having presented both principles, the legitimate question we can pose is: why are coordination (avoiding negative effects) and coherence (avoiding contradictions) important as principles? Given our perspective based on the structure of governance in multilevel states, the answer is that they have a moderating function in the centralization/decentralization dynamics. In this sense these principles have the function of graduating centralization/decentralization in practice, as the levels of centralization/decentralization can never be taken in absolute terms.

The character of the moderating role of these principles highlights how they can work to generate potential solutions in the inevitable situations of tension among the levels of government.[10] Considering the procedural dimension (principle of coordination), most of the key tensions in how to govern immigration in multilevel and multinational states are related to how to interpret the constitutional framework, rule of law, and the allocation of power. In this case each driving force pushing towards centralization/decentralization raises different concerns. Applied to the efficiency criteria, the principle of coordination raises questions such as: if we have to combine a multilevel governance framework and effectiveness, is there a single way to fashion that system or can we think of different systems according to different levels/units of governments to achieve the same efficiency result? Applied to the national identity criteria, procedural concerns can be formulated as follows: the choice among various systems aimed at ensuring a certain level of self-government among different levels can clash with the constitutional framework of the distribution of competences. How should this tension be dealt with?

With regard to the normative dimension of the collaborative framework (principle of coherence), concerns are related to good governance, which can be defined broadly as the capacity to govern immigration issues following the principle of coherence among units of government. This good governance framework raises different questions when it is applied to the efficiency and the national identity criteria. The efficiency criterion poses the question of whether, within the same multilevel governance framework, different immigration policies can work at the same time or not. The concern here is that there is a need to reach a minimum threshold to maintain coherence and efficiency at the same time. When applied to the national identity criteria the question is the following: if different approaches to immigration are accepted in some

units based on national identity arguments, how do we ensure coherence in a broad multilevel framework?
Schematically, this section can be summarized in Table 2.1.

Table 2.1   Two principles: cooperation and coherence

		Principles	Key questions given potential tensions
Sharing a common framework of collaboration To work together With the same criteria or with different criteria on how to interpret the driving forces of efficiency and national identity	*Procedural dimension* Dealing with common interests	Coordination to avoid negative effects of a decision at one level on others at the same level (horizontal) or at another level (vertical) of government	*Constitutional framework, rule of law, and allocation of power* • Efficiency criteria: Is there a single way to fashion the system or can different systems at different levels of government achieve the same efficiency result? • National identity criteria: How can the tension be balanced between allowing different systems to ensure a degree of self-government and respecting the constitutional framework of distribution of competences?
	Normative dimension Dealing with different interests	*Coherence* to avoid contradiction since there may be conflicting interests and approaches at different government levels (both vertical and horizontal dimension).	*Good governance* • Efficiency criteria: In a given multilevel governance framework, do we find a single immigration governance policy or policies? • National identity criteria: If different approaches to immigration are accepted in some units based on national identity arguments, how do we ensure coherence?

Potential scenarios of immigration governance

Based on the two previous steps, we can identify at least three potential scenarios for the structure of immigration governance: the centralist, the cooperative, and the asymmetric scenarios. In developing the scenarios, we build on Spiro's (2001) seminal article related to the federalism-immigration nexus, which proposes three models of immigrant federalism, namely centralist, cooperative, and devolutionary federalism. He defines cooperative immigrant federalism as a model where 'central government retains primary control and supervision over immigration decision-making, but enlists sub-national authorities as junior partners and allows them some discretion to assert or account for particular sub-national needs' (Spiro, 2001: 67). Spiro's model does not, however, have multinational states in mind, nor does it envisage the possibility of national identity driving the centralization/decentralization debate. Asymmetrical federalism can occur when each unit has a measure of autonomy to manage the impact of immigration in economic, cultural, social and even demographic terms; but the degree of autonomy will vary among the units. This variation usually exists due to national identity differences.[11]

In presenting these three scenarios and linking them with the two previous steps of our argument, we take into account the two levels of governance proposed by Dahl. The distinctive feature of multilevel governance is that 'who decides' (level of decision-making) and 'who does' (level of implementation) do not necessarily coincide on the same level of governance. This is precisely why it is called multilevel. Instead, different scenarios are possible, as the tables below illustrate.

Each scenario relates to the different possibilities in the relationship between central government and the sub-state units in immigration governance, in terms of the level of decision-making and implementation. In general, the centralist and cooperative scenarios do not allow different vertical relations among units, so as to link efficiency and

Table 2.2 Scenarios in the structure of immigration governance in multilevel states

	Who decides? (Decision-making level)	**Who does?** (Implementation level)
Centralist	Hegemony	Subsidiarity
Cooperative	Consensual	Intergovernmentality
Asymmetric	Polycentric	Self-government

coherence. The asymmetric scenario, in contrast, does allow different vertical relations among units. This is why, as the following tables show, the all/some distinction is important to introduce here. By 'all' we mean all units without exception; by 'some' we highlight the fact that not all units within the same multilevel system share the same allocation of power and the same possibilities for self-governance. We now discuss each scenario separately.

In the centralist scenario, the central government retains primary control and supervision of coordination/coherence of immigration decision-making and implementation, leaving to all units (without any distinction) the administrative implementation of those issues that are more efficiently dealt with at the lower administrative level (subsidiarity), but without any power at the level of decision-making (hegemony).

Table 2.3   The centralist scenario of immigration governance

Centralist		Who decides?	Who does?
Central government		Yes (hegemony)	Yes
Sub-state units	All	No	Yes (subsidiarity)
	Some	No	No

In the cooperative scenario the central government retains primary control and supervision of coordination/coherence over immigration decision-making but enlists all units (again, without any distinction) as partners and allows them some administrative discretion to assert or account for particular unit needs at the implementation level. This cooperative relationship is general for all units and can establish a structure to reach a consensual decision-making process on certain immigration policies (consent) and can leave other exclusive competencies to all units, but without endangering the coordination and coherence among other units and central government (intergovernmentality).

Table 2.4   The cooperative scenario of immigration governance

Cooperative		Who decides?	Who does?	
Central government		Yes	Yes	(Intergovernmentality)
Sub-state units	All	Yes (Consent)	Yes	
	Some	No	No	

Finally, in the asymmetric scenario the central government allows the coexistence of several centres of decision-making based on efficiency/ national identity criteria (polycentric) but does not extend this to all units. Coordination and coherence are controlled and supervised by consent. At the level of implementation, it can also leave self-management to certain unit authorities to assert or account for particular (national-) unit needs (self-government).

Table 2.5   The asymmetric scenario of immigration governance

Asymmetric		Who decides?		Who does?
Central government		Yes	(Polycentric)	Yes
Sub-state units	Some	Yes		Yes (self-government)
	All	No		Yes

Mapping immigration policy in multinational states

Having mapped out different scenarios of immigration governance based on the institutional structure in multilevel systems, we now shift our attention to the substance of the relevant policy areas by assessing how multilevel governance and immigration mutually influence each other. We highlight three elements of policy on immigration – admissions, reception, and citizenship – and discuss what the character of these policy areas suggests for how immigration is governed in multilevel systems. These policy areas are examined because they are core elements of immigration policy in terms of the scenarios outlined above. We therefore set aside other sectoral policy areas such as health or education that may impact on migration and migrants, but that are not core components of immigration policy. As in the previous section, particular attention is given to understanding the relationship between immigration and multilevel politics in the context of multinationality.

The interests of central-state and sub-state actors in immigration

Historically, immigration, integration, and citizenship policies have been powerful tools of nation-building and the national interests of states, because they are channels by which the state can (attempt to) shape the composition and characteristics of its national population (Norman, 2006).[12] Nation-building through immigration entails determining who can enter the territory, what the criteria are for membership of the nation and of the legal citizenry, and what the formal and informal demands are regarding how newcomers should adapt to the national society. Of course, in the 19th century, such policies were applied as much to regional minorities and the diversity already existing on the national territory as they were to immigrant newcomers (Weber, 1976). How important are these policy areas for contemporary nation-states? At first glance, central states have an interest in controlling and ensuring the uniformity of admissions and citizenship policies across the territory, because even in the contemporary era of arguably diminished and shared sovereignty, the power to decide who may enter the territory and become a member of the citizenry remains a key power of the sovereign state. As the previous section foreshadowed in its discussion of coordination and coherence, the central-state's interest in controlling immigration might be grounded in functional goals. For instance, it might seek to avoid possible externalities of differential immigration rules across the territory, such as 'backdoor' migration whereby newcomers admitted into the territory by one region subsequently move freely to the rest of the country. Alternatively, and recalling the national sustainability or national-interest arguments outlined earlier, another reason for the central state to ensure policy uniformity across the units is the historical utility of immigration as part of bilateral relations and broader foreign policy (Spiro, 2001).

Where states confront immigration in the context of existing multinationality and ongoing debates about identity in the multilevel state, a further set of central-state motivations with respect to immigration might arise. Insofar as the central state has an interest in pursuing a centralist nation-building project and seeks to assert an overarching national identity across the territory, then it is likely to have an interest in maintaining control of the policy levers related to immigrant admissions that could affect the linguistic, cultural, and identity compositions of the population (Norman 2006). Conversely, given that admissions, reception, and citizenship policies have significant downstream impacts on the demographic, linguistic, and cultural make-up of the multinational state, it is unsurprising that sub-state units assert an interest not just in implementing but also in deciding on immigration policy with the goal of mediating the impact of immigration and integration on their own national identity and society. These possibly divergent interests at central-state and sub-state levels of government reflect our earlier point that national sustainability arguments can be deployed to advocate for both centralization and decentralization processes in multilevel states.

The implications of immigration policies for the demographic, linguistic, and cultural balance of the statewide population distinguishes the governance challenge in multinational states from those multilevel states without a multinational character. Cross-nationally, however, and as the case studies in this volume show, there is no consistent pattern in multinational and multilevel polities with regard to either 'who decides' or 'who does' in the fields of admissions, reception, and citizenship (Barker, 2012). However, as we discuss below, similarity across multilevel states is more likely in the governance of integration. We now consider the three dimensions of policy individually and identify what tensions may arise between central-state and sub-state levels of government and which scenario of immigration governance appears most likely in the context of each policy area.

Admissions policy

As we explained earlier, admissions policy is most closely connected to core state functions and, as such, lends itself to a centralized approach. This is not just because of sovereignty goals, but also because of the practical challenge of reconciling principles of free movement within the territory with any differentiation in the decision-making on admissions across the territory. Max Frisch's famous statement that, in recruiting guest-workers, European countries 'asked for manpower, but people came', highlights that decisions on immigration admissions have much broader societal impacts, which in turn have implications for the governance of immigration in a multilevel system.

Language is a key identity marker of many sub-state nations. Admissions policies are salient for the linguistic dimension in a multinational society insofar as immigration flows have the potential to influence the linguistic or cultural composition of the national society in general, and the linguistic balance or imbalance between the sub-state society and the majority nation in particular. For instance, where immigration has the effect – deliberate or not – of buttressing the majority linguistic group at the expense of the language or culture of the sub-state society, tensions can arise between the sub-state unit and the central state (Banting and Soroka, 2012). To the extent that admissions criteria, especially in active immigration recruitment countries, have the effect of privileging the immigration of nationals of some groups over others (Joppke, 2005), the power to set admissions policies is a relevant tool of national self-determination and a potential site of struggle between central-state and sub-state levels. The degree of contestation is, though, mediated by whether language is central to the sub-state national identity, and whether language issues form a major stake in the autonomy project vis-à-vis the central state (Barker, 2012).

While the literature on sub-state nationalism and migration often focuses primarily on the core identity dimensions of language and ethnicity, material factors such as economic interests may also be a feature of vertical contestation between levels of government. One important reason for this is that immigration is a powerful lever for economic development. Sub-state regional units often have different interests in immigration to those of the central state and/or those of other sub-state units, given their specific regional economic development and labour-market needs. Moreover, regions and localities may be either more favourable or more opposed to immigration, depending on the geographic concentration of immigrants and the perceived local economic impacts of immigration (Money, 1999). Tensions can therefore arise as sub-state units seek either differentiated rules for immigration on a territorial basis (for example, in federations like Australia) or else the actual transfer of power over immigration policy to regions so that they may pursue their particular economic interests (Joppke and Seidle, 2012).

Clearly, as Eve Hepburn also notes in Chapter 3 of this volume, distinctive regional economic interests can – and do – exist in multilevel settings, both with and without multinationality. However, a key difference in multinational systems is that the power to pursue particular economic and labour-market goals via immigration policy is valued not merely for economic ends as such, but also more fundamentally as a means of asserting self-determination. To the extent that immigration powers are controlled exclusively or predominantly by the central state, then sub-state governments may view this as hampering their ability to self-determine. Self-determination goals, defined by the sub-state unit in economic, linguistic, cultural, and/or political terms, may consequently drive the sub-state unit to seek a role not just in implementing, but also in deciding the content of migration and integration policy, thereby enabling the effects of immigration on the sub-state society to be mediated (Zapata-Barrero, 2009).

Given the degree of contestation over admissions policy, which scenarios might result? From the perspective of the central state, we are likely to observe a push for centralized policy-making, whereby the central state controls decision-making overall, with only limited administrative power decentralized to the sub-state units. While some participation in decision-making power could be allowed, the state is unlikely willingly to decentralize meaningful decision-making power across the territory. We do observe examples of sub-state units participating in the immigration process in multilevel states to ensure that regional preferences or local labour-market needs are taken into account within points-based immigration systems (Hugo, 2008; Pandey and Townsend, 2011).

However, most of these examples reflect differentiation of policy at the level of specific policy settings, rather than enabling the sub-state level to influence either the broader policy goals or the fundamental paradigm within which policy is made (Hall, 1993). Thus, the central state will generally try to ensure that participation in decision-making processes on immigration remains limited in scope and ultimately controlled by the centre.

The central state is likely to agree to meaningful power-sharing in immigration policy-making only in cases when it is forced, as part of broader multilevel contestation, to respond to individual sub-state claims to specific interests in the character (for example, identity, language, and skills) or size of the immigrant population. In other words, the central state is most likely to decentralize elements of decision-making on admissions where the claim to policy differentiation forms part of a sub-state unit's ongoing claim for self-determination and identity recognition. In such cases, the asymmetric scenario is most likely, as the central state seeks to restrict the decentralization of actual decision-making power to only those sub-state units with particular identity-based claims.

Reception policy

On the surface, reception policies – that is, the policies pertaining to welcoming newcomers and giving them tools to participate in mainstream society, language integration, cultural adaptation, education, and social services for immigrants – could appear more likely to generate tension between different levels of government in multinational states, given that reception policies directly touch on the issues of identity, language and culture that are so often the object of vertical and horizontal contestation. In practice, however, reception policies are more amenable than admissions policies to power-sharing between levels of government along both decision-making and implementation dimensions, for at least two reasons. First, unlike admissions and citizenship, policies associated with reception are less and less viewed as intrinsic to the core functions of the modern state. This is especially true now that the imposition of linguistic, cultural, or religious homogeneity commonly seen in the 19th century is considered unacceptable in liberal-democratic states.[13] The central state is therefore less likely to demand a unified statewide approach to reception on sovereignty grounds. Second, migrants' differential adaptation across the territory is not just of lesser importance to the central state but could even be viewed as beneficial so as to ensure that migrants adapt more quickly to particular local cultures or societal contexts. At a functional level, and consistent with subsidiarity principles, services relevant to migrant integration, such as education, culture, and social services are in any case commonly subject to some form of decentralization in multilevel polities. Sub-state governments – or in some cases even municipal authorities – are therefore already accustomed to implementing policy in areas related to migrant integration and a variety of approaches is tolerated or even actively encouraged by the central state in many countries.

Of the three areas of admissions, reception, and citizenship, it is in reception that we expect to see the most meaningful decentralization of policy-making power, rather than mere administrative decentralization. Except in cases where it asserts a strong centralist nation-building project to ensure cultural uniformity across the territory, perhaps using national sustainability arguments, the central state has little interest in enforcing a highly centralist approach. Instead, it is likely to restrict itself to maintaining oversight over the broad parameters of policy to ensure consistency with its underlying policy goals regarding societal cohesion and national identity.

The cooperative scenario is therefore the most likely outcome; however, an asymmetric distribution of policy power is possible in situations where a linguistic or cultural foundation underpins one or more sub-state autonomy projects in the state and thereby creates a reason for differentiation in the character and outcomes of reception policy across the multilevel system. Thus, whether or not a cooperative or asymmetric scenario emerges is shaped by how and how much the politics of immigration intersects with the politics of multinationality in the multilevel state. The case study chapters in this volume illustrate the diversity of policy choices evident across the cases.

Citizenship policy

Similar to admissions powers, citizenship deals with belonging in the society. However, whereas admissions policy governs the right to move into and around a territory and to work in it, citizenship policy implies a more fundamental decision regarding the full set of civic, social, and political rights and duties in the political community, as well as membership in the national community past, present, and future. As such, citizenship is the least amenable of the three policy components to power-sharing between central-state and sub-state levels precisely because of its finality as a marker of membership in the national community in both a legal and identity sense. The centralist scenario in which the central state controls decision-making and implementation remains the most likely. This does not imply, however, that there is no contestation between levels of government. In a multinational state, a key assertion of sub-state self-determination claims is that the sub-state government should also have the right to forge its own national community and to delineate its boundaries of membership in line with its own identity concerns. The nature of its political relationship with the central state may influence how the sub-state unit seeks to delineate membership boundaries. For instance, in pursuing a territorial autonomy project vis-à-vis the central state, sub-state nations are arguably increasingly likely to adopt a territorial or residence-based conception of membership (Keating, 2001). Whereas the implication of the earlier literature on nationalism was that sub-state units would adopt a thick, ethnic conception of membership and therefore an exclusionary and defensive position vis-à-vis immigrants (Hobsbawm and Ranger, 1992), an alternative contention with empirical support is that sub-state units have reason to welcome and validate newcomers as potential members of the sub-state national community (Kymlicka, 2001), especially where this serves to buttress the sub-state nation vis-à-vis the nation-state in either political or identity terms (Schuck, 2009; Zapata-Barrero, 2009).

At a very concrete level, the more that the central state seeks explicitly to define the content of national citizenship, the more that tension is likely to characterize the vertical relationship, as sub-state units contest the central state's definition or vision of citizenship. For instance, as tests and civic integration demands are introduced as prerequisites to naturalization and the acquisition of citizenship (Goodman, 2010), sub-state units can increasingly question whether the values and cultural characteristics defined by the civic integration requirements reflect the identity and cultural diversity that exists across the territory of the host society, or the different interpretations of the country's political history (Meehan, 2010). Both at this micro-level of policy content and at the much broader level of debating who should have the power to set the boundaries of membership in the political community, tensions might arise between the sub-state unit and the central state about who controls citizenship policy settings. Yet, despite contestation between levels, the importance of citizenship policy to a state's overall self-definition suggests it will resist attempts to deviate from the centralist scenario.

The intersecting politics of immigration and multinationalism

In general, we hypothesize that as we move from citizenship to admissions to reception policy, there is a greater logic in, and probability of, allowing the sub-state level to participate not just in implementing, but also in deciding policy. This is so, on one hand, because, as the logic of subsidiarity suggests, reception policies that deal with concrete matters relating to migrants' integration patterns and their relationship with the communities in which they live are arguably most appropriately addressed at the sub-state level.[14] Moreover, viewed from the perspective of the central state, it is in reception policy that state sovereignty is least challenged, although elements of a centralized nation-building project may need to be conceded. Asymmetric policy-making is unlikely in the case of citizenship policy, but may occur in admissions and reception policy as the central state responds to particular identity-based autonomy claims emanating from sub-state units. In this case we should see the national identity driving force as outweighing the efficiency driving force.

Table 2.6 summarizes the discussion above and links likely scenarios to the policy areas of citizenship, admissions, and reception. The multiple possible configurations of policy power in the multinational state reflect the fact that, as in other policy areas, the distribution of policy power is not predetermined, but rather results from processes of political negotiation. In order to understand when and where these policy areas are likely to become highly politicized and to lead to a push for asymmetric immigration governance in the multinational and multilevel state, we need to identify both the bases of the autonomy projects and the configuration of the sub-state claims and power in the multinational society. The character and extent of tensions between levels of government is driven in part by the degree to which immigration and integration patterns, as well as citizenship policy and trends, are perceived to impinge on the national autonomy project at the sub-state level (Barker, 2012).

Table 2.6 Scenarios of immigration policy-making

	Without multinationality	*With multinationality*
Citizenship policy	Centralist	Centralist
Admissions policy	Centralist/Cooperative	Centralist/Cooperative/Asymmetric
Reception policy	Cooperative	Asymmetric

From the sub-state perspective, immigration – via admissions and reception policies – could be seen as having either negative or positive potential, given its own autonomy goals and the character of the immigration flows. These considerations therefore also influence the degree to which the sub-state unit seeks to push decentralization in immigration policy. If the sub-state unit defines its national community and autonomy project along linguistic lines, then the impact of central-state admissions policy on the sub-state language is likely to be of particular concern and will provoke sub-state claims in this area. Conversely, if an economic or political project is central to the national autonomy project, then the degree to which the central-state admissions policy impinges on the sub-state's ability to realize its own political and economic goals will likely drive the political salience of immigration for the sub-state unit (Barker, 2012).

Policies on immigration, especially in the areas of admissions and citizenship, are closely implicated in questions of nation-building, sovereignty, and self-determination. These issues, in addition to the identity content, are what push central states to assert a controlling role in decision-making over citizenship and admissions, while allowing more scope for aspects of reception that are perceived as less intrinsic to state functioning and sovereignty. Even in the cooperative scenario, the participation allowed may be limited to altering policy settings, as a central state will almost certainly seek to retain overarching control of the policy goals and the overall policy paradigm. However, in multi-level systems that are conceived as highly decentralized, and where the weight of power lies with constituent units, then the force of a centralist nation-building project is minimized. So too, then, is the central-state drive to control fully all aspects of admissions and citizenship policy likely to be correspondingly diminished.

Conclusion

This chapter has set out a framework for studying the governance of immigration and integration policies in multilevel states with particular application to those states also characterized by multinationality. The first section set out the components of a heuristic model that helps us to understand immigration policy governance in a multilevel context. It noted that two considerations – efficiency and national identity – are at play in driving centralization or decentralization dynamics in any multilevel state. As in any policy area in a multilevel state, certain principles further shape how policy competencies might be distributed between levels of government, both vertically and horizontally. Examples were given of how the principles of coordination and coherence could be applied in the policy area of immigration. Based on these structural and institutional elements, drawn from multilevel governance theory, the section derived three main scenarios – centralist, cooperative, asymmetric – of 'who decides' and 'who does' in immigration. The second part of the chapter developed scenarios for immigration policy governance, drawing on the characteristics of the policy area itself.

Similarly acknowledging the possibility for both centralization and decentralization dynamics in immigration policy in multilevel systems, we suggested that the subfields of citizenship and admissions policy are more likely to lead to a centralist, or in some cases cooperative, scenario, given the nation-building and sovereignty concerns of central states. In contrast, reception policy is more amenable to decentralization and asymmetry because of the lesser challenge posed to sovereignty, but also because regional or local variation in reception policies can be reconciled with the logic of subsidiarity common to multilevel governance.

Overall, we stressed that the precise configuration of 'who decides' and 'who does' in admissions, reception, and citizenship policy is an empirical question, rooted in context-specific factors such as the bases of the sub-state national self-determination claims, the particular economic, linguistic and demographic landscape across the multilevel state, and the degree to which immigration is perceived as impinging on sub-state national autonomy claims. The empirical analysis of immigration policy governance in the case studies that follow elaborates on the character of, and reasons for, the distribution of powers in each case.

Finally, it is important to reiterate the extent to which political negotiation between levels of government (and especially between sub-state and central-state levels) shapes who decides, who implements, and what kind of immigration and integration policy ultimately results. Behind any discussion of political negotiation is, necessarily, an acknowledgement of power politics and the interests of diverse political actors in the multilevel state. It is here that we can see clearly the link between governance and the role of party politics, as Eve Hepburn outlines in Chapter 3 of this volume. In the face of tensions and competing interests between central and sub-state units regarding which policy competencies in immigration and integration should be decentralized and to what degree, attention to power relationships is important. In particular, as Hepburn elaborates, the broader territorial question, often institutionalized in the form of a territorial-politics cleavage in the party system, impacts on how party political and intergovernmental debates on immigration and integration policy will unfold.

Notes

1. Other authors refer to the concentration/deconcentration distinction (Rocher and Rouillard, 1996) that focuses on state-power control. Concentration means that the state concentrates control of power. We adopt the decentralization/centralization distinction because it contains both a political and an administrative dimension, and thus better fits the governance focus of this section. Decision-making and administrative implementation do not necessarily coincide, and there can be administrative decentralization without political decentralization.

2. One of the most recent works on this issue distinguishes seven federal countries concerned with immigration issues (Australia, Belgium, Canada, Germany, Switzerland, Spain and United States) (Joppke and Seidle, 2012). See also the comparative legal analysis between the United States, Belgium, and Italy in Strazzari (2012).

3. Given space constraints, we will not explore in detail the implications involved in each of these three scenarios, but we will briefly describe them and show how they can play a function in our heuristic model. Some chapters in this volume will illustrate the implications of the various scenarios.

4. See, among others, Chattopadhyay and Ostien Karos (2009), Burgess (2009), and Gagnon (2009).

5. On this dimension, see Joppke and Seidle's (2012) edited volume on migrant integration policy in federal countries.

6. See on this issue, Schuck (2009).

7. This national identity criterion is often linguistically based, as several of the case study chapters in this volume discuss.

8. 'National sustainability' includes political arguments that survival of the national tradition is the legitimate basis of a state or territory claiming national recognition.

9. We can say that the principle of cooperation belongs to the same basis of structure of multilevel governance evidenced in the European Union. See, for instance, Kaiser and Prange (2004). For the principle of coherence, there is less literature. Reference to the principle of coherence, as applied to immigration policies, can be found in the section 'Migration policies and governance' of the International Labour Organization (2010: 143–190) report.

10. Conflicts and tensions are inherent to the very nature of multilevel systems. See, among others, the first section of Villiers (1994) and Burgess (2009).

11. See, for instance, Gagnon (2009), Gagnon and Keating (2012), Gagnon and Tully (2001), and Gagnon and Requejo (2011).

12. Of course, the degree to which policy outcomes match policy goals has frequently been debated in the political science literature on immigration. See, for instance, Freeman (1995).

13. For an argument that the recent turn to civic integration policies constitutes a degree of regression in the approach to migrants' adaptation and can be described as 'repressive liberalism', see Joppke (2007).

14. This point could apply to states both with and without multinationality.

References

K. Banting and S. Soroka (2012) 'Minority Nationalism and Immigrant Integration in Canada', *Nations and Nationalism*, 18(1): 156–176.

F. Barker (2012) *Immigration and Contested Nation Building: Explaining the Political Salience of Immigration in Multi-National Societies.* (Barcelona: Universitat Pompeu Fabra, GRITIM Working Paper).

M. Burgess (2009) 'Managing Diversity in Federal States: Conceptual Lenses and Comparative Perspectives' in A. Gagnon (ed.) *Contemporary Canadian Federalism: Foundations, Traditions, Institutions.* (Toronto: University of Toronto Press).

R. Chattopadhyay and A. Ostien Karos (eds) (2009) *Dialogues on Diversity and Unity in Federal Countries. A Global Dialogue on Federalism, Booklet Series Vol. 7.* (Ottawa: Forum of Federations).

R.A. Dahl (1961) *Who Governs? Democracy and Power in an American City.* (New Haven: Yale University Press).

J, Erk and E. Koning (2010) 'New Structuralism and Institutional Change: Federalism Between Centralization and Decentralization', *Comparative Political Studies*, 43(3): 353–378.

A.-G. Gagnon (2009) *The Case for Multinational Federalism.* (London: Routledge).

A.-G. Gagnon and M. Burgess (2010) *Federal Democracies.* (London: Routledge).

A.-G. Gagnon and M. Keating (eds) (2012) *Political Autonomy and Divided Societies: Imagining Democratic Alternatives in Complex Settings.* (Gordonsville, Virginia: Palgrave Macmillan).

A.-G. Gagnon and J. Tully (eds) (2001) *Multinational Democracies.* (Cambridge: Cambridge University Press).

S.W. Goodman (2010) 'Integration Requirements for Integration's Sake? Identifying, Categorizing and Comparing Civic Integration Policies', *Journal of Ethnic and Migration Studies*, 36: 753–772.

P. Hall (1993) 'Policy paradigms, Social Learning, and the State – The Case of Economic Policy Making in Britain', *Comparative Politics*, 25: 275–296.

E. Hobsbawm and T. Ranger (1992) *The Invention of Tradition.* (Cambridge and New York: Cambridge University Press).

G. Hugo (2008) 'Australia's State-specific and Regional Migration Scheme: An Assessment of Its Impacts in South Australia', *Journal of International Migration and Integration*, 9(2): 125–145.

International Labour Organization (2010) *International Labour Migration: A Rights-based Approach.* (Geneva: International Labour Organization).

C. Joppke and F.L. Seidle (eds) (2012) *Immigration Integration in Federal Countries.* (Montreal: McGill-Queen's University Press).

C. Joppke (2005) *Selecting by Origin: Ethnic Migration in the Liberal State.* (Cambridge, MA: Harvard University Press).

C. Joppke (2007) 'Beyond National Models: Civic Integration Policies for Immigrants in Western Europe', *West European Politics*, 30(1): 1–22.

R. Kaiser and H. Prange (2004) 'Managing Diversity in a System of Multi-level Governance: The Open Method of Co-ordination in Innovation Policy', *Journal of European Public Policy*, 1(2): 249–266.

M. Keating (2001) *Plurinational Democracy. Stateless Nations in a Post-sovereignty Era.* (Oxford: Oxford University Press).

W. Kymlicka (2001) *Politics in the Vernacular: Nationalism, Multiculturalism, and Citizenship*. (Oxford: Oxford University Press).

E. Meehan (2010) 'Active Citizenship: For Integrating the Immigrants' in B. Crick and A. Lockyer (eds) *Active Citizenship. What Could it Achieve and How?* (Edinburgh: University of Edinburgh Press).

J. Money (1999) *Fences and Neighbors: The Political Geography of Immigration Control*. (Ithaca, NY: Cornell University Press).

W. Norman (2006) *Negotiating Nationalism: Nation-Building, Federalism, and Secession in the Multinational State*. (New York: Oxford University Press).

M. Pandey and J. Townsend (2011) 'Quantifying the Effects of the Provincial Nominee Programs', *Canadian Public Policy*, 37(4): 495–512.

F. Rocher and C. Rouillard (1996) 'Using the Concept of Deconcentration to Overcome the Centralization/Decentralization Dichotomy: Thoughts on Recent Constitutional and Political Reform' in P. Fafard and D. Brown (eds) *Canada: The State of the Federation 1996*. (Kingston: Institute of Intergovernmental Relations).

P.H. Schuck (2009) 'Taking Immigration Federalism Seriously', *The Forum*, 7(3): Article 4.

P. Spiro (2001) 'Federalism and Immigration: Models and Trends', *International Social Science Journal*, 53(167): 67–73.

D. Strazzari (2012) 'The Scope and the Legal Limits of the "Immigration Federalism"': Some Comparative Remarks from the American, Belgian and the Italian Experiences', *European Journal of Legal Studies*, 5(2): 95–137. [http://www.ejls.eu/11/140UK.pdf]

B. De Villiers (ed.) (1994) *Evaluating Federal Systems*. (Dordrecht: M. Nijhoff Publishers).

E. Weber (1976) *Peasants into Frenchmen: The Modernization of Rural France*. (Stanford, CA: Stanford University Press).

R. Zapata-Barrero (ed.) (2009) *Immigration and Self-government of Minority Nations*. (Bruxelles: Presses interuniversitaires européenne-Peter Lang).

R. Zapata-Barrero (2013) *Diversity Management in Spain. New Dimensions, New Challenges*. (Manchester: Manchester University Press).

3
Multilevel Party Politics of Immigration: Territorial Rescaling and Party Competition

Eve Hepburn

Introduction

Immigration is one of the most pressing concerns in Western democracies, becoming a key source of polarization amongst political parties and public opinion (Boswell, 2003; Odmalm, 2012). However, while the integration of immigrants is increasingly managed at the sub-state regional level, as demonstrated by Ricard Zapata-Barrero and Fiona Barker in Chapter 2, thereby becoming an important issue in the agendas of sub-state territorial actors as we shall see below, studies on immigration have focussed almost exclusively on the central- or nation-state level. This limited state-level focus prohibits a full understanding of the party politics of immigration in multilevel states. This is because states are no longer (if they ever were) homogenous political entities with the same statewide parties competing on the same statewide policy issues across the entire space of a given country. Instead, we have witnessed a dramatic decentralization of powers to sub-state territories, which has enabled regional political actors to advance distinct sub-state policy agendas, leading to policy divergence across states (Loughlin, 2001; Keating, 2001). This process has been described as spatial or territorial 'rescaling', whereby power and authority is dispersed across several territorial levels within states (Keating, 2009). In response, political parties have themselves undergone degrees of territorial rescaling by transforming themselves from unitary organizations into decentralized multilevel creatures (Deschouwer, 2003; Hopkin, 2003; Bradbury and Mitchell, 2006; Thorlakson, 2006; Fabre, 2008; Detterbeck and Hepburn, 2010). As a result, sub-state regional branches of parties are allowed to fashion their own policy programmes and campaigns in order to cater to the interests of the regional citizenry and to compete with home-grown stateless nationalist and regionalist parties (SNRPs) which advocate greater self-determination for the territory. Often, this requires parting from central-party policy to develop more appropriate policies for the sub-state region. Therefore, similar to the levels of government themselves, as Zapata-Barrero and Barker have shown us in Chapter 2, different levels of political parties may also adopt more synchronized or divergent positions on immigration policy matters.

The territorial rescaling of states has led to increasing policy differentiation and divergence across states, as regions seek tailored policy solutions to regional problems (Keating, 2009). Yet so far, studies have focussed on traditional social policy issues such as childcare, health, or education, whereby regional parties have 'broken' from central-party agendas to meet the specific socioeconomic and cultural needs of the sub-state territory. However, immigration represents another key policy issue that has become decentralized in certain states – especially in relation to reception and migrant integration – leading to possibilities of regional policy divergence. Furthermore, immigration has become a source of competition between political parties at the sub-state regional level, and to that end it deserves careful attention. A focus on the multi-level party politics of immigration has generally been lacking from the literature (see, Zapata-Barrero, 2009a; Hepburn, 2009b), and the aim of this chapter is to begin a discourse that seeks to redress this imbalance.

The dynamics of regional party systems are often distinct from state-level party systems – not only in immigration matters but also in other policy areas. In particular, the issues contested in regional party systems are often influenced by a 'territorial cleavage', which in some cases takes prominence over the left-right dimension (Hepburn, 2010). This cleavage revolves around three issues of territorial concern:

1. the politics of territory, that is, issues of political autonomy, self-determination, and representation within state structures (here, parties often take positions along an independence – unitarism continuum)
2. the culture of territory, such as issues of language, identity, and culture (here, the main polarizing issue tends to be language, whereby, in the case of the existence of a regional minority language, parties take positions along a unilingualism – bilingualism continuum)
3. the economics of territory, whereby parties may seek to follow local forms of economic development, and support either increasing state subsidies or increased economic autonomy for the region (thereby

taking positions along an economic dependence – autonomy continuum).

These three dimensions of 'territorial interests' interact with issues of immigration and demographic change in distinct ways at the sub-state level that diverge from state-level norms. Regarding the territorial politics of immigration, regional parties may welcome immigrants into the ranks of the sub-state region (which may also constitute a stateless nation) to augment the regional population and bolster claims for self-determination; or alternatively, they may perceive immigrants as political agents of the centre sent to weaken demands for self-government or independence (Hepburn, 2009b; Banting and Soroka, 2012). On territorial cultural interests, sub-state parties may view immigrants as a threat to the regional culture and traditional way of life. In particular, when the region has its own language, immigration can be seen as 'diluting' the linguistic ranks of the territory. This is especially true if the language is perceived to be 'threatened' by the expansion of the dominant national (statewide) language (Zapata-Barrero, 2007). Alternatively, regional parties may view immigrants as enriching the culture of the sub-state region or stateless nation if they endorse a multicultural vision of society (Kymlicka, 2001). Finally, on the issue of territorial economic interests, regional parties may view immigration as a way to boost the regional economy by filling particular skills gaps in the labour force; or alternatively, they may perceive immigrants as taking jobs from the locals (see, Dustmann, 2003).

Yet the effects of territory are not only restricted to the sub-state level. Various dimensions of the territorial cleavage (political, economic, and cultural) may also become key issues within the *statewide* party system. This may occur when a statewide party that has a strongly concentrated support base in a particular region seeks to highlight the problems of that region by placing it on the national political agenda. Perhaps more common is when a stateless nationalist or regionalist party (SNRP) advances its territorial claims within the statewide electoral arena. In short, both statewide parties and regional parties may develop strategies at multiple levels – regional, state, and (beyond the scope of this collection) Europe – to address issues of territory (for more on territorial strategies in the EU see Hepburn, 2010).

These territorial issues interact with immigration in several ways. At the statewide level, parties must account for the uneven settlement and impact of migrants across different parts of the country – so, for instance, migrants tend to settle in urban rather than rural regions. As a result, migrant integration takes different forms in different places, which parties must address. The decentralization of party structures also enables regional branches of parties to approach immigration in distinctive ways, which may involve developing a custom-made regional approach to migrant integration. This may be especially important if the sub-state territory also considers itself a 'nation' with claims to distinctiveness. In this case, sub-state elites may be preoccupied with promoting a distinctive nation-building project and conception of citizenship that diverges from, or even conflicts with, the state-building project.

This chapter seeks to develop an explanatory framework for understanding multilevel party competition on immigration issues. It begins by considering the general trend towards territorial rescaling and the effect of this on parties and party systems. It then goes on to examine classical theories of party competition, in particular the spatial and ownership theories. The chapter examines two issues that do not conform to left-right ideological polarization: territory and immigration. It then explores how the issues of immigration and territory interact in multilevel party systems, with a particular focus on the neglected sub-state regional level. Following this, the chapter examines how parties – including statewide parties (and their regional branches) and SNRPs – have adopted distinctive stances on immigration at different levels, which are often influenced by their positions on the territorial cleavage. This final section puts forward several possible explanatory factors, which are then tested in the case studies, for why political parties adopt different positions on immigration at different territorial levels; in particular, why regional party stances may differ from statewide party responses.

Theories of party competition

Immigration has become a key source of political conflict in Western democracies (Boswell, 2003; Lahav, 2004; Koopmans et al., 2005; Odmalm, 2012). However, there is still a paucity of comparative research on the salience of immigration in the policy agendas of political parties, which is still generally perceived as a 'niche' issue (see, Meguid, 2008; Alonso and da Fonseca, 2012). Furthermore, there is an ever bigger dearth of research on how political parties at the sub-state regional level compete on immigration. Most approaches to party competition still tend towards a 'state-centric' bias, emphasizing ideology as the critical axis upon which parties compete.

Political parties are commonly classified and differentiated from one another by their location on a left-to-right spectrum, conventionally ranging from Marxism at the extreme Left, with Fascism at the extreme-right. In the late 1950s, Downs (1957) developed a 'proximity theory' of party competition. He argued that parties compete by taking diverging positions along a set of issue dimensions based on the assumption that voters will support a party whose position on an issue most closely resembles their own. More specifically, they will 'strive to distinguish themselves ideologically from each other and maintain the purity of their positions' (Downs, 1957: 126–127). This is more likely in proportional electoral systems than majoritarian systems, whereby the greater number of parties in the proportional representation (PR) system encourages parties to distinguish themselves more clearly, and possibly more radically, on policy grounds.

Building upon Downs' analysis, Sartori (1976) argues that party competition arises from the extent to which parties differ on ideological grounds, that is, the existence of 'left-right polarization'. This means that party systems, which are understood as 'the system of interactions resulting from interparty competition' (Sartori, 1976: 44), can be categorized by the number of ideological 'poles' upon which parties pivot, and the 'distance' between parties on a left-right continuum. Party systems are 'bipolar' if there are two ideological poles around which parties obtain support, and 'multi-polar' if support pivots along various points along a left-right continuum. Others have argued that there are dimensions other than ideology which are important in party competition, such as issues relating to gender, race, sexual orientation, Europe, immigration, and the environment. Yet even then, ideology is still seen as a 'multiple-ordering dimension' under which other issues are accommodated (Maor and Smith, 1993). In a different vein, some scholars contend that the salience of a given issue may be just as important as the ideological distance between parties in determining the way they compete. Budge and Farlie (1983) argue that parties seek to make their concerns most prominent in campaigns, rather than emphasizing how their position on an issue is distinguishable from other party positions. In 'owning' certain issues, parties will attract those voters who are concerned with this issue (so left-wing parties emphasize social welfare while right-wing parties are seen to 'own' the issue of law-and-order). However, the 'ownership' approach, as conceptualized by Budge and Farlie and which is focused exclusively on socioeconomic matters, is unable to account for issues that are not associated with a particular left-right ideology.

Territory is one such issue whereby constitutional change or the defence of territorial interests may be pursued by any or all of the main 'class-based' parties, as well as regionalist and green parties (Hepburn, 2010;

Alonso, 2012). A growing body of literature in nationalism and regionalism studies has shown that political activity often pivots around issues of culture, language, boundaries, and self-determination (Lynch, 1996; De Winter and Türsan, 1998; Jones and Keating, 1995; Keating, 2001). The territorial heterogeneity of states, according to Lipset and Rokkan (1967), is a result of territorial cleavage 'structures' and different patterns of political conflict in different places. These territorial cleavages have never gone away, despite the modernizing and centralizing impulses of modern nation-states. Indeed, some scholars have argued that the territorial cleavage is now experiencing a renaissance as states decentralize (Hough and Jeffery, 2006; Swenden and Maddens, 2008; Hepburn, 2010). The resilience of the territorial cleavage has led political parties to take greater account of issues of territory in their political agendas, encouraging them to contest the 'ownership' of the territorial dimension (alongside other left-right dimensions) in multilevel states (Alonso, 2012).

In particular, a certain type of political party – the stateless nationalist or regionalist party (SNRP) – has made the issue of territory its *pièce de résistance* (Hepburn, 2009a). These parties have been defined as 'geographically concentrated peripheral minorities which challenge the working order and sometimes the democratic order of a nation-state by demanding recognition' (Müller-Rommel, 1998). The defining characteristic of these parties is the demand for territorial empowerment, which often includes the goal of self-determination (De Winter and Türsan, 1998; Hepburn, 2009a). In particular, SNRPs are distinguished by three characteristics: (1) they are organized within a given territory; (2) they seek to represent a population which shares a common identity; (3) their strategies aim to secure territorial self-determination (de Prat, 2002). Importantly, SNRPs span a range of ideological positions, including the extreme left (Scottish Socialist Party), the centre-left (Eusko Alkartasuna), the centre-right (Convergència i Unió), and the extreme-right (Vlaams Belang). Indeed, some scholars have argued that SNRPs are the only party family in Europe that is located across the entire left–right dimension (Tronconi, 2005; Gomez-Reino, 2008; Hepburn, 2009a).

Immigration is another issue that is not associated exclusively with a particular ideology. As Odmalm (2012: 1) argues, 'immigration "messes" up party classification ... Parties that are supposed to be on the "Right" are suddenly on the "Left" (and vice versa) once immigration is taken into account'. Although early research made a connection between immigration and far-right populist parties, which campaigned primarily on an anti-immigrant platform, several recent studies have shown that immigration has become a concern for all mainstream parties (Mudde, 2007;

Davis, 2012; Odmalm, 2012). For instance, Van Spanje (2010) identifies a 'contagion effect' of anti-immigrant parties, whose electoral success influences other parties' policy positions on immigration. In an analysis of 75 parties within eleven West European states, he finds that the policies of left-wing parties were as influenced by anti-immigrant parties as rightwing parties. As such, he posits that anti-immigrant parties have a contagion effect on entire party systems (Van Spanje, 2010). Alonso and da Fonseca (2012) also show that the immigration issue has gained saliency in the agendas of both centre-right and centre-left parties, so that the positions of both have been converging in an anti-immigrant direction in the face of electorally successful far-right parties. Further research shows that the adoption of anti-immigrant positions by the mainstream parties has, in turn, facilitated anti-immigrant success. Dahlström and Sundell (2012) demonstrate that mainstream parties legitimize anti-immigrant parties by taking a tougher position on immigration. Clearly, immigration has become a key concern across the party system in Western states, not only influencing the rise of far-right parties, but also affecting the policy agendas of mainstream left and right parties.

However, while these developments can be identified at the state level, might one discover a rather different set of findings when examining the effects of immigration on sub-state regional party systems? The following section will explore how the twin issues of territory and immigration may produce a different set of outcomes at the regional level as opposed to the state level.

Immigration, sub-state regions, and territorial interests

The trend towards regionalization and federalism within many states means that sub-state regional electoral arenas have become important focal points for territorial interest representation (Jeffery, 1997; Hough and Jeffery, 2006; Marks, Hooghe and Schakel, 2008; Keating, 2009). Decentralization has led to the creation of regional executives and parliaments, regional policy communities, and regional electoral arenas. In longstanding federal states such as Austria, Canada, and Germany, as well as newly decentralized or federalized states such as the UK, Spain, Italy, and Belgium; regional tiers of government have accumulated extensive executive, legislative, and fiscal powers that lie outside the control of the state. This has resulted in the empowerment of the sub-state regional level, and the development of specific policies to address regional concerns.

As a result of territorial rescaling, immigration has become not only an important issue and policy competence at the state level; it has also become a key concern for sub-state regions, some of which are steadily gaining increased powers over immigration policy. However, the sub-state regional level has so far been virtually absent in the field of immigration studies, despite the fact that it is increasingly responsible for the social, economic, and cultural integration of immigrants (see, Joppke and Seidle, 2012).

Where there has been research done on party competition on immigration, scholars have focussed exclusively on the state level (Meguid, 2008; Green-Pedersen, and Krogstrup, 2008; Alonso and da Fonseca, 2012; Odmalm, 2012; Davis, 2012). Party competition at multiple territorial levels of a state is a field of research that has barely been touched by scholarship. Yet the trend towards decentralization and federalism within OECD states mean that sub-state regional assemblies have been empowered with control over large sections of social, environmental, and economic policy; including health, education, housing, culture, the environment, planning and economic development (Keating, 2001; Loughlin, 2001; Marks, Hooghe and Schakel, 2008). These policy areas 'overlap' with immigration, which tends to be controlled by the 'centre' – that is, the state government, as Zapata-Barrero and Barker have shown in Chapter 2. They overlap because immigration affects the sub-state region's demographic growth, labour market, economic development and the delivery of public services (such as schooling, health and social care, and housing). Furthermore, as the case studies in Part II of this volume demonstrate, some regions have also been allocated direct competencies for migrant integration and reception. As such, and as the case studies in Part III show, sub-state regional parties have increasingly taken a stance on immigration issues, despite this being a policy area traditionally associated with the centre (Hepburn, 2009b).

The way in which territory influences party positioning on immigration becomes all the more heightened in states of a multinational (or 'plurinational') nature, which may or may not contain SNRPs. Most debates on immigration assume 'that the receiving society and the receiving state coincide' (Zapata-Barrero, 2007: 3). However, this is certainly not the case in multinational states, in which one or more sub-state nation, with its own language, culture and political identity, exists within the shell of the state. For Banting and Soroka (2012: 157), 'the existence of multiple and potentially competing political identities can complicate the integration process. This is particularly the case if the central state and the substate nation promote different conceptions of citizenship and different nation-building projects – in effect, competing for the affections of newcomers'.

Furthermore, immigration presents particular opportunities and challenges for stateless nations within multinational states that have distinct political identities and cultures, as Zapata-Barrero and Barker made clear in Chapter 2 (see also, Kymlicka, 2001). According to Banting and Soroka (2012: 157) 'immigration into the homeland of national minorities such as Quebec, Flanders or Catalonia can ... generate added tensions. Such immigration has the potential to dilute the culture of the national minority, affect the prospects for nationalist mobilization, and upset historic balances between the substate nation and the majority in the country as a whole'.

Finally, sub-state nations may use their devolved powers not only to also assert their autonomy vis-a-vis the central government, but also to highlight their 'distinct society' claims by defining their own conditions for migrant integration. This may include special conditions for access to permanent residence or citizenship (which may be more restrictive of more liberal than that at the central-state level).

Immigration and parties in multilevel states

So how have political parties operating within multilevel states responded to the issue of immigration, and to what extent has it become entwined with issues of territory? Have regional immigration concerns influenced statewide-level debates? And have statewide immigration concerns influenced regional-level debates? Indeed, has immigration become an important point of competition, or even polarization, between sub-state parties at all – be they nationalist, regionalist, conservative, socialist, liberal, or green? Finally, to what extent (if at all) have SNRPs and regional branches differed from statewide parties in their approach to immigration?

Most obviously, the issue of immigration is a fundamental concern to SNRPs. As we saw above, SNRPs are primarily focussed on the goal of territorial empowerment, which includes seeking to protect or maintain the identity, culture, and interests of the regional population and to obtain greater autonomy for the region based on its (cultural, linguistic, historical, and political) distinctiveness – a priority that distinguishes them from statewide parties (for a fuller description of the goals of SNRPs see, Hepburn, 2009a). As such, immigration poses a particular challenge for SNRPs to include 'non-nationals' in their region- or nation-building projects. In particular, immigration may be perceived by SNRPs as posing distinct challenges to preserving regional identities, cultures, and languages. Traditionally, SNRPs have sought to defend these territorial interests from encroachment by the 'centre', that is the majority population of the state. Immigrants, in opting to integrate into the majority culture by learning the majority language, for instance, may be included in the perceived threat of the centre by SNRPs (Zapata-Barrero, 2007). However, if immigrants choose (or are required) to integrate into the minority culture and learn the regional language, then SNRPs will presumably view immigrants in a more positive light as the ranks of the region will have been augmented. SNRPs have also been among the greatest critics of central-state immigration policies and advocates of greater regional control of immigration policy. To that end, SNRPs have often taken their demands to the statewide level, arguing for a decentralization of state immigration systems.

Immigration has also become an important policy issue for regional branches of statewide parties, which must respond to the immigration concerns of SNRPs while at the same time maintaining a coherent immigration policy across different levels of a multilevel party. As noted above, one important characteristic of regional party systems is that statewide parties must operate in a peculiarly regional context, and compete on regional issues. This has led to intra-party demands for the organizational decentralization of political parties (Detterbeck and Renzsch, 2003; Fabre, 2008; Wilson, 2009; Detterbeck and Hepburn, 2010). Furthermore, it is well-documented that political parties operating at the sub-state regional level often diverge in their policy agendas from parties at the nation-state level on issues such as education, healthcare, and immigration (Bradbury and Mitchell, 2001).

Importantly, the decentralization of political parties may lead to intra-party conflict as different levels of parties diverge in the areas of policy, campaigning, and their activities in public office. For instance, the Quebec Liberal Party, Catalan Socialist Party, and Scottish Labour Party have all – to varying extents – sought to distinguish (or even separate) themselves from their statewide counterparts over contested policy issues, including multiculturalism and social policy. Furthermore, in cases where statewide parties must compete with SNRPs – such as Flanders, Catalonia, Quebec, Scotland, and Northern Italy – regional branches have sometimes adopted more radical territorial positions, including support for greater self-determination, to defuse support for secession as well as to exert greater control over policy issues that strongly affect regional populations, such as immigration (Fabre, 2008; Hepburn, 2010, 2011). In particular, if immigration becomes a key concern of SNRPs in their development of a nation-building project, then it must also become a concern of regional branches of statewide parties. This is because they too need to be seen as representing 'territorial interests' and defending the needs and identity of the territory (from potential external threats) (Hepburn, 2009a). Furthermore, regional party positioning on territorial issues may be motivated by attempts to align the party with public opinion (i.e., support for greater self-determination for the region). However, it may also demonstrate a 'gap' with public opinion on issues they consider to be best decided at the elite level (and here, the positions of party leaders on immigration often diverge from those of party followers – on the Spanish case, see, Zapata-Barrero, 2009b).

Of course, there is no straightforward correlation between territory and immigration in determining party competition, as there is no straightforward correlation between ideology and immigration (Odmalm, 2012) or territory and ideology (Hepburn, 2009a). SNRPs and regional branches of statewide parties have responded in various ways to the challenges and opportunities associated with immigration. Just as some parties may welcome immigration as a tool to vitalize the economy, boost the regional population and underpin the 'inclusive' nature of the sub-state community, other parties may perceive immigration as a threat to the sub-state identity, culture and labour market, without caring if outsiders view their positions as exclusionary (Hepburn, 2009b). There is a need, therefore, to examine the positions of SNRPs and regional branches of statewide parties on immigration, and to explore to what extent they are distinctive from the positions of national-level parties, and why. As this discussion has sought to demonstrate so far, the context in which regional parties compete on immigration may be very different from that of the statewide level. This is because, as we saw above, the dynamics of regional party systems are often different from those of statewide party systems, due to the distinctive nature of the regional political culture and economy. In particular, regional party systems may be strongly influenced by a territorial cleavage, with parties taking distinct positions on self-determination, the protection of cultural identities, languages, and traditional economies. This would lead us to assume that regional parties might adopt quite different positions on immigration from statewide parties in multilevel states.

Identifying explanatory factors for regional and statewide party positions on immigration

The following section seeks to provide an explanatory framework for understanding the positioning of regional and statewide parties on immigration, and for identifying potential areas of divergence between the two. It develops several hypotheses to account for the immigration stances of national parties operating in statewide systems on one hand, and SNRPs and regional branches of statewide parties operating at the regional level on the other. These factors are: (1) demographic issues, (2) economic issues, (3) linguistic and cultural issues, (4) party ideology, (5) electoral system, (6) party polarization and (7) the relative degree of government control over immigration policy. This list is certainly not exhaustive and there may be other specific factors that account for party positioning on immigration in particular countries. Instead, it seeks to identify general factors that explain the positioning of parties within multilevel states. Furthermore, not all of these variables may be applicable for one case; instead, it is anticipated that there may only be one or two (clusters of) explanations for party positioning on immigration at a particular time in a particular case.

1. Demography

A first factor that could account for divergence between statewide and regional party positions on immigration relates to the overall demographic situation of the state in question, and the specific demographic position of the region within that state. Demographic status includes: current levels of immigration to the state/region, the direction of migratory trends, and the (forecasted) stability of the state/regional population. On the first matter, if a state has received high overall levels of immigrants, then it is more likely that statewide parties adopt more restrictive stances on immigration; alternatively, in cases where a state has received low numbers of immigrants, parties are likely to have a more positive approach based on a greater need to attract and/or retain skilled immigrants. Regional parties are likely to adopt similar positions to statewide parties unless (1) the region has received significantly higher levels of immigration compared to the national average in which case regional parties are more likely to advocate less immigration than statewide parties, or (2) the region has received significantly lower levels of immigration compared to the national average in which case regional parties will take more pro-immigration stances than statewide parties. On the second issue, in states that are net importers of immigrants, statewide parties are likely to have more restrictive stances that states that have high levels of out-migration, as population decline may be a concern in the second scenario. Similarly, regional parties may adopt more restrictive/open positions on immigration based on the in-migration and out-migration of the region. Linked to that, parties are more likely to adopt positive approaches towards immigration if long-term demographic decline (owing to low fertility rates or an ageing population) are forecast for sub-state regions; in contrast, regions that have flourishing demographic rates are more likely to incite positions from statewide parties that the territory is 'full up' and requires no further immigration. Again, regional parties are likely to adopt similar positions unless the region faces long-term demographic decline compared to the national average in which case regional parties may take more positive positions than statewide parties. On the basis of this analysis, we can hypothesize that:

H1.1 Immigration is viewed positively by *statewide* parties if there are low levels of immigration and demographic decline and negatively if there are high levels of immigration and robust demographic levels.

H1.2 Immigration is viewed positively by *regional* parties if there are low levels of immigration to the *region* and demographic decline compared to the national average and negatively if the *region* received significantly high levels of immigration on top of already robust demographic levels.

2. Economy

A second potential explanatory variable for statewide and regional party positioning on immigration is economic. To put it simply, in poorer states that have a skills shortage in the labour market, statewide parties are more likely to support increased immigration, in particular targeting migrants that possess certain labour-market skills that are required by the national economy to sustain economic growth. In contrast, wealthy states that are performing well and have no labour shortages are less likely to demand substantially increased levels of immigration. Regional parties are likely to adopt similar positions to statewide parties unless (1) the regional economy is much weaker than the national economy as a whole and there is a significant labour shortage, which encourages parties to view immigration as necessary to boost growth; or (2) the regional economy is much stronger than the national economy as a whole, which causes regional parties to see no need for high levels of immigration. Based on this, we can hypothesize that:

H2.1 Immigration is viewed positively by *statewide* parties if the national economy is in decline and there is a labour shortage, and negatively if the national economy is flourishing and there is no labour shortage.

H2.2 Immigration is viewed positively by *regional* parties if the *regional* economy is underperforming compared to the national average and there is a significant labour shortage and negatively if the *regional* economy is outperforming the national economy and there is no *regional* labour shortage.

3. Linguistic and cultural barriers

Third, language and culture – and the extent to which they present 'barriers' to migrant integration – may be an important determinant of statewide and regional parties' positions on immigration. In particular, statewide parties may be opposed to immigration if the current immigrant population has been perceived as having difficulties learning the national language or adopting the cultural norms of the host society. Similarly, linguistic proficiency in the minority language of the region is also a key barrier for becoming a citizen of the region, in cases where the sub-state language differs from the language of the state (i.e., French in Quebec, English in the rest of Canada; Catalan or Basque versus Castilian in Spain). Regional parties may therefore oppose immigration if they believe it might reduce the size of the regional population who speak the minority language, whereby minority language speakers might be threatened or 'submerged' within the state. This may happen in cases whereby immigrants choose to adopt the language of the majority (rather than the minority) for reasons of social mobility. In contrast, regional parties are more likely to welcome immigrants if (1) the newcomers selected for entry are already fluent in the minority language or willing to learn it or (2) if there are strong immigrant education policies in place for the region which encourages migrants to integrate into the culture, language, and identity of the region.

H3.1 Immigration is viewed positively by *statewide* parties if immigrants share and/or learn the national language and negatively if immigrants have difficulties/opposition to learning the national language.

H3.2 Immigration is viewed positively by *regional* parties if immigrants make efforts to learn *the regional minority* language and negatively if immigrants speak/adopt the majority language of the state rather than the minority language of the *region*.

4. Party ideology

A fourth factor determining a statewide or regional party's stance on immigration is its ideological profile. Some scholars have argued that left-wing parties favour more pro-immigrant multicultural stances while right-wing parties are more traditionalist and anti-immigrant (Jupp, 2003; Lahav, 2004), which is just as relevant for statewide as regional parties. Of course, as discussed earlier, immigration rarely maps neatly onto parties' ideological profiles, and left-wing parties are as susceptible to the contagion effect of anti-immigrant parties as right-wing parties (Van Spanje, 2010; Alonso and da Fonseca, 2012; Odmalm, 2012). Furthermore, parties are often split on the issue of immigration (Zaslove, 2004). However, given the continuing appeal of viewing immigration through a binary left-right ideological lens, we will still put this forward as a possible hypothesis to be tested for both statewide and regional parties:

H4.1 Immigration is viewed positively by (centre-)left *statewide* and *regional* parties.

H4.2 Immigration is viewed negatively by (centre-)right *statewide* and *regional parties*

5. Electoral system

A fifth factor that may influence the positioning of statewide and regional parties on immigration is the structure of the electoral system. Studies have shown that majoritarian or 'first-past-the-post' systems tend to punish extreme policy positions, as they are usually based on competition between two dominant parties, with the creation of single-party governments that have a majority in parliament (see, Odmalm, 2012). In this scenario, we expect to see that majoritarian systems produce a dynamic of party competition that converges on a moderately pro-immigrant position. In contrast, electoral systems based on proportional representation encourage a wider variety of policy positions, including more extreme positions, with the resultant creation of coalition governments. In this scenario, proportional systems may increase polarization between parties, thereby encouraging parties to adopt more anti-immigrant positions. These hypotheses apply to both regional and statewide parties:

H5.1 Immigration is viewed more positively by *statewide and regional parties in majoritarian electoral systems* that discourage polarization.

H5.1 Immigration is viewed more negatively *by statewide and regional parties in proportional or mixed-member electoral systems* that encourage polarization.

6. Party polarization

It is also worthwhile separating out party polarization as an independent explanatory factor, as polarization is influenced not only by the electoral system but also by the types of parties competing. In particular, the existence of electorally relevant anti-immigrant parties – which have appeared in all types of electoral systems – may increase polarization and push other parties to a more anti-immigrant position (Dahlström and Sundell, 2012). Even in cases where anti-immigrant parties do not compete, if there is a high degree of polarization, that is, parties taking extreme opposite views on the issue, this may create a negative climate for immigration. Finally, the existence and position of SNRPs on immigration may also influence party competition. If electorally relevant SNRPs adopt a negative attitude towards immigration, this may have a 'contagion' effect on regional branches of statewide parties that seek to represent territorial interests; however, in cases where SNRPs adopt a positive position on immigration, this may encourage regional branches to adopt more liberal stances. So:

> H6.1 Immigration is viewed positively *by statewide* and *regional* parties if there are low levels of party polarization on immigration (in particular, if there is no electorally successful anti-immigrant party competing in the party system) and negatively if there are high levels of party polarization on immigration (in particular, if there is an electorally successful anti-immigrant party competing in the party system).

> H6.2 Immigration is viewed positively by *regional* parties if the predominant SNRP is in favour of immigration and negatively if the predominant SNRP opposes immigration, thereby demonstrating a 'regionalist' contagion effect.

7. Policy control over immigration

Our final factor explaining why regional parties may adopt diverging positions on immigration compared to statewide parties is the extent to which immigration has been decentralized in multilevel states. This is, of course, not an issue in unitary states. In cases where a region has no competence or control over the levers of immigration there is often demand for more powers in this area, at least in the area of migrant integration, which affects other regional competencies such as health, education, and housing. In such cases, regional parties may unite in calls for more powers over immigration, reducing polarization on the issue, and acting as a 'territorial bloc' in opposition to statewide parties. However, in cases where a region has a high degree of control over immigration, such as determining a regional points system, then there may be more contestation over how to manage the details of the policy controlled by the regional government, resulting in more attention to, and polarization on, immigration. In short, regions lacking immigration powers may experience low contestation/polarization on immigration, while regions with maximum control over immigration may experience high contestation/polarization. This leads us to hypothesize that:

> H7.1 Immigration is viewed positively by regional political parties if the region has limited control over immigration policy, which results in low levels of contestation and polarization on immigration policy.

> H7.2 Immigration is viewed negatively by regional parties if the region has extensive control over immigration policy, which leads to high levels of contestation and polarization on immigration policy.

Conclusion

The decentralization and federalization of states has created or strengthened regional party systems in which parties may adopt distinctive positions on policy issues that 'break' from the statewide party line. The issue of immigration is no exception. Despite being a policy area traditionally controlled by the central-state government, the impact of immigration on areas of regional competence – such as the delivery of public services, economic development, and social cohesion – as well as the decentralization of policy competencies in the sphere of migrant integration – has encouraged sub-state regional political parties to adopt stances on immigration based on the needs and interests of the regional citizenry, society, and economy that diverge from the positions of statewide parties. In particular, the existence of a 'territorial cleavage' based on political, economic, and cultural territorial interests (such as demands for self-determination and the protection of minority languages) intersects with immigration in particular ways at the regional level. This leads to the possibility of quite diverse stances of regional parties on immigration compared to national statewide parties.

This regional-statewide diversity in party positions is especially pronounced if there is an electorally successful SNRP operating in the sub-state territory. The SNRP party family, given its focus on the preservation of regional cultures, languages, and economies, has an important stake in determining who is considered part of the sub-state region or nation. Although the focus in the literature has overwhelmingly been on radical-right responses to immigration (that is, parties which focus mainly on the threats to national-state identities), it is no less important to SNRPs that focus on preserving sub-state regional identities.

In some cases, immigration may be viewed as undermining the culture, identity, and language of the sub-state nation in question. However, in others, SNRPs may view immigration as a positive development that increases the ranks and clout of the sub-state nation. As such, we can postulate no single correlation between nationalism/regionalism and immigration. SNRPs have adopted a variety of approaches on immigration, ranging from outright xenophobic and anti-immigrant stances, to valorizing immigrant-origin groups as an important resource for the stateless nation or region. SNRPs do, however, tend to have a clear effect on the positions of their competitors: regional branches of statewide parties. In similarity to anti-immigrant parties, the stances of SNRPs on immigration (as well as territory – that is, demands for self-determination) may have a 'contagion' effect on other parties. So if an SNRP adopts a positive position on immigration based on the territorial needs of the sub-state region/nation, this may colour the views of other parties to similarly adopt positive approaches. Contrarily, if a SNRP adopts a negative position, they, like the anti-immigrant parties themselves, may encourage other parties to become restrictive.

As the dynamics of regional party systems often differ from the dynamics of statewide party systems, there is a need to explore how immigration is viewed by parties at both levels, in particular the under-researched sub-state level, and how party stances at both levels diverge and intersect. This chapter has sought to address this need, by developing a general explanatory framework for regional and statewide party positioning on immigration. In particular, it has developed several hypotheses to account for party competition in multilevel states, drawing on socioeconomic, cultural, and political determinants. These hypotheses will be used to form the basis for the empirical chapters in Part III of the book. Contributors to the Political Parties section have been encouraged to draw on the hypotheses presented above in their own cases. But rather than requiring all authors to test all of the hypotheses in their case(s), we have invited them to engage selectively with the hypotheses in a way that reflects the importance they attribute to different explanatory variables in their particular case(s). This will allow individual authors to examine a particular argument or proposal in greater depth. Beyond this volume, it is also hoped that these hypotheses will prove useful for other scholars wishing to explain political parties' positions on immigration in multilevel states and will encourage future work on multilevel immigration approaches that challenge the assumption that immigration is an exclusively 'national' issue contested only by statewide parties.

References

S. Alonso and S.C. da Fonseca (2012) 'Immigration, Left and Right', *Party Politics*, 18(6): 865–884.

S. Alonso (2012) *Challenging the State. Devolution and the Battle for Partisan Credibility*, (Oxford: Oxford University Press).

K. Banting and S. Soroka (2012) 'Minority Nationalism and Immigrant Integration in Canada', *Nations and Nationalism*, 18: 156–176.

C. Boswell (2003) *European Migration Policies in Flux*. (Wiley-Blackwell).

I. Budge and D.J. Farlie (1983) *Explaining and Predicting Elections. Issue Effects and Party Strategies in Twenty-three Democracies*. (London: George Allen and Unwin).

C. Dahlström and A. Sundel (2012) 'A Losing Gamble. How Mainstream Parties Facilitate Anti-immigrant Success', *Electoral Studies*, 31: 353–363.

A. Davis (2012) *The Impact of Anti-Immigrant Parties on Mainstream Parties' Immigration Positions in the Netherlands, Flanders and the UK*. Unpublished PhD Thesis. (Florence: European University Institute).

L. De Winter and H. Türsan (1998). *Regionalist Parties in Western Europe*. (London and New York: Routledge).

K. Deschouwer (2003) 'Political Parties in Multi-layered Systems', *European Urban and Regional Studies*, 10(3): 213–226.

K. Detterbeck and E. Hepburn (2010) 'Party Politics in Multi-level Systems: Party Responses to New Challenges in European Democracies' in W. Swenden and J. Erk (eds) *Exploring New Avenues of Comparative Federalism Research*. (London: Routledge).

K. Detterbeck and W. Renzsch (2003) 'Multi-level Electoral Competition: The German Case', *European Urban and Regional Studies*, 10: 257–269

A. Downs (1957) *An Economic Theory of Democracy*. (New York: Harper).

E. Fabre (2008) 'Party Organization in a Multi-level system. Party Organizational Change in Spain and the UK', *Regional & Federal Studies*, 18(4): 309–329.

M. Gómez-Reino (2008) 'A Niche or an Expanding Universe for Ethnoregionalist Parties in Europe? Party Demands in Contemporary European Politics'. Paper presented at the conference 'European Identities: Nationalism, Regionalism and Religion', University of Notre Dame, London centre, 17–18 October.

C. Green-Pedersen and J. Krogstrup (2008) 'Immigration as a Political Issue in Denmark and Sweden', *European Journal of Political Research*, 47(5): 610–634.

E. Hepburn (ed.) (2009a). *New Challenges for Stateless Nationalist and Regionalist Parties*. Special issue of *Regional & Federal Studies*, 19(4–5).

E. Hepburn (2009b) 'Regionalist Party Mobilisation on Immigration', *West European Politics*, 32(3): 514–535.

E. Hepburn (2010) *Using Europe. Territorial Party Strategies in a Multi-level System.* (Manchester: Manchester University Press).

E. Hepburn (2011) 'Citizens of the Region. Party Conceptions of Regional Citizenship and Immigrant Integration', *European Journal of Political Research,* 50(4): 504–529.

J. Hopkin (2003) 'Political Decentralisation, Electoral Change and Party Organisational Adaptation. A Framework for Analysis', *European Urban and Regional Studies,* 10(3): 227–237.

D. Hough and C. Jeffery (eds) (2006) *Devolution and Electoral Politics.* (Manchester: Manchester University Press).

B. Jones and M. Keating (eds) (1995) *The European Union and the Regions.* (Oxford: Clarendon).

C. Joppke and F.L. Seidle (2012) *Immigrant Integration in Federal Countries.* (Montreal: McGill-Queen's University Press).

J. Jupp (2003). 'Immigration, Asylum and Extremist Politics – Europe and Australia', paper presented at the conference The Challenges of Immigration and Integration in the European Union and Australia, 18–20 February, University of Sydney, available at http://www.utexas.edu/cola/centers/european_studies/content/conferences/ immigration_policy/PDF/papers/jupp.pdf (accessed 5 September 2008).

M. Keating (2001). *Plurinational Democracy. Stateless Nations in a Post-Sovereignty Era.* (Oxford: Oxford University Press).

M. Keating (2009) 'Rescaling Europe', *Perspectives on European Politics and Society,* 10(1): 34–50.

R. Koopmans, P. Stratham, M. Giugni and F. Passy (2005) *Contested Citizenship. Immigration and Cultural Diversity in Europe.* (Minneapolis: University of Minnesota Press).

W. Kymlicka (2001) 'Minority Nationalism and Immigrant Integration' in W. Kymlicka (ed.) *Politics of the Vernacular.* (Oxford: Oxford University Press).

G. Lahav (2004). *Immigration and Politics in the New Europe. Reinventing Borders.* (Cambridge: Cambridge University Press).

S. Lipset and S. Rokkan (eds) (1967) *Party Systems and Voter Alignments.* (NY: The Free Press).

J. Loughlin (2001) *Subnational Democracy in the European Union: Challenges and Experiences.* (Oxford: Oxford University Press).

P. Lynch (1996). *Minority Nationalism and European Integration.* (Cardiff: University of Wales Press).

M. Maor and G. Smith (1993) 'On the Structure of Party Competition: The Impact of Maverick Issues' in T. Bryder (ed.) *Party Systems, Party Behavior and Democracy.* (Copenhagen: Copenhagen Political Studies Press).

G. Marks, L. Hooghe and A. Schakel (2008) Regional Authority in 42 Countries, 1950–2006: A Measure and Five Hypotheses, *Regional and Federal Studies,* 18(2/3): 121–140

B. Meguid (2008) *Party Competition Between Unequals: Strategies and Electoral Fortunes in Western Europe.* (Cambridge: Cambridge University Press).

C. Mudde (2007) *Populist Radical Right Parties in Europe.* (Cambridge: Cambridge University Press).

F. Müller-Rommel (1998) 'Ethnoregionalist Parties in Western Europe' in L. De Winter and H. Türsan (eds) *Regionalist Parties in Western Europe*. (London: Routledge).

P. Odmalm (2012) 'Party Competition and Positions on Immigration: Strategic Advantages and Spatial Locations', *Comparative European Politics*, 10: 1–22.

G. Sartori (1976) *Parties and Party Systems: A Framework for Analysis*. (Cambridge: Cambridge University Press).

W. Swenden and B. Maddens (eds) (2008) *Territorial Party Politics in Western Europe*. (Basingstoke: Palgrave Macmillan).

L. Thorlakson (2006), 'Party Systems in Multi-level Contexts' in D. Hough and C. Jeffery (eds) *Devolution and Electoral Politics*. (Manchester: Manchester University Press).

F. Tronconi (2005) 'Identita` Etnica e Competizione Politica. Un'Analisi del Voto ai Partiti Etnoregionalisti in Europa Occidentale', *Rivista Italiana di Scienza Politica*, 35(1):77–106.

J. Van Spanje (2010) 'Contagious Parties: Anti-Immigration Parties and Their Impact on Other Parties' Immigration Stances in Contemporary Western Europe', *Party Politics*, 16(5): 563–586.

A. Wilson (2009) 'Coalition Formation and Party Systems in the Italian Regions', *Regional and Federal Studies*, 19(1): 57–72.

R. Zapata-Barrero (2007) 'Setting a Research Agenda on the Interaction Between Cultural Demands of Immigrants and Minority Nations', *Journal of Immigrant & Refugee Studies*, 5(4): 1–25.

R. Zapata-Barrero (2009a) *Immigration and Self-government of Minority Nations*. (Brussels: Peter Lang).

R. Zapata-Barrero (2009b) 'Policies and Public Opinion Towards Immigrants: The Spanish case', *Ethnic and Racial Studies*, 32(7):1101–1120

A. Zaslove (2004). 'Closing the Door? The Ideology and Impact of Radical Right Populism on Immigration Policy in Austria and Italy', *Journal of Political Ideologies*, 9(1): 99–118.

Part II
Governance

4

Divided on Immigration, Two Models for Integration. The Multilevel Governance of Immigration and Integration in Belgium

Ilke Adam and Dirk Jacobs

Introduction

Since the federal elections of 2007, and especially since the new elections in 2010 which led to a new government after a world record-breaking 541 days of negotiations, elites from both sides of the language frontier in Belgium have had extreme difficulty in agreeing on nearly anything. As a result, the possibility of dividing the country has been seriously discussed. Although the final government formation in December 2011 brought a temporary 'armed peace'[1] between the political elites of both linguistic communities, this is widely considered as a temporary and very delicate solution until the federal elections of 2014. In these elections, the Flemish nationalist party NV-A, favouring an independent Flanders, is expected to gain such electoral success that the future of Belgium will – again – no longer be certain. Although not the main source of conflict, immigration and migrant integration policy are areas in which Flemish and Francophone political elites tend to hold diametrically opposing views. From the 1990s onwards, this linguistic cleavage was apparent in all government negotiations and parliamentary debates on immigration and citizenship issues, which both fall under the jurisdiction of the central state.

After the devolution of migrant integration policy to the regions in 1980, regional policy responses have gradually begun to diverge. From the start of the academic debate on 'national models of integration' (Brubaker, 1992), it is clear that there is no such thing as 'one Belgian national model' for migrant integration (Martiniello, 1995; Adam, 2013). Regional migrant integration policies in Belgium were for a long time categorized under the assimilationist *versus* multiculturalist binary (Martiniello and Rea, 2004; Martiniello, 1995; Rea and Jacobs, 2005; Rea, 1994). Francophone integration policies were said to conform to the former, and Flemish policies to the latter. Policy change in Flanders from 2000 onwards, which introduced compulsory civic integration trajectories for migrants has, however, complicated the picture of Flemish multiculturalist *versus* Francophone assimilationist policies (Adam, 2011, 2013). Following the conceptual chapter on the multilevel governance of immigration by Ricard Zapata-Barrero and Fiona Barker (Chapter 2) this contribution first analyses the division of competencies over immigration and migrant integration in Belgium, as well as intergovernmental relations. We will show how Belgium combines a 'divided' centralist immigration policy with a devolutionary migrant integration policy (Spiro, 2001). Secondly, the chapter will compare the different policy positions of Francophone and Flemish parties on central-state immigration and citizenship issues, as well as the divergent regional migrant integration policies. From this comparison, we are able to demonstrate that there is no such thing as one Belgian 'migrant integration model'. When comparing regional migrant integration policies, we will mainly focus on the policy frames inspiring them, the chosen policy instruments, and their centralized *versus* decentralized features. Thirdly, the chapter will offer a possible explanation of these divergent Flemish and Francophone policy responses. The two last sections of this chapter also link with Eve Hepburn's chapter on the multilevel party politics of immigration (Chapter 3) since they analyse party positioning as well as policies and try to explain the differences between the positioning of Flemish and Francophone parties at the federal level as well as between the different regional policies.

Who governs? The division of policy-making power and intergovernmental relations

The gradual transformation of Belgium from a unitary state into a federal system with a large degree of autonomy for the federated entities (the so-called Communities and Regions) is a response to the Flemish nationalist movement and the subsequent Francophone responses (Deschouwer, 2012; Swenden and Jans, 2006). While at first being essentially a movement for cultural and linguistic emancipation in a state dominated by Francophones, the Flemish struggle for cultural recognition has gradually developed into a form of sub-state nationalism striving for political autonomy and, ultimately, independence (Deprez and Vos, 1998). From 1970 onwards, political autonomy was granted to six meso-level authorities (three Communities and three Regions) in a large number of policy fields, but excluding policy areas such as finance, taxation, justice, defence, and social security. which remain prerogatives of the federal state. These meso-level authorities are organized according to linguistic and territorial lines. The *regions* are organized along territorial lines: the Flemish region, the Walloon region, and the Brussels region. The three *communities* are organized according to linguistic lines: the Flemish community, the French community, and the German community. The regions have jurisdiction over policies related to territorial issues, such as area-development planning, transportation, economic development, environmental issues, housing, and employment. The communities have authority over policies related to personal services, such as culture, education, media, and some social services.

One major asymmetry exists however in the institutional configuration of the meso-level authorities in the north and the south of Belgium: while the Flemish region and the Flemish community have merged – thereby composed of one Flemish parliament, one Flemish government, and one Flemish administration – the French Community and the Walloon Region have not. In Francophone Belgium, where political elites are more attached to the Belgian national identity, Walloons and Francophone Brusselers are divided over the definition and institutional configuration of their regional political community. As a result, the political elites have not decided which political institutions should be privileged, the French Community or the Walloon and Brussels Regions.

The division of policy-making power over immigration and immigrant integration

With regard to immigration and migrant integration policy, one can roughly say that the federal state is competent with regards to immigration policy *sensu strictu* (admissions, removals, and residence rights), and the regions have authority over promoting migrant integration (reception and the promotion of substantial equality for immigrants and ethnic minorities). The federal state as well the regions have full legislative and executive power over the competencies that have been assigned to them. The special law of 8 August 1980, which concretized the second Belgian state reform, does stipulate that the meso-level authorities have jurisdiction over 'the reception and integration of immigrants'. Nevertheless, several policy competencies of the federal state also strongly influence migrant integration, not least, citizenship attribution (nationality), anti-racism and (partially) anti-discrimination, but also the attribution of several rights to immigrants, like civic rights, political rights (voting) and most but not all social rights (rights to social welfare). We can thus rightly argue that although the sub-state authorities are, according to the special law of 1980, officially competent over 'reception and integration of immigrants', when one defines migrant integration policy in a sociological way as all policies that promote the participation of immigrants in the host society, and this by the attribution of equal rights as well as by stimulating substantial equality (Adam, 2011; 2013), migrant integration policy can be considered as a shared competence between the federal state and the meso-level authorities.

According to Peter Spiro's frameworks on immigration federalism (Spiro, 2001), presented in Chapter 3 of this book, we can categorize Belgian immigration federalism as centralist with regards to immigration *sensu strictu* (admissions, removals, residence), the attribution of most immigrants' rights (civil, political, and partially social rights), and citizenship acquisition. With regards to migrant integration policy (the promotion of de facto participation, which includes reception policy and the attribution of certain social rights, most importantly the right to public education), the Belgian immigration federalism can be considered as devolutionary, since the sub-state level has been attributed legislative as well as administrative powers with regards to these policy areas. Belgian federalism has excluded the cooperative model as much as possible. In the immigration context, there is one notable exception to that rule (the laws have to be voted and implemented before June 2015). Regions have been attributed the administrative power to deliver study permits to foreign workers but the central state stays competent in developing the regulatory framework.

Let us now explain which (of the six) meso-level authorities are competent for promoting migrant integration. In 1980, competency over the 'reception and integration of immigrants' was attributed to the Flemish and the Francophone communities. This division of competencies changed however in 1993, but only with regard to the French community. In 1993, due to the French Community's budgetary problems, jurisdiction over social policy matters – including migrant integration – was transferred from the French community (which includes the Walloon and Brussels territories) to the Walloon Region and the French Community Commission of the Brussels-Capital Region (FCC).

Since then, three meso-level authorities have legislative and administrative jurisdiction over migrant integration policy, and each followed a different policy path: the Flemish Community, the Walloon Region, and the French Community Commission of the Brussels-Capital Region. Despite the existence of three different policies (two Francophone, one Flemish) only two media debates and two political fora (in political parties) can be detected: a Flemish and a Francophone one. This dual rather than threefold division of the debate on migrant integration policy reflects the *de facto* most important building blocks of the Belgian federation, which are the linguistic communities.

Intergovernmental immigration relations

Compared to other federal states, Belgium corresponds more to the characteristics of an ideal-type dual federation (Deschouwer, 2012). The central state and the federated entities have full legislative and executive power over the competencies that are assigned to them. Federal and regional legislation are on equal footing, the rules of the federal level do not have precedence over regional legislation. Because of this absence of a hierarchy of norms, cooperation between the central state and the meso-level authorities is less of a daily need and practice than in a cooperative federation where the central state sets the frame and the regions implement. By assigning the power to 'decide' and to 'do' (Dahl, 1961) to the same authority, the Belgian federation has been designed to prevent intergovernmental relations as much as possible (Swenden and Jans, 2006: 886). However, despite this wish to prevent the need for cooperation, it seems unavoidable in numerous policy fields, especially in the case of the Europeanization of devolved policy areas (Beyers and Bursens, 2006).

Ever since the devolution of the competence over migrant integration to the meso-level authorities in 1980, the central state's attempts to claim policy-making power over migrant integration – which surpassed its legal prerogatives of nationality law making and the attribution of formal rights – were considered illegitimate by the largest meso-level authority, the Flemish Community. Moreover, the small initiatives the central state took in this policy field had little or no impact on Flemish policy-making. The Francophone authorities, not involved in a nation-building project, were generally more supportive of the central state's initiatives on migrant integration.

The only exception to the rule of Flemish opposition to the central state's initiatives on migrant integration was the 1989–1993 period during which the Royal Commissariat for Immigrants Policy was set up by the central state to make policy recommendations regarding migrant integration. The influence of the Commissariat's policy reports is clearly observable in Flemish and Walloon policy documents, particularly through the follow-up of its recommendations by the regions (Adam, 2013). We assume that this temporary policy-making legitimacy of the federal authorities can be attributed to the fact that the Royal Commissioner was Flemish and Christian Democrat (like the Flemish minister for integration), as well as the sense of urgency and need for policy learning in Flanders, which was surprised by the rise of the extreme-right party Vlaams Blok in the 1988 (local) and 1991 (national) elections (Coffé, 2005).

Subsequent federal initiatives on migrant integration or cultural diversity issues had far less – though not to say any – policy impact (Adam and Rea, 2010). The 2004 Commission for Intercultural Dialogue and the 2010 Interculturality Sessions, both initiated by Francophone federal ministers for equal opportunity, consisted of a large federal consultation process of experts and civil-society actors on how to live together in a culturally diverse society, which resulted in a report making policy recommendations (Delruelle and Torfs, 2005; Foblets and Kulakowski, 2010). Different than in 1993, these recommendations were not taken into account by the regional authorities. The federal ministers launching the policy recommendations in 2004 and 2010 were Francophone, and of a different political party family than the Flemish regional ministers for integration. In 1993, the Flemish as well as the federal ministers were Flemish and Christian Democrat.

Notwithstanding the fact that two official mechanisms for intergovernmental cooperation have been created since the devolution of migrant integration policy to the regions and that political parties still function as informal cooperation mechanisms – albeit less and less (Swenden and Jans, 2006) – one can rightly argue that integration-related cooperation between the regions, and between the regions and the federal state, has been very limited. The federal authorities, when involved in immigration policy-making (a federal competence), do not, or only to a very limited extent consult the regional authorities. The regions, when involved in migrant integration policy-making (a regional competence) do not consult with other regions or the federal state.

The first formal tool of intergovernmental cooperation on migrant integration was the Interministerial Conference for Immigrants Policy, created in 1989 as one of several Interministerial Conferences which were introduced by constitutional legislation (Poirier, 2002). During a ten-year period (1989–1999), they were presided over by the Flemish, Christian Democrat prime ministers Wilfried Martens and Jean-Luc

Dehaene. They were organized at the initiative of the prime minister and granted access to the exchange of information between representatives of the federal and meso-level governments with competencies related to immigrant integration. These conferences allowed for some convergence, mostly due to establishing common (federally financed) projects. However, these projects were additional to the regional migrant integration policies and did not prevent the regions from following different policy paths. Policy coherence amongst the different regional policies was not the conference's objective. As a principle observant confirmed to us,[2] Flemish Community ministers participated in the Interministerial Conferences, although with little enthusiasm. They were required to do so by the federal prime minister who was from the same party as the Flemish ministers responsible for integration. The political party thus only functioned partially as a mechanism of intergovernmental cooperation. It allowed the exchange of information and the creation of common federally financed projects but it had no influence on stimulating regional policy coherence. In 1999, with the accession to power of the purple-green coalition (Francophone and Flemish; liberals, social-democrats, and greens) and the relegation of the Christian Democrats to the opposition after 48 years of government participation, the Interministerial Conferences became a lot less prominent as an intergovernmental relations tool and the Interministerial Conference for Migrants Policy stopped working.

Officially speaking, another formal coordination and exchange platform was created in 1993: the federal Centre for Equal Opportunities and Opposition to Racism (CEOOR), which now constitutes the Belgian Equality body in the light of the European anti-discrimination directives. In addition to its central mission on anti-discrimination, the CEOOR was assigned the task of 'promoting coherence and dialogue over integration policy of the different regions'.[3] However, the regions, in particular the Flemish Community, did not consider the CEOOR as a legitimate policy-making actor but as a competitor that stepped on their competencies. As Marco Martiniello (2012: 95) rightly argues, migrant integration is considered by the regions (meaning the Flemish Community) as their 'private hunting ground' (*chasse gardée*). Therefore, the CEOOR has had difficulties in implementing its coordination task.

Different regional approaches

This section examines the different policy positions of Francophone and Flemish parties on the central state's immigration and citizenship policies, as well as the different regional migrant integration policies. At the central-state level, the different policy positions of Francophone and Flemish parties can be categorized under the 'restrictive-liberal' binary, while the distinction between Flemish and Francophone regional policies is a lot more complex to portray.

Let us start by very briefly explaining the different policy positions of the Francophone and Flemish parties on the central state's immigration and citizenship policies (see also the chapters by Dandoy and Erk in this volume). Belgian history clearly shows that Flemish parties have tended to call for firmer immigration policy and are more opposed to the extension of foreigners' rights than Francophone parties. Francophone parties have been, for instance, more open towards granting voting rights to foreigners at the local level (Jacobs, 1999), and they have also defended more liberal nationality legislation than the Flemish for whom immigrants first have to prove they are 'integrated' before they can be naturalized. For Francophone political parties, on the contrary, naturalization has long been seen as a process that stimulates integration (Rea, 2000). During the difficult governmental negotiations of 2007 when the Flemish demanded much tighter nationality legislation and limitations on family reunification, the Francophones wanted a regularization of undocumented migrants. This divergence between Francophone and Flemish party positions on immigration and immigrant rights were also reflected in the government negotiations that led, in 2006, to the simultaneous implementation of several European immigration and asylum directives[4] and a reform of the Belgian asylum system. In this package deal, Francophone demands (mainly from the *Parti Socialiste* – PS) for a humanitarian subsidiary protection statute were weighted against the Flemish demand (Flemish liberals, VLD and Flemish Socialists, SP.a) for a more restrictive family reunification procedure (Vink, Bonjour and Adam, 2014).

Different from the Flemish and Francophone party positions at the federal level, the distinction between the Francophone and Flemish regional responses towards migrant integration cannot be categorized under the restrictive/liberal dichotomy. Schematically, one can say that the Francophone approach to migrant integration is very much inspired by the French Assimilationist-Republican Model. The emphasis is on social and economic inclusion and the necessity of a common citizenship. Its approach can be typified as a laissez-faire assimilationist stance (Adam, 2011, 2013), in which assimilation into the mainstream Francophone culture is expected from migrants. Colour-blind social policies have long been considered the best strategy towards immigrant assimilation. Cultural government intervention, in an assimilationist or a multiculturalist direction, is considered to reify differences. The only thing the government should do is refrain from developing targeted or multiculturalist policies that are considered to cement differences. Immigration is not seen as a threat in Francophone Belgium as long as it does not lead to multiculturalism.

In contrast, Flanders emphasizes its language competence and the importance of ethnic-cultural identities, two issues that have played a prominent role in the history of the Flemish nationalist movement (see Chapter 11 by Erk in this volume). Additionally, the state is given a much more important role in dealing with the management of cultural diversity (Adam 2011, 2013). Today, Flanders has a hybrid policy towards immigrant incorporation which can be typified as combining an interventionist assimiliationist policy towards (mostly) newcomers (through obligatory integration trajectories that insist on learning common norms and values) and a more multicultural, targeted ethnic-minorities policy for established ethnic minority groups (Adam, 2013; Loobuyck and Jacobs, 2010). The influence of the Dutch model on the development of Flemish integration policies has been quite emphatic (Jacobs, 2004).

Two different events at the end of the 1980s brought migrant integration to the forefront of the government's agenda for the French and Flemish communities: the prospect of creating the Brussels Region in 1989 (a region with a high percentage of foreigners and therefore future immigrant electorate in Francophone Belgium) and the electoral breakthroughs of the extreme-right party, Vlaams Blok in Flanders (1988 and 1991). Greater policy attention to the integration question did lead to different types of policy changes in the French community and in the Flemish community. On the Francophone side, it led to abandoning the policy programme promoting immigrant cultures in favour of a colour-blind assimilationist policy.[5] In Flanders, this more prominent positioning of the integration question in the government's agenda reinforced formerly initiated multiculturalist policies.

Today, Flemish integration policy is mainly regulated by the civic integration law (*inburgeringsdecreet* 2003, 2006, 2008[6]) and the integration law (*integratiedecreet* 2009, formerly the ethnic minorities law 1998).[7] The civic integration part of the 2013 law regulates the organization of the integration trajectories, compulsory for most new migrants and for some categories of old migrants (depending on welfare, unemployment benefits, or social housing). The trajectories mainly include language courses, a civic integration course (focusing on rules and regulations, common norms, and values), vocational training, and counselling by an individual tutor. Non-compliance is sanctioned with an administrative fine. Since the federal government has exclusive competence over immigration and nationality law, the sanction for non-compliance could not be related to the residence permit or citizenship acquisition. A decade after its implementation, Flemish civic integration policy has developed into a centralized and professionalized policy with a large network of implementing actors; most importantly, the reception offices, the Houses of Dutch, and the Flemish employment office.

Notwithstanding the introduction of compulsory civic integration courses (that can be categorized as corresponding to an interventionist-assimilationist policy frame), former multiculturalist policy instruments were not withdrawn in Flanders but rather reinforced (Adam, 2007; Jacobs, 2004). The legal cornerstone of the Flemish multiculturalist integration policy – the ethnic minorities law of 1998 – was modified in 2009 and 2013. The law mainly organizes the work of the Flemish administration, of sub-regional integration centres, of public local integration services, and of the Minorities Forum. The integration centres have had the responsibility of supporting mainstream organizations in adapting their services towards a culturally diverse public, thereby promoting culturally conscious mainstream services. The local integration services are subsidized to support local authorities in developing a local integration policy. The Minorities Forum, an umbrella organization of ethnic minorities associations and their federations, was created to allow its members to prepare joint positions to allow for interest representation at the regional level. While the policy instruments of the former ethnic minorities law have not been withdrawn or rolled back, the multiculturalist terminology was removed in 2009. The backlash against multiculturalism in Flanders seems to have been expressed mainly through political rhetoric and the introduction of assimilationist policy measures, but not through the concrete withdrawal of formerly institutionalized policy instruments that valorize and publicly finance cultural diversity and immigrant associations. Immigrant associations, their federations, and their umbrella organization (the Minorities Forum) have never been seriously questioned as relevant policy instruments and their (relatively limited) budgets have only risen over time. The 'ethnic minorities policy' has been re-labelled an 'integration policy' and the formerly labelled target group of ethnic minorities is currently labelled 'new Flemings'.[8] While previously, a former immigrant was for several generations categorized as an 'allochtoon' and could seemingly only become a 'new Belgian' but not a 'new Fleming', now a former immigrant seems, at least on paper, able to become a Fleming.

The Walloon migrant integration policy is organized through the law of 4 July 1996 on the integration of foreigners and persons of foreign origin, which was slightly modified in 2009. The sub-regional integration centres are Walloon's central policy instruments. These centres are also important policy actors in the Flemish integration policy. Unlike the Flemish community, however, the Walloon region does not clearly define the policy frame within which these integration centres function. Nevertheless, Walloon policy-makers seem less hostile to multicultural policy instruments than Francophone Brusselers, as they modestly finance immigrant associations and their cultural activities. The Walloon region only vaguely describes the centres' mandates, and it does not establish a coordination structure that contributes to the harmonization of the sub-regional or local integration centre policies. This process leads to a *de facto* decentralization of Walloon integration policy in which the underlying policy frame is determined at the sub-regional or local rather than the regional level. This is much like the importance of municipalities in deciding integration policy in the regions of Italy, especially Emilia-Romagna, as revealed in Chapter 7 by Campomori and Caponio. Moreover, the budget devoted to this policy in Wallonia is extremely low in relation to that of Flanders.[9]

Unlike several neighbouring countries and Flanders, no compulsory integration courses have (yet) been set up for immigrants. Although this might change very soon, up until now, a structured, harmonized offering of non-compulsory language and civic integration courses is likewise unavailable. The absence of a structured, harmonized supply does not mean that language courses or activities promoting civic integration are not available at all. Rather, they are mostly local, bottom-up initiatives organized by a palette of very different organizations, without regional coordination or quality standards.

Since the summer of 2012, integration courses have been on the Francophone regional policy agenda. At the time of writing, the governments of the Walloon Region and the French Community Commission of the Brussels Region have been drafting legislative proposals to set up integration trajectories for immigrants. Different to Flanders, these legislative proposals do not foresee making participation in courses compulsory. Nevertheless, they will oblige new migrants to attend a meeting during which their needs with regards to language and social integration will be assessed.[10]

In Brussels, two different migrant integration policies have been implemented in the same territory: a Flemish and a Francophone one, and this without any institutional and little intergovernmental cooperation. Since 1993, Francophone authorities in Brussels (the French Community Commission of the Brussels Region, COCOF) have held legislative power over migrant integration, while Flemish Brussels' authorities (the Flemish Community Commission of the Brussels Region) have not. As a consequence, the Flemish integration policy in Brussels is more or less the same as in Flanders, while the Francophone Brussels policy is different than the Walloon one. One major difference exists, however, between the implementation of the Flemish civic integration trajectories in Flanders and in Brussels: in Flanders the trajectories are compulsory, in Brussels they are not. Constitutional provisions prevent Flemish integration courses from becoming compulsory in bilingual Brussels. Francophone Brussels' migrant integration policies have long followed a more pronounced colour-blind, French-style assimilationist policy path than those of Wallonia. Inspired by the French republican approach, general social policies targeting poor neighbourhoods are the preferred policy tools. The 2004 law on social cohesion organizes the policy path followed since 1993. Coordinated by 19 local authorities, around 200 non-profit organizations set up social and cultural activities towards 'all Brusselers', mainly in deprived neighbourhoods. While this 'social cohesion policy' is officially recognized as the Francophone Brussels migrant integration policy, references to immigrants or integration are deliberately left out. Immigrant associations (when portrayed as such) or activities leading towards ethnic homogeneity among groups have been explicitly excluded from the social cohesion funds (CRAcs, 2007), fearing they would lead to segregation (*ghettoization*) and ethnicized social relations. In case the French Community Commission votes on the legislative proposal with regard to migrant integration courses, which is highly probable, the traditionally colour-blind assimilationist policy of the French Community Commission will become more colour-conscious.

As has become clear following this analytical description, regional migrant integration policies gradually diverged after devolution. Policy coherence between regional policies was certainly not an objective of devolution. On the contrary, is policy divergence, at least in multinational states, not the main objective of devolution (Keating and McEwen, 2005)? These divergent migrant integration policies do however have consequences for immigrants' rights and duties, depending on if they live in Flanders, Brussels, or Wallonia. To give a few examples, during the 2003–2014 period, if an immigrant settled in Flanders, he or she might be obliged – or, to phrase it positively, 'have the right' – to follow an integration trajectory including a language course, a civic integration course, and individual labour market assistance. In Wallonia, a new migrant is not (yet) obliged to follow such a trajectory, but neither is there (yet) a structured and professional offer of these courses available if he or she wishes to do so. Other examples concern the public recognition of religious and cultural rights. If immigrant children go to school in Flanders or a Flemish school in Brussels, they are allowed to be legitimately absent for a religious festival day of one of the six recognized religions, while in Francophone schools this is not the case. If immigrants want to create an immigrant association and get subsidized by the regional authorities for cultural activities, this is a lot easier in Flanders than in Wallonia, and in Brussels immigrants are better-placed to address the Flemish instead of the Francophone institutions with such a demand.

Explaining the differences

Explaining the differences between the Francophone and Flemish approaches towards immigration and migrant integration is not a straightforward exercise. Depending on whether one wants to understand the restrictive *versus* liberal approach of Flemish and Francophone political parties towards immigration at the federal level, or the different regional migrant integration polices, interpretations will point in different directions. Nevertheless, we argue, and demonstrate with empirical data, that the combination of patterns of party politics and sub-state nationalism delivers explanatory insights into most of these differences.

Different patterns of party politics

Since the separation of the traditional political parties in the 1960s and 1970s (Delwit, 2003), Belgium has had a regionalized party system with a Flemish variant and a French-speaking variant (see chapter 10 by Dandoy). Since that time, there have been no more statewide parties, but neither are there only regional parties. Flemish and Francophone parties are present in regional as well as in federal elections and parliaments. Except for Brussels and some of its surroundings, the electorate of one linguistic community cannot vote for political parties of the other, even though the federal government is composed of political parties from both communities (De Winter, Swyngedouw and Dumont, 2006). In recent decades, these two political landscapes have evolved differently with regard to the number of parties and their electoral successes. The Flemish party system has become more fragmented than the Francophone one and, while the Flemish party system has to count with an electorally successful extreme-right party (Vlaams Blok), the Francophone extreme-right party Front National has always remained very weak (Coffé, 2005). As a consequence, and as electoral research shows, immigration and migrant integration have become more determining elements for voters during elections in Flanders than in French-speaking Belgium (Coffé, 2005: 120), even when this element is controlled by taking into account the major socioeconomic variables which constitute electoral behaviour. Large comparative research (Koopmans, Michalowski and Waibel, 2012) shows the importance of electoral factors, in particular the presence of a successful extreme-right party, in explaining the types of migrant integration policies. We can therefore legitimately assume that the different degree of party polarization on immigration in Flanders and Francophone Belgium has had an impact on the positions of Francophone and Flemish political parties with regard to the central state's immigration and citizenship policies, as well as on the Flemish and Francophone regional migrant integration policies, which confirms one of the hypotheses laid out by Hepburn in Chapter 3.

As we have shown in the previous section, different patterns of party politics in Flanders and Francophone Belgium seem to explain very well the different restrictive *versus* liberal positions of Flemish and Francophone political parties with regard to the central state's immigration and citizenship policies. The party politics variable is however less convincing in completely capturing the central features of divergence in regional integration policies, *id est* the more intensive policy activity of the Flemish community on integration, its more intensive cultural interventionism, its multiculturalist features, and its greater degree of centralization. The patterns of party politics do however seem to explain why Flanders developed integration courses for immigrants and why Francophone Belgium did not until 2013.

We can demonstrate the importance of party politics for the establishment of compulsory civic integration courses by means of discursive references to the electoral climate at the moment these courses were proposed by Flemish political actors. These discursive references can be traced back to the first electoral successes of the Flemish extreme-right party Vlaams Blok. Since 1991, the Flemish mainstream right (Flemish liberal party) proposed compulsory language courses for immigrants as a reaction to the electoral success of Vlaams Blok. The Liberal Party president at that time (Guy Verhofstadt) explained the VB's electoral success '...because they [the extreme-right] seem to be preoccupied with the real problems of the people like the disturbed contact with immigrants ...', which are problems '... which traditional parties do not take into account'.[11] This mainstream right has also been shown to be the principal policy entrepreneur in the final setup of the compulsory integration courses in Flanders in 2003 (Adam, 2013). A representative of the Flemish liberals legitimates these compulsory integration courses by 'the need to give a signal to the population [that we are not too lax with immigrants]'.[12] This helps to explain the importance attributed to immigration in the manifestos of the Liberal Party, as identified by Dandoy in Chapter 10. Meanwhile, because of the absence of anti-immigrant politicization in the Francophone party system, the Francophone liberal party (PRL, later MR), always seemed to have more to lose than to win by claiming a tougher migrant integration policy. Their coalition-seeking strategy with the Francophone socialists – for whom the immigrant electorate is of primary importance in the Brussels region (Teney et al., 2010) – explains their abstention for engaging with anti-immigrant politicization and tougher migrant integration policies (Adam, 2011, 2013).

The stronger politicization of immigration in Flanders compared to Francophone Belgium, due to the presence of an electorally successful extreme-right party, cannot be isolated from the Flemish sub-state nation-building process. In this way, the electoral success of the extreme-right party in Flanders, compared to the failure of the Francophone extreme-right party, can be explained by the strong and professional organization of Vlaams Blok, which could lean on the radical right wing of the Flemish nationalist movement and which disposed, from the onset, of ideologically trained party activists and leaders (Coffé, 2005).

Flemish minority nationalism and the near absence, or more fragmented nature, of sub-state nationalism in Francophone Belgium (Swenden and Jans, 2006) are equally important in explaining several differences between Flemish and Francophone migrant integration policies.

Divergent processes of nation-building

While it seems nearly impossible to distinguish between a sub-state nation and a region (Keating, 2001: 24), it is clear that meso-level authorities are not all involved in nation-building to a similar extent, or even at all. This differing degree of involvement in sub-state nation-building is empirically noticeable in Belgium. While Flanders is actively involved in a sub-state nation-building project, there is no such clear nation-building project in Francophone Belgium (Erk, 2005; Deschouwer, 2012).

This different degree of involvement in sub-state nation-building impacts on policy development in general, and on migrant integration in particular. Whereas policy development in Flanders serves to legitimize its actual and claimed autonomy (Erk, 2003; Kerremans, 1997), this is not the case in Francophone Belgium. With regard to migrant integration policy-making, it is clearly observable that the Flemish authorities invest a lot more time and resources in policy development than the Francophone authorities, the different budgets spent on integration can serve as a simple indicator, as well as the large differences in the number of policy documents produced (Adam, 2013). Although the different levels of politicization help explain different levels of investment in policy-making, the sub-state nation-building project in Flanders and its search for internal legitimacy must be added to the explanatory cocktail. The search for legitimacy is in our view also responsible for the more centralized features of Flemish integration policies in comparison with the more decentralized Walloon policies. By developing clearly centralized regional policies, the policy ownership is more easily attributable (McEwen, 2005) to the legitimacy-seeking and autonomy-claiming Flemish Community.

Beyond the search for internal legitimacy for the sub-state nation-building project, the need for external legitimacy may, in Flanders like in Québec (Barker, 2010; Chapter 11 by Erk in this volume), explain some of the progressive and tolerant features of the migrant integration policies, which, counter-intuitively, seem to have been reinforced in parallel with the increasing electoral success of the Flemish extreme-right party Vlaams Belang (direct successor to the Vlaams Blok) from 1988 onwards (Adam, 2013). These 'progressive' features are firstly, the fact that the Flemish integration policy became increasingly more multiculturalist; secondly, that these multiculturalist policy instruments survived in Flanders when they were being rolled back everywhere else in Europe where they had previously existed (Joppke, 2004) and thirdly, that Flanders invested more in anti-discrimination policies than its Francophone counterpart (Adam, 2006). The Flemish authorities acknowledge that the success of Vlaams Blok/Belang and recent nationalist demands and policies strengthens the perception of an intolerant Flanders outside its borders; and that something has to be done to change that reputation.[13] The Flemish government's hiring of an 'image manager'[14] demonstrates that the Flemish authorities are concerned about their external legitimacy.

Most importantly, however, it can be argued that next to the search for internal and external legitimacy, the need for boundary-setting by the Flemish nation-building authorities has inspired its interventionist cultural integration policies. Flemish nation-building has led to the need to define the collective 'us', which in turn leads to the definition of 'the other'. Both of these definitions are central to migrant integration policies. In Francophone Belgium, where elites and citizens tend to identify more with Belgium than with Flanders (Billiet, Maddens and Frognier, 2006), the definition of 'who we are' and 'who is the other' is considered to be a task of the Belgian federal authorities, which are competent over nationality law. By way of its interventionist cultural integration policies, nation-building Flanders invests in the definition of the Flemish 'us'. Moreover, it is in debates over migrant integration as opposed to the more general debates over extending Flemish autonomy, that the modest attempts towards a de-ethnicization of the Flemish identity can be found. In 2007, the Flemish liberals (VLD) proposed replacing the term 'allochtonous' (allochtoon) – the official term used to describe someone with an immigrant background – with the term 'new Fleming'. Although this group label is far from hegemonic, it indicates an elite concept of a civic Flemish identity that until now has been reserved only for the Belgian identity. Since 2009, the Flemish nationalist party, N-VA, has used this terminology in the description of its annual award to a 'new Fleming' who has 'contributed by his or her merits to the enrichment of Flanders and is an example for the new Flemings and for Flemings in general'.[15]

Conclusion

This chapter has shown that Belgium combines a 'divided' centralist immigration federalism with a devolutionary integration federalism. We qualify the centralist immigration federalism as 'divided' because of the very different views of the Flemish and Francophone political parties who, together, govern the central state, but function in different party systems. With regard to migrant integration policy-making, we can legitimately claim that Belgium does not count as 'one' but 'two' governance systems, and this seems to be unique with regard to the other multinational states studied in this volume. The existence of two instead of one integration governance system can be explained because regional authorities have legislative *and* administrative power over migrant integration, because their policies substantively diverge and because there is no horizontal intergovernmental cooperation. Although the central state still holds legislative and administrative power over several policy areas that are key to migrant integration, not least citizenship attribution, vertical intergovernmental cooperation on migrant integration issues has become extremely rare. The complexities and difficulties of coordinating migrant integration policy issues certainly do not contribute to policy efficiency. International organizations even perceive them as an explanation for the weak results of the labour-market participation of immigrants in Belgium in a comparative perspective (OECD, 2012). The different integration governance systems on each side of the linguistic border also results in a differentiation of immigrants' rights within the Belgian state.

The recent Europeanization of immigration and migrant integration policies might however modestly alter the centrifugal tendencies of immigration and integration governance in Belgium. First accounts on the Europeanization of Belgian immigration and migrant integration (Van Puymbroeck, Adam and Goeman, 2010; Vink, Bonjour and Adam, 2013) have shown that European hard and soft law instruments (such as the Family reunification directive, the European Integration Fund, and the National Contact Points for Integration) have, although modestly, stimulated regional policy convergence, brought the party positions of Francophone and Flemish political parties closer to each other, re-launched vertical and horizontal intergovernmental cooperation on migrant integration, and have brought the central state back in on a lost policy competence. Europe might thus constitute a – further to be studied – centripetal force in Belgian immigration and migrant integration governance.

Notes

1. Reference to Luc Huysse's book on Belgian's consociational democracy, 'De gewapende vrede' ('The armed peace').
2. Interview with the former *chef de cabinet* of the Royal Commissioner for Migrants Policy and consecutively director of the Centre for Equal Opportunities and the Fight against Racism.
3. Art 2 § 2 of the Law of 15 December 1993 as amended by the Law of 10 May 2007.
4. Family migration, 2003/86; minimal standards for the qualification and status as refugees, 2004/83 and 2004/81 on victims of trafficking in human beings.
5. We understand a laissez-faire assimilationist or universalist policy frame to mean a policy vision in which a certain form of cultural homogeneity is deemed necessary for better socioeconomic and political participation by immigrants and for promoting social cohesion in a culturally diverse society. However, the proponents of such a vision consider this cultural conformity to be a process that will naturally come to pass within a society, without the

need for explicit promotion by the state. The laissez-faire assimilationism is colour-blind. The conviction is that a certain form of cultural conformity will actually be achieved without developing a specific, targeted, group-oriented social policy, which would only accentuate the differences. The general rules are considered to be neutral, and a general social policy is considered to be the best guarantee of the socioeconomic integration of immigrants and their descendants. By contrast, an interventionist, assimilationist philosophy believes that the state has a duty to actively advance an explicit policy that is focused on the promoting the majority culture (a common language, common values and norms, and a common history). For a detailed presentation of Adam's bi-dimensional conceptual space for situating migrant integration policy frameworks, see Adam (2013a).

6. Law on the Flemish civic integration policy of 28 February 2003, amended by the laws of 14 July 2006 and 1 February 2008.
7. Both decrees are at the time of this writing due to be integrated into a new integration decree. Flemish Parliamentary documents (2012–2013), 1867 (1).
8. This categorization is not part of the decree, which would have implied a legal definition, but it is part of the accompanying policy documents and discourses.
9. In 2009, the Flemish budget for migrant integration policy was nearly 18 times larger than in Wallonia (author's calculations, sources available upon request).
10. Le Soir, Le parcours d'intégration se concrétise, Mardi 5 juillet 2012; Le Soir, Accord wallon sur le parcours d'intégration, 24 December 2012.
11. Verhofstadt G. (1992) Tweede Burgermanifest.
12. Interview with the advisor of the Flemish Liberal vice-minister in the Flemish Government negotiations on the proposal for a decree that organizes compulsory integration courses. Decreet Vlaams inburgeringsbeleid, 6 November 2006.
13. Strategische Adviesraad Internationaal Vlaanderen, Beeldvorming van Vlaanderen in het buitenland, Advies 2008/22.
14. De Morgen, Vlaamse overheid zoekt imagomanager, 9 March 2009.
15. http://www.n-va.be/agenda/uitreiking-ebbenhouten-spoor, consulted on 30 January 2011.

References

I. Adam (2013) *Les entités fédérées belges et l'intégration des immigrés. Politiques publiques comparés.* (Bruxelles: Editions de l'Université de Bruxelles).
I. Adam (2011) 'Des approches différenciées de la diversité. Les politiques d'intégration des personnes issues de l'immigration en Flandre, en Wallonie et à Bruxelles' in J. Ringelheim (ed.) *Les droit et la diversité culturelle.* (Brussels: Bruylant).
I. Adam (2006) 'La discrimination ethnique à l'embauche à l'agenda politique belge', *Formation emploi: Revue française des sciences sociales*, 93: 11–25.
I. Adam and A. Rea (2010) *La diversité culturelle sur le lieu de travail: pratiques d'aménagements raisonnables en Belgique.* (Brussels: Centre pour l'Egalité des Chances et la Lutre contre le Racisme).

I. Adam (2007) 'Multiculturalism, Alive but Changing? Policy Change in Flanders as a Test Case', *Paper Presented at the ECPR General Conference*, Pisa.

F. Barker (2010) 'Learning to Be a Majority: Negotiating Immigration, Integration and National Membership in Quebec', *Political Science*, 62(1): 11–36.

J. Beyers and P. Bursens (2006) 'The European Rescue of the Federal State: How Europeanisation Shapes the Belgian State', *West European Politics*, 29(5): 1057–1078.

J. Billiet, B. Maddens and A. P Frognier (2006) 'Does Belgium (Still) Exist? Differences in Political Culture between Flemings and Walloons', *West European Politics*, 29(5): 912–932.

H. Coffé (2005) 'Do Individual Factors Explain the Different Success of the Two Belgian Extreme Right Parties', *Acta Politica*, 40(1): 74–93.

CRAcs (2007) *Rapport annuel sur l'application du décret du 13 mai 2004 relatif à la cohésion sociale*. (Brussels: COCOF).

E. Delruelle and R. Torfs (2005) *Eindverslag Commissie voor Interculturele Dialoog*. (Brussels: Centrum voor Gelijkheid van Kansen en Racismebestrijding).

K. Deprez and L. Vos (1998) *Nationalism in Belgium: shifting identities, 1780–1995*. (London: Routledge).

K. Deschouwer (2012) *The Politics of Belgium: Governing a Divided Society*. (Basingstoke: Palgrave Macmillan).

M. Foblets and C. Kulakowski (2010) *Einverslag Rondetafels van de Interculturaliteit*. (Brussels: Centrum voor Gelijkheid van Kansen en Racismebestrijding).

D. Jacobs (2004) 'Alive and Kicking? Multiculturalism in Flanders', *International Journal on Multicultural Societies*, 6(2): 280–299.

D. Jacobs (1999) 'The Debate Over Enfranchisement of Foreign Residents in Belgium', *Journal of Ethnic and Migration Studies*, 25(4): 644–663.

C. Joppke (2004) 'The Retreat of Multiculturalism in the Liberal State: Theory and Policy', *British Journal of Sociology*, 55(2): 237–257.

M. Keating and N. McEwen (2005) 'Introduction: Devolution and Public Policy in Comparative Perspective.', *Regional & Federal Studies*, 15(4): 413–421.

R. Koopmans, I. Michalowski and S. Waibel (2012) 'Citizenship Rights for Immigrants: National Political Processes and Cross-national Convergence in Western Europe', *American journal of sociology*, 117(4): 1202–1245.

P. Loobuyck and D. Jacobs (2010) 'Nationalism, Multiculturalism and Integration Policy in Belgium and Flanders', *Canadian Journal of Social Research – Revue canadienne de recherche sociale*, 3(1): 29–40.

M. Martiniello (2012) 'Belgium' in C. Joppke and L. Seidle (eds) *Immigrant Integration in Federal Countries*. (Montreal and Kingston: McGill-Queen's University Press).

M. Martiniello (1995) 'Philosophies de l'intégration en Belgique', *Hommes & Migrations*, 1193: 24–29.

M. Martiniello and A. Rea (2004) *Affirmative action: des discours, des politiques et des pratiques en débat*. (Brussels: Bruylant-Academia).

M. Martiniello, A. Rea and F. Dassetto (2007) *Immigration et intégration en Belgique francophone: état des savoirs*. (Brussels: Bruylant-Academia).

N. McEwen (2005) 'The Territorial Politics of Social Policy Development in Multi-level States', *Regional and Federal Studies*, 15(4): 537–554.

OECD (2012) *Settling In: OECD Indicators of Immigrant Integration 2012*. (Paris: Organisation for Economic Co-operation and Development).

J. Poirier (2002) 'Formal Mechanisms of Intergovernmental Relations in Belgium', *Regional & Federal Studies*, 12(3): 24–54.

N. Van Puymbroeck, I. Adam and H. Goeman (2010) 'The Europeanisation of the "Belgian" Integration Policy: Soft European Instruments and Their Impact' in Dierckx, D., Van Herck, N. and J. Vranken (eds) *Poverty in Belgium.* (Leuven: Acco).

A. Rea (2000) *Immigration, Etat et citoyenneté. La formation de la politique d'intégration des immigrés de la Belgique*, Brussels: PhD Thesis, Political Science Department: Université Libre de Bruxelles.

A. Rea (1994) 'La politique d'intégration des immigrés et la fragmentation des identités. Le modèle belge à l'épreuve de la crise économique et de la fédéralisation de l'Etat, *Revue internationale d'action communautaire*, 71: 81–92.

A. Rea and D. Jacobs (2005), 'Construction et importation des classements ethniques. Allochtones et immigrés aux Pays-Bas et en Belgique', *Revue européenne des migrations internationales*, 21(2): 35–59.

P. Spiro (2001) 'Federalism and Immigration: Models and Trends', *International Social Science Journal*, 53(167): 67–73.

W. Swenden and M. Jans (2006) 'Will It Stay or Will It Go? Federalism and the Sustainability of Belgium', *West European Politics*, 29(5): 877–894.

C. Teney, D. Jacobs, A. Rea and P. Delwit (2010) 'Ethnic Voting in Brussels: Voting Patterns among Ethnic Minorities in Brussels (Belgium) During the 2006 Local Elections', *Acta Politica*, 45(3): 273–297.

M. Vink, S. Bonjour and I. Adam (2013) 'The Politicization and Europeanization of Family Migration Policies in Belgium and the Netherlands: Contrasting Dynamics in a Consensual Context' in Vollaard, H., Beyers, H. and P. Dumont (eds) *European Integration and Consensus Politics in the Low Countries.* (London: Routledge).

L. De Winter, M. Swyngedouw and P. Dumont (2006) 'Party System (s) and Electoral Behaviour in Belgium: From Stability to Balkanisation', *West European Politics*, 29(5): 933–956.

5
Canadian Federalism and the Governance of Immigration

Raffaele Iacovino

Introduction

The recent societal debate over 'reasonable accommodations' in Quebec, which culminated in the *Consultation Commission on Accommodation Practices Related to Cultural Differences* (Bouchard and Taylor, 2008), is perhaps most notable to observers in that it was about the larger question of migrant integration in and for Quebec. Indeed, the usual story over the sharing of the immigration file in Canada has been to present it as a case of *de facto* asymmetry – with two nation-building projects competing through their respective affirmations as primary host societies (Gagnon and Iacovino, 2007: 92) in a situation where policy choices and collective identity are mutually reinforcing (Barker, 2010; Labelle and Rocher, 2009). In what is essentially a policy field marked by inevitable interdependence, Quebec and the federal government have managed to carve out a governance framework that has remained in place for around 20 years – and has come to represent something of a standard bearer for demonstrating the flexibility of the Canadian federation in light of its socio-political and regional diversity. Indeed, immigration is often touted as a prime example that Canada's constitutional architecture is fundamentally flexible and can evolve to accommodate collective demands without engaging in drastic constitutive introspection and formal change.

In recent years Canada has introduced a considerable degree of decentralization in both admissions and reception by extending and signing a patchwork of agreements with all of the other provinces and territories (PTs). Through Canada's informal style of bargaining between federal and provincial government executives, the structure of governance in immigration has largely been the result of a series of bilateral agreements that has rendered Canada's immigration regime extremely complex. However, this narrative of a flexible governance framework that has successfully adapted to regional diversity misses part of the picture and masks some very salient distinctions between Quebec and the other PTs. This chapter will disentangle this complex institutional framework and sets of agreements and will argue that the governance framework for immigration in Canada operates simultaneously along two distinct 'logics', or justificatory schemes. These schemes render it difficult to classify intergovernmental relations along a single continuum applicable to all provinces. Quebec's powers relative to the federal government in this policy area are qualitatively singular and are governed by constitutive considerations that have no counterpart in other federal-provincial relationships, which can be more aptly characterized as ideologically driven in delineating the rise of decentralization and devolution as policy priorities. The chapter will briefly outline the main constitutional architecture designating roles in immigration and then move to assess the more substantive determinants of the country's governance framework – federal-provincial bilateral agreements.

Governance structure

Constitutional framework[1]

Canada's formal constitutional framework in the policy field of immigration has remained in place since its founding in 1867. Under Section 95, immigration is a concurrent power, with the federal government paramountcy.[2] This is perhaps the feature that most explicitly contributes to the federal government's capacity to ensure some uniformity and coherence among the provinces and to limit the scope of policy divergence. Indeed, federal paramountcy in a shared jurisdiction allows much room for central authorities to pick and choose the particular aspects of the immigration process that they are willing to share or devolve entirely.

Along with this stipulation of concurrent power, other constitutional provisions impact on the governments' capacities in immigration and integration. Perhaps most notably, Section 91 (25) grants the federal government exclusive control over naturalization and aliens, leaving it as the sole order of government empowered to structure the formal terms of citizenship.[3] Moreover, this affords the federal government unrestricted responsibility over the terms of admission, as a final arbiter of sorts, which again allows for much leverage even in cases of negotiated devolution.[4]

While federal control of naturalization creates somewhat of a hierarchical relationship, the social and political determinants of immigration and integration policy are broad, thus provinces do hold some authority when considerations on the planning and management of immigration affect larger social, economic and cultural outcomes that reside within provincial jurisdictions.[5] As such, provincial control over matters such as civil and property rights, and health and education allow some policy space to determine the terms of coordination and collaboration with central authorities, specifically in the area of settlement programmes. This provides provinces with some legal and normative avenues to constrain unilateral action by the federal government and moderates the potential to exploit federal paramountcy.[6] At a minimum, the federal government is thus compelled to consider the effects of immigration and integration policy on governing capacities and priorities, leading to structural incentives to collaborate and coordinate desired policy outcomes.

In 1982, the entrenchment of the *Charter of Rights and Freedoms* in the repatriated constitution included Section 6 (2) which guarantees mobility rights not only to Canadian citizens but to permanent residents as well.[7] As such, both provinces and the federal government must be cognizant of internal migratory patterns and the question of coherence in order to ensure that desired admissions are not adversely affected by internal displacement. In other words, while agreements in principle may allow particular governments to meet specific needs, newcomers cannot be subject to restrictions relating to their place of residence or employment, which tempers somewhat the range of options available through centralized admissions policy. Moreover, since this provision is underpinned by considerations related to international human rights obligations, and more specifically in the case of Canada, freedom from discrimination based on residence in the pursuit of a livelihood, governments are in effect forced to ensure some exchange of information and policy coherence. Indeed, mobility rights in a framework marked by differentiated admissions criteria could potentially allow some applicants to circumvent one set of criteria by entering through another admissions framework and then simply moving to the jurisdiction in which they would not have qualified in the first instance.[8]

The constitutional framework highlighted above, however, does little to shed light on the complex configuration of Canada's governance regime in this policy field. Indeed, disentangling the responsibilities associated with the various facets of immigration requires a closer look into the evolution of bilateral agreements between specific provincial governments and the federal government over time. The following section will illustrate that as a shared file, immigration is precisely the kind of jurisdiction in which actors in multinational states may exercise a certain political adaptation without necessarily upsetting the federation's symmetry at a formal level. It is this patchwork of political arrangements rather than the constitution itself that more adequately reveals the scope, nature, and dynamics of provincial roles in selection, admissions and settlement policies.

The intensification of provincial governance: bilateral agreements

Aside from some provincial interest in immigration in the late 19th century, as a holdover of colonial government concerns prior to Confederation, immigration for much of the 20th century was almost entirely managed by the federal government.[9] As early as 1868, prompted in large part by the Quebec government's pressing for more clarity in regard to the roles of respective governments, the first federal-provincial conference was convened. It resulted in Canada's first Immigration Act in 1869 where provinces could actively engage in recruitment abroad (mostly in Britain) as well as establish settlement policies, yet the federal government maintained extensive control over most aspects of the file.[10] Also, the informal practice of provincial governments advising the federal government in matters relating to volume was initiated. Soon after, in 1874, the agreement was amended and provinces were thereafter not permitted to recruit abroad due to conflicts with federal government priorities, leading to perceptions that governments were acting at cross-purposes, and creating ambiguity from the perspective of potential migrants. Instead, an agent could be placed within federal offices, a practice that was gradually discontinued when the federal government simply assumed this responsibility. For nearly 80 years onwards, immigration became highly centralized,[11] with the federal government restricting its collaboration with provincial governments to settlement activities, which required provincial cooperation.[12]

As aforementioned, the real battleground in immigration has occurred in the intergovernmental arena, where bilateral negotiations have become the mechanism of choice for the designation of particular roles. Throughout the late 1960s and early 1970s, Quebec consistently petitioned the federal government to negotiate an agreement that would expand the province's responsibilities. Further to Quebec's demands, in Canada's landmark Immigration Act of 1978, the federal government paved the way for increased provincial activity in immigration by explicitly stipulating that the minister could 'enter into an agreement with any province ... for the purpose of facilitating the formulation, coordination and implementation of immigration policies and programs'.[13] This opening for provincial input had been set in motion in a 1974 Green Paper released by the federal government, where the intention to include provincial governments in the planning and management of immigration was formally declared, and this would lay the groundwork for the patchwork of negotiated arrangements between the provinces and the federal government. Quebec was the first province to press for greater institutionalization of immigration governance.

Quebec

Through most of the 20th century into the 1960s, Quebec had largely dismissed federal government overtures for joint cost-sharing arrangements. Under Premier Maurice Duplessis in particular, it did not support the largely British immigration favoured by Ottawa, nor did it seek to employ public resources for settlement policies aimed at newcomers, which were deemed to constitute a threat to the French-Canadian nation. Indeed, Quebec's clerical and conservative elites viewed immigration as a threat to a traditional rural and Catholic conception of the nation and as a potential challenge to the long-standing dominance of the Church and the professional middle class in controlling questions relating to collective identity (Behiels, 1991). Quebec had thus been an exception in the pre-1970 era of centralized policy because while other provinces were content with the nation-building efforts and resources of the federal government, Quebec's position was one of disinterest. Along with exclusionary education policies, this resulted in most immigrants opting for integration into the Anglophone minority, which exacerbated the divide. Quebec viewed federal government policies with suspicion and promoted pro-*nataliste* policies rather than more actively seeking powers in immigration (Behiels, 1986).

By the mid-1960s, labour-market pressures due to economic growth re-awakened provincial interest in immigration. The main catalyst, however, was Quebec, where the Quiet Revolution transformed ethnocultural conceptions of collective identity towards a socio-political discourse centred on language, territory, and the state. Quebeckers, through the language of nationhood, could build a majoritarian liberal-democratic society and cease to assume a defensive posture as a permanent minority. Combined with a significant decline in the province's birth rate, immigration came to represent a key pillar in ensuring its economic, cultural, and socio-demographic flourishing; and along with many other social policy fields, the state was targeted as the appropriate agent of intervention. Neo-nationalists were primarily concerned with the perverse effects of leaving immigration to central authorities, most notably with regard to the fear of a declining percentage of Francophones in the country, and thus a waning of influence (for an early study, see Dumareau, 1952). The main concern was twofold: not only was Quebec getting a smaller share of immigrants, but those that were settling continued to integrate into the Anglophone stream. In 1968, the government created a Ministry of Immigration, and throughout the following two decades, engaged in a determined campaign to claim management and planning powers in various areas of immigration.

The first accord signed was the Lang-Cloutier[14] agreement in 1971, which predated the Immigration Act. This arrangement allowed Quebec representatives to be employed in Canadian embassies and to engage in advising Canadian immigration officers stationed abroad about social conditions that were specific to Quebec. Subsequently, the 1975 Andras-Bienvenue Accord moderately expanded the role of Quebec agents, as they were allowed to direct interviews with candidates. Moreover, agents were to be more active in the selection process by making recommendations to visa officers. However, Quebec officers were nevertheless limited to an advisory role, as formally recognized immigration officers worked under the banner of the Canadian government.

In 1978, *The Quebec-Canada Accord in Matters of Immigration and Selection of Foreigners*,[15] or the Cullen-Couture agreement, granted Quebec a more pronounced role in the selection of immigrants from its own network of offices abroad. Quebec also received the capacity to control temporary immigration movement for workers and students. While respecting the general framework of the Canadian Immigration Act, Quebec was able to nevertheless secure a significant portion of its objectives as to the volume and the composition of its immigration. The federal government retained control over borders and the admission and selection of refugee claimants. Moreover, Quebec had to abide by the categories of immigrants as defined by federal legislation – independent immigrants, family class, and individuals in distress.

In 1991, in the wake of the failed Meech Lake Accord, which sought to entrench Quebec's *de facto* immigration powers in the constitution, the two parties signed the *Canada-Quebec Accord Relating to Immigration and Temporary Admission of Aliens* (Gagnon-Tremblay/McDougall Accord), which remains in force to this day. This was the most comprehensive agreement to date, and it attempted to more adequately assign responsibilities to correspond to Quebec's demands. Briefly, the federal government is responsible for the annual volume to Canada, criteria of residency (length, authorization of study and work), categories of immigrants, criteria for family sponsorship and assisted relative cases, and asylum claims. Quebec received exclusive responsibility in three domains relative to permanent immigration: total volume for its territory, the selection of candidates that seek settlement in Quebec[16] (with the exception of claimants for the status of refugee and family reunification), and the management and follow-up of sponsorship arrangements and their duration, according to criteria established by federal legislation.

In terms of temporary immigration, Canada must receive Quebec's consent in matters that concern the issuing of work and student permits, the admission of international students (except in cases where the latter participate in a Canadian government assistance program with developing states), and the authorization given to a visitor to Quebec to receive medical treatment. In short, while Canada sets the broad guidelines through its designation of classes of immigrants, Quebec has much room to manoeuvre according to how it chooses to meet its own needs.

In addition, Quebec immigration officials abroad are granted a certain formality. Quebec officials review files of applicants, interview them, and ultimately grant approvals for entrance. This process is intended to clearly demonstrate that the selection process is undertaken by Quebec authorities in order to help alleviate potential confusion among immigrants. Moreover, since the officers represent the government of Quebec rather than Canadian officers applying Quebec's criteria, it reduces the potential for individual officers using their own discretion against the interests of Quebec.

One of the underlying aims was to strengthen Quebec's capacity to maintain its demographic weight in Canada and to promote the notion that the process of admitting and integrating immigrants bolsters Quebec's status as a minority nation and host society in its own right. As such, the accord allowed Quebec to receive a percentage of immigrants that is equal to the percentage of its population in Canada – with a clause allowing for 5 per cent more. Furthermore, the federal government agreed to consult Quebec with regard to the total volume of immigrants that will be destined for Canada. Quebec also agreed to receive an equal proportion of refugees. While Canada accords refugee status, Quebec has a say in selecting those candidates that are more suitable to meeting Quebec's criteria. Visitors are also subject to Quebec's consent prior to being admitted. In short, Quebec directly controls 'economic' immigrants while having a significant input into the application of selection criteria in other categories. It is also important to note that this accord transferred to Quebec reception services and linguistic and cultural integration as well as the financial resources necessary to meet this responsibility, which must either remain constant or increase on an annual basis.[17] While there are no formal requirements to report activities to the federal government, the accord does include two broad clauses mandating Quebec to respect some uniformity in settlement provision:

• the reception and integration services offered by Quebec correspond, when considered in their entirety, with those offered by Canada in the rest of the country
• these services are offered without discrimination to all permanent residents in the province, whether or not they have been selected by Quebec[18]

Finally, the agreement contains no termination clause and amendment is contingent on consent from both parties.

Migrant integration in Quebec: challenging Canada's conception of citizenship

Quebec's integration regime is extensive in scope and one aspect of its orientation that merits elaboration is that such policy initiatives in effect straddle the line between citizenship and integration. As such, while Quebec does not control the formal levers of citizenship, it has tailored its integration and settlement capacities to reinforce a regime of differentiated citizenship in emphasizing distinct terms of belonging.[19] This is an important aspect of Canada's immigration regime, building on the recognition that citizenship is more than a mere legal category – it is also buttressed by identity concerns: 'Citizenship is not just a certain status, defined by a set of rights and responsibilities. It is also an identity, an expression of one's membership in a political community' (Kymlicka and Norman, 1994).

As such, in the area of socio-political integration, the story is one of competing national projects between Canada and Quebec. Institutionally, the federal government controls naturalization policy and thus delineates formal citizenship status; it has instituted a policy of multiculturalism within a bilingual framework[20]; and it has constitutionally entrenched a Charter of Rights and Freedoms since 1982. Each of these pillars of socio-political integration is meant to integrate newcomers into a political community structured around Canada as an undifferentiated territorial/political unit, and the rights regime is not nuanced to allow for the institutional acknowledgment of Quebec's specificity. Naturalization allows the federal government to welcome newcomers through the granting of formal citizenship, as well as to engage in early efforts at political socialization through citizenship tests which outline a particular conception of the terms of belonging and a specific view of the country's history. Multiculturalism within a bilingual framework, which is expressed through the *Multiculturalism Act*[21] and the *Official Languages Act,*[22] as well as enjoying certain fundamental protections through constitutional entrenchment, also allows central authorities to employ the institution of citizenship to carve out a place for itself as the guarantor of key identity markers. Both also define belonging in Canada away from territorial/collective conceptions of language rights as well as a multinational institutional architecture that would involve the constitutive acknowledgement of the existence of multiple host societies. Finally, the Charter of Rights and Freedoms, the subject of much controversy in Quebec since it did not sign the constitutional package in which it was entrenched, formally denies certain fundamental equality rights that in effect serve as constraints on Quebec's capacity to independently determine the boundaries of its integration model, including the scope of religious, linguistic, and ethno-cultural diversity.[23]

As noted above, Quebec enjoys none of these formal levers of citizenship, yet has managed to use the tools at its disposal to gradually challenge this conception of Canadian citizenship virtually every step of the way. Perhaps the most salient of these initiatives has been Quebec's interventions in the area of language legislation. Since the early 1970s, Quebec has instituted a series of linguistic policies that directly challenge formal Canadian bilingualism with regard to framing the terms of membership, culminating in the *Charter of the French Language,*[24] which explicitly identifies French as the official language of Quebec: '[French is] the language of Government and the Law, as well as the normal and everyday language of work, instruction, communication, commerce and business.' The aim is to establish French as the common public language. While a full treatment is not possible here,[25] the Charter of the French Language provides that the language of instruction in Quebec is to be predominantly French, while the English stream is available only to children whose parents or siblings have attended English schools in Canada, effectively ensuring that newcomers will be integrated through the French education system. In terms of more immediate settlement policies aimed specifically at newcomers, the Quebec government has also instituted a succession of specific programs aimed at the francization of newcomers, including the *Programme d'aide financière pour l'intégration linguistique des immigrants* (PAFILI), and the *Programme d'intégration linguistique pour les immigrants* (PILI).[26]

Quebec has also elaborated its own model of 'interculturalism' as an integration framework, meant to affirm its status as a primary host society contesting the primacy of Canadian multiculturalism (see Gagnon and Iacovino, 2007; Labelle, 2008).[27] Debates continue to proceed regarding the actual salience of interculturalism, since it has never been the subject of a legislative pronouncement and has remained a guiding principle of sorts through both policy statements and re-construction by intellectuals and policy practitioners.[28] Moreover, its actual substantive singularity relative to multiculturalism continues to elicit much deliberation, as does the evolution of its primary normative objectives in defining the place of minority and majority cultures in the public sphere (Iacovino and Sévigny, 2010).[29] Regardless of these ongoing debates, one constant is the promotion of the conception of Quebec as a pluralist host society – emphasizing French as a common public language, the primacy of liberal-democratic institutions and values, and evolving conceptions of cultural pluralism with regard to relations between majority and minority cultures.

In recent years, the Parti Québécois, as well as some prominent public intellectuals (Lisée, 2007; Seymour, 2010),[30] have called for the institutionalization of internal Quebec citizenship as a means to bolster Quebec's integration capacities and to more effectively manage the markers of collective identity. The proposed legislation, *The Quebec Identity Act* (Bill 195)[31] tabled by Pauline Marois as a member of the National Assembly, sought to more definitively contest Canadian legal authority in this area (see Chapter 11 by Erk for more details on the Parti Québécois' position on immigration). The Bill proposed initiatives such as adding a preamble to the *Quebec Charter of Human Rights and Freedoms* that would safeguard equality between the sexes; affirming the secular nature of public institutions, the predominance of the French language, and the protection of Quebec culture. More controversially, the Bill sought to go beyond an interpretive clause in the Quebec Charter and proposed actual constraints on citizenship rights by requiring, for example, proof of French proficiency and knowledge of Quebec culture to obtain a citizenship certificate, which is necessary in order to attain certain political rights, such as running for office in provincial, municipal, or school board elections. As an enforcement mechanism, the Bill proposed that a three-year contract with newcomers settling in Quebec be instituted, outlining the criteria required to obtain the certificate. This aspect of the Bill was widely contested, and most observers agreed that it would not survive legal challenges since it directly challenges Canada's rights regime, including most notably the right for all citizens to run for office without discrimination.[32] While such rhetoric may simply reflect electoral politicking in a context of heightened societal sensitivity,[33] it does signal a tendency to view Quebec's toolkit in the area of migrant integration as somewhat limited, or stunted, because it must constantly contend with a parallel conception of the terms of belonging that is sometimes irreconcilable with Quebec's approach.

In closing, one noteworthy feature of Canada's governance in the area of immigration, however ambiguous, is precisely this distinction between migrant integration as a vehicle for the flourishing of a distinct national identity – where integration initiatives straddle the formulation of citizenship boundaries – and integration conceived as reception and settlement services (delivery) meant to complement established identity markers of citizenship. The following subsection will highlight the trend towards decentralization in the rest of Canada, where this key distinguishing feature in relation to national integration is largely absent.

Decentralization and the other provinces

While not grounding their claims in national identity considerations, during the late 1970s other provinces began to press for some form of bilateral consultative framework in immigration relating to economic and labour-market needs. By the end of the 1970s and into the early 1980s, all of the provinces established consultative bilateral committees with the federal government, aimed mostly at determining the appropriate volume to particular provinces. With the openings provided by the Green Paper in 1974 and the Immigration Act in 1978, the federal government sought to walk a tightrope between appearing to offer the other provinces the same attention it provided to Quebec while hoping that demands would not get too unwieldy. In the mid-1970s, the federal Minister of Immigration Robert Andras offered to sign agreements with other provinces but many did not have the institutional infrastructure to cope with accepting new roles, nor were they inclined to bear the financial costs associated with setting up agents abroad for recruitment and selection (Hawkins, 1988: 181–182). Moreover, there was little popular support for these initiatives, which were viewed as potentially fragmenting Canada as a unified political community. While there was some concern about Quebec's capacity to offer more attractive incentives to immigrants, particularly potential investors, most were assured that Quebec's aims were to increasingly recruit within Francophone countries and were selecting from a distinct pool of potential candidates. In general, the provinces were happy to continue to allow the federal government to undertake the bulk of the responsibilities with most aspects of the immigration file.[34] The agreements that were concluded rested largely on information exchange, policy consultation, and the targeting of specific categories of immigrants that affected provincial policy fields, such as teachers and entrepreneurs, yet none gave the provinces powers over selection (Vineberg, 1987: 315). By the mid-1980s and into the 1990s, most provinces gradually signed agreements with the federal government, yet none came close to the extent of powers concluded with Quebec and were generally consultative in nature. The most pressing concerns related to labour needs in economic planning, particularly in the Western provinces, which wanted more input into targeting certain types of workers; as well as more say in business immigration. Another area of concern that was identified as requiring greater regularized coordination was compensation for settlement services, which the federal government had been increasingly happy to offload. Some provinces expressed concern that Quebec was receiving a disproportionate share of settlement transfers, since its immigration intake in many instances did not reflect its proportion of the country's population.

Perhaps the most notable transition to decentralization, and a change from Canada's exclusive control of the selection and admission of immigrants was instituted in the mid-1990s with the introduction of the *Provincial Nominees Program* (PNP). This allowed provinces to nominate a number of immigrants for admission, through their own selection criteria that was centred largely on economic objectives. Applications would then be approved by the federal government upon satisfying certain health, criminal, and security credentials – the beginning of a 'two-tiered immigrant selection system' (Baglay, 2012: 136). The federal government has outlined four primary objectives related to PNPs:

• To increase the economic benefits of immigration to provinces and territories (PTs), based on their economic priorities and labour-market conditions
• To distribute the benefits of immigration across all PTs
• To enhance federal-provincial/territorial (FPT) collaboration
• To encourage development of official language minority communities[35]

In introducing this programme, the federal government nevertheless maintains control over admissions volume and security considerations, as well as the tools to continue to steer policy priorities through the extensive use of reporting requirements.

At its outset, the programme capped the number of immigrants to be nominated through this class, but since 2006 this cap has been lifted. With this initiative, provincial governments now enjoy the capacity of directly tailoring criteria for immigration to meet their particular needs, including the ability to attract immigrants to desired locations without implicating mobility rights through centralized planning (Baglay, 2012: 126).[36] Moreover, from the perspective of the federal government, this allowed for a certain 'marketization' of immigration outcomes – a more cost-effective twofold process of decentralization (to provinces) and devolution (from the public to the private sector), since this approach allowed both more employer input into identifying immigration needs as well as inviting much more participation from civil society in providing settlement services (Dobrowolsky, 2012: 3). Alexandra Dobrowolsky (2012: 2) summarizes the thrust of this new approach:

> '... (a) attract highly skilled immigrants; (b) expand low wage, tempo-
> rary foreign worker programs; (c) diversify immigration "entry
> doors" and make some more flexible; (d) cut admission and settle-
> ment costs; (e) encourage settlement in less well-populated areas; (f)
> tighten border controls and crack down on undocumented migrants;
> (g) "change citizenship rules to reduce risks of undesired costs and
> unrealized benefits to the state"; and (h) "sell immigration to the
> Canadian public ... through a policy rhetoric that emphasizes the
> hoped-for benefits of immigration while downplaying risks and
> disappointing outcomes"'.[37]

Moreover, the present Conservative Government has intensified a commitment to more diversified and streamlined pathways to permanent residency. For example, the Canadian Experience Class, initiated in 2008, targets temporary workers and international students already in Canada and permits them to bypass the existing points system as an avenue to permanent residency if they can demonstrate proficiency in one official language. As a condition of acceptance, however, such applicants must plan to live outside the province of Quebec.[38] Other examples include the recently launched Federal Skilled Trades Program, which allows the needs of particular industries to be considered when processing eligible immigrant applications, and the Start-Up Visa program, meant to recruit entrepreneurs by linking them with private-sector organizations with experience in working with fledgling ventures.

While the federal government has noted that PNPs have success-fully regionalized immigration, as well as reducing processing times, it has nevertheless pointed out some worrying trends with regards to monitoring, accountability, and coherence in the desired outcomes, sparking calls for further collaboration. To this effect, in expressing concerns about programme integrity, fraud has been identified as an area of concern, where a wide gulf between the capacities of Canadian Visa Officers Abroad (CVOA) and the verification capacities of PTs has been noted. Also, Canadian immigration officials have expressed concern about follow-up data outlining the performance of provincial programmes, particularly in the business stream. In more general terms, the federal government has expressed concern over a serious lack of measures or benchmarks available to assess the economy and efficiency of the wide variety of programs on offer, requiring the setting of bench-marks through collaboration in order to more adequately compare the costs of programmes from both federal and provincial governments. A second broad area of concern involves the commitment of provinces to meet the federal objective of directing applicants to Official Language Minority Communities, with only three PTs identifying this objective as a priority for their programmes.

The federal government thus recently recommended a series of initia-tives to attempt to rectify these shortcomings, including collaboration to establish minimum standards with provinces and territories on basic language ability, including official language minorities, since mobility was a concern here; more standardized measurement and reporting indi-cators with regards to labour-market strategies in order to more effectively identify shortages; increased training and coordination, including clari-fying respective roles between CVOAs and PTs to more effectively tackle fraud as well as to monitor the capacity of PNP applicants to establish themselves economically in the various jurisdictions; greater input from Citizenship and Immigration Canada to encourage the commitment to Official Language Minority Communities; and finally, to collaborate on establishing a monitoring and reporting framework with common performance measures.[39]

To this end, the federal government and the PTs have recently agreed on an action plan: the *Joint Federal-Provincial-Territorial Vision for Immigration*[40] which addresses shared strategic objectives, key actions, and expected results on priority areas ranging from levels planning, economic immigration and settlement/integration. The joint vision focuses almost exclusively on addressing economic pressures relating to efficient and performance-based settlement outcomes, labour-market needs, and volume directly tied to economic demand. Moreover, the priority is to collaborate on identifying evidence-based performance measures that can contribute to a common framework for assessment in all three areas. In terms of key measures, the vision plan calls for a common application management system to process 'expressions of interest' in order to coordinate planning with regards to volume and to strengthen the accountability and integrity of the various economic immigrant programmes. It also calls for the development of a 'Pan-Canadian Framework for Settlement Outcomes' to ensure enforcement of common standards and the establishment a set of principles and guidelines for partnership models with regards to settlement.

Indeed, in the broad area of settlement policies, the federal government has recently decided to reverse its commitment to decentralize and devolve responsibilities due to an extremely complex set of relationships. The federal government had in fact devolved virtually all of its settlement responsibilities to provinces as well as non-governmental service providers through contractual relationships, and to varying degrees provinces have followed suit with their own devolution projects.[41] Leslie Seidle (2010) has provided a useful categorization of the main settlement delivery frameworks of the various agreements with provinces, excluding Quebec, which enjoys comprehensive control and receives funding through a single annual grant. Outside of Quebec, federal government funding for settlement programmes is contingent on the proportion of immigrants in each jurisdiction. In British Columbia and Manitoba, the first provinces to sign comprehensive agreements, devolution to provincial control was the preferred mechanism as the provinces were virtually responsible for the entirety of service delivery; and federal funding was contingent on a host of reporting mechanisms, accountability frameworks, service plans, commitments to Official Language Minorities, and an acknowledgement of federal funding.[42] In the case of Alberta, a 'co-management model' (Seidle, 2010: 15) was established through a *Statement of Understanding regarding Settlement Programs and Services for Immigrants in Alberta.*[43] Service providers under this model submitted a single application received by CIC and Alberta Employment and Immigration (AEI) where a joint-review process was followed by determinations as to the successful applications and the partitioning of funding relationships – in effect matching certain service providers with either the provincial or federal government. Ontario also enjoyed a unique model, involving a Joint Steering Committee to oversee priorities and implementation, with a mechanism to include input from the City of Toronto through a memorandum of understanding (Seidle,

2010: 9–10).[44] The basic thrust of the approach was to establish working groups to ensure the harmonization of settlement delivery services. Finally, the remaining provinces continued to rely on federal government settlement programmes, often through third-party providers, and their role remained limited to consultation and the sharing of data. The broad picture was one of the federal government maintaining a steering role, particularly through initiatives to develop common national standards in settlement outcomes, as highlighted above. As indicated above, however, this concern over variation in service delivery and standards across the country has prompted the federal government to unilaterally opt to centralize the design, delivery, and management of settlement services altogether, as well as to bypass the involvement of provincial governments in soliciting proposals from service providers. Indeed, as of 2014, all settlement services in Canada (except Quebec) are directed by the federal government through a national settlement funding formula based on a province's share of immigrant intake, and settlement will be coordinated through two regional offices in Calgary and Ottawa.

Conclusion

While a cursory overview of the designation of roles in immigration points to a highly decentralized structure with much variety in federal-provincial relationships, the driving forces lying beneath the fragmentation of the governance regime have remained surprisingly steadfast. With regards to Quebec, more traditional considerations premised on constitutive federal principles of autonomy, mutual recognition, and non-subordination in multinational contexts has resulted in a very stable and relatively uncontested consensus regarding an acceptable degree of special status for the province. As highlighted above, this fundamental asymmetry in itself is not the source of enduring political conflict. Rather, the ambiguities associated with competing host societies employing the tools of social and political integration in their respective projects for national integration – challenging the actual boundaries and markers of citizenship – lies at the heart of Quebec-Canada tensions in the policy field. In Quebec, federalism trumps multilevel governance.

In contrast, the 'logic' driving federal-provincial arrangements outside of Quebec is more closely aligned with the sort of multilevel governance that takes its cues from functional considerations such as efficiency, coordination, non-duplication, flexibility and so on. The primacy of the federal government as a steering agent for national integration is not a salient source of political conflict and therefore does not significantly impact negotiated outcomes. The rapid rate of decentralization in recent years is a response to regional economic diversity and the recognition that member states require greater capacity to more adequately direct immigration priorities to meet a variety of economic challenges. In short, the driving forces at work here are ideological rather than constitutive. Policy priorities in selection and settlement in the intergovernmental governance framework outside of Quebec are noteworthy precisely because they will always be circumscribed by a privileged standing of centralized markers of citizenship that is non-negotiable.

Notes

1. The author would like to acknowledge the excellent research assistance of Emmet Collins, Doctoral candidate, Department of Political Science, Carleton University.Although devolution in Canada has resulted in an increasing role for municipal governments in immigrant integration, particularly in regards to implementing and coordinating the delivery of settlement programmes, this chapter will limit its observations to federal and provincial governments.
2. Section 95, in relation to federal paramountcy, stipulates that: 'In each Province the Legislature may make Laws in relation to Agriculture in the Province, and to Immigration into the Province; and it is hereby declared that the Parliament of Canada may from Time to Time make Laws in relation to Agriculture in all or any of the Provinces, and to Immigration into all or any of the Provinces; and any Law of the Legislature of a Province relative to Agriculture or to Immigration shall have effect in and for the Province as long and as far only as it is not repugnant to any Act of the Parliament of Canada.' http://lois.justice.gc.ca/eng/Const/page-4.html#h-24
3. Section 91:...it is hereby declared that (notwithstanding anything in this Act) the exclusive Legislative Authority of the Parliament of Canada extends to all Matters coming within the Classes of Subjects next hereinafter enumerated; that is to say,...25. Naturalization and Aliens http://lois.justice.gc.ca/eng/Const/page-4.html#h-24
4. Section 91 (11) also provides the federal government exclusive control over quarantine which, although somewhat anachronistic today, does provide the federal government with justification for medical and health screening as a condition of admission
5. This is due to the juridical doctrine whereby provincial jurisdiction shall not be deemed repugnant to federal powers in immigration if 'it bears essentially upon a matter within exclusive provincial jurisdiction' (Mercier, 1944: 868–869).
6. Indeed, one point of contention historically has involved the thorny issue of defining the stage at which the federal government's responsibility for providing assistance to immigrants through settlement services shifts to the provincial social assistance regime. In Canada, social assistance is a provincial responsibility yet unemployment insurance is a federal government

program. Determining whether or not newcomers meet the criteria to qualify for settlement assistance, social assistance, or unemployment insurance has historically involved much negotiation and careful coordination because of inevitable linkages. Provinces have consistently argued that they should not be forced to compensate for federal government admissions policies that fail to adequately account for employment prospects, particularly in cases where immigrants have been engaged in continuous employment, which could trigger the transition away from settlement assistance, yet not for a long enough period to qualify for unemployment insurance.

7. Section 6 (2): Every citizen of Canada and every person who has the status of a permanent resident of Canada has the right: (*a*) to move to and take up residence in any province and (*b*) to pursue the gaining of a livelihood in any province; http://laws-lois.justice.gc.ca/eng/Const/page-15.html

8. Still others, in making the case for stringent centralization in admissions policy, fear that Canada already practices such discrimination due to the fact that Quebec may deny a federally approved applicant direct entry to its territory if this person does not qualify under Quebec's selection framework (see Kostov, 2008: 100). However, the preamble to the Quebec-Canada Accord specifically recognizes that mobility rights are guaranteed under the *Charter*.

9. For an historical overview of intergovernmental relations in immigration, see Vineberg (1987).

10. If the provinces choose recruitment policies, their agents abroad have to accept federal government accreditation.

11. One significant exception was Ontario, which received the bulk of immigrants to Canada and recruited heavily from its offices in London and Glasgow to meet labour needs for its burgeoning manufacturing sector.

12. In one notable case, however, provincial lobbying resulted in the federal government heeding to the demands of British Columbia to impose a head tax on Chinese immigrants in an effort to regulate Chinese immigration. See Vineberg (1987: 303).

13. The Act also outlined the broad framework of Canada's selection regime by identifying three main classes of immigrants: economic, family, and refugee. In 2002, the Act was replaced by the Immigration and Refugee Protection Act, and the relevant section is cited from the latter: 8. (1) The Minister, with the approval of the Governor in Council, may enter into an agreement with the government of any province for the purposes of this Act. The Minister must publish, once a year, a list of the federal-provincial agreements in force.

14. The agreements are commonly referred to by the names of the respective ministers of immigration at the time of signing

15. http://www.cic.gc.ca/english/department/laws-policy/agreements/quebec/can-que.asp#admission

16. Quebec has established its own selection grid that is similar in principle to that of the federal government, yet allows the province to alter the relative weight of priorities. For example, Quebec allocates a disproportionate number of points to the ability to speak French relative to English (16 to 6), while the federal government assigns equal status to both languages. Also, in terms of criteria associated with 'adaptability', Quebec attributes points for: Personal qualities, Motivation, Knowledge of the province of Quebec; visit to and ties with Quebec; previous visits to study or other visits; and

family in Quebec. The federal selection criteria, on the other hand, emphasizes family, work, and post-secondary education.See http://www.cic.gc.ca/english/resources/evaluation/fswp/section7.asp#sub3 for a comparative grid of the selection criteria for independent immigrants.

17. Compensation for integration and settlement services went from approximately $101M to $283M from 1998 to 2012. http://www.cic.gc.ca/english/resources/publications/dpr/2012/01.asp. One noteworthy feature is that it accounts for the extra costs associated with French-language instruction.

18. http://www.cic.gc.ca/english/department/laws-policy/agreements/quebec/can-que.asp#reception

19. Quebec's most recent policy statement outlining its general framework is *La Diversité: une valeur ajoutée*, and can be accessed at: http://www.micc.gouv.qc.ca/publications/fr/dossiers/PlanActionFavoriserParticipation.pdf

20. Bilingualism in Canada is formally pan-Canadian in scope, premised on individuals from coast to coast rather than on the territorial principle. See McRoberts, 2004.

21. http://laws-lois.justice.gc.ca/PDF/C-18.7.pdf

22. http://laws-lois.justice.gc.ca/eng/acts/O-3.01/FullText.html

23. It must be noted that traditionally, Quebec's objection to the Charter has been on procedural grounds – its propensity to act as a centralizing and homogenizing forces – rather than on its substantive provisions for equality protection. Indeed, Quebec's own *Charter of Human Rights and Freedoms* predates the Canadian Charter. For more on this interpretation, see Bélanger and Campeau (Commissioners) (1991: 34).

24. http://www2.publicationsduquebec.gouv.qc.ca/dynamicSearch/telecharge.php?type=2&file=/C_11/C11_A.html

25. The Charter also made provisions for the Francization of commercial enterprises with a certain number of employees as well as placing restrictions on commercial signs in languages other than French.

26. http://www.micc.gouv.qc.ca/publications/fr/divers/Pili.pdf

27. Quebec nationalists have criticized Canadian multiculturalism as a policy meant to undermine Quebec's status as a majoritarian political community within Canada; or as a hub of integration as a distinct host society with an explicit recognition that rights and responsibilities of integrating in Quebec are distinct. For a thorough overview, see Labelle, 2008; see also Chapter 11 by Erk in this volume.

28. 'Often mentioned in academic papers, interculturalism as an integration policy has never been fully, officially defined by the Québec government although its key components were formulated long ago.' (Bouchard and Taylor (Abridged Report), 2008: 39). In a more recent essay, unencumbered by his role as co-commissioner, Charles Taylor (2012: 418) elaborates on the basic thrust of Quebec's motivation for developing its own integration framework: ' ... the idea that one could simply dethrone the ancestral identity, and declare that Quebec had no official culture, could never take hold in this province. It sounded too close to an abandoning of the struggle. ... So the contrast is clear: the "multi" story decentres the traditional ethno-historical identity and refuses to put any other in its place. All such identities coexist in the society, but none is officialized. The "inter" story starts from the reigning

historical identity but sees it evolving in a process in which all citizens, of whatever identity, have a voice, and no-one's input has a privileged status'.

29. The model has undergone variation since its initial formulation in 1981, from cultural convergence to a common public culture, to a more civic formulation, and so on. See Iacovino and Sévigny (2010: 249–266).

30. Michel Seymour (2010), in making a case for an internal Quebec constitution, notes that one of the main incentives for Quebec to adopt its own citizenship is that Canadian citizenship allows for unilingual English speakers to obtain citizenship and settle in Quebec, which is directly at cross-purposes with the core of Quebec's integration efforts.

31. Québec, projet de loi no. 195, *Loi sur l'identité québécoise*, Première Session, Trente-Huitième Législature, Éditeur offciel, 2007. http://www.assnat.qc.ca/fr/travaux-parlementaires/projets-loi/projets-loi-38-1.html

32. Indeed, the response from the legal community was swift. See, for example, Campagnolo et al. (2007).

33. Indeed, the Liberal Government also attempted to appeal to the perceived identity malaise by instituting a 'values pledge' as a condition of selection. Immigrants have to sign a form as part of the process of obtaining a Quebec selection certificate attesting to having read and understood a brief description of the common values at the core of Quebec society.http://www.micc.gouv.qc.ca/publications/fr/mesures/Mesures-ValeursCommunes-Brochure2008.pdf

34. The first agreements were concluded with Saskatchewan and the four Maritime provinces

35. http://www.cic.gc.ca/english/resources/evaluation/pnp/section5.asp#a2

36. In 2009, Canada's Auditor-general identified over 50 selection categories under the various provincial programs governed by PNPs. Moreover, selection criteria range from simple categories relying on a pass/fail accreditation to more developed provincial selection grids based on a points system, and targets include skilled and semi-skilled workers; business/investor class immigrants; international student graduates and those with family/community connections. See Baglay (2012) p. 126.; see also, http://www.cic.gc.ca/english/hire/provincial.asp

37. Dobrowolsky (2012), p. 2; points (g) and (h) were cited from Simmons (2010: 257–260).

38. http://www.cic.gc.ca/english/immigrate/cec/index.asp; This programme indirectly allows more provincial input as well, since provinces are responsible for post-secondary education, they can increase their funding for international students who would then be eligible for permanent residency through this channel.

39. http://www.cic.gc.ca/english/resources/evaluation/pnp/section5.asp#a2

40. For a detailed grid, see http://www.cic.gc.ca/english/department/media/backgrounders/2012/2012–11–16.asp. The joint vision also explicitly states that Quebec 'fully assumes sole responsibility for establishing immigration levels, and for the selection, Francization and integration of immigrants. In areas under its responsibility, Québec develops its policies and programs, legislates, regulates and sets its own standards.'

41. Until this recent devolution, three programs constituted the bulk of federal government activities in settlement: Immigrant Settlement and Adaptation

Program (ISAP); Language Instruction for Newcomers to Canada (LINC); and a Host Program (Seidle, 2010: 5).
42. See Annex A of the Canada-Manitoba Immigration Agreement, http://www.cic.gc.ca/english/department/laws-policy/agreements/manitoba/can-man-2003a.asp; as well as Annex A of the Canada-British Columbia Immigration Agreement, http://www.cic.gc.ca/english/department/laws-policy/agreements/bc/bc-2010-annex-a.asp. Also, it must be noted that the Resettlement Assistance Program, aimed mostly at refugee claimants, remains in the hands of the federal government.
43. See the Agreement for Canada-Alberta Cooperation on Immigration, which includes a direct reference to the Statement of Understanding; http://www.cic.gc.ca/english/department/laws-policy/agreements/alberta/can-alberta-agree-2007.asp.
44. See also Annex D of the Canada-Ontario Immigration Agreement, http://www.cic.gc.ca/english/department/laws-policy/agreements/ontario/ont-2005-annex-d.asp

References

S. Baglay (2012) 'Provincial Nominee Programs: A Note on Policy Implications and Future Research Needs', *Journal of International Migration and Integration*, 13(1): 121–141.

F. Barker (2010) 'Learning to be a Majority: Negotiating Immigration, Integration and National Membership in Quebec', *Political Science*, 62(1): 11–36.

M.D. Behiels (1991) *Québec and the Question of Immigration: From Ethnocentrism to Ethnic Pluralism, 1900–1985*. (Ottawa: Canadian Historical Association).

M.D. Behiels (1986) 'The "Commission des écoles catholiques de Montréal" and the Neo-Canadian Question: 1947–1963', *Canadian Ethnic Studies*, 18(2): 38–64.

G. Bouchard and C. Taylor (Co-Commissioners) (2008) *Building the Future, a Time for Reconciliation* (Québec: Commission de consultation sur les pratiques d'accomodement reliées aux différences culturelles).

A. Dobrowolsky (2012) 'Nuancing Neoliberalism: Lessons Learned from a Failed Immigration Experiment', *Journal of International Migration and Integration*, DOI 10.1007/s12134–012–0234–8 Published Online: 15 February 2012.

P. Dumareau (1952) 'L'Aspect et l'avenir démographique du Canada français', *L'Actualité économique*, 28(1): 5–26.

A.-G. Gagnon and R. Iacovino (2007) *Federalism, Citizenship and Quebec: Debating Multinationalism*. (Toronto: University of Toronto Press).

F. Hawkins (1988) *Canada and Immigration: Public Policy and Public Concern*. (Montreal: McGill-Queen's University Press).

R. Iacovino and C.-A. Sévigny (2010) 'Between Unity and Diversity: Examining the Quebec Model of Integration' in S. Gervais, C. Kirkey and J. Rudy (eds) *Quebec Questions*. (Toronto, Oxford University Press).

C. Kostov (2008) 'Canada-Quebec Immigration Agreements (1971–1991) and Their Impact on Federalism', *The American Review of Canadian Studies*, 38(1): 91–103.

W. Kymlicka and W. Norman (1994) 'Return of the Citizen: A Survey of Recent Work on Citizenship Theory', *Ethics*, 104(2): 352–381.

M. Labelle and F. Rocher (2009) 'Immigration, Integration and Citizenship Policies in Canada and Quebec: Tug of War Between Competing Societal Projects' in R. Zapata-Barrero (ed.) *Immigration and Self-Government of Minority Nations.* (Brussels: Peter Lang).

M. Labelle (2008) 'Les intellectuels québécois face au multiculturalisme: hétérogénéité des approches et des projets politiques', *Canadian Ethnic Studies*, 40(1): 33–56

J.-F. Lisée (2007) 'Rien d'inédit dans la citoyenneté interne...', *Le Devoir*, 23 October.

K. McRoberts (2004) 'Struggling Against Territory: Language Policy in Canada' in T. Judt and D. Lacorne (eds) *Language, Nation, and State: Identity Politics in a Multilingual Age.* (New York: Palgrave Macmillan).

J. Mercier (1944) 'Immigration and Provincial Rights', *The Canadian Bar Review*, 22: 868–869.

F.L. Seidle (2010) *The Canada-Ontario Immigration Agreement: Assessment and Options for Renewal.* (Toronto: Mowat Centre for Policy Innovation).

M. Seymour (2010) 'Une constitution interne comme remède au malaise identitaire québécois' in Bernard Gagnon (ed.) *La Diversité québécoise en débat.* (Montréal: Québec Amérique).

A.B. Simmons (2010) *Immigration and Canada: Global and Transnational Perspectives.* (Toronto: Canadian Scholars).

C. Taylor (2012) 'Interculturalism or multiculturalism?', *Philosophy and Social Criticism*, 38(4–5): 413–423.

R.A. Vineberg (1987) 'Federal-Provincial Relations in Canadian Immigration', *Canadian Public Administration*, 30(2): 299–317.

6
Managing Immigration in a Multinational Context. Border Struggles and Nation-Building in Contemporary Scotland and Catalonia

Jean-Thomas Arrighi de Casanova

> Who wants to be responsible? Whenever anything goes wrong, the first thing they ask is: 'who's responsible for this?'
> — Jerry Seinfeld, *The Blood*, 1997

Introduction

As Michael Keating already observed more than a decade ago, the liberal state is being simultaneously challenged from above with the consolidation of supranational institutions, laterally by the advance of the market and civil society, and from below with the resurgence of national and regional identities (Keating, 2001). Too big for small issues, too small for big issues, the state seems increasingly unable to address contemporary challenges and is subsequently constrained to delegate its prerogatives to other tiers of government or to surrender its authority to allegedly more efficient market forces. The well-established literature on immigration suggests that the capacity of the liberal state to accept or reject aliens as it sees fit has been equally contested. For some, the emergence of an international human rights regime, best embodied by the European Union, has considerably constrained its ability to control its borders as it pleases (Soysal, 1994). Others have stressed how immigration policies have been subordinated to corporate interests and the dynamics of economic push and pull factors exacerbated by globalization (Freeman, 1995; Hollifield,

2004). In contrast to the vast literature on the growing role played by supranational institutions and civil society, research exploring whether or not the authority of the state in the realm of immigration is also being eroded from below by lower tiers of government is still scarce. This chapter contributes to fill this gap in the literature by examining to what extent and in what ways sub-state governments engaged in far-reaching nation-building projects have challenged the capacity of their respective central administrations to regulate what has been referred to in Chapter 2 of this volume as admissions policies. In order to do so, this chapter systematically compares immigrant admissions policies and the discourses underlying them between 1999 and 2011 in two well-known cases of protracted nationalist mobilization, Scotland and Catalonia, against the background of statewide policy developments. The empirical analysis is based on a wide review of secondary sources as well as a broad range of primary sources including policy drafts, press articles, parliamentary transcripts, government research papers, and elite interviews conducted between January 2009 and May 2010 in Barcelona and Edinburgh.[1]

This chapter is divided into four sections. The first section briefly introduces the comparative framework and justifies the selection of cases. The second section examines how the Scottish Executive has sought to administer its own admissions policy between the advent of devolution in 1999 and the second victory of the Scottish National Party with an absolute majority of seats in the 2011 devolved elections, against the background of an ever more restrictive statewide policy framework. The third section reviews successive attempts by the Catalan Generalitat to challenge the centralized policy regime since immigration to Spain rose sharply in 1999 until the return of *Convergència i Unió* (CiU) in office after seven years spent in opposition. The last part compares the findings in light of the existing literature on regional economic development and territorial politics and shows why substate governments' 'administrative failure' to gain control over admissions policy may well be interpreted as a 'political victory'.

Immigration in a multinational context: comparing Scotland and Catalonia

For Nick Griffin, leader of the British National Party (BNP), Britain should urgently 'close the door to more [immigration] because this is the most overcrowded country in Europe and is way beyond its proper carrying capacity in population terms'.[2] In a similar vein, the French

Minister of Immigration and National Identity [sic] legitimized the need to introduce stricter border control on the grounds that 'France's hosting capacity is simply limited', which requires putting an end to the 'migratory chaos which consists in accepting migrants without restrictions'.[3] Comparable arguments have regularly been deployed in Germany, the United States, Australia, Switzerland, and other industrialized countries where the supposedly uncontrollable influx of immigrants has been presented as exceeding the nation's capacity to cope with the consequences. But does the BNP leader refer to the London conurbation where inward flows have indeed been considerable since 1945, or to the English North East, Scotland, or Cornwall where the main concern has been protracted emigration? Is the French Conservative government solely concerned with the situation in the Ile-de-France and the Bouches-du-Rhône as the main recipients of international flows or with the notorious *diagonale du vide* stretching from the Meuse to the Landes where the population density barely exceeds 30 inhabitants per km^2, a heritage of the 19th and 20th century rural exodus?

By shifting the unit of analysis from state to regional level, migration trends can shift dramatically, not only in quantitative terms, but also with regard to the cultural and socioeconomic composition of migrant stocks. In consequence, the costs and benefits of migration flows, be they internal or external, are unevenly distributed across the territory of a single sovereign state, a phenomenon which may reinforce existing territorial inequalities or create new ones (Arrighi, 2012: 56–61; Ballesteros, 2003). Yet, immigration policies have generally been considered 'a part of national foreign relations and as such to require ultimate central government control' (Spiro, 2001: 68). While the regulation of immigration can become a prominent intergovernmental issue in centralized and mononational states, the phenomenon is likely to acquire more salience in a multinational context in which the question of 'who governs' in matters of immigration is closely connected to self-determination claims and the accommodation of national pluralism as stipulated by Zapata-Barrero and Barker in Chapter 2 of this volume (see also Zapata-Barrero, 2009; Kymlicka, 2001).

This chapter examines policy-making and intergovernmental relations in the realm of immigrant admissions in two cases of protracted nationalist mobilization, Catalonia and Scotland, whose similarities facilitate their systematic comparison. Stein Rokkan (1983: 28) saw both of them as clear examples of 'failed-centre peripheries that tried to build up their own core structures but fell victim to more effective drives of incorporation launched by other centres'. They are both self-proclaimed stateless nations with nationalist cleavages that cut across socioeconomic and ideological lines. They have been leaders of devolution processes that have had profound constitutional implications and have affected the rest of their respective states. In their domestic politics, they treat themselves as similar, with leaders showing interest in one another, and their media regularly covering their respective news and political developments. In 2008, a meeting of representatives from Flanders, Québec, Scotland, and Catalonia was held with the aim of sharing good practices and discussing mutual experiences in matters of immigration. Catalonia and Scotland also exhibit critical differences, the most important of which for the purpose of this chapter being their past and present experiences of migration, which illustrate historically rooted uneven patterns of economic development. Hence, Spain has long conceived of itself as a country from which 'one leaves', and the United Kingdom as one to which 'one comes'. On the contrary, shifting the unit of analysis from the state to the sub-state level reverses this trend, as Catalonia has since the late 19th century been subject to intense waves of internal influx, whereas Scotland has historically been a land of protracted emigration. In relative terms, the Catalan population went from representing 11 per cent of that of Spain as a whole in 1900 to 16 per cent in 2010. In sharp contrast, the resident population of Scotland shrank from representing 12 per cent of the United Kingdom in 1901 to 8 per cent today.

Between 1911 and 1930, 600,000 people settled in Catalonia from other parts of Spain. Between 1950 and 1975, this figure reached 1.4 million, of which the majority of immigrants came from Andalusia, Murcia, and Galicia; by 1975, 38 per cent of the Catalan resident population was born elsewhere in Spain. The influx almost completely dried out between 1975 and 1990 as the net migration balance throughout this period was consistently negative. However, it began again by the middle of the decade and gained considerable vigour at the turn of the century. Unlike in earlier periods, immigrants no longer came from the rest of Spain but from a variety of countries, reflecting the growing internationalization of the Catalan economy. By 2010, the proportion of foreign-born residents amounted to 16.2 per cent of the population, against 2 per cent a decade earlier. Out of the 1.2 million foreign residents, almost a quarter came from Africa, another quarter from Latin America, and another 15 per cent from Asia. The same year, official figures released by the Catalan Institute of Statistics (IDESCAT) revealed that 19.7 per cent of the population residing in Catalonia was born in another part of Spain and 17.4 per cent in another country.

As Scotland's population remained remarkably stable in the past 100 years, the population of England rose from 29 to 56 million (Lisenkova and Wright, 2008). While uneven fertility and mortality rates did play a role in the relative demographic decline of Scotland vis-à-vis its southern neighbour, distinct historical records of migration flows account for most of the discrepancy. Some 2 million people emigrated from Scotland in the 19th century, and as many did so in the 20th (McCrone, 2001). On the basis of the 2001 Census figures, the Scottish Government's Social Research unit estimated that 835,000 individuals born in Scotland resided elsewhere in the United Kingdom, while another 250,000 lived overseas.[4] As for immigration, a growing number of individuals born in England have migrated to Scotland since the 1950s, their proportion of the total population rising to 8.1 per cent in 2001. Since the European Union's enlargement in 2004, inward flows to Scotland have grown considerably, mainly from Poland, so that between 2001 and 2010, the *General Office for Statistics in Scotland* registered a population increase of 230,000 that is almost exclusively attributed to immigration. In 2009, 6 per cent of the Scottish population was born outside the United Kingdom. Among them, 67 per cent self-identified as white, 16 per cent as Asian, 5 per cent as black, and 4 per cent as Chinese.[5] In spite of a steady increase in immigration since devolution, the proportion of foreign-born residents in Scotland remains to date far lower than south of the border.

Scottish immigration policy (1999–2011): devolution and the limits of control

In Britain, admissions policies under successive Conservative governments between 1979 and 1997 have been widely qualified as both restrictive and effective (Hussein, 2001). Since the implementation of the first *Immigration Act* in 1962, the British government has consistently managed to keep immigration at a significantly lower level than its continental neighbours such as France, Germany, or the Netherlands. As Christian Joppke (1999: 133–134) put it, '[i]f Fortress Europe is being built on the foundation of its lowest common denominator, it is the Fortress Britain turned inside out'. After seventeen years of Conservative rule, New Labour took office in 1997 with an open-borders agenda for those bringing desirable skills, although it lacked a clear strategy to achieve this aim in practice (Somerville, 2007). From 1997, the net migration balance grew sharply, stabilized in 2000, and rose again in 2004 in the wake of the European Union's enlargement and subsequent flows of East

European migrants into the fast expanding British labour market. With a net migration rate above the 250,000 threshold in 2004, it seemed the executive was no longer able to control borders effectively. However, New Labour's ideological stance combined with business pressures have played a much greater role in this rapid increase than the supposed loss of sovereignty resulting from globalization or Europeanization (Duvell and Jordan, 2003). Indeed, until the middle of the decade, the government still perceived immigration as essential for the country's continuing prosperity. But in 2005, the publication of the five-year strategy for asylum and immigration, *Controlling Our Borders: Making Migration Work for Britain*[6] came as a response to rising public concerns in the aftermath of the 2004 EU enlargement.[7] In 2008, a points-based immigration system was introduced with the aim of reinforcing control for 'unwanted' migrants, while broadening the channels of entry for skilled and highly skilled ones.

In 1999, the first government of post-devolution Scotland was confronted with a radically different migration landscape. In sharp contrast to the public debate south of the border, immigration in Scotland has not turned into a salient political issue as a result of a traumatic episode shedding light on the governments' alleged inability to control the influx of foreigners or a popular belief there are 'too many' of them. Instead, it gained currency in the wake of the publication of the 2001 census figures, and was framed as a demographic crisis,[8] as opposed to a societal one. Failing fertility, life expectancy that remains low by West European standards, and sustained emigration coupled with weak immigration were some of the most worrying issues made explicit in the *Report on Scotland's Population in 2001*.[9] While Britain's population was expected to grow from 60 million to 64 million by 2025, that of Scotland, with current trends remaining constant, would soon start to decrease, down to 4.5 million by 2050 (Lisenkova and Wright, 2008). With compelling evidence that the Scottish population was ageing faster than that of England and Wales,[10] the report left little room for optimism. For the vast majority of Scottish politicians, it constituted no less than 'an illustration of the failure of Scotland's economy over the past decades.'[11] It found particular resonance in Scottish politics, where depopulation is a long-standing concern that at least since the 1960s has been perceived both as a brain drain and a symptom of increased dependence on London (Arrighi, 2012: 106–115).

In the new institutional context, what was rapidly referred to in the public debate as the 'population crisis', which had become 'the single biggest challenge facing Scotland as we move further into the 21st century',[12] could not remain unanswered. But 'it was rather easy, before devolution, to invoke the Scottish cultural stereotypes...since these statements in general had few consequences' (Keating et al., 2003: 152). It eventually became more difficult *after* devolution to systematically blame the Westminster government for making decisions portrayed as damaging to Scotland and adopting rhetorical postures that have no consequences for actual policy-making. Consequently, political actors have had to adapt to new rules and address 'Scottish questions with Scottish answers',[13] thereby running the risk of annihilating 'the village story of consensualism' carefully cultivated throughout the long road to home rule (Keating et al., 2003: 153). For the first democratically elected Scottish administration, addressing the population crisis meant simultaneously encouraging immigration and limiting long-standing emigration to the rest of Britain and beyond. However, the 1998 (Scotland) Act, which placed immigration in the list of matters reserved to the Westminster Parliament, considerably limited the Scottish governments' room for conducting its own admissions policies.

The collaboration between the Home Office in London and the Labour-led Scottish Executive resulted in the adoption of the *Fresh Talent Initiative* in 2004 that was based on the assumption that long-standing demographic decline could be reversed by 'promoting Scotland as an attractive location to live, work, study and do business'.[14] The Scottish National Party's (SNP) 2003 manifesto proposed the devolution of immigration competences and the creation of a Green Card aimed at attracting up to 50,000 highly skilled immigrants per year. By contrast, Scottish Labour initiatives focused on softer levers which could be implemented within the existing UK-wide framework[15] (for more details on Scottish party positions on immigration, see Chapter 12 by Hepburn and Rosie in this volume). The overarching policy purpose of the *Fresh Talent Initiative* was to raise awareness abroad and promote Scotland as a welcoming and dynamic nation. The Scottish Executive-funded website has ever since provided exhaustive information to prospective migrants. On the homepage, available in Chinese and Polish, Scotland is described as 'a multicultural mix of 5 million people. People have been coming to live here from all over the world since centuries. So you can be sure of a warm welcome'.[16] The campaign was complemented by the creation of a Relocation Advisory Service (RAS) with offices in Glasgow, which provides personalized information about business and academic opportunities in Scotland in order to ease the relocation process.

The most emblematic initiative of the Scottish government is the *Fresh Talent: Working in Scotland Scheme* (hereafter FTwiss), which entitled international graduates from Scottish universities to live and work in Scotland for two years without the need for a work permit,[17] whereas international students in English and Welsh universities saw their visa expire immediately after graduation.

Since raising the demographic growth rate to the EU average by 2011 was one of the SNP's main campaign promises,[18] profound changes in admissions policy were to be expected when the party won the 2007 elections and was able to form a minority government for the first time in the short history of devolution. The Aberdeen and Grampian Chamber of Commerce ordered a report in 2009 to be submitted to the Office of National Statistics to evaluate the pros and cons of the Canadian and Australian regionalized systems. The author of the report concluded that: 'evidence gathered from Canada clearly shows that a points-based system with regional elements works better and more effectively than country-wide procedures. Bespoke factors for Scotland could easily be factored in through bonus points or lower thresholds for those who agree to work, live and stay here for a minimum period of time, a process that could not only help us to find skilled people for jobs but will also help to boost the declining population in a targeted and controlled way.' On the basis of these findings, the SNP government advocated the creation of a regionalized point-based system in order to take into account Scotland's distinct economic and demographic interests. But in 2008, the Scottish proposal was firmly rebuffed by the Home Office, where it was argued that creating 'a two tier system for Scotland at the same time as the Irish and British governments are working to close the existing "back doors" does not make sense'.[19] Instead, the newly-created Skills Advisory Board (SAB) and Migration Advisory Committee (MAC), in charge of assessing the optimal number and skills of migrants to the UK economy, were asked to issue a distinct list of jobs to be filled by migrants in Scotland, including very specific activities such as ballet dancer and sheep shearer. In relative terms, the MAC 2007 report revealed that the Scottish economy had almost three times as many vacancies for skilled workers as companies in England.[20] Besides, the March 2008 Green Paper *A Points-Based System* did touch upon the issue of territorial disparities and specified that 'skilled and highly-skilled migrants [could be encouraged] to stay in Scotland in the longer-term, for example through a reduced qualifying period for some Tier 1 and Tier 2 migrants who can demonstrate they have lived and worked in Scotland for an appropriate period of time'.[21] But these concessions were far from incorporating a fully fledged regional dimension similar to the Canadian Provincial Nominee Immigration Programme in operation since 1967 and allowing provincial governments to select immigrants according to their economic needs (see Chapter 5 by Iacovino in this volume). Besides, in 2008, FTwiss was mainstreamed into the UK-wide points-based system, and Scotland *de facto* lost its competitive advantage. For the Scottish Labour party, this also proved the success of devolution, portrayed as a catalyst for policy innovation, and of its own policy, which encouraged London policy-makers to expand it to the rest of the United Kingdom. Conversely the SNP saw it as another illustration of Westminster's pernicious attitude towards devolution and its long-standing inability to take into account Scottish sectional interests. This discontent was broadly shared among Scottish public opinion beyond SNP circles. As the *Scotsman's* editor commented: 'Scotland has different needs from the rest of the UK, and it would be far easier for us to influence population and economic growth by having the ability to set our immigration policy'.[22]

By 2011, the gap between Westminster's concern with border control and Holyrood's fear of another brain drain exacerbated by adverse economic conditions had grown wider than ever. One of the first decisions made by the Conservative/Lib-Dem coalition after they took office in May 2010 was to impose a so-called 'immigration cap' on the influx from outside of the European Union. In response, Alex Salmond pleaded that Scotland should be exempt from UK immigration rules, and that a wave of migrant workers should be allowed north of the border in order to 'flood the recession and boost the country's economy'.[23] But his demands were immediately rejected by the British Immigration Minister Damien Green, for whom the government was 'committed to getting immigration back to sensible levels, after it had been allowed to get out of control for too long'.[24] Ultimately, after ten years of sustained efforts to acquire greater autonomy to address what has officially been referred to as Scotland's 'greatest challenge in the twenty-first century', Westminster's sovereignty over admissions policy has remained largely unaffected.

Catalan immigration policy (1999–2011): 'Much Ado About Nothing'?

In sharp contrast with the United Kingdom where immigration control has regularly appeared on the political agenda since the 1962 *Commonwealth Immigrants Act*, the first piece of legislation in Spain was issued as late as 1985, one year before the country joined the European Community (EC). To that date, there were less than 250,000 foreign nationals living in Spain, a figure about ten times below that of Spanish nationals living abroad. Until the mid-1990s, the concomitant processes of democratic consolidation and economic opening were not translated into a sharp rise in immigration. But by the end of the decade, the Spanish economy initiated a period of unprecedented growth, boosted by the labour-intensive construction and tourism sectors. In 1999, the Institute of National Statistics (INE) recorded 127,000 entries. Five years later, this figure had risen to 684,000, came close to a million in 2007, and was then divided in two in 2009 in the turmoil of the economic crisis. In 2010, the number of foreign nationals officially figuring on local registries amounted to 5,708,940, converting Spain into one of the main recipients of international migration in the course of a single decade (Arango and Finotelli, 2009).

Already in 2000, the General Regime of entry, implemented at a time of severe economic recession and mass unemployment, was rightly perceived as unable to address the needs of a booming economy characterized by a substantial labour shortage. Within this framework, Spanish businesses could not recruit abroad until it was formally acknowledged that no native worker could fill the position. The *Organic Law 4/2000* provided for the creation of a parallel track of entry – the so-called Quota Regime – based on the functional evaluation of needs, and granting Autonomous Communities a key role in determining the contingent. But this proved to be ill-suited to Spanish businesses, and in particular to Catalan small and medium-sized enterprises (SMEs) which lacked the resources to anticipate their needs (Roig, 2007: 293). Besides, the scheme was far from covering the overall demand for foreign labour in a context of sustained economic growth. Hence, in 2004, merely 31,000 foreign workers were granted a work permit through the quota system, while there were 688,000 applicants for the extraordinary regularization that took place a year later (Serra et al., 2005). The decision to complement the quota system with a list of hard-to-fill positions issued by respective provinces and targeting skilled-labour shortages was equally disappointing, not least because the visa system managed by Spanish consulates was essentially ineffective. As Gonzalez-Enriquez (2009) compellingly showed, the lack of resources dedicated to the effective recruitment of workers abroad and to border controls has been an enduring feature of Spanish immigration policy over the past 15 years. Ultimately, the 'cheap' approach prevailed, 'allowing immigrants to come in irregularly, as "bogus tourists", and then regularizing their status, either through collective amnesties or administrative arrangements' (Gonzalez-Enriquez, 2009: 144). Hence, since 1986, successive Spanish governments have recurrently decreed 'extraordinary'[25] regularizations in order to contain the rise of the underground economy and reap the benefits of this sudden influx of additional taxpayers and contributors to social security (Gala, 2007: 376).

Although the international influx to Catalonia started relatively earlier than in the rest of Spain, the phenomenon remained largely unnoticed until the early-1990s. Internal migrations had stopped abruptly in 1975, and the net migration rate was consistently negative in the 1980s (Miret, 1997). This trend, unseen since the early 19th century, can be attributed to a combination of two factors. First, while the Catalan economy was temporarily penalized by its old industries and the profound structural reforms undertaken to make it more competitive in European markets, other Spanish territories were growing at a fast pace. Hence, the territorial gap that had characterized Spanish economic development ever since the 19th century was gradually being plugged (Garrido-Yserte and Mancha-Navarro, 2009). Second, large numbers of internal migrants who had settled in Catalonia were now returning home, encouraged to do so by the pre-pension schemes implemented at the time by the Spanish government as a means of fighting unemployment by decongesting the labour market. But progressively, Catalonia went from being a 'springboard' to more appealing and yet seemingly unreachable destinations as Western European states were tightening their immigration policies, to a 'land of attraction' in the wake of its economic recovery. As the stock of internal migrants willing to move away from their communities and accept poorly paid jobs had dried out as a result of economic growth and falling birth rates, immigration channels from abroad were progressively institutionalized. From then on, the phenomenon grew at a faster pace than in other Autonomous Communities so that by 2010, the proportion of foreign-born residents in Catalonia amounted to 16.2 per cent of the population, against 2 per cent a decade earlier (GENCAT, 2010).

According to the 1978 Constitution, drafted at a time when immigration from abroad was insignificant, immigration is an exclusive competence of the central state, together with the regulation of resident aliens' legal status and naturalization. But by 1999, as Catalonia was confronted with a fast-accelerating influx of international migrants, the Generalitat sought to gain some control over admissions policy. In an official visit to Montréal in May 2001, the representative of the Generalitat[26] signed the *Québec-Catalonia Agreement on Immigration* and returned to Spain with the intention of advocating a regionally differentiated immigration policy along Canadian lines. The administration led by the centre-right nationalist party CiU formalized its proposal and lobbied the

Conservative government to introduce a mechanism of shared competences as part of a broader reform of the legislation under scrutiny. But
besides the fact that the Conservative party (PP) no longer needed CiU's
parliamentary support following its victory with an absolute majority of
seats in the 2000 general elections, the statewide Spanish Socialist party
(PSOE) was equally reluctant to support a reform delegating power over
a matter commonly understood as an 'act of sovereignty' (Santolaya,
2007: 67). Jordi Pujol, in his last term as the President of the Catalan
Generalitat, responded to this rebuff in a dramatic vein by insisting
that the Generalitat had 'to be able to run its own immigration policy,
as immigration is, for Catalonia, a question of being or not being'.[27]
The degradation of intergovernmental relations between Barcelona and
Madrid combined with a Catalan Socialist Party (PSC) far ahead in the
polls during the 2003 Catalan election campaign pushed the CiU-led
Generalitat to bypass the central state by opening immigration offices
in Poland, Morocco, and Colombia. This initiative officially aimed to
link Catalan employers with foreign candidates,[28] and to make sure, in
the terms of Artur Mas, then *Consellor en cap* of the Generalitat, that
'newcomers know the reality and the culture of Catalonia'.[29] Hence, the
'Catalan embassies' were mandated to provide prospective immigrants
with Catalan classes in order to familiarize them with the 'cultural
specificities' of Catalan society.[30] By using its paradiplomatic[31] network
to pursue a more targeted immigration policy, the Generalitat sought to
mitigate the deficiencies of the statewide framework, increase its international visibility in sending countries, and facilitate the recruitment of
skilled workers. But the Spanish consulates in charge of delivering visas
were unwilling to cooperate and were in any case already overloaded
(Moya Malapeira, 2006: 65). Besides, the Catalan initiative was taken to
the Constitutional Court by the central government and partially struck
down in October 2003[32] on the grounds that it constituted an invasion
of state competencies. A few weeks later, CiU, despite its narrow advance
over the Socialists, was not able to constitute a coalition so that the left-
wing tripartite coalition made up of the PSC, Esquerra Republicana de
Catalunya (ERC), and the Catalan Green party (ICV) took control over
the Generalitat; putting an end to Pujol's six consecutive terms in office
(1980–2003). Shortly after, the decision was made to close the existing
offices abroad and not establish new ones.

The 2003 change of leadership in Catalonia was soon followed by
the no less surprising return of the PSOE to office in Madrid at the
2004 general elections. As far as admissions policies are concerned, the
consequences were twofold. Firstly, it marked a clear shift away from a

security-driven to a socioeconomic-driven agenda. Immigration respon-sibilities, which had been placed under the remit of the Government Office of Alien and Immigration Affairs, accountable to the Ministry of the Interior, by the former Conservative government, were transferred to the Ministry of Labour and Social Affairs. Secondly, the commitment of Prime Minister José Luis Rodriguez Zapatero during the campaign to back up the much-awaited reform of the Catalan Statute opened the way for a revision of the constitutional *status quo*. The New Statute, approved both by a referendum and the Catalan Parliament in 2006, provided the Generalitat with a new set of prerogatives in immigration matters.[33] As of October 2009, the Employment Services of Catalonia (*Servei d'Occupacio de Catalunya* (SOC)) are responsible for issuing and renewing working visas whose validity is limited to the four Catalan provinces of Lleida, Barcelona, Gerona, and Tarragona.[34]

However, this competence is strictly administrative, thereby consider-ably limiting the Generalitat's potential incidence on immigration other than by accelerating the application process (that within the existing framework took on average up to six months). Besides, the central state remains exclusively competent in the delivery of residence permits, thus requiring a cooperative exercise of competencies between multiple levels of administration. Yet the 2009 reform states that 'the coordina-tion should not be made at the expense of the self-government capacity of each Autonomous Community', an addition that was sought and gained by CiU in return for its parliamentary support for the legislation. Another significant concession was the greater involvement given to the Generalitat in 'the state decisions in matters of immigration with a special interest for Catalonia',[35] notably in regard to the Quota Regime. Yet the Autonomous Community of Madrid, whose President Esperanza Aguirre is well-known for her virulent opposition to Catalan nation-alism, brought the case to the Constitutional Court on the grounds that holders of working visas issued in Catalonia could end up working in Madrid.[36] For the CiU leader Artur Mas, this was no less than 'an idea inherited from the Franco state denying Catalonia's legitimate right to self-government'.[37] At the time of writing, the decision of the Constitutional Court is still pending. While these long-awaited changes do alter the power of the state in setting the rules of entry into Spain, they can hardly be compared with the far-reaching competencies of Canadian provinces in general and Québec in particular. Overall, there is a broad consensus cutting across party lines in Catalonia that the Generalitat would be better off running its own immigration policy (see Chapter 13 by Franco-Guillén and Zapata-Barrero for more details on Catalan parties' perspectives on integration policies). Carles Campuzano, CiU MP in charge of immigration at the Spanish Parliament, summarized this frustration as follows: 'one thing we can blame the central government for is the absence of control over migration flows. The mechanisms of entry into Spain have overwhelmingly favoured irregular channels'.[38] Like in Scotland, and in spite of the fact that the Autonomous Community of Catalonia has been relatively more affected by the influx of international migrants to Spain since the turn of the century than the rest of the state, admissions policies have remained by and large the prerogative of the central government.

Comparative analysis: an administrative failure, or a political victory?

The study of the Catalan and Scottish cases corroborates a core assumption of Chapter 2 of the present volume: the question of 'who governs' in the realm of admissions policies is likely to be particularly salient in a multinational context in which the political boundaries of the state are internally contested as a result of ongoing dynamics of rival nation-building. However, sustained efforts undertaken by the Catalan and Scottish governments to gain greater leverage for regulating the number and provenance of foreign citizens entering their jurisdictions within the framework of a regionalized system were not translated into a partial devolution of admissions policies. In spite of the fact that they have been confronted with diametrically opposed migration issues – the Scottish government's fear of sustained emigration contrasting sharply with the Generalitat's growing concern with protracted immigration from abroad – both cases tell a similar story, qualified by Andrew Davis as a 'frustrated policy transfer' (Davis, 2009: 423). The underlying reason for the absence of devolution in admissions policy was also already touched upon in Chapter 2 of this volume: as argued by Ricard Zapata-Barrero and Fiona Barker, central governments are reluctant to delegate powers over a matter they see as essentially linked to their sovereignty. In the British and Spanish contexts, this has been facilitated by the logic of institutional path dependency, as central administrations inherited a quasi-monopoly over immigration powers from their pre-devolution centralized structure. In Scotland, immigration, as well as nationality, figures in the list of areas reserved to Westminster, as specified in schedule 5 of the Scotland Act (1998). Similarly, Article 149.2 of the 1978 Spanish Constitution states that immigration, together with emigration, the legal status of resident aliens, asylum, and nationality are exclusive competences of the central state. Whether in 1978 Spain or in 1997 Britain, the formal distribution of immigration powers was hardly touched upon during the parliamentary debates that preceded major constitutional reforms. But the rapid acceleration of immigration into Spain and the United Kingdom at the turn of the century brought the issue to the forefront of politics and became intertwined in the 'nationality question'.

While the underlying reason for the absence of policy transfer is rather straightforward, interpreting its implications for the Catalan and Scottish nation-building projects is a more complex task. From the perspective of nationalist parties and sub-state governments, this can be understood as an 'administrative failure' shedding light on the limits of territorial self-government in matters that are perceived as strategic by the state, as well as compelling evidence that the latter – like the reed in the fable – bends but does not break. However, this can also be interpreted as a 'political victory' for sub-state governments and nationalist parties engaged in protracted nation-building projects in the political, cultural, and economic spheres for two interrelated reasons. Firstly, they primarily legitimized their demands on economic grounds and consistently stressed the inadequacy of the statewide framework in addressing their territorial interests. Secondly, admissions policy is one area in which governments are more likely to pursue a 'blame-avoidance' rather than a 'credit-claiming' strategy. Accordingly, nationalist parties and sub-state governments in Scotland and Catalonia have skilfully used their lack of competence to criticize actions undertaken by their respective central governments which have failed to take into consideration the sectional interests of their constituencies.

Regarding the first aspect, the emphasis placed on economic considerations may seem quite puzzling to the tenants of a long-standing orthodoxy which sees minority nationalism as a parochial and essentially ethnic ideology that cannot be reconciled with immigration. Besides having no normative foundations and failing to account for empirical developments in a variety of cases, this widely held view overlooks the fact that, irrespective of their anxieties about cultural conformity, nationalist elites have to convince their constituencies that further political autonomy will not undermine their economic prospects.

The comparative analysis of Scotland and Catalonia shows that, in the same way as 'support for free trade can be part of a political strategy by nationalist leaders seeking further autonomy or outright independence' (Meadwell and Martin, 1996: 80; see also Hamilton, 2004), sub-state governments can incorporate immigration within a broader 'nation-building' strategy of socioeconomic development, connecting the territory with transnational flows of labour in order to bolster endogenous growth and to strengthen their competitive advantage in a globalized context (Keating, 1998). However, in both cases, these aims have been undermined by statewide policies pursing distinct objectives and failing to address territorial disparities.

In Catalonia, immigration from abroad has gained significance at a time of rapid economic internationalization. Whereas the weight of trade with the rest of Spain has slightly decreased between 1994 and 2007, international trade has grown twice as high, thus diminishing the reliance of the Catalan economy on the Spanish market (Parellada and Álvarez, 2007; Alonso, 2007: 39–72). While immigrants have unquestionably contributed to economic growth in the past decade, their relatively low-skilled profile and concentration in low-productivity sectors such as tourism, catering, and construction, has meant that overall productivity has decreased in absolute terms between 2001 and 2006 (Fernández-Huertas Morata and Ferrer-i-Carbonell, 2006). Immigration has also had detrimental effects on the diversification of the Catalan economy, whose over-reliance on the construction sector put considerable strain on the housing market and made the region more vulnerable to global economic cycles. Hence, nationalist parties have been able to legitimize their claims that the Generalitat should be given the means to manage its own admissions policy on solid economic grounds.

In Scotland, initiatives undertaken to 'Attract Fresh Talents to meet the Challenge of Growth'[39] were largely inspired by Richard Florida's pioneering book in which he argued that attracting the so-called 'creative class', whose members choose to live in stimulating, tolerant, and 'bohemian' environments, was key to boosting economic growth in the era of the knowledge economy (Florida, 2002). While Florida's demonstration may be flawed – numerous inquiries have shown that economic factors remain by far the most significant determinant cause of labour mobility (Houston et al., 2008) – boosting Scotland's ability to attract and retain highly skilled workers became a crucial component of the broader economic strategy later adopted with the *Smart, Successful Scotland* plan.[40] Notwithstanding the fact that the net migration rate has been consistently positive since 1999, Scotland's demographic and economic objectives can hardly be satisfied within the framework of a restrictive statewide policy, the aim of which is to reassure an increasingly anxious public opinion in England.

The second aspect is closely related to the previous one and proceeds from the premise that political discourses can hardly be taken for face value, irrespective of the dynamics of territorial politics. Instead, it fully takes into consideration one crucial component of intergovernmental relations, which is particularly important in a multinational context; that is the use of blame-shifting strategies by political actors, whether operating at the centre or in the periphery. While some authors have focused on how central governments selectively devolved competencies to lower tiers of government in order to shift the blame for unpopular policies (Pierson, 1996), others highlighted how blame-shifting strategies, far from being the monopoly of central administrations, were widespread among regional political elites seeking to minimize their responsibility for negative policy outcomes (Morgensen, 2012). Immigration is one area of public policy in which governments and political parties are especially prone to make use of blame-shifting postures, not least because of the ever-growing gap between policy aims and outcomes (Hollifield, 2004), and the presence of greater ideological divergences within parties than between them (Schain, 2008).

Seen from this perspective, the absence of policy transfer is not necessarily at odds with sub-state preferences, as political elites retain the opportunity to blame their respective central governments, which retained an exclusive competence over a matter which offers limited electoral rewards and the outcome of which largely fails to meet policy goals. This blame-shifting strategy is encapsulated in the words of First Minister Alex Salmond: 'I long for the day, as First Minister in the Scottish Parliament, that we can legislate for an immigration system that reflects the priorities, the needs and the attitude of this country.'[41] Likewise, for the recently elected president of the Generalitat, Artur Mas: 'Catalonia is a diverse and complex society. Immigration should be managed by the Generalitat rather than from some distant Madrid-based office.'[42] While the PSC and Scottish Labour found it harder to blame their party comrades in power at the centre, non-statewide nationalist parties have not faced similar constraints and have exploited this privileged position, hence giving some substance to their claim of being the sole representatives of Scotland and Catalonia's territorial interests.

Conclusion

This chapter systematically compared immigrant admissions policies and the discourses underlying them between 1999 and 2011 in two well-known cases of protracted nationalist mobilization, Scotland and Catalonia, against the background of statewide policy developments. The results shows that the question of 'who governs' has increasingly become a divisive and salient intergovernmental issue in both cases, thus corroborating a core assumption of Chapter 2 of the present volume. However, in spite of the fact that both the Scottish and Catalan governments have actively sought to acquire greater control over the regulation of immigration in their own jurisdiction, their demands have been largely unfulfilled. Indeed, the British and Spanish governments have proved equally reluctant to share their prerogative in a matter they saw as closely associated with their sovereignty. But the fact that the distribution of immigration competencies has remained largely unaffected should not be interpreted as a clear victory of central administrations eager to assert their authority over their turbulent yet politically subordinated peripheries. On the contrary, their intransigence has not only fed intergovernmental tension, but also has had the paradoxical effect of giving credence to those who claim that the current institutional framework inhibits Scotland and Catalonia's economic and political flourishing.

Notes

1. Research for this contribution has been carried out as part of a PhD dissertation, which was successfully defended in the department of Social and Political Science of the European University Institute (Florence) in 2012. I take this opportunity to express my gratitude to Prof. Ricard Zapata-Barrero who gave me the opportunity to spend three months in the Interdisciplinary Research Group on Immigration (GRITIM) at the Pompeu Fabra University in Barcelona, and Prof. Charlie Jeffery who offered me a visiting scholarship at the Institute of Governance of the University of Edinburgh.
2. Nick Griffin, quoted in MidDay.com, 14 June 2009.
3. Brice Hortefeux, speaking at the French National Assembly, 18 September 2007.
4. *Scotland's diaspora and overseas-born population*, Scottish Government Social Research. Report prepared by Carr J. and Cavanagh, L. 2009, p. 8.
5. *Regional Characteristics of foreign-born people living in the United Kingdom*, Office of National Statistics, report prepared by Reid A. and Miller, C. 2010.
6. *Controlling our borders: Making migration work for Britain – Five year strategy for asylum and immigration* (2005) presented to Parliament by the Secretary of State for the Home Department by Command of Her Majesty.
7. A Yougov survey in December 2004 found that 75 per cent of Britons think 'there are too many immigrants coming into the country'. Another survey carried out in 2005 found that 58 per cent of Britons thought the government's policies on immigration and asylum were 'not tough enough' (Ensor et al., 2005).
8. *'The Birth of a population crisis'* in the Scotsman, 14 September 2002.
9. Publication of the General Register Office for Scotland, 2002.
10. Although the extent to which population ageing actually constitutes a handicap is not clear, the negative effects it could engender, chief among them

sky-rocketing pensions and state-subsidized healthcare for a 'greying' electorate, are nevertheless worrying (Calwell et al., 2002).

11. In *The Official Report* published by the Scottish Administration, March 2003.
12. *New Scots, attracting Fresh Talents to meet the challenge of Growth*, published by the Scottish Executive, February 2004.
13. This slogan was a rallying cry in the 1990s for the partisans of devolution.
14. Ibid.
15. Equality and Human Rights Commission (EHRC). *Room for Manoeuvre? The Options for Addressing Immigration-Policy Divergence between Holyrood and Westminster*, report prepared by Sarah Kyambi, 2009.
16. See scotlandistheplace.com, [last accessed 18 September 2009].
17. *Fresh talent: Working in Scotland Scheme, an Evidence Review*, Scottish Government Social Research (2008) a report prepared by Cavanagh L. and Eirich, F.
18. SNP 2007 Party Manifesto, p.7.
19. *Managing Migration: A Public Sector Dialogue on Migration into Scotland*, published by COSLA, 2008.
20. *'You're welcome to come and live in Scotland, but only if you can...'* in the Scotsman, 29 January 2007.
21. *A Points-Based System: Making Migration Work for Britain* presented to Parliament by the Secretary of State for the Home Department, March 2006.
22. Alex Orr, *'Damaging to Scotland'* in the Scotsman, 2 April 2008.
23. *'David Cameron rejects Salmond's bid to flood recession hit Scotland with migrant workers'* in EU Times, 22 June 2011.
24. Ibid.
25. One may question the extent to which regularizations in the Spanish context can be qualified as 'extraordinary'. Indeed, they occurred periodically, in 1986, 1991, 1996, 2000, 2001, and 2005.
26. Fundación CIDOB (2001) *Anuario Internacional CIDOB 2000, edición 2001*.
27. Jordi Pujol, speaking soon after the end of his last term at the head of the Generalitat, quoted in el Pais, *'Pujol pide el traspaso de competencies sobre inmigracion'*, 23 August 2004.
28. *'Cataluña contratará inmigrantes a través de nuevas oficinas de empleo en el extranjero'* in El Mundo, 10 January 2002.
29. Press release by CDC, *'Artur Mas: El nou estatut perpetra contractar immigrants desde Catalunya'*, 6 November 2002.
30. Ibid.
31. While speaking of fully fledged diplomacy at the sub-state level is contentious, the 'paradiplomatic' activities of regional governments which seek to defend their economic, political, and cultural interests in multiple arenas and loci of authority on the international scene has been extensively researched in the literature (see, for example, Keating and Aldecoa, 1999).
32. *'Mas asegura que mantendrá las "embajadas" catalanas pese a la medida del Constitucional'* in El Mundo 2 November 2003.
33. Presidència del Govern del Estat. *Reial Decret 1463/2009, de traspàs de funcions i serveis a la Generalitat de Catalunya en materia d'immigracio*. DOGC 5469 – 22 September 2009.
34. Besides executive powers, matters of work inspection were also devolved to the Generalitat that, at least in discourse, expressed its will to be tougher. But while Catalan elites have long blamed the central government for failing to

stop irregular immigration, it is difficult to say whether the Catalan administration will actually be more efficient. Although measuring the proportion of irregular workers is arguably difficult, Colectivo Ioé (2008: 50) suggested that they represented 15 per cent of the Catalan workforce in 2007, a figure slightly higher than statewide estimates.

35. *Catalan Statute, 2006*, art. 138.2.
36. '*Aguirre recurre que Cataluña pueda dar permisos de trabajo a extranjeros*' in La Vanguardia, 7 October 2009.
37. Ibid.
38. Interview published in elsingulardigital, 27 October 2009.
39. '*New Scots, attracting Fresh Talents to meet the challenge of Growth*', published by the Scottish Executive, February 2004.
40. *A Smart Successful Scotland: Ambitions for the Enterprise Networks*, Scottish Executive, 2004.
41. Quoted in the Scotsman, 28 September 2009.
42. Interview with Artur Mas, '*partidario de un "itinerario de integración" para inmigrantes*', in Amo Dominicana, 22 November 2010.

References

J. Alonso (2007) 'Cataluña 1994–2007: una economía en transición' in Escrivá J. (ed.) *Economía Catalana: Retos de Futuro*. (Barcelona: BBVA and Generalitat de Catalunya).

J.-Th. Arrighi de Casanova (2012) *Those Who Came and Those Who Left: The Territorial Politics of Migration in Scotland and Catalonia*. (PhD Dissertation, Florence, European University Institute).

J. Arango and C. Finotelli (2009) 'Past and Future Challenges of a Southern European Migration Regime: the Case of Spain', *IDEA Working Papers*, 8: 1–44.

A.G. Ballesteros (2003) 'Notas sobre la Desigual Distribución de los Inmigrantes en España', *Papeles de Geografía*, 37: 65–75.

Colectivo Ioé (2008) *Trabajo Sumergido, precariedad e inmigracion en Catalunya: una primera aproximacion*. (Barcelona, Fundacio Jaume Bofill).

A. Davis (2009) 'False and Frustrated Policy Transfer: Spanish Immigration Policy and Catalonia', *Policy and Politics*, 37(3): 423–438.

F. Duvell and B. Jordan (2003) 'Immigration Control and the Management of Economic Migration in the United Kingdom: Organisational Culture, Implementation, Enforcement and Identity Processes in Public Services', *Journal of Ethnic and Migration Studies*, 29(2): 299–336.

J. Fernández-Huertas Morata, and A. Ferrer-i-Carbonell (2007) *Immigration in Catalonia*. (Barcelona: Institut d' Analisis Economic – IAE-CSIC).

R. Florida (2002) *The Rise of the Creative Class, and How it's Transforming Work, Leisure and Everyday Life*. (New York: Basic Books).

G. Freeman (1995) 'Modes of Immigration Politics in Liberal Democratic States', *International Migration Review*, 29(4): 881–902.

J. Hollifield (2004) 'The Emerging Migration State', *International Migration Review*, 38(3): 885–912.

C. Gala (2007) 'Inmigrantes extracomunitarios y Seguridad Social en Cataluña' in E. Argullol i Murgadas (ed.) *Inmigración y transformación social en Cataluña, Vol. II – Estudio Jurídico comparado*. (Barcelona: Fundación BBVA).

R. Garrido-Yserte and T. Mancha-Navarro (2009) 'The Spanish Regional Puzzle: Convergence, Divergence, and Structural Change' in J. Cuadrado-Roura (ed.) *Regional Policy, Economic Growth, and Convergence: Lessons from the Spanish Case.* (New York: Springer).

C. Gonzalez-Enriquez (2009) 'Spain, the Cheap Model: Irregularity and Regularisation as Immigration Management Policies', *European Journal of Migration and Law*, 11(2): 139–157.

P. Hamilton (2004) 'Converging Nationalisms: Québec, Scotland, and Wales in Comparative Perspective', *Nationalism and Ethnic Politics*, 10(4): 657–685.

D. Houston, A. Findlay, R. Harrison and C. Mason (2008) 'Will Attracting the "Creative Class" Boost Economic Growth in Old Industrial Regions? A Case Study of Scotland', *Geografiska Annaler*, 90(2): 133–149.

C. Joppke (1999) *Immigration and the Nation State.* (New York: Oxford University Press).

M. Keating and F. Aldecoa (1999) *Paradiplomacy in Action: The Foreign Relations of Subnational Governments.* (London: Frank Cass).

M. Keating (1998) *The New Regionalism in Western Europe: Territorial Restructuring and Political Change.* (Cheltenham: Edward Elgar).

M. Keating (2001) *Nations against the State: The New Politics of Nationalism in Quebec, Catalonia, and Scotland.* (Basingstoke: Palgrave Macmillan).

M. Keating, L. Stevenson, P. Cairney and K. Taylor (2003) 'Does Devolution Make a Difference? Legislative Output and Policy Divergence in Scotland', *The Journal of Legislative Studies*, 9(3): 110–139.

W. Kymlicka (2001) *Politics in the Vernacular: Nationalism, Multiculturalism, and Citizenship.* (Oxford: Oxford University Press).

K. Lisenkova and R. Wright (2008) 'Ireland and Scotland: Converging or Diverging Demography?', *Scottish Affairs*, 64: 18–36.

A. Hussein (2001) *British Immigration Policy under the Conservative Government.* (London: Ashgate).

H. Meadwell and P. Martin (1996) 'Economic Integration and the Politics of Independence', *Nations and Nationalism*, 2(1): 67–87.

N. Miret (1997) 'L'évolution du Panorama Migratoire en Catalogne Sud (1950–1975)', *Revue Européenne des Migrations Internationales*, 13(3): 47–69.

D. Moya Malapeira (2006) 'La evolución del sistema de control migratorio de entrada en España' in E. Aja and J. Arango (eds) *Veinte Años de Inmigración en España: Perspectiva Jurídica y Sociológica (1985–2004).* (Barcelona: CIDOB).

P. Morgensen (2012) '"It's the Central Government's Fault": Elected Regional Officials' Use of Blame-Shifting Rhetoric', *Governance: An International Journal of Policy, Administration, and Institutions*, 25(3): 439–461.

M. Parellada and M. Álvarez (2007) 'El comercio de Cataluña con el extranjero' in J. Luís Escrivá (ed.) *Economía Catalana: Retos de Futuro.* (Barcelona: BBVA and Generalitat de Catalunya).

P. Pierson (1996) 'The New Politics of the Welfare State', *World Politics*, 48(2): 143–179.

E. Roig (2007) 'La entrada por razones laborales en Cataluña' in E. Argullol Murgadas (ed.) *Inmigración y transformación social en Cataluña, Vol. II – Estudio Jurídico comparado.* (Barcelona: Fundación BBVA).

S. Rokkan (1983) *Economy, Territory, Identity: Politics of West European Peripheries.* (London: SAGE).

P. Spiro (2001) 'Federalism and Immigration: Models and Trends', *International Social Science Journal*, 53(167): 67–73.

P. Santolaya (2007) 'Extranjería y Nuevos Estatutos de Autonomía', *Revista d' Estudis Autonomics i Federals*, 4: 159–184.

M. Schain (2008) 'Why Political Parties Matter', *Journal of European Public policy*, 15(3): 465–470.

A. Serra, P. Mas, A. Xalabarder and G. Pyniol (2005) *Current Immigration Debates in Europe: Spain*. (Brussels: Migration Policy Group Report Series).

Y. Soysal (1994) *Migrants and Postnational Membership in Europe*. (Chicago: University of Chicago Press).

W. Somerville (2007) *Immigration under New Labour*. (Bristol: Polity).

R. Wright and M. Ellis (2000) 'Race, Region and the Territorial Politics of Immigration in the US', *International Journal of Population Geography*, 6: 197–211.

R. Zapata-Barrero (ed.) (2009) *Immigration and Self-Government of Minority Nations*. (Brussels: Presses inter-universitaires Peter Lang, collection Diversitas).

7
Migrant Reception Policies in a Multilevel System: Framing and Implementation Structures in the Italian Regions

Francesca Campomori and Tiziana Caponio

Introduction

The national policy agenda on immigration in Italy has crystallized around issues of border controls and security, placing much less emphasis on integration. Yet integration has represented a significant challenge since the 1980s (when immigrants became a visible presence in Italy) and it still remains of crucial importance, given that in 2012 foreign residents comprised 7.5 per cent of the total population (almost five million).

Unlike 'old' north-west European immigration countries, Italy has adopted neither an assimilationist nor a multicultural/pluralist stance regarding integration. Rather, and in similarity to other countries in Southern Europe (King, 2001; King, Lazaridis and Tsardanidis, 1999), Italy has been characterized by a lack of systematic national integration policies or a coherent inclusion model. To this end, Ambrosini (2001) has talked of an 'implicit' inclusion approach, suggesting that for a long time immigrants in Italy have been ignored by official policies or subjected to limited emergency measures.

Nevertheless, regional and local governments have always been at the front line in coping with everyday immigrant reception and integration needs. Initially, sub-state regional units often acted in an informal way, in the absence of specific legislation and specific funding for integration measures. Yet over time, the formal responsibility of Italian regions in this policy area has continuously increased, and reception policy became an entirely regional matter with the 1998 Immigration Law. Moreover, the federalist reform of the Italian state that was approved in 2001 assigned complete autonomy to the regions in the field of social policy, immigration issues included, thus acknowledging a *de facto* regional responsibility with regard to migrant integration. As such, regions represent the most interesting and appropriate level for investigating migrant integration policies and policy governance regarding immigration in Italy.

This chapter intends to bring light to the policy dimension of governance in relation to migrant reception in Italy (for a definition of migrant reception policies see Chapter 2 by Zapata-Barrero and Barker in this volume). Three regions will be compared which represent the so-called three (political and social) 'Italies': Veneto for the North, Emilia-Romagna for the Centre-North, and Calabria for the South. Veneto has been governed since 2000 by a centre-right majority including the openly anti-immigrant Northern League party (Lega Nord), while Emilia-Romagna in the same period has been governed by a centre-left majority encompassing the ex-Communist party and left-wing Catholics. Even if these two regions are politically at odds, they have in common a high level of economic development, social capital, and administrative efficiency. As regards the third case, Calabria embodies the traditional problems of most of the southern regions; namely, a high rate of unemployment (11.9 per cent in 2010), a thriving black economy, deep-rooted political corruption, and an inefficient administration. Politically, since the post-war years up until 1992, Calabria has been a stronghold of Christian Democracy (DC). After the break-up of that party, this region has been characterized by an alternation between centre-left and centre-right coalitions. Since 2010, it has been governed by centre-right parties.

Giving these contextual differences, this chapter centres on the following questions: how do regions view and interpret immigration and immigrants in their territory? What regional policy styles have been developed to deal with integration and, in particular, what policy control does the region exert on immigrant policy? In other terms, how is migration governed at the sub-state level with respect to reception policies? Hence, in this contribution we will primarily focus on the reception policy dimension of the governance of migration in Italy.

The chapter is organized as follows. The next section introduces an overview of state-regional governance relations with regard to migrant reception in Italy. Section 3 provides information on the social, economic and political contexts of the regions considered and elucidates the research methodology. Section 4 undertakes an in-depth analysis of the policy documents approved by the three cases under investigation in order to see how regions frame the immigration issue and how reception policies are decided upon and implemented. Both aspects are crucial in order to shed light on Dahl's famous tension between 'who decides' and 'who does' in Italian immigrant reception policies. As we shall see, the regions formally enjoy institutional competence in this respect, and throughout the last decades they have been able to establish distinct discourses on migrant integration. So while implementation rests upon local authorities and/or third-sector organizations, the regions have a considerable say in deciding the policies to be carried out. This has led to the emergence of quite a complex and scattered scenario, where formally cooperative intergovernmental relations are challenged by local authorities' autonomous decision-making powers. In section 5 we carry out a comparative assessment of the results of the analysis, in order to understand what counts and why in the governance of reception policies. The final section attempts to summarize the main features of the Italian governance of immigrant reception policies, by weighting them against the principles of coherence and cooperation in multilevel governance systems.

The migrant integration policy framework: the crucial role of sub-state units

Until recently, the national level has had a very broad and often vague definition of integration (Caponio and Zincone, 2011), leaving the responsibility for undertaking more specific actions about reception to regional and local tiers of government. In this respect, and with reference to the reception dimension of migration policies, Italy can be included in the 'cooperative scenario' of policy-making in multilevel systems that Zapata-Barrero and Barker outline in their conceptual framework (Chapter 2), since the decentralization of both decision-making ('who decides') and implementation ('who does') has been the norm.

Briefly chronicling the development of reception policies in Italy, it can be noted that at the beginning of the 1980s the main cities of central and northern Italy – that is, Milan, Rome, Turin, and Bologna – became recipients of immigration. The immediate impact of this was on housing and social exclusion, and in response local authorities set up housing plans and immigration offices, often working in close collaboration with third-sector associations (Campomori, 2008; Caponio, 2010). In Southern Italy, Catholic voluntary associations assumed a pivotal role, compensating for the absence (or the delay) of public intervention. Indeed, in the acknowledgement of certain social rights, civil society organizations and the municipalities have preceded the state and its institutions in terms of promoting healthcare for irregular migrants and the acceptance of their children in public schools (Ambrosini, 2012; Zincone, 2011).

While the first Immigration Law was approved in 1986, it was not significant in terms of integration policies: the law indicated the regions and local authorities as responsible for cultural programmes and social inclusion, respectively, but no specific funding was provided. This gap has only been partially plugged by the second Immigration Law in 1990, which devoted economic resources to integration but used a narrow approach to their application. Regions and local authorities only received funding in order to set up first-aid shelters, and in any case only until 1993. Nevertheless, throughout the decade many Centre-North cities, often funded by the regions, undertook innovative interventions in areas such as: foreign minors' admission at schools, immigrants' access to hospitals, intercultural education, and support for immigrant associations and civic participation. As a consequence, differentiated integration policies surfaced that led to a strongly local-based system of access to civil and social rights (Zincone, 2011).

The third Immigration Law of 1998 explicitly aimed at establishing a distinctive migrant integration model in Italy – so-called 'reasonable integration' (Zincone, 2001) – and overcoming the existing fragmentation of local policies. In doing so it formally assigned competence over the formulation of reception policies to regional authorities: a National Fund for Immigrant Policy (NFIP) was introduced, to be allocated to the regions to finance programmes of interventions to be agreed upon with the municipalities in specific annual and triennial migrant integration plans. Devolution of decision-making powers to the regions was strengthened under the federalist reform approved in May 2001 by the then centre-left government: the NFIP merged into a general Social Policy Fund (SPF) and regional governments gained complete autonomy in deciding if and to what extent to engage in supporting migrant integration. Following through the social assistance reform approved in 2000 (law n.328/2000), local authorities have also had a considerable say in approving local social services plans, together with third-sector organizations and other institutions (schools, hospitals and so on), to deliver public services in the territory.

Hence, if it is true that today the regions enjoy considerable power in deciding who is to be integrated and how, the definition of concrete reception and integration measures – as well as their implementation – is in principle devolved to local partnerships between municipal administrations, civil society organizations, and other public institutions (the so-called 'Social Areas Plans' – *Piani sociali di zona*). The cooperative scenario informing the general division of labour between the central state and the regions on social policy matters also seems to underpin relations between the regions and local tiers of government.

However, this general pattern was challenged in the second half of the 2000s in two main respects. On the one hand, since 2005 increasing budget constraints and continuous cuts to the national SPF have considerably reduced regional financial resources for social policies in general and, as a consequence, also for immigrant reception policies. On the other, the approval in July 2009 of a national law introducing a so-called Integration Agreement *(Accordo di Integrazione)* seems to underscore a centralistic turn in immigrant reception policies in Italy. The Integration Agreement has to be signed by an immigrant at the moment that he or she requests his or her first residence permit. The agreement commits him or her to fulfil specific integration requirements within two years in order to obtain the permit renewal, with a particular emphasis on mastery of the Italian language and on knowledge of the country's history, institutions, and civic culture.[1] This new nationalist reception policy was implemented just recently (March 2012). But, it has not challenged established regional authority on integration matters since the regions have been involved in the implementation of language and civic culture courses through specific funds provided by the Ministry of the Interior. Again, the cooperative scenario seems to prevail.

In this chapter, we intend to deconstruct the multilevel governance of immigrant reception policies in Italy by considering the regions not only as administrative bodies, but first and foremost as political institutions. Thus, the political orientations of regional governments might be expected to make a difference to the kind of integration models being pursued, especially in a context of limited financial resources. Centre-right regions may be regarded as either avoiding any intervention that favours immigrants or as limiting their action to the recognition of basic rights and services. In contrast, centre-left governments might in theory be characterized by a more open stance towards immigrants and pursue more favourable policies. How do these different political orientations combine with vertical and horizontal governance relations with respect to the different framings of migrant integration? Arguably, the regions can either pursue a model centred on a strict control of local-level immigrant reception policies, or leave local-level horizontal governance networks substantial room to manoeuvre. Horizontal governance, involving not only public authorities but also civil society organizations, adds complexity to the standard cooperative model of centre-periphery relations in Italy, bringing left-right considerations about the primacy of either the public sector or civil society into the delivery of social services. In this chapter we shall address this political dimension of the multilevel governance of reception policies, which in Italy clearly cuts across vertical relations in accounting for different regional (and local) models of migrant integration.

Empirical research: case studies and methodology

The case selection takes into account two main cleavages in Italy: on one hand, the North/South cleavage, triggered by discrepancies in economic performance and social capital (Putnam, 1993); on the other hand, the political culture cleavage (left-wing versus right-wing coalitions), that since the post-war period has characterized the Centre-North of Italy in particular.

As for the former, Calabria is representative of the problems in Southern Italy, which were previously mentioned in the Introduction and which are often referred to collectively as the *Questione Meridionale* ('Southern issue') to indicate the heavy imbalance between the North and the South of the country. This includes weaker and inefficient welfare provisions and therefore a low level of social protection in the South. Instead, Veneto and Emilia-Romagna are two of the best performing regions in the country both in terms of economic development and social protection. Both regions are part of the so-called industrial districts area (Bagnasco, 1977; Trigilia, 1986), which encompasses the Centre-north and the northeast of Italy and is characterized by the presence of lively networks of primarily export oriented small- and medium-sized firms.

As for the second cleavage, Veneto and Emilia-Romagna represent opposite political traditions that are historically linked to the emergence of different systems of social policy and public service provision (Fargion, 2005; Messina, 2001). On one hand, Emilia-Romagna has been traditionally characterized by its prevailing Communist 'red' subculture (together with Liguria, Tuscany, and Umbria), while Veneto has always been part of the Catholic 'white' area (including some provinces of Lombardy, east Piedmont, and Friuli-Venezia Giulia). During the post-war period, such political polarization gave rise to different policy and administrative styles whose legacies are still evident today. Whereas in Veneto, according to the Catholic principle of subsidiarity, regional authorities have always been particularly prone to devolving responsibilities for service delivery to private actors and voluntary associations, in Emilia-Romagna, a policy-making model characterized by a strong coordinating role of the region can be discerned, albeit in the context of a tradition of municipal autonomy.

From the beginning of the 1990s, the immigration issue began to be especially politicized in Veneto, where the Northern League has deployed a strong anti-immigrant political discourse emphasizing the perceived risks of competition in the job market and increased public insecurity. In contrast, the centre-left coalitions, which have been governing in Emilia-Romagna, have adopted a positive view of immigration, usually describing it as an opportunity for social and cultural enrichment (for an in-depth analysis of party positions on immigration in Northern Italy and Emilia-Romagna, see Chapter 9 by Schmidtke and Zaslove in this volume). As for Calabria, immigration has not been presented by politicians as an issue requiring much political intervention, at least with regard to reception policies. However, episodes of violence point out risks of radicalization in the local population: in January 2010, violent riots exploded in the village of Rosarno because of racial harassment against black immigrant workers. Notwithstanding the national media coverage, local and regional political leaders did not take a clear stance on the issue.

To find out if the two cleavages mentioned above, that is the socio-economic and cultural-political cleavages, have actually led to different ways of framing immigration and different systems of governance of immigrant reception, this research undertakes a qualitative analysis of the main regional policy documents on the topic; the so-called 'annual and triennial integration programmes'. These are executive agendas in the sense that they set the guidelines for local-level implementation processes and provide the related financial resources. Hence, these documents can be regarded as informing policy practice, that is, as yielding the policy frames that determine regional actors' policy actions.

The analysis of the programmes has been grounded in two dimensions: (a) the naming and framing of immigrants and immigration, and; (b) the implementation process as it is designed in the programmes, in order to understand what policy control the regions actually exert over reception policies. As for the first dimension, we look at the labels (Schön and Rein, 1994; Scholten, 2011) attached to immigration as a phenomenon and to immigrants as new residents. In other words, what are the policy narratives (Boswell, Geddes and Scholten, 2011) used by regional decision-makers in order to depict immigration and immigrants? As for the second dimension, it has to be pointed out that regional documents can be more or less constraining in the identification of policy priorities to be implemented at a local level, and they can also leave a considerable margin of initiative to local administrations. Therefore, in order to understand if a certain discourse on migrant integration and reception is actually translated into concrete policy actions, we need to reconstruct how the programming documents foresee the implementation process, that is how the regions identify and then recommend priorities to the implementing agencies; if they steer local authorities' actions, leaving them little space of manoeuvre; or if, instead, they devolve most of their decision-making to local authorities. Whereas in the first case, we expect a regionally centralized system of governance, in the second a more cooperative scenario will emerge.

Framing and governance structures of Italian regions' reception policies

Emilia-Romagna: a culture-friendly model devolved to local authorities

The Emilia-Romagna approach to labelling immigrants seems to underscore the acknowledgement on the part of regional authorities of their increasing numbers and permanent settlement in the region. The heading of the 1999 programme talks about 'activities of welcome and assistance in favour of immigrants'.[2] Beginning with the 2000 programme, the words 'assistance' and 'welcome' disappeared, and the more general heading 'activities in favour of immigrants' was adopted. In 2004 this was definitively replaced with the expression 'actions for immigrants' social integration',[3] while immigrants started to be explicitly defined as 'citizens' following the approach of the 2004 regional immigration law. This framing of immigrants as would-be citizens is reinforced by the strong critical stance towards the centre-right 2002 national immigration law, which is accused of keeping immigrants in a permanently precarious legal status.

With regard to the definition of the phenomenon of immigration, the 2001[4] programme emphasized 'the opportunities and enrichment brought by immigration' in terms of cultural diversity and hoped for the establishment of 'a multicultural society...based upon immigrants' full status of citizens'. Nevertheless, in subsequent years, the appreciation of immigration as a cultural asset was overcome by a greater emphasis on economic aspects. In the triennial programme 2006–2008,[5] we find an appraisal of the European Union's The Hague programme (2004: 11) which argues that 'if immigration flows are regulated and well managed, each single state can get gains: stronger economies, better social cohesion and [a] better sense of security'. The programme particularly emphasizes the necessity of putting pressure on national policymakers for more favourable legislation, allowing for a greater match between new inflows and the needs of the regional economic system. Furthermore, the introduction to the 2009–2011 programme stated that 'the perception according to which integration costs are higher than the economic advantages is wrong'. Since the 2000 programme, Emilia-Romagna has encouraged immigrants' representation in local government and promoted activities in favour of their associations. In 2002 a further step was taken, since the programme that year deemed it important to establish consultative councils at the provincial level in order to improve immigrants' opportunities to be actively engaged in the host society. From 2004 onward, the programmes took another step forward by arguing that foreign citizens' representative bodies should be directly elected from within the community of legally resident immigrants. Intercultural initiatives have also received considerable attention, covering a wide array of interventions: Italian language and civic education courses; cultural mediators in school education and social services; intercultural communication activities to be promoted in schools; and professional training in journalism for young immigrants.

Another recurrent issue regards the setting up of structures at the local level devoted to monitoring, informing, and providing legal assistance to immigrants who have experienced discrimination. The 2004 regional law on immigration, in fact, has launched the creation of a regional centre on discrimination, with the task of preventing discrimination, supporting policies devoted to remove the disadvantaged conditions of immigrants, and monitoring the phenomenon.

To sum up, immigrants are defined as 'new citizens' and the building of a multicultural society is positively regarded in Emilia-Romagna (especially by its political parties – see Schmidtke and Zaslove in Chapter 9 for more on this). A 'culture-friendly' framing of integration can be highlighted, which rests on a soft or liberal understanding of multiculturalism (Castles and Miller, 2003), in the sense that it does not go so far as to endorse a policy of recognition, but simply acknowledges the positive value of cultural diversity for the host society. As for the implementation process, it must be pointed out that the identified policy priorities are very general and therefore not particularly constraining for local authorities, which actually enjoy considerable autonomy in defining the concrete policies to be carried out. Between 1999 and 2004, resources were assigned to the nine provinces in Emilia-Romagna, which were held responsible for deciding how much to invest in each policy issue, even though in the period 2002–2004 the regional programmes also explicitly reserved a small budget line, around 10 per cent of the total, for intercultural projects promoted both by public sector and civil society organizations (including immigrant associations). Since 2004, the implementation structure has become more complex. Seventy per cent of the total regional budget was assigned to the 'social areas plans' (38 in total) which are small and medium-sized municipalities' joint ventures established in order to promote an integrated system of social services delivery (see above regarding the social assistance reform, that is Law 328/2000). As a consequence, provinces have assumed a secondary role, benefiting from the remaining 30 per cent of the resources to be devoted primarily to tasks of monitoring the phenomenon on the territory (provincial immigration observatories) and coordinating local interventions in the areas of intercultural activities, discrimination, political representation, and services for asylum-seekers and refugees. Clearly, a high degree of devolution to local tiers of government characterizes the implementation model adopted in Emilia-Romagna, which is consistent with a social policy tradition of municipal autonomy. The region has a mainly planning and administrative role, which consists of collecting, evaluating, and then funding the provincial and social areas integration programmes.

Veneto: socioeconomic framing and regional primacy

In Veneto, immigration is framed mostly as a phenomenon which must be regulated in order to be socially sustainable and consistent with regional economic development priorities. An emphasis on 'legality and regularity' surfaces in all of the analysed policy programmes: in particular, the importance of fighting illegal immigration is noted, while the programmes explicitly state that social interventions should only target legal immigrants. Given this emphasis on control, in the first two programmes the word 'integration' is never mentioned, although it has become more and more relevant since 2004,[6] when it started to occur in the headings of some of the identified policy priorities (see: 'Education and Social Integration' and, from 2007, 'Pact of Welcome and Integration').[7]

Until 2003, immigrants were usually referred to as 'extracomunitari'. This word literally means 'people from a non-European Union country', but it has a negative and pejorative meaning, as indicated by the fact that it is never used for US or Canadian citizens for instance. In contrast to what we have seen in Emilia-Romagna, the term 'citizen' is never used, except once in the 2001–2003 programme[8] where it could be considered an accidental occurrence since the word 'extracomunitario' appeared more frequently in this document. At the same time, immigrants are constantly compared to past Venetian emigrants[9] and their descendants. Both the 2001–2003 and the 2004–2006[10] triennial programmes give these latter a preference in access to social provisions as opposed to the subordinate position associated with 'extracomunitari'.

An analysis of the priorities reveals a framing of the issue of migrant integration predominantly based on housing, employment and regulation of immigrant workers inflows and vocational training. Throughout the period studied, housing was the main item in the programmes' total budget (35–40 per cent). The 2002[11] programme argued that housing was an essential requirement for integration and allocated significant economic resources for the building of around 100 housing units devoted to immigrants and return emigrants of Venetian origin. The 2004–2006 programme declared an appreciation for those employers engaged in supporting their foreign employees in finding suitable accommodation, while at the same time emphasized the need to avoid competition with the native population and to prevent housing and social decay. Since 2007, the region has been committed to launching an Ethnic Housing Fund for low-income immigrants and native people alike.

According to the Veneto programmes, employment is the second precondition for effective integration. In order to accomplish that, since 2001 the programmes have provided for a wide array of actions such as professional training either in Veneto or in the country of origin before arrival. The programmes also stress the need for greater regional involvement in (national) decisions about annual entry quotas; to that aim, since 2004 Veneto has been collaborating with the Ministry of Labour on the implementation of a system for monitoring labour shortages in the small and medium-sized factories of the region. Vocational training is another important item reiterated year after year. Various actions are included under this heading: Italian language and civic education courses, courses on labour safety regulations, training for employees in public and private services dealing with immigrants, cultural mediators' training courses, and schooling and social integration for foreign children. Vocational training projects favouring the return of immigrants to their countries of origin are also mentioned. From the triennial plan of 2004–2006 onwards, schooling and social integration of immigrant children has been identified as a new autonomous policy priority to which a specific budget has been assigned. This primarily involves refresher courses for school teachers, support in learning the Italian language, intercultural education programmes, and cultural mediation.

Compared to Emilia-Romagna, a quite different framing of immigrants' integration has emerged. The labelling process underscores a clear concern for social cohesion, economic development, and the cultural identity of the region. Comparing 'extracomunitari' and return emigrants of a Venetian origin stresses the cultural otherness of the former while constructing the idea of a regional community bound together by a common ethnic origin. Veneto regional authorities pursue a socioeconomic approach to integration, providing for individuals' basic needs such as access to housing and employment, while discouraging long-term integration into the local community as indicated for instance by the funding of projects of re-insertion into the migrants' countries of origin. Furthermore, access to more expensive and valuable welfare resources such as housing is not unconditional: if initially ethnic Venetian return migrants were given preference, since 2004 housing programmes have been re-framed in more universalistic terms, targeting the disadvantaged population in general.

Veneto also displays a different style with respect to Emilia-Romagna as far as the implementation structure is concerned: since the beginning, it has listed well-specified areas of intervention that have been maintained for the entire decade, just with marginal changes in some of the foreseen actions. As in Emilia-Romagna, local authorities are held responsible for carrying out policies, yet these have less room to manoeuvre. The budget is allocated to the policy priorities described above and local governments cannot choose which one to favour, but rather are required to elaborate specific projects on each matter. Provinces receive on average 50–60 per cent of the regional programmes' total budget for vocational training and housing policies. Since 2002, specific agreements between the region and the provinces have been signed, establishing the budget assignment for each province and the actions to be implemented. The 2001–2003 regional programmes also allocated 25 per cent of the total budget to public agencies and civil-society organizations (including non-profit associations) which submitted integration projects. Beginning in 2004, another 25 per cent of the regional budget was devoted to municipalities responsible for the schooling and social integration of immigrant children: for this purpose the drafting of plans with civil society associations, schools, and so on was encouraged. Finally, around 10 per cent of the budget is destined every year to activities implemented directly by the region, such as the Regional Immigration Observatory. Hence, similarly to Emilia-Romagna, Veneto plays mainly a planning and administrative role, but unlike Emilia-Romagna it is also more involved in the direct implementation of specific policy actions. Yet, what seems to characterize the Veneto regional government policy implementation style is the greater specification of both policy priorities and implementation structures, resulting in a greater degree of control over local tiers of government involved in policy implementation.

Calabria: a social assistance framing implemented through public bids

The Calabria region has always been characterized in the Italian context as an area of first arrival rather than of settlement of foreign migrants. Since the end of the 1980s, its coasts have been the landing territory for thousands of irregular immigrants arriving primarily from Northern Africa but also from Turkey. As a consequence, this region has been traditionally concerned with temporary accommodation provided by the first-aid shelters established after each humanitarian emergency through ear-marked national funding, the last one being in 2011 due to the political collapse of several North-African regimes. Civil society organizations, especially of a Catholic background, have also been particularly active in this respect, coping with the basic needs of both regular and undocumented migrants in an informal way. Settlement and integration do not seem to represent top priorities for the Calabrian regional government. As a consequence, this region displays extremely concise programmes and the priorities are not detailed at all, especially before 2007. This situation is made worse because of the absence of triennial plans, which in the other regions examined have the function of describing in broad terms the regional specific approach to immigration.

Similarly to Veneto, 'extracomunitari' has been the label most often used for immigrants in Calabria until 2008, even if in the 2003 and 2004[12] programmes the words 'immigrant citizens' were also used. In the first half of the decade, the region set the following priorities: housing, either first-aid shelters or other forms of accommodation aimed at supporting settlement; vocational training; intercultural mediation and link workers; support for immigrants' cultural, religious, and economic initiatives; and language courses. In 2007,[13] the region envisaged only two priorities: facilitating immigrant access to the housing and the labour markets and special assistance for foreign minors (especially unaccompanied ones) and for vulnerable immigrants. From 2008, regional priorities began to be better specified and more issues were considered, such as school integration, to be pursued through both the provision of language courses for foreign pupils and promoting a greater commitment of parents in school activities; and the prevention of social marginalization, including specific actions in favour of migrant women like vocational training and information campaigns on how to obtain protection in the case of discrimination or violence.

Considerable emphasis has also been placed on housing. The 2008 programme encouraged the presentation of projects oriented at recovering buildings to convert into first-aid shelters or flats to be rented to immigrants. Nevertheless, it seems that it has been very difficult to implement these actions effectively. In the 2010 programme,[14] the region had to admit that while the 2008 programme had foreseen a budget of 500,000 Euros for housing, only three projects were presented for a total funding of less than 80,000 Euros. Since 2007, immigration has been included amongst the ten priorities of the regional Social Plan, which contains general planning about welfare polices. This programme encouraged increased partnership between public and private actors together with a closer collaboration among neighbouring local authorities in formulating immigrant interventions (in Emilia-Romagna and Veneto this was pursued least since 2002, following the 2000 national reform of social assistance policies). Ultimately, Calabria seems to have pursued an approach that is centred on social assistance (housing in particular) and just more recently on school integration.

Concerning the implementation style, Calabria's programmes are designed as calls for applications (public bids), where applicants can in some cases be local authorities and in others third-sector associations or schools. In concrete terms, the region lists some priorities, and the applicants have to present a project which complies with them. Until 2004, public and private actors could apply without distinction for the entire set of priorities specified in the programmes, while since 2005, associations have only been allowed to apply for cultural activities and language courses. Therefore, local authorities have become the main implementing actors, though they can engage associations in the implementation process. Moreover, if, until 2007, there was just a single budget for the entire call for applications, then subsequently each priority started to be associated with a specific budget. Therefore, in comparison with the other two regions, Calabria lies in between Emilia-Romagna and Veneto: priorities are identified with rather bound and determined actions whose specification is completely left to local agencies (mainly local authorities) selected through the call for applications. The main difference between Calabria and the other two regions is with respect to the funding method: in Calabria local-level governments do not necessarily receive a budget. Instead, the funding is assigned to the proponents of the selected projects.

What counts in the governance of reception policies in Italy?

The specific configuration of the Italian system of multilevel governance has a strong impact on immigrant reception policy, which must be considered in the context of social assistance policies more broadly since the above-mentioned federalist reform (2001) has delegated most welfare competencies to the regions. Looking at immigrant reception and integration policies (though almost the same could be said for social assistance), there are two interrelated levels of autonomy: on one hand the regions whose increasing decision-making powers have enabled them to decide to what extent and how to tackle migrant integration issues; on the other there are local authorities, which enjoy considerable leverage in the design of specific policy actions. The regions seem to be prone to devolving not only implementation competences but in some cases policy formulation to local authorities.

This is particularly noticeable in Emilia-Romagna, where 70 per cent of the budget has been assigned to municipal joint ventures, whereby local authorities draft their own reception programmes, even if they have to be based on the very general policy priorities specified by the region. Social areas programmes are therefore not purely executive documents; instead they can re-formulate and place more or less emphasis on regional priorities, according to the municipalities' specific framing of immigration and integration. A cooperative scenario has emerged where, however, there has been a low level of coherence across local territories in terms of the concrete policy actions carried out. Also in Veneto, despite the greater role played by the region in specifying the policy goals and hence in constraining the implementing agencies (especially due to the fact that each priority has a dedicated budget), the region does not completely control implementation and the local tiers of government enjoy some autonomy in this respect. Again, a cooperative model can be singled out, even though the greater central control exerted by the region is likely to ensure a higher consistency between the regional policy discourse and the policies concretely implemented at a local level. As for Calabria, the public tendering system does not guarantee that local authorities receive regular funding; the policy goals pursued by the region, even if rather circumscribed, are not at all well profiled, hence giving the municipal governments that have been able to 'win' the bids a large margin of manoeuvre in the specification and interpretation of the reception measures to be implemented. An asymmetric scenario is likely to prevail here.

From the comparison carried out so far, the relevance of the North-South cleavage in accounting for differences in regional immigrant reception governance comes to the fore. In the first place, Southern regions' planning – including Calabria – is less institutionalized than in the Centre-North regions (Campomori and Caponio, 2013). This means that Southern regions are much less consistent in drafting immigrant programmes: in Calabria the absence of triennial programmes – which provide a long-term perspective and analysis of problems is noticeable. Furthermore, Calabria's planning does not seem to take into account the needs of the territories: the municipal governments which are successful in getting regional funds are usually the most enterprising and efficient ones in project delivery, but this does not mean that they are also the most in need. Veneto and Emilia-Romagna, instead, make use of sociodemographic indicators in order to establish the share of funding to be devoted to local authorities. Last but not least, in Calabria's programmes, immigration seems to be perceived mainly as a condition of precariousness: immigrants are regarded as facing a greater risk of poverty because of unstable jobs, insecure housing, risks of being trapped into deviant activities, and in need of special assistance. The interventions envisaged are generally of an emergency-related and reactive kind, which are aimed at facing problematic conditions rather than dealing with long-term integration processes.

Regarding the political culture cleavage, which primarily pits Veneto against Emilia-Romagna, the research depicts clear differences in the labelling of immigration and in the related policy narratives. The two regions' policy discourses reflect the opposite political cultures which have traditionally characterized them. Whereas Emilia-Romagna's culture-friendly frame evokes a left-wing political culture open to immigrants and their integration, Veneto's socioeconomic frame reflects a right-wing rhetoric on integration through the labour market. Nevertheless, moving from the labelling to the actual foreseen priorities, elements of similarity and convergence between the two regions have also emerged. Since 2005 Emilia-Romagna has started to put more emphasis on labour-market necessities and economic issues related to immigration, while Veneto has been increasingly involved in actively supporting school integration and intercultural issues.

What then counts in the governance of immigration in Italy? Considering the findings of this research, the regional and, even more, the local dimension makes a difference both in terms of decision-making ('who decides') and implementation ('who does'). A local citizenship has emerged, which corresponds with the ancient, but unfortunately still alive, North/South cleavage. In contrast, the role of the cultural-political variable does not seem to be as important in the sense that it does not seem able to produce significant differences in the actual governance of immigration, even if it accounts for opposing rhetoric that mirrors the different constituencies of the two governing coalitions. Yet, the scenario is more complex at an urban level where, especially since the late 1990s, restrictive policies and practices have been emerging (Ambrosini, 2012). In particular, the major outcome of Berlusconi's security policies, which were strongly driven by the Northern League, has been the approval of two so-called Security laws (Law 125/24 July 2008 and Law 94/15 July 2009) which among other measures have assigned increased powers in managing security issues to city mayors (see for instance Caponio and Graziano, 2010). The result, especially in northern Italy, has been a flourishing of anti-immigrant ordinances and resolutions. Therefore, many governing coalitions at the urban level have been engaged in policies of exclusion in order to gain political support, even though anti-discrimination associations, advocacy groups, and courts have often been successful in reacting against these measures (Ambrosini, 2012). These policies reveal the emergence of a fragmented scenario, where regional programmes set the scene, but it is at a local and urban level that relevant decisions are actually taken and carried out in terms of fostering immigrant inclusion or exclusion. This is not surprising because even in unitary states like the Netherlands and the United Kingdom, local governments play a crucial role in developing their own migrant integration policies (for more details see Chapter 8 by Scholten in this volume).

Conclusion

This chapter has sought to highlight the governance of immigrant reception in Italy at the regional level, given its central role in planning migrant integration and reception measures and in allocating funding for implementation. At least from a formal perspective, by looking at existing laws and regulations, the governance of reception policy in Italy seems to be underpinned by a cooperative scenario where the central government retains some control and supervision over the coherence of the overall system, as recently pointed out by the introduction of the Integration Agreement. The regions enjoy considerable power both in decision-making ('who decides') and the implementation ('who does') of measures to be undertaken. Nevertheless, the picture is far more fragmented and complicated if we look at the governance of reception policies starting from an analysis of regional integration programmes. Our study has revealed the crucial relevance of municipal authorities that, especially in Emilia-Romagna but also in the other two regions, have considerable say in deciding the actions to be undertaken and how to implement them. The vertical dimension of immigrant reception policy governance in Italy seems to proceed in a 'bottom-up' rather than in a 'top-down' manner. At the same time, the horizontal dimension assumes significant relevance because of the policy networks that are actively mobilized on the ground in order to deal with immigrant reception needs. Third-sector organizations are not only key partners in the 'social areas plans', but also – in the case of Veneto and to some extent Calabria – they are implementing agencies directly charged with carrying out specific projects.

This complex patchwork of centre-periphery/state-society relations gives rise to the emergence of different regional, and even local, policy frames, which clearly contradict the principle of coherence which is supposed to inspire the multilevel governance of immigration in multilevel settings (see Chapter 2 by Zapata-Barrero and Barker). As far as reception and integration policies in Italy are concerned, the regions not only have different rhetoric and policy discourses, stemming from the political ideologies of governing parties, but they also leave local-level horizontal governance considerable room to manoeuvre, with the result that local reception policies can vary across municipalities and territories within a region. This lack of coherence is coupled with the weakness of the coordination principle: more generous municipalities in terms of public services available and/or cities characterized by dense networks of NGOs have often lamented the risk of attracting higher numbers of immigrants vis-à-vis the disengagement of public and voluntary actors in other areas of the country and especially in the South (see Campomori, 2008). At the same time, exclusionary practices are likely to emerge in those cities where anti-immigrant parties such as the Northern League control local government.

Therefore, the multilevel governance of immigrant reception policies in Italy appears to be extremely fragmented and always potentially in conflict, especially at the local level where the pressure of immigrant integration challenges and the changing attitudes in the electorate are most keenly felt.

Notes

1. http://www.interno.gov.it/mininterno/export/sites/default/it/assets/files/22/0185_Accordo_dI_Integrazione_Italiano.pdf. Last accessed: January 2013.
2. Delibera del Consiglio Regionale n. 1174, 14 July 1999.
3. Delibera del Consiglio Regionale n. 615, 16 November 2004.
4. Delibera del Consiglio Regionale n. 203, 20 June 2001.
5. Delibera del Consiglio Regionale n. 804, 7 February 2006.
6. Delibera della Giunta Regionale n. 3637, 19 November 2004.
7. Delibera della Giunta Regionale n. 3041, 2 October 2007.
8. Delibera del Consiglio Regionale n. 20, 26 June 2001.
9. From the 1860s up to the 1970s, Veneto has been a region of Italian mass emigration. At the present time, in most cases Venetian emigrants or their children are likely to have become third-country nationals, especially from Argentina and Brazil. Some of them have returned to Italy, especially during the Argentinean economic crisis in 1999–2002, Yet, their number is far lower compared to that of new foreign immigrants: in 2011, neither Argentina nor Brazil were among the first 15 countries of origin of foreigners living in Veneto (Caritas/Migrantes, 2011).
10. Delibera del Consiglio Regionale n. 53, 10 November 2004.
11. Programma di iniziative di interventi in materia di immigrazione anno 2002.
12. Decreto dei dirigenti della Regione Calabria n. 14961, 17 October 2003; deliberazione della Giunta Regionale n. 769, 25 October 2004.
13. Decreto n. 9936, 9 July 2007.
14. Decreto n. 2235, 3 March 2010.

References

M. Ambrosini (2001) *La fatica di integrarsi. Immigrazione e lavoro in Italia.* (Il Mulino: Bologna).

M. Ambrosini (2012) ' "We Are Against a Multi-ethnic Society": Policies of Exclusion at the Urban Level in Italy', *Ethnic and Racial Studies*, i-First article, 1–20.

A. Bagnasco (1977) *Tre Italie. La problematica territoriale dello sviluppo italiano.* (Il Mulino: Bologna).

C. Boswell, A. Geddes and P. Scholten (2011) 'The Role of Narratives in Migration Policy-making: A Research Framework', *The British Journal of Politics and International Relation*, 13(1): 1–11.

F. Campomori (2008) *Immigrazione e cittadinanza locale. La governance dell'integrazione in Italia.* (Carocci: Roma).

F. Campomori and T. Caponio (2013) *'Le politiche per gli immigrati. Istituzionalizzazione, programmazione, trasparenza'* in S Vassallo (ed.) *Il divario incolmabile. Rappresentanza politica e rendimento istituzionale nelle regioni italiane.* (Bologna: Il Mulino).

T. Caponio (2010) 'Grassroots Multiculturalism in Italy: Milan, Bologna and Naples compared' in T. Caponio and M. Borkert (eds) *The Local Dimension of Migration Policymaking.* (Amsterdam: Amsterdam University Press).

T. Caponio and P.R. Graziano (2011) 'Towards a Security-oriented Migration Policy Model? Evidence from the Italian Case' in E. Carmel, A. Cerami and T. Papadopoulus (eds) *Migration and Welfare in the New Europe. Social Protection and the Challenges of Integration.* (Bristol: Policy Press).

T. Caponio and G. Zincone (2011) *Study on the National Policy Frame for the Integration of Newcomers – Italy.* Research paper for the PROSINT Project, mimeo.

Caritas/Migrantes (2011) *Dossier statistico immigrazione. 21° Rapporto.* (Roma: Idos).

S. Castles and M.J. Miller (2003) *The Age of Migration,* 3rd edn. (Basingstoke: Palgrave Macmillan).

V. Fargion (2005) 'From the Southern to Northern question: Territorial and Social Politics in Italy' in N. McEwen and L. Moreno (eds) *The Territorial Politics of Welfare.* (London: Routledge).

R. King (ed.) (2001) *The Mediterranean Passage: Migration and New Cultural Encounters in Southern Europe.* (Liverpool: Liverpool University Press).

R. King, G. Lazaridis and C. Tsardanidis (eds) (1999) *Eldorado or fortress? Migration in Southern Europe.* (New York: Palgrave Macmillan).

P. Messina (2001) *Regolazione politica dello sviluppo locale. Veneto ed Emilia-Romagna a confronto.* (Utet: Torino).

R. Putnam (1993) *Making Democracy Work: Civic Traditions in Modern Italy.* (Princeton: Princeton University Press).

P. Scholten (2011) *Framing Immigrant Integration. Dutch Research-Policy Dialogues in Comparative Perspective.* (Amsterdam: Amsterdam University Press).

D.A. Schön and M. Rein (1994) *Frame Reflection: Towards the Resolution of Intractable Controversies.* (New York: Basic Books).

C. Trigilia (1986) *Grandi partiti e piccole imprese.* (Bologna: Il Mulino).

G. Zincone (2001) *Secondo rapporto sull'integrazione degli immigrati in Italia.* (Bologna: Il Mulino).

G. Zincone (2011) 'The Case of Italy' in G. Zincone, R. Penninx and M. Borkert (eds) *Migration Policymaking in Europe: The Dynamics of Actors and Contexts in Past and Present.* (Amsterdam: Amsterdam University Press).

8
The Multilevel Dynamics of Migrant Integration Policies in Unitary States: The Netherlands and the United Kingdom

Peter Scholten

Introduction

Multilevel governance does not apply only to multinational states or the relationship between nations and regions. Also in more unitary states, the concept of multilevel governance captures the relationship between the central state and regional and local authorities like provinces and cities. In fact, studies have shown that relations between central and local governments in unitary states are often not as well structured as their state-centric structures suggest. Local governments, especially large cities, often do much more than implementing national policies in a top-down manner, but often play a key role in the formulation of their own policies as well as influencing the formulation of national policies.

This multilevelness of policies regardless of unitary or federal state structures seems to apply in particular to migrant integration. From a sociological perspective, migrant integration appears to be primarily a local process. The local level is where migrants go to school, find jobs, mix with their neighbours, participate in social life, and raise their kids. Research has also indicated that migrants tend to feel more connected to the cities or regions in which they live, than to the countries they live in or to supranational identities like Europe (Welle and Mamadouh, 2009). However, more than in many other policy areas, migrant integration has been characterized in policies, politics, and also academia in terms of distinct 'national models of integration' (Brubaker, 1992; Cornelius et al., 1994; Koopmans and Statham, 2000). These models represent state-centric problem definitions as well as state-centric structures of policy formulation and implementation. Furthermore, European institutions have attempted to get more involved in specific areas of migrant integration (Geddes, 2005; Guiraudon, 2000), though much more slowly than in the domain of migration policies.

However, throughout Europe there has been a proliferation of migrant integration policies on the regional as well as the local level (Alexander, 2007; Caponio and Borkert, 2010). Recognizing that migrant integration is a multilevel policy field (Zincone and Caponio, 2006) does not mean that policy processes and policy efforts at the various levels are necessarily harmonious and congruent. In fact, there are many examples of the decoupling of policy processes at various levels, leading to diverging or even conflicting policy frames and sometimes even conflicting policy measures and messages to target groups (Poppelaars and Scholten, 2008; see also Chapter 7 by Campomori and Caponio in this volume). This can hamper the effective multilevel governance of migrant integration and have a negative impact on policy effectiveness.

This chapter asks how relations between central and local migrant integration policies have been organized in the Netherlands and the United Kingdom, and to what extent this organization has led to convergence or divergence in terms of the framing of migrant integration policies. This investigation involves a focus on both the structure of multilevel governance, that is, governance relations between central and local governments, as well as more cultural elements of policy framing, that is, to what extent migrant integration policies are framed similarly or differently at these levels. With reference to the literature on national models of integration, top-down relations can be expected between policy levels as well as convergence in terms of policy framing around specific national models. In contrast, critics have argued that relations between levels can be characterized by decoupling as well, resulting in divergent policy frames or even policy conflicts. From a multilevel governance perspective, we would expect coordinated relations between national and local levels and limited divergence in terms of policy framing though without policy conflict.

This chapter focuses on two (decentralized) unitary states in order to reveal the mechanisms of multilevel governance at play in this kind of state. The Netherlands was the first European country to develop centrally coordinated migrant integration policies at the end of the 1970s. Ever since then, it has maintained a relatively strong national coordination framework and has strongly connected migrant integration to national issues like national identity and the welfare state

(Scholten, 2011). In contrast, the United Kingdom never developed a centrally coordinated policy in this area. As far as migrant integration was addressed in terms of race relations or community cohesion, it was devolved to the regional (i.e., Scotland) and local level (Spencer, 2011). In order to study multilevel dynamics, at least two cities are studied in both the United Kingdom and the Netherlands: Glasgow and London (and within London one borough from inner London and one from outer London) and Rotterdam and Amsterdam, respectively. Focusing on two states as well as a total of four local governments allows us to capture not just the vertical dimension of multilevel governance, but also the horizontal dimension. Do relations between national and local governments allow for divergence not just vertically but also horizontally between cities within countries? And is there something specific to local-level migrant integration policies, even across different countries?

The structure and culture of multilevel governance

Reflecting the book's overall focus, the multilevel dynamics of migrant integration will be conceptualized both in terms of the 'structure' of relations and interactions between policy levels as well as the 'culture' of problem definition and framing of migrant integration issues on these levels (Scholten, 2011). The former refers primarily to how the processes of multilevel governance are structured and organized, for instance whether there are hierarchical top-down structures or more bottom-up structures that lend local policy-makers more discretionary space. The latter refers primarily to the outcomes of policy-making at the various levels, in terms of the types of policies that are adopted and the level-specific conditions (such as problem developments, politics) that shape these policies.

Cultures of policy framing: beyond national models of integration

In politics, policy-making as well as academia, migrant integration is often discussed in terms of 'national models of integration'. These are historically rooted and nationally situated ways of framing and acting upon migrant integration, like the French republican model (Bowen, 2007), the British race-relations model (Hansen, 2000) or, at least for a long time, the Dutch multiculturalist model (Entzinger, 2003; Scholten, 2011). These national 'paradigms' are inherently bound to nation-states, 'not just because of their context dependency and insufficient clarifications on the conditions of generalizability, they are national because the modes of presenting and questions are political constituted by the nation states for which migration becomes a problem or a challenge' (Thränhardt and Bommes, 2010: 10). Also, as Favell (2001) shows, these models are reified in the context of 'exclusively internal national political dynamics' especially when migrant integration is politicized on the national level. The assumption behind these national models is that frames of migrant integration are set at the local level and that as far as local governments are involved in policy implementation this involvement should be under a strong national coordination framework and within the scope of the national policy frame. Perhaps the most used reference in this context is the French case, where the colour-blind and assimilation-oriented republican model is deeply engrained in national politics (Bleich, 2003; Brubaker, 1992; Schain, 1999).

In contrast to this national paradigm, there has been a growing interest in migrant integration policies at the local level in particular (Alexander, 2007; Caponio and Borkert, 2010; Penninx, 2004). This has revealed that in many cases, local and regional migrant integration policies 'frame' the issue in very different ways than at the national level, and they can also make very different policy choices. Caponio and Borkert (2010) speak of a distinctly 'local dimension' to migrant integration policies which on average are more pragmatic and accommodating than national policies. This is due in particular to local opportunity structures being more open to migrant groups than national opportunity structures, for instance because of policy-making taking place primarily 'behind closed doors' (Guiraudon, 1997) and with much greater proximity between local governments and local migrant organizations. Some studies have shown that this has led to a growing divergence of national and local policies and sometimes even conflicts between policy levels (Jørgensen, 2012; Poppelaars and Scholten, 2008). Even in the French case, there have been examples where local policies were much more colour-oriented and group-specific than as anticipated on the national level (Baldwin-Edwards and Schain, 1994; Bertossi and Duyvendak, 2012; Bowen, 2007).

Finally, besides local and national policies, European institutions have been attempting to get more involved in specific sub-areas of migrant integration (Boswell, 2008; Geddes, 2005; Guiraudon and Lahav, 2000; Guiraudon, 2000; Joppke, 2007; Zincone and Caponio, 2006). This is for instance clearly illustrated by the European Common Basic Principles of Integration and by the Europeanization of anti-discrimination policies in particular (Bertossi, 2007; Geddes, 2004). In many cases, EU involvement in migrant integration is driven by spin-offs from other more Europeanized policy areas, like migration policies. Rather than taking the form of direct regulation, EU involvement mostly comes in the form of soft or open measures of coordination. The EU-supported development of the Migration Policy Index (MIPEX) by the Migration Policy Group (MPG) is a good example of how the European Union tries to bring about more policy convergence and policy learning between various states.

Structures: defining multilevel governance

The structure of governance in multilevel settings refers to how relations between various levels are organized. Unitary states are generally assumed to have state-centric or top-down governance structures. These structures mean that central governments formulate policies that have to be implemented, in multilevel settings, at the regional and local levels. It leaves very little room for local governments to formulate their own policies or to respond to specific local conditions. This state-centric model contrasts with local or devolved modes of governance that leave considerable discretion to local governments to formulate their policies. In this type of local governance mode, central governments mostly just provide a generic policy framework or promote the exchange of best practices at the local level rather than formulate a single and coherent national policy.

Multilevel governance is often defined very broadly as any form of governance in multilevel settings, which assumes that any form of governance in such settings will effectively involve multiple levels. However, as institutionalists have shown, governance in such settings can also involve forms of decoupling, or the parallel development of policies at two levels without mutual coordination. In fact, studies in the area of migrant integration show instances of conflicting policy messages and even policy conflicts between national and local governments, revealing a decoupling of policies at both levels (Poppelaars and Scholten, 2008: Jorgensen, 2012).

Therefore, I will define multilevel governance as a specific mode of governance that can emerge in multilevel settings if the structure of relations between levels involves some form of coordinated action and the frames of migrant integration are similar or at least congruent between the levels (Scholten, 2013). This definition means that evidence of coordinated mutual relations have to be found in order to speak of 'multilevel governance'. Such coordinated relations can involve institutionalized venues where national and local governments jointly coordinate policy efforts, but also more ad-hoc and informal networks that policy-makers from both levels share and use for policy coordination.

The multilevel dynamics of migrant integration policies in the United Kingdom

The United Kingdom is a unitary state, though the central Westminster government delegates specific competencies to regional and local governments (in particular to Scotland, Wales, and Northern Ireland). This is clearly reflected in the multilevel character of migrant integration policies in the United Kingdom in which central as well as regional and local governments play a key role. This makes the United Kingdom an excellent case for studying the multilevel dynamics of migrant integration policies. In the following analysis, I will first look at the evolution of national policies and national policy structures. Subsequently, I will analyse migrant integration policies in two UK cities, London and Glasgow, and discuss their relationship to the national policy framework.

UK national policies

Migrant integration emerged relatively early on the UK national agenda, framed as an issue of 'race relations'. Already in the 1960s, the conservative politician Roy Jenkins put the idea of integration on the agenda in what has been defined as his 'rivers of blood' speech. Jenkins' speech basically warned that integration would not be effectively promoted and public order could be dramatically disturbed in the form of racial tensions and unrest. At the end of the 1950s there had indeed already been cases of urban unrest related to race relations, such as in Nottingham and Notting Hill. Such early agenda-setting events led to the formulation of policies aimed at promoting racial equality, equality of opportunity, and good race relations, in many ways resembling the American experience in preventing ethnic tensions (Bleich, 2011). This was codified in three respective Race Relations Acts in 1965, 1968, and 1976.

The race relations policy that thus emerged was strongly devolved to the local level. As Hansen (2000) shows, the role of the national government in this area was limited also because the issue of migrant integration could not be connected to a clear national identity, a topic that was often ignored because of the strong regional identities in the united Kingdom. Rather, the British framed their nation as a 'community of communities', embracing diversity (Parekh, 2000). Distinctive for the logic of policy formulation in this period was its pragmatic character

(Favell, 1998; Joppke, 1999). Favell (1998: 96) speaks in this respect of 'calculated, piecemeal, evolutionary, anti-philosophical pragmatism' in which symbolic debates about national identity and a British model of migrant integration were avoided.

In terms of the structure of policy coordination, this race-relations frame allowed the national government to delegate policies to the local level. Besides local governments, local Community Relations Councils and later Race Equality Councils played a key role in policies until well after the turn of the millennium. At the national level, the Home Office was responsible for the coordination of the race-relations policies but never really developed a strong coordination framework.

In the 2000s, Britain would break away from this race-relations discourse quite radically. As early as the late 1990s and even up to 2000, there was a brief deepening of race-relations discourse, focusing in particular on combating forms of institutional racism (such as in the Macpherson report, 1999) and reinventing British multicultural identity (such as in the Parekh report, 2000). However, several incidents put migrant integration high up on the British political agenda and triggered a sharp turn in policy direction. This included in particular the 2001 ethnic riots in Bradford, Burnley, and Oldham and the 9/11 attacks in New York, and gained further momentum after the 2005 London bombings. These events led to broad public concerns about segregation and radicalization in the United Kingdom (Finney and Simpson, 2009; Kundnani, 2007; McGhee, 2008). In a memorable speech, the head of Britain's Commission for Racial Equality, Trevor Phillips, warned that if no proper course of action was taken, Britain would be 'sleepwalking into segregation' (Phillips, 2005). In response to these events, a community cohesion policy was developed which, much more than promoting racial equality, was oriented at promoting relations between minority groups, building social capital, preventing parallel lives, and developing a shared sense of 'Britishness' (Cantle, 2001). Promoting community cohesion would be the solution to the problem of growing segregation. The race-relations frame that had prevailed in preceding decades was now discarded as proof that multiculturalism had failed in Britain (Grillo, 2010). Furthermore, attention shifted away from the traditional focus on 'race' to a focus on religion and Islam in particular (Modood, 2005).

This community cohesion policy marked a shift toward a somewhat more centrally coordinated and communitarianist approach (Flint and Robinson, 2008). The revaluation of Britishness in relation to community cohesion, as propagated by former Home Secretary David Blunkett but later also by Prime Minister Gordon Brown, defined migrant integration as a national issue (McGhee, 2008). However, the policy window that was created in the aftermath of the events in 2001 did not lead to the formulation of a coherent national policy strategy aimed at migrant integration. No coherent policy structure emerged, and as Spencer (2011) shows, there were discrepancies between the policy arguments of the Home Office and the Department of Communities and Local Government. Spencer describes the lack of 'vertical integration' in the United Kingdom's national policy framework in terms of persistent 'policy silos' that complicate the development of a coherent integration policy. Apart from the development of a politically strongly supported discourse on what the United Kingdom's policies in this domain should achieve, actual policies remained fragmented and often with ad-hoc responses to specific issues for specific categories of migrants (such as refugees). Furthermore, most of the policy measures directed at community cohesion were still situated at the local level.

Gradually, this community cohesion discourse seems to have faded away from the national political agenda. In 2007, a Commission on Integration and Cohesion clearly argued that community cohesion was something to be achieved at the local level. The 2010 Localism Bill also created a setting for devolution of this type of policy. Furthermore, national resources for community cohesion policies declined. In 2012, after several complications in the formulation process, the coalition government of David Cameron did launch an integration strategy. However, it provided few concrete policy initiatives and only reconfirmed the lack of coherence in the policy framework, on the vertical level (departments) as well as the horizontal level (devolution).

Local policies: London

London is by far the city with the largest immigrant population in the UK. About one-third of the London population was born outside the UK (Gidley and Jayaweera, 2010). This includes a large proportion of refugees, family migrants as well as labour migrants, especially from Central and Eastern European (CEE) countries, whose immigration to London peaked in the 1990s and early 2000s. However, London's diversity surpasses that of first-generation migrants; especially from the British Commonwealth, there are many British citizens with an immigrant background. Both new and old immigrant categories together make London into a city characterized by what Vertovec (2007) defines as 'superdiversity'.

There is no single policy framework for the whole of London. Though the Greater London Authority (GLA) represents a central authority for the greater London area, it is relatively 'weak' in comparison to city governments in the Netherlands or France, and it delegates many powers to the level of 'boroughs' (Tewdwr-Jones, 2009). The GLA is mostly limited to issues that span several boroughs, like transportation. Between boroughs, there are significant differences in terms of the relative size of migrant populations, as well as in terms of the distribution of specific migrant groups which leads to significant differences between, for instance, London's West End and its infamous East End, as well as between inner and outer London (Gidley and Jayaweera, 2010).

Reflecting the superdiverse character of the city as well as the importance of immigration for London's economy, the GLA has adopted a strongly entrepreneurial role when it comes to immigration and issues related to integration. This is, for instance, reflected in its integration approach for refugees. The 'London Enriched' programme that Boris Johnson launched to this aim (Greater London Authority, 2009) provides an integration framework that is both more ambitious and more comprehensive than national policies in this area. It develops a comprehensive approach to areas of language, housing, employment, health, community safety, children, and community development. Furthermore, it sets a much more positive tone: 'refugees living in security and dignity, sharing with all Londoners the same chances for a decent quality of life and the opportunity to contribute to London and its development' (ibid: 5). Unique to the British case is that London Enriched also involves a broadening of the policy scope to other types of migrants, beyond refugees (ibid: 5).

On various occasions, the London Mayors Ken Livingstone and (his successor) Boris Johnson also dissociated themselves from national policy discourses on the restriction of immigration and the importance of Britishness as a concept for integration (see also Keith, 2005). According to Livingstone, if one thing defines Britishness 'it is its emptiness as a concept' (ibid). Furthermore, the need for an immediate implementation of a community cohesion policy, which had emerged on the national agenda in 2001 in response to urban unrest in the West Midlands, was also not so immediately felt in London.

For the implementation of this framework, the GLA relies heavily on the boroughs. In an effort to develop a coherent policy framework in which relevant actors are involved, the responsibility for the coordination of the refugees integration strategy was devolved to the GLA in 2006 (Vachelli et al., 2011). In this context, the mayor leads the London

Strategic Migration Partnership in which various relevant administrative bodies are involved as well as boroughs, NGOs, and the border control agency of the UK government.

It is impossible to get a good understanding of London's policies in this area without looking at the boroughs. One of the boroughs that has stood out in terms of its proactive approach in the area of race relations and community cohesion, is Tower Hamlets (located in inner London/the East End). This borough is characterized by a particularly high concentration of Muslims from Bangladesh: over one-third of the borough population (Butler et al., 2011; Dench et al., 2006). There is also a clear presence of Bengalis in local politics, making Tower Hamlets the council with the highest percentage of Muslim councillors in the UK. Tower Hamlets has been very active in the area of community cohesion from the very beginning. It was widely recognized as an example for local community cohesion policies as well as for its efforts to promote cross-cultural contact (being awarded the Beacon status and the pathfinder status in 2003) (Cantle, 2005; Tower Hamlets Borough Council, 2003). An important characteristic of Tower Hamlets' policies was that it mainstreamed community cohesion policies into its broad community plans that spanned various sectors of local policies. It did not develop a separate policy approach. This mainstreaming also seems to hide that, in spite of the shift in discourse, there was much more continuity in policy practices. The exemplary status that was awarded to Tower Hamlets was interpreted more as a form of recognition for the experience and expertise that the borough had developed over the years.

Enfield is an outer-London borough that has experienced significant immigration, particularly in the period 2001–2006 (Vachelli et al., 2011). In contrast to Tower Hamlets, its immigrant population consists primarily of Caribbean and black African groups (Butler et al., 2011). Enfield too has developed its own policy approach both in the area of race relations, with a powerful Enfield Racial Equality Council (EREC), as well as in the area of community cohesion. Echoing the national policy approach, it stresses the focus on building trust between people, increasing a sense of belonging, as well as building strong and positive relationships between people. At the same time, it continues most of its race-relations approach, oriented at preventing discrimination, recognizing diversity, and creating similar life opportunities for all (Enfield Borough, 2003; Enfield Borough, 2007). It is fair to say that Enfield's community cohesion policies were developed alongside its race-relations policies, rather than substituting for them. Enfield stands out in stressing the role of local leadership, in particular the figure of a Cabinet member for community safety and the voluntary sector; Enfield does not just consider community cohesion a local issue, but also an issue that has to be targeted by local government (Enfield Borough, 2003: 69–70). Like Tower Hamlets, Enfield too is considering how to broaden the scope of its policy approach for the integration of various migrant groups.

For London we can conclude that the GLA as well as the boroughs have been very active within the scope of the national policy framework. Faced with the city's diversity, London's governments have tried to put the opportunities offered by race-relations policies as well as community cohesion policies and the refugee-integration framework to its maximum use. However, in response to the rapid changes in demographic composition and the diverse nature of migrant groups, boroughs like Enfield and Tower Hamlets seem to be evolving pragmatically toward a more comprehensive approach to migrant integration. This is also reflected in the entrepreneurial role of the GLA in this respect, making London a powerful advocate for a more comprehensive integration approach on the national level.

Local policies: Glasgow

The case of Glasgow differs from London in many respects, in terms of the immigration context as well as the policy setting. First of all, immigrants make up a much smaller proportion of Glasgow's population than in London, and involve in particular refugees and CEE migrants. Furthermore, Glasgow has an ageing population, creating an important economic and demographic pull for immigration to Glasgow. This may explain the overall positive attitudes toward immigration in Glasgow. There have been no incidents like the race riots in England, though the murder of a refugee in the area of Sighthill (in Glasgow) in 2001 did create some concern about race relations in Glasgow. There was a strong feeling that these riots and the parallel-lives discourse, as well as the 2005 London bombings, were interpreted as not relevant in the Scottish context. In fact, the juxtaposition of the Scottish approach against the English approach seems to have only reinforced the Scottish discourse of openness and accepting diversity (for more on how the Scottish political approach to immigration differs from the UK approach, see Chapter 6 by Arrighi de Casanova and Chapter 12 by Hepburn and Rosie).

As the largest city in Scotland, Glasgow develops its migrant policies in the context of Scottish government. Whereas immigration and race relations are not devolved, community cohesion does belong to a broader range of issues that have been devolved to the Scottish government. This means, for instance, that the national turn toward community cohesion policies after 2001 did not apply to Scotland and cities like Glasgow.

This has created a setting in which Glasgow (and in a broader context Scotland) has been able to set a much more welcoming and positive tone toward migrants than on the UK level. On the Scottish level, this was exemplified amongst others by the One Scotland campaign, stressing that the Scots were an open people that welcomed migrants and diversity. Within Scotland, there were positive experiences with the reception of migrants within local communities, often recognizing the importance of these migrants for the revitalization of the local economy (McGarrigle, 2010; Pacione, 2005). The positive tone to migrant integration was also shared by the Scottish Nationalist Party (SNP). The Scottish government has even developed measures to induce migrants to stay in Scotland for longer periods. For instance, the 'Fresh Talent Initiative' allowed foreign students in Scotland to stay to work for a couple of years, hoping that these students might eventually stay for a longer period. Similarly, in Glasgow a Bridges project was conducted that basically involved a work scheme for asylum-seekers, as well as a development partnership (ATLAS) that was set up at the local level to promote the integration of asylum-seekers in particular.

At the same time, Glasgow (and Scotland at large) had to face the UK's national sovereignty in the area of migration management. In this context there have been many cases of fruitful and sometimes less constructive interaction between Glasgow and Scotland and the national government. One particularly positive experience was an asylum-seeker dispersal programme, which involved an agreement between the city of Glasgow and the UK Borders Agency (UKBA) to resettle refugees (primarily from the London area, and primarily families) to Glasgow. Concurrent to this programme, Glasgow developed various measures to 'integrate' these refugees into Glasgow society to make sure that once their admission was finalized the migrants would stay in Glasgow. However, the interviews reveal that there have also been less successful efforts, amongst others by the strategic migration partnership of the Scottish association of local authorities (COSLA).

Wrapping up the discussion of the UK case, it becomes clear that there has never been something like a coherent British model of migrant integration policies. Instead, we find a highly fragmented policy reality where policy philosophies on the various levels are weakly articulated and where there are important differences between government levels. First of all, on the national level, there have been considerable changes in policy framing over time, especially from a race-relations frame until the 1990s to a community cohesion frame that emerged in the early 2000s. Both frames have however never been articulated as a coherent national policy framework and at no point did a central coordination structure emerge. It is also important to realize that the very concept of 'integration', except from some recent initiatives in that direction, has never really been embraced in the UK context. Secondly, policies at the local level clearly had their own dynamics. Policies in Glasgow and Scotland were much more open to migration and diversity and also went much further in attempting to promote the integration of asylum-seekers. Also, London's policies, especially in the borough of Tower Hamlets, were a much more positive approach to diversity.

The multilevel dynamics of migrant integration policies in the Netherlands

The Netherlands has become a highly diverse society, especially since the 1960s and 1970s. Like the UK, it has attracted various types of migrants, including colonial migrants as well as labour and asylum migrants. In contrast to the UK, the Netherlands is a decentralized unitary state where the central government plays a leading and coordinating role in many policy areas, including migration and integration. Yet, the multilevel character of integration policies has also become increasingly manifest in the Dutch case. This includes not just the obstacles the national government feels it faces in the European context, but increasingly also local governments that are trying to develop their own answers to the local situation they face.

Dutch national policies

The Netherlands was among the first European countries to formulate a centrally coordinated migrant-incorporation policy in the early 1980s. It is the policies in this period that have often been taken as exemplary of the Dutch multicultural model of integration. This model involved a strong belief in the recognition and institutionalization of cultural pluralism in promoting a process of cultural and socioeconomic emancipation of migrant groups (Duyvendak and Scholten, 2011). Indeed, the Ethnic Minorities Policy that the Dutch central government formulated in the late 1980s reflected some traits of the multicultural model. It was directed at specific target groups only and stressed the role of socio-cultural emancipation as a condition for socioeconomic participation.

The Ethnic Minorities Policy of this period was coordinated by the Minister of Home Affairs. This Minister was able to fulfil a strong coordination role, especially as many policy measures of the Ethnic Minorities Policy fell in the areas of other ministers, in particular those of Culture, Social Affairs, Education, and Justice. Also, Home Affairs ministers were mostly powerful figures in Dutch politics, who were often also deputy prime ministers that could provide significant political leverage. Furthermore, policy legitimacy was derived from the involvement of migrant organizations through a 'National Consultation and Advisory Structure for Migrants' and from academic expertise such as reports from the authoritative Scientific Council for Government Policy and the Advisory Committee on Minorities Research (Guiraudon, 1997; Scholten, 2011). This technocratic policy framework enabled a strong national leadership to formulate the policies that were to be implemented in the 1980s.

However, migrant integration re-emerged on the national policy agenda in the late 1980s and early 1990s in a way that challenged both its multiculturalist orientation and its strong central coordination. An integration policy was formulated that was more liberal-egalitarian in its focus on the socioeconomic participation of individual migrants. The main goal of government policies was to promote full and equal citizenship in terms of participation in the socioeconomic and political sphere, with cultural emancipation shifting toward the background. In terms of coordination, this meant that the coordinating role of the Department of Home Affairs became weaker as more responsibilities were shifted to sectoral departments such as Housing, Education, and Social Affairs. However, the Home Affairs minister continued to be responsible for the coordination of policy measures between various departments.

However, by the end of the 1990s, migrant integration again re-emerged on the agenda. The issue was now increasingly connected to broader concerns about urban developments. This led to the establishment of a special minister (without a separate department) for Integration and Large Cities, who was situated in the Department of Home Affairs. A strength of this positioning in the Department of Home Affairs was that this minister could act as a liaison between central and local governments.

Just after the turn of the millennia, migrant integration re-emerged yet again on the political agenda, resulting in what was to become an assimilationist turn in Dutch integration policies. An 'Integration Policy New Style' was formulated that put much more stress on issues of culture and public order. Whereas the integration policy had stressed 'active citizenship', the Integration Policy New Style stressed the 'common citizenship', which meant that 'the unity of society must be found in what members have in common ... that is that people speak Dutch, and that one abides to basic Dutch norms' (TK 2003–2004, 29203, nr. 1: 8.). Persisting social-cultural differences were now considered a hindrance to migrant integration. Moreover, the integration policy was linked to broader concerns about migration (such as imposing compulsory civic integration tests in the country of origin as well as after arrival in the Netherlands) and about the re-imagination of national identity and social cohesion in Dutch society. It was in this period that the framing of the 'multicultural model' took place as a 'counter-discourse' against which new policy developments were to be juxtaposed.

In response, a special minister was established for migration and integration who would be situated in the Department of Justice. This stressed the law-and-order approach to integration that had emerged, as well as the connection between integration and immigration policies at the central level of government. It was this minister for migration and integration that would take the lead in the formulation of the pre- and post-admission civic integration programmes that would become the most important measure of integration policies in the 2000s.

Finally, since 2010 there have been clear indications that the central government is retrenching from the domain of migrant integration, while putting more focus on limiting immigration. The conservative minority-government coalition that was formulated in 2010, supported by the anti-immigrant Freedom Party in parliament, only established a minister for migration and asylum, while for some time delegating the responsibility for integration to the Home Affairs Minister (which was changed back after two years). This means that there is no longer a special government minister for integration. Migrant integration is increasingly framed as an individual responsibility of the involved migrants themselves.

Local policies: Amsterdam

Amsterdam and Rotterdam are the two largest cities as well as the two most diverse cities in the Netherlands, with large populations of Moroccan, Surinamese, and Turkish migrants (Crul and Heering, 2008; Uitermark, 2010). Often, Amsterdam is perceived as an exemplary case for the so-called Dutch multicultural model of integration (Lucassen & Penninx, 1995). Indeed, for a long time it seemed that Amsterdam's migrant integration policy largely developed in pace with national developments. Until the 1970s, Amsterdam followed what Alexander (2007) describes as a guest-worker approach that was not oriented at settlement and integration but rather assumed a 'minimal responsibility' for migrants. In the late 1970s and 1980s, Amsterdam developed a more pluralist 'minorities policy'. This policy formed a response to the national developments in this period, but also to the mounting social problems that the city was faced with in the 1970s, particularly in the sphere of housing. In a 1978 policy memorandum on foreign workers in Amsterdam, the government observed that most foreign workers would indeed settle permanently. In this period, national and local policy developments unfolded more or less simultaneously, also with a more or less similar policy model as a result. There were also indications that the development of national policies in this period were directly inspired by policy developments in Amsterdam.

Amsterdam's minorities policy in the 1980s was 'based on the idea that minorities should integrate while also maintaining their cultural identity' (City of Amsterdam, 1982). Most attention was devoted to political-legal aspects of migrant integration, in particular to cooperation with migrant organizations and to anti-discrimination (and anti-racism) measures. This also involved many group-specific measures, such as the establishment of ethnic minority advisory councils and many measures in the socioeconomic domain, intensive cooperation with migrant organizations, promoting ethnic entrepreneurship, affirmative-action policies in the city government itself, and very tolerant policies toward the establishment of (mainly Muslim) religious facilities.

In a 1989 memorandum (City of Amsterdam, 1989), the city concluded that 'after a decade of efforts of both government and private initiatives the position of ethnic minorities groups seems not to have improved' and 'the effects of the minorities policy which took form from the beginning of the seventies...appear not to be encouraging'. Migrant integration re-emerged on the local agenda in this period. Additionally, the first National Minorities Debate that took place in 1992 also found its way onto the local political agenda of Amsterdam during the local elections of 1994. This did, though more gradually than on the national level, mark a turning point away from Amsterdam's pluralist policies of the 1980s. The new climate brought the anti-immigrant Centre Party into the City Council with four seats in 1990. The replacement of the Mayor Ed van Thijn, a proclaimed multiculturalist, further facilitated a policy frame-shift in the years to follow (Alexander, 2007: 186).

This resulted in a newly formulated diversity policy, involving a reframing from 'group-specific policies' toward 'problem-oriented policies' (see City of Amsterdam, 1999). Many group-specific measures were abandoned, at least in formal policy, for a more generic and individual- or citizen-oriented approach. Wolff (1999) describes the three main aims of the new diversity policy as guaranteeing equal opportunities, combating discrimination, and promoting individual participation. As part of such a more generic approach, the role of migrant organizations was significantly decreased, in favour of a more individualized and diverse 'migration council' that did not represent any group in particular. In addition, Amsterdam developed, in correlation with national developments and developments in a number of other cities, civic integration programmes on the local level. Even going beyond the requirements of the Civic Integration of Newcomers Law that entered force in 1998, Amsterdam developed civic integration programmes for specific categories of newcomers such as 'old comers' (long-term resident migrants that still suffered from language or other associated integration problems). Amsterdam's often proactive and tolerant policies toward cultural and religious matters of the 1980s were largely abandoned, claiming that these matters belonged to the private realm rather than the public realm (Maussen, 2006: 69).

Migrant integration re-appeared prominently on the local political agenda after the turn of the millennium. This re-emergence occurred somewhat later than on the national level, probably because the Labour party maintained control over Amsterdam after the 2002 municipal elections. Furthermore, the terrorist killing of the filmmaker Van Gogh in Amsterdam in November 2004 was a particularly powerful focus event. As a policy follow-up to this event, Amsterdam published a new memorandum 'We, the people of Amsterdam'. This memorandum made a more explicit issue-connection between migrant integration and anti-radicalization policies. This new policy initiative seemed to reinforce the trend toward what Maussen (2006) describes as a dialogical approach to migrant integration, involving an approach primarily oriented at participation and interethnic contact. This local dialogical approach stressed the diverse possibilities for identification with the city of Amsterdam as a means of creating social cohesion at the city level, contrasting sharply with emerging policies on the national level in that period. In public debate, Amsterdam's Mayor Cohen's slogan 'keeping things together' became exemplary of this pragmatic approach.

This shows that, whereas Amsterdam's policies developed largely in pace with national developments until just before the turn of the millennium, the local formulation of a diversity policy and a bit later the assimilationist turn at the national level mark clear points of divergence between national and local policies, as did its more pragmatic approach to 'keeping things together', promoting intercultural dialogue and continuing to invest in migrant integration issues altogether.

Local policies: Rotterdam

In the city of Rotterdam, the development of local migrant integration policies followed a somewhat different path. Until well into the 1970s, the city of Rotterdam followed a guest-worker approach similar to that at the national level and in Amsterdam. However, the issue of migrant integration emerged in the local policy agenda relatively early, following ethnic riots in 1972 in the city district Afrikaanderbuurt. The industrial character of Rotterdam's local economy meant that the city was strongly affected by the economic recession in the 1970s. This recession hit the immigrant population particularly hard, with problems of social segregation, deprivation and criminality concentrated in specific sections around the city's centre (Odmalm, 2005: 48). This meant that the city of Rotterdam was faced relatively early on with the consequences of the discrepancy between the norm of not being an immigration country and the fact of increasing and prolonged settlement of migrants in specific neighbourhoods; social problems and ethnic tensions pushed migrant integration onto the local policy agenda well before this happened on the national level.

Consequently, Rotterdam adopted a policy aimed at integration by the end of the 1970s, ahead of developments on the national level. In contrast to national policies, Rotterdam's policies were much more oriented at combating social deprivation and housing problems than at cultural emancipation. In this context, it proposed a regulation for the spatial dispersion of migrants (City of Rotterdam, 1979), which however was never implemented due to fierce criticism from society and from experts.

In contrast with Amsterdam's pluralist policies, Rotterdam's policies combined elements of a pluralist with a more dialogical approach (Maussen, 2006). A 1985 policy memorandum states that 'minorities should to a great extent adapt [to Dutch society] ... integration inevitably means learning the Dutch language, knowledge of and participating in Dutch social relations and the acquisition of some Dutch norms and values ... however, foreigners do not need to become like average Dutchmen' (cit. in Maussen, 2006: 113). The policy's main focus was on integration in the spheres of the labour market, education, and housing, but also on stimulating interethnic contact. Moreover, the role of migrant organizations was not so much oriented at the accommodation of group differences, but rather at promoting the integration of these specific communities into Rotterdam society.

Rotterdam was not only a frontrunner in developing migrant integration policies; it became a key policy entrepreneur in the turn towards an integration policy at the national level. In 1988, it issued a Memorandum on Minorities Policy in which it advocated specific policies that were mainly targeted at socioeconomic areas in order to influence a national report from the Scientific Council for Government Policy that would be issued later (1989). In this context, Rotterdam continued to advocate more policy decentralization, as it considered national policies aimed at social renewal a failure. During the 1990s, Rotterdam largely continued this policy approach aimed at integration through socioeconomic participation.

Like Amsterdam, Rotterdam did mark a brief shift at the end of the 1990s to a diversity policy that was more oriented at promoting (and even celebrating) the diversity of the city. The tone of this diversity policy was much more positive than the earlier integration policies aimed primarily at social deprivation; thereby it reflected the gradual improvement of the socioeconomic position of many migrants in Rotterdam throughout the late 1990s. Also, Rotterdam developed policies oriented at 'social mixing', for instance by promoting differentiated housing in neighbourhoods in order to prevent the concentration of deprivation or social problems in specific urban areas. Rotterdam continued to cooperate with migrant organizations even under the banner of the diversity policy where these migrant organizations were taken as instruments for the integration of these groups, rather than as instruments for the accommodation of cultural differences.

Rotterdam was a frontrunner in the early 1990s in the agenda setting of civic integration programmes for newcomers. Already in 1991, Rotterdam began a municipal Project Integration for Newcomers (Van den Bent, 2010: 152). Much earlier than was the case for national policies, Rotterdam made participation in these courses mandatory for migrants that received social benefits (ibid.: 153). With these programmes, the policies shifted attention from settled minority groups to the ongoing influx of newcomers to the city.

The years 2002–2003 marked a major turning point in Rotterdam's local politics (Van den Bent, 2010). In these years, Pim Fortuyn made his first moves on the Dutch political stage, as leader of the centre-right populist party 'Liveable Rotterdam' that eventually won the 2002 local elections. In these elections, migrant integration was framed in relation to issues as criminality, Islam, radicalization, and the decline of social cohesion. This marked a turning point not just in local policy discourse, but also in actual policies in the area of migrant integration. Rotterdam developed a more assimilationist policy that concentrated in particular on neighbourhoods where migrants were relatively overrepresented (Uitermark and Duyvendak, 2008).

One of the policy initiatives involved the introduction of the 'Rotterdam Code', or a set of basic rules of social behaviour for everybody in Rotterdam. In addition, the Alderman Pastors (from the Liveable Rotterdam party) attempted to develop a policy that would provide a total end to ethnic minority settlement in specific neighbourhoods ('allochtonenstop'), which he was forced to abandon under fierce political pressure. However, subsequently the municipality pushed the national government to adopt a law on 'Special Measures for Urban Areas', which provided the municipalities with means for preventing the settlement of people from low-income categories or with social-security benefits in designated urban areas (Uitermark and Duyvendak, 2008). This was also called the 'Rotterdam law' as it was pushed only by Rotterdam, but also implemented only in Rotterdam. In addition, Rotterdam adopted new measures to promote interethnic contacts in particular, such as the project ('Welcome to Rotterdam') where 'old' and 'new' citizens of Rotterdam met on an individual basis.

In a very similar way to the United Kingdom, the Dutch case reveals a discrepancy between national and local integration policies. In fact, since the 2000s, there seems to be a progressive divergence between both levels. Unlike the UK, the Netherlands has until very recently had a centrally coordinated policy framework. Especially the minorities policy in the 1980s involved a strongly centrally coordinated and well-articulated national policy framework. This changed in the 1990s when the integration policy involved a weaker central coordination structure and was more closely linked to urban policies; this was a brief period in which Dutch national and local governments seemed to cooperate in a more effective structure of multilevel governance. In contrast, the assimilationist turn since the 2000s seemed to be driven by very specific national factors that in some respects conflicted with the more pragmatic approach on the local level, especially in Amsterdam.

Conclusions

Whereas migration studies have tended to focus on and contribute to the reification of national models of integration, this chapter shows that the reality of migrant integration policies is much more fragmented and multifaceted. This reality applies not just to federal states, but also to unitary states like the Netherlands where 'methodological nationalism' has been very strong. The vertical fragmentation between national and local migrant integration policies that was found in both the United Kingdom and the Netherlands provides a rationale for the evolving research agenda on multilevel governance in this policy field. In the Netherlands, migrant integration policies were formulated in a relatively centralized way at the national level; however, rather than mere policy implementers, the analysis of Rotterdam and Amsterdam shows that local policies have sometimes taken very different turns from the national levels. In the United Kingdom, migrant integration policies have been largely devolved to the local level. However, in the UK case, a complex relationship has also emerged between local-level policies and evolving national policy frameworks such as community cohesion and integration policies.

In terms of vertical fragmentation, various contributions to the literature have suggested that there is something specific to the 'local dimension' of migrant integration policy-making. In particular, local policies would be more pragmatic and more accommodative in terms of coping with cultural diversity. Though many local governments do indeed seem to be more welcoming and positive in terms of diversity, this does not apply to all local cases. For instance Rotterdam has for a long time been more integrationist than the national level and other Dutch cities. In fact, my analysis shows that the differences between local governments in terms of their integration approach are very significant as well. Just as there are no national models of integration there also does not seem to be one local model of integration.

Furthermore, the analysis in this chapter shows that local governments are more than just implementers of national policies. Responding to local (political, policy problem) circumstances, they develop their own migrant integration policies that clearly do not necessarily accord with national policies. On various occasions, local governments have also acted as policy entrepreneurs trying to influence policy developments at the national level. Take, for instance, the 'vertical-venue shopping' by Rotterdam to get national support for policies of spatial dispersion ('the Rotterdam law'), or the efforts by the GLA to get a broader approach to the integration of refugees and other types of migrants on the agenda.

This chapter also revealed the horizontal fragmentation of policy responsibilities and policy dynamics over time. National models of integration assume consistent and coherent national policy discourses and coordination mechanisms. In the UK as well as in the Netherlands, the institutional responsibility for migrant integration has been fragmented between sectoral departments and contested over time. In both countries, various policy frames came and went over the past decades. Moreover, various departments have been involved in coordinating parts of migrant integration policies, and recently in both countries the tendency to mainstream migrant integration across sectoral departments has increased.

The findings of this chapter legitimize further inquiry into the dynamics of migrant integration policies in multilevel settings. It remains an empirical question whether the multilevel dynamics of migrant integration policy-making involves effective forms of multilevel governance. Defined as a form of governance in multilevel settings, specific to multilevel governance is that there is some form of coordinated interaction across policy levels. This chapter casts doubt on whether we can thus speak of effective multilevel governance in this domain. Both the UK and the Dutch case provide examples of the decoupling of policies at various levels. The Dutch case in particular seems to lack proper forms of cross-level policy coordination, though the Rotterdam case reveals that instances of more strategic 'vertical-venue shopping' or attempts by local governments to create more scope for their policies by influencing national policies. However, decoupling and policy conflicts seem to have been much more characteristic of national-local policy relations than effective forms of multilevel governance.

References

M. Alexander (2007) *Cities and Labour Immigration: Comparing Policy Responses in Amsterdam, Paris, Rome and Tel Aviv*. (Farnham: Ashgate).

M. Baldwin-Edwards and M. Schain (1994) *The Politics of Immigration in Western Europe*. (Abingdon: Routledge).

C. Bertossi and J. W. Duyvendak (2012) 'National Models of Immigrant Integration. The Costs for Comparative Research', *Comparative European Politics*, 10(3): 237–247.

C. Bertossi (2007) *European Anti-Discrimination and the Politics of Citizenship: Britain and France*. (Houndmills: Palgrave Macmillan).

E. Bleich (2003) *Race Politics in Britain and France: Ideas and Policymaking since the 1960's*. (Cambridge: Cambridge Univ Press).

E. Bleich (2011) 'Social Research and "Race" Policy Framing in Britain and France', *The British Journal of Politics & International Relations*, 13(1): 59–74.

C. Boswell (2008) 'The Political Functions of Expert Knowledge: Knowledge and Legitimation in European Union Immigration Policy', *Journal of European Public Policy*, 15(4): 471–488.

P.J. Bowen (2007) 'A View from France on the Internal Complexity of National Models', *Journal of Ethnic and Migration Studies*, 33(6): 1003–1016.

R. Brubaker (1992) *Nationhood and Citizenship in France and Germany*. (Cambridge/ Mass: Harvard University Press).

T. Butler, C. Hamnett, S. Mir and M. Ramsden (2011) *Ethnicity, Class and Aspiration: Understanding London's New East End*. (Bristol: Policy Press).

T. Cantle (2001) *Community Cohesion*. (London: Home Office).

T. Cantle (2005) *Community Cohesion: A New Framework for Race Relations.* (Houndmills: Palgrave Macmillan).

T. Caponio, T. and M. Borkert (2010) *The Local Dimension of Migration Policymaking.* (Amsterdam: Amsterdam University Press).

Commission on Integration and Cohesion (2007). *Our Shared Future.* (London: CIC).

W.A. Cornelius, P.L. Martin and J.F. Hollifield (1994) *Controlling Immigration: A Global Perspective.* (Stanford: Stanford University Press).

M. Crul and L. Heering (2008) *The Position of the Turkish and Moroccan Second Generation in Amsterdam and Rotterdam: The TIES Study in the Netherlands.* (Amsterdam: Amsterdam University Press).

G. Dench, K. Gavron and M.D. Young (2006) *The New East End: Kinship, Race and Conflict.* (London: Profile).

J. Duyvendak and P. Scholten (2011) 'Beyond the Dutch "Multicultural Model"', *Journal of International Migration and Integration,* 12(3): 331–348.

Enfield Borough (2003) *Enfield – A Borough for All. Enfield Council's Community Cohesion Strategy 2007–2009.* (Enfield: Enfield Borough Council).

Enfield Borough (2007) *Enfield's Future. A Sustainable Community Strategy for Enfield 2007–2017.* (Enfield: Enfield Borough Council).

H. Entzinger (2003) 'The Rise and Fall of Multiculturalism: The Case of the Netherlands' in Bommes and Morawska (eds) *Toward Assimilation and Citizenship: Immigrants in Liberal Nation-States.* (Houndmills/Basingstoke: Palgrave).

A. Favell (1998) *Philosophies of Integration: Immigration and the Idea of Citizenship in France and Britain.* (Houndmills: Palgrave Macmillan).

A. Favell (2001) 'Integration Policy and Integration Research in Europe: A Review and Critique' in Aleinikoff et al. (eds) *Citizenship Today: Global Perspectives and Practices.* (Washington: Brookings Institution Press).

N. Finney and L. Simpson (2009) *'Sleepwalking to Segregation'?: Challenging Myths about Race and Migration.* (Bristol: Policy Press).

J. Flint and D. Robinson (2008) *Community Cohesion in Crisis. New Dimensions of Diversity.* (Bristol: Policy Press).

A. Geddes (2005) 'Migration Research and European Integration: The Construction and Institutionalization of Problems of Europe' in Bommes and Morawska (eds) *International Migration Research: Constructions, Omissions and Interdisciplinarity.* (Aldershot: Ashgate).

A. Geddes (2004) 'Britain, France, and EU Anti-discrimination Policy: The Emergence of an EU Policy Paradigm', *West European Politics,* 27(2): 334–353.

B. Gidley and H. Jayaweera (2010) *An Evidence Base on Migration and Integration in London.* (Oxford: Centre on Migration, Policy and Society, University of Oxford).

Greater London Authority (2009) *London Enriched: Reference Document: Supporting Evidence for the Strategy.* (London: GLA).

R. Grillo (2010) 'British and Others' in Vertovec and Wessendorf (eds) *The Multiculturalism Backlash: European Discourses, Policies and Practices.* (Abingdon: Routledge).

V. Guiraudon (1997) *Policy Change Behind Gilded Doors: Explaining the Evolution of Aliens' Rights in France, Germany and the Netherlands, 1974–94.* PhD Thesis, Harvard University.

V. Guiraudon (2000) 'European Integration and Migration Policy: Vertical Policy-Making as Venue Shopping', *Journal of Common Market Studies*, 38(2):251–271.

V. Guiraudon and G. Lahav (2000) 'A Reappraisal of the State Sovereignty Debate', *Comparative Political Studies*, 33(2):163–195.

R. Hansen (2000) *Citizenship and Immigration in Post-War Britain: The Institutional Origins of a Multicultural Nation.* (Oxford: Oxford University Press).

C. Joppke (1999) *Immigration and the Nation-State: The United States, Germany, and Great Britain.* (Oxford: Oxford University Press).

C. Joppke (2007) 'Beyond National Models: Civic Integration Policies for Immigrants in Western Europe', *West European Politics*, 30(1):1–22.

M.B. Jørgensen (2012) 'The Diverging Logics of Integration Policy Making at National and City Level', *International Migration Review*, 46(1): 244–278.

M. Keith (2005) *After the Cosmopolitan? Multicultural Cities and the Future of Racism.* (Abingdon: Routledge).

R. Koopmans and P. Statham (2000) *Challenging Immigration and Ethnic Relations Politics.* (Oxford: Oxford University Press).

A. Kundnani (2007) *The End of Tolerance: Racism in 21st Century Britain.* (Michigan: Pluto Press).

M. Maussen (2006) *Ruimte voor de Islam? Stedelijk beleid, voorzieningen, organisaties.* (Amsterdam: Het Spinhuis).

J.L. McGarrigle (2010) *Understanding Processes of Ethnic Concentration and Dispersal.* (Amsterdam: Amsterdam University Press).

D. McGhee (2008) *The End of Multiculturalism?: Terrorism, Integration and Human Rights.* (Maidenhead: Open University Press Milton Keynes).

T. Modood (2005) *Multicultural Politics: Racism, Ethnicity, and Muslims in Britain.* (Minnesota: University of Minnesota Press).

M. Pacione (2005) 'The Changing Geography of Ethnic Minority Settlement in Glasgow, 1951–2001', *The Scottish Geographical Magazine*, 121(2):141–161.

B.C. Parekh (2000) *The Future of Multi-Ethnic Britain: Report of the Commission on the Future of Multi-Ethnic Britain.* (London: Profile Books Ltd).

R. Penninx (2004) *Citizenship in European Cities: Immigrants, Local Politics, and Integration Policies.* (Farnham: Ashgate).

T. Phillips (2005) *After 7/7: Sleepwalking to segregation.* Speech, 22 September 2005.

C. Poppelaars and P. Scholten (2008) 'Two Worlds Apart', *Administration & Society*, 40(4): 335–357.

M.A. Schain (1999) 'Minorities and Immigrant Incorporation in France: The State and the Dynamics of Multiculturalism' in Lukes (ed.) *Multicultural Questions.* (Oxford: Oxford University Press).

P. Scholten (2011) *Framing Immigrant integration: Dutch Research-Policy Dialogues in Comparative Perspective.* (Amsterdam: Amsterdam University Press).

P. Scholten (2013) 'Agenda Dynamics and the Multilevel Governance of Intractable Policy Controversies. The Case of Immigrant Integration Policies in the Netherlands', *Policy Sciences*, 46: 217–236.

S. Spencer (2011) *The Migration Debate.* (Bristol: Policy Press).

M. Tewdwr-Jones (2009) 'Governing London; The Evolving Institutional and Planning Landscape' in R. Imrie, L. Lees and M. Raco (eds) *Regenerating London.* (Abingdon: Routledge).

D. Thränhardt and M. Bommes (2010) *National Paradigms of Migration Research.* (Osnabruck: V&r Unipress).

Tower Hamlets Borough Council (2003) *Community Cohesion: Identifying Opportunities for Future Action.* (London: Tower Hamlets Borough Council).

J. Uitermark and J.W. Duyvendak (2008) 'Civilising the City: Populism and Revanchist Urbanism in the City of Rotterdam', *Urban Studies,* 45(7):1485–1503.

J. Uitermark (2010) *Dynamics of Power in Dutch Integration Politics.* PhD Thesis University of Amsterdam.

E. Vachelli, E. Kofman and A. D'Angelo (2011) *Local Integration Policies for Newcomers in the UK.* (London: Middlesex University).

E. Van den Bent, (2010) Proeftuin Rotterdam: bestuurlijke maakbaarheid tussen 1975 en 2005. PhD Thesis, Erasmus University Rotterdam.

I. Van der Welle and V. Mamadouh (2009) 'Territoriale identiteiten en de identificatiestrategieen van Amsterdamse jongvolwassenen van buitenlandse afkomst: over evenwichtskunstenaars en kleurbekenners', *Migrantenstudies,* 25(1): 24–41.

S. Vertovec (2007) 'Super-diversity and Its Implications', *Ethnic and Racial Studies,* 30(6): 1024–1054.

G. Zincone and T. Caponio (2006) 'The Multilevel Governance of Migration' in Penninx, Berger and Kraal (eds) *The Dynamics of International Migration and Settlement in Europe.* (Amsterdam: Amsterdam University Press).

Part III
Political Parties

9
Politicizing Migration in Competitive Party Politics: Exploring the Regional and Federal Arenas in Germany and Italy

Oliver Schmidtke and Andrej Zaslove

Europe has witnessed a contradictory development in the field of migration over the last decade. On the one hand, most European countries have adopted policies to recruit in particular highly skilled immigrants and to include them more fully within the workforce and society at large. On the other hand, however, higher levels of immigration and cultural diversity have sparked an, at times, aggressive backlash against immigrants. In this context, right-wing populist parties have become successful contenders in elections across Europe, and anti-immigrant rhetoric has been repeatedly employed also by centrist and left-wing actors in competitive party politics (Bale, 2003; Bale et al., 2010; Mudde, 2007). In the post 9/11 environment (cross-border security issues, threats of terrorism, economic uncertainty), European party systems seem to be particularly vulnerable to the exploitation of anti-immigrant sentiments for electoral gains.

The lion's share of research on the link between immigration and parties focuses on the national (statewide) level. However, what is not clear is whether, with the growing policy role for sub-state regions regarding the task of managing migration and integration, whether regional party politics is vulnerable to similar dynamics regarding the exploitation of anti-immigrant sentiments for political gain. In this chapter, we examine whether there is a different logic or dynamic at play in politicizing migration-related issues at the national and regional level. The question is whether regions simply replicate dominant framing strategies and the strategic use of migration issues in competitive party politics that can be found at the national level. Do regions striving for greater autonomy simply follow modes of political mobilization similar to nationalist modes of identity formation and the exclusion of the 'other'? In other words, do regions tend to lean more strongly toward exploiting migration issues in terms of identity claims and populist concerns vis-à-vis 'foreigners'? Or is there a tendency toward a less ideologically divisive approach in regional party politics and, as a result, a more pragmatic reasoning in developing policies?

In order to investigate this dynamic, we focus on two regions in Germany and Italy (countries with a federal or federalizing governance structure) that are characterized by opposing traditional political identities (North Rhine Westphalia and Emilia-Romagna with a legacy of social-democratic or communist rule; Bavaria and Lombardy with a tradition of conservative dominance). The focus of the empirical analysis is on dominant regional parties, their discursive and programmatic approaches to issues of migration and integration, and the policies in this field adopted under their governments.

With the selection of regional contexts that reflect two different national contexts and contrasting regional political cultures, the chapter will explore how migration-related issues are politicized and employed in competitive party politics. Our working hypothesis is based on the empirical observation that regional contexts provide distinctive political arenas in which these issues are debated and policy options developed. Beyond the idiosyncrasies of regional politics, we assume that the pattern of diverging political preferences along regional-state and intra-regional lines can be related to structural features shaping these different levels of governance. These features range among others from the socio-economic position of the region in the national context to the legacy of regional-federal relations and the regional political culture.

The national context in Italy: political opportunity structures, parties, and immigration

Italy is a particularly interesting case regarding the questions addressed in this chapter. On the one hand, Italy only became an immigration country in the 1980s. Thus, it had to adjust rather quickly to these new developments. It did not have an immigration law until 1986. In the next two decades, however, it produced three important laws (Martelli in 1990; Turco-Napolitano in 1998; Bossi-Fini in 2002). Competitive party politics at the national level and the relationship between the region and the nation-state were important in the construction of Italian immigration policies. After 1989 and the fall of communism, Italy developed into the so-called Second Republic: the party system dramatically changed, moving towards a bipolar system. However, it also remained highly fragmented with a large number of smaller parties (Diamanti, 2007). And in addition, competition not only between the left and the right (inter-coalition competition) but also competition within the left and the right blocks remained high (intra-coalition competition) (Wilson, 2009). Two other important developments created new opportunities for the politicization of migration. First, there was the formation of Forza Italia (FI). Forza Italia was created just before the 1994 elections by the media mogul Silvio Berlusconi. The party was intended to be a centre-right liberal market-oriented party replacing the formerly powerful Christian Democratic Party. The second development was the electoral rise of the Lega Nord (LN). As important as the rise of the LN was for Italian politics, for the current discussion, its relationship with FI was crucial. The LN began as a regional, federalist, anti-corruption, market-oriented party. With the fall of the First Republic and the surge in the LN between 1990 and the 1994 elections, it appeared that it might be possible for the LN to become the dominant centre-right party (Diamanti, 1995; Biorcio, 1997). However, FI proved to be a more moderate version of the LN, and in the process, it became a competitor of the LN, stealing the more moderate centre-right voters (Biorcio, 1997). It soon became apparent that in order for the LN to remain an important political force it needed to radicalize and to secure its own identity in its strongholds in the northeast, in particular in Lombardy and in the Veneto (Diamanti, 1995, 2009). The LN began to focus on questions of identity, federalism, and opposition to immigration. Emerging from a non-Fascist past meant that it had a protective shield (Ivarsflaten, 2006). Unlike the *Movimento Sociale Italiano* (MSI) it was able to mobilize on the theme of migration.

Migration as a political and policy issue at the federal and regional level

As the 1990s progressed, the opportunity for the regional and the local levels to influence immigration policy began to grow. Important institutional features also transformed Italian politics, creating a multilevel structure (Cento Bull, 2002; Wilson, 2009; Campomori and Caponio, 2013; Cotta and Verzichelli, 2007). In addition, the party structure also dramatically changed at the regional level. This was in part a reflection of the national changes in politics: the creation of the new party system. The regional party system is, on the one hand, highly influenced by the national party system. The larger core parties on the left and the right also compete at the regional level. However, the regional party systems are also determined by strong subcultures. To be sure, this has been a long-lasting condition of Italian politics (Hellman, 1992). However, they have been modified since the 1990s (Diamanti, 2009).

Immigration and integration in Emilia-Romagna: politics in a centre-left region

Emilia-Romagna is a region dominated by the centre-left. In the post-war era, the Italian Communist Party prevailed in regional elections until the early 1990s. Since then the reincarnation of the Italian Communist Party (PCI) into a social-democratic party replaced the PCI as the hegemonic party in the region. First as the Democratic Party of the Left (PDS), then as the Left Democrats (DS), and finally with the Democratic Party (PD). On the other side of the political spectrum the centre-right is composed of several parties. In the post-war era, the Christian Democratic Party was the dominant centre-right party. However, with the emergence of the so-called Second Republic the centre-right has been represented by FI and its smaller allies, such as Alleanza Nazionale (AN), the LN, and the Christian Democrats. In 2009 FI and AN merged and became the People of Freedom (PDL).

Party competition and immigration

The dominance of left-wing parties within the region has structured migration as a political issue at the regional level. The positions of the left and the right, and the parties within the left and the right regarding migration, can be categorized by specific frames.[1] The parties on the left frame the debate regarding immigration in terms of universal rights and entitlements. In this respect migration is interpreted as a structural challenge to social cohesion and civil society such as cultural reciprocity, legality, and the need to foster political participation. Second, immigration is framed in terms of structural transformations: the focus is on push factors that require migrants to come to Europe and Italy, but also in terms of the regional demand for immigrants. Third, the left-wing parties emphasize the need to integrate immigrants by way of increasing cultural mediation between immigrants and the host society. The term used by the left is interculturalism; here the focus is on providing immigrants and Italians with the knowledge, resources, and the ability to communicate with one another.

Finally, the left-wing parties recognize the need to provide the resources and the legal means to legalize immigrants in Italy, while there is considerable focus on the need to facilitate political participation. Although the priority of the centre-left is to provide voting rights at the municipal level and to amend the existing citizenship laws, they have not been able to accomplish this, and therefore they have focused on alternative forms of political representation. Although these frames do not radically differ from the national level, the DS/PD within Emilia-Romagna has been more forceful in pursuing them and in transforming them into policies (Schmidtke and Zaslove, forthcoming).

The centre-right is highly critical of these positions. Its frames are shaped by concerns for security, law-and-order, and integration as assimilation. The overarching theme that characterizes the centre-right is security. Here there is a tendency to link immigration with crime and law-and-order. The focus is on controlling illegal immigration. A common refrain for the centre-right parties is to argue that the provisions provided by the Bossi-Fini law (i.e., the 2002 national legislation), especially regarding controlling illegal immigration and linking work and immigration, better address the ills of immigration.

Despite these highly diverse positions between the left and the right, it is the left that has been the most influential in setting the agenda at the regional level regarding migration. This is due in part to its electoral hegemony, to its strong link with civil society organizations, and it is also due to the leadership role played by regional presidents. Vasco Errani, the regional president since 1999, has been a leading exponent of creating a regional integration policy: a policy that, in its inclusive orientation, is explicitly used to counter national immigration policies (Errani, 2010). As a result, Emilia-Romagna has been able to forge a very different integration policy than what has occurred at the national level. The region has, therefore, been at the forefront in building institutions and in creating policies to enable immigrants to integrate (Campomori and Caponio, 2013; see also Campomori and Caponio, in Chapter 7 for an in-depth examination of the positive cultural framing of immigration in Emilia-Romagna).

Lombardy: the centre-right and the politics of immigration

The party system in Lombardy is very different to that in Emilia-Romagna. On the one hand, the centre-right parties are dominant, while on the other, there has been considerable intra-coalition competition between the two largest centre-right parties, FI/PDL and the LN. A defining characteristic of the party system in Lombardy is its highly decentralized nature. Although FI/PDL is a national (statewide) party, the party at the regional level has been highly dependent on the role of the regional leader Roberto Formigoni (Wilson, 2009: 201–205). The second most important party on the right is the LN. The party dominates especially in the provinces of Bergamo, Brescia, Como, Lecco, Sondrio, and Varese. The LN, even though its central office is in Milan, has fared less well here, with the exception of holding the mayorality of the city between 1993 and 1997.

The centre-left has not been very strong electorally or organizationally in the region. It is characterized by fragmentation and is dominated by centralized leadership: attempts for more autonomy have been challenged by the national wings. The situation is complicated by a lack of strong regional leadership (Wilson, 2009: 210). The left played with the idea at times of creating an alliance with the LN, although this was challenged by the national level due to the xenophobia of the LN and also because of the national alliance of the centre-right parties (Wilson, 2009: 210). The left has lost votes due in part to socioeconomic changes, de-industrialization, and due to a new political issue: the influx of migrants and growing concerns over crime and security. The party has not been able to respond to these issues effectively (Wilson, 2009: 211–212).

Party competition and immigration

As noted, Roberto Formigoni has exerted strong regional control over FI. Formigoni is a centre-right politician with local roots, with a strong Catholic background and dense networks. His staunch centre-right positions are clearly evident in the party's platform, especially regarding migration and integration. The party focuses on three themes: work, language, and family. The task of integrating newcomers is addressed via the market and active employment (with tools such as certificate translation and linguistic training). Of particular importance is language training. Finally, integration via building a strong family is emphasized (Formigoni, 2012). As a regional councillor notes: 'precisely in this manner can you talk about a "Lombard model" of integration'.[2]

The other key political player is the LN. On the one hand, immigration does not play a key role in the electoral platforms of the LN at the regional level. The 2010 election platform for example had only a couple of references to immigration, noting that immigration was primarily a national concern (LN, 2010). However, on the other hand, the LN has politicized migration during election campaigns and by way of public demonstrations. For example, during the regional election campaign in 2010 migration played an important role. The LN focused, along with other core themes such as federalism, on the need to control immigration and on the need to prioritize Italians over immigrants.[3] In addition, the LN has been active on the streets with anti-mosque petitions and raising objections to special Islamic schools and teaching Arabic in schools (*La Repubblica*, 2005, 2009, 2010). The LN's influence is formidable in its strongholds in Lombardy.[4] Although its electoral success is less pronounced in Milan,[5] it nevertheless has an important presence. However, despite the electoral success of the LN and its vocal opposition to immigration, it has not been able to significantly influence regional policies.[6]

Party competition regarding migration is more intense in Lombardy than in Emilia-Romagna. The question becomes, however, whether this has had a tangible influence on regional immigration and integration policies. Research demonstrates that, in fact, immigration (and in particular integration) policies in Lombardy lag behind other regions with high numbers of immigrants, such as Emilia-Romagna: laws, policies, and resources are less extensive and less developed (Campomori and Caponio, 2013; Campomori and Caponio, in this volume). Even though it would be incorrect to argue that legislation is overly restrictive, resources are often insufficient and active regional government involvement is often minimal. The policy process in Lombardy can be characterized as a 'hands-off' market-oriented approach and is thus different from the active integration process and the focus on cultural mediation found in Emilia-Romagna.

The national context in Germany: stalemate at the national level

The reforms and the political stalemate of the 2000s: the national arena

The politics of migration in Germany appears paradoxical at first sight. While the guest-worker programmes of the 1950s and 1960s brought many migrants – often permanently – into the country (2.6 million already in 1973 when the active recruitment was stopped), immigration only gradually developed into an issue of public debate and party politics in the 1980s. Germany's legacy of the *Gastarbeiter* (guest-worker) scheme, its exclusivist notion of nationhood and its post-war political culture contributed to this peculiar 'delay' that allowed the former Chancellor Helmut Kohl to maintain that 'Germany is not a country of immigration' until 1998. It was only in the late 1990s that, with the Social Democratic (SPD) – Green government under Chancellor

Schroeder, migration-related issues moved into the spotlight of political debate and policy-making.

In 1999, the Red-Green government introduced a new Citizenship Law. With the modernization of the outdated German nationality laws, the traditional ancestry principle was supplemented by elements of a territorial tradition (*jus soli*) in 2000 which facilitates the acquisition of German citizenship by birth. While the law passed both chambers of parliament without problems, the issue of dual citizenship became one of the most controversial issues in the domestic debate. It provided a supreme opportunity for the ailing Christian Democratic Union – Christian Social Union (CDU/CSU) to regain momentum after their devastating loss in the 1998 general elections. In February 1999, the SPD-Green government's proposed dual nationality law became the centrepiece of the CDU election campaign in Hesse. The CDU mobilized a massive signature campaign against the federal government's proposal to permit foreigners to become naturalized Germans and to routinely keep their old passports.[7] In exit polls at the time, opposition to the government's dual nationality proposal was second only to worries about unemployment. After only 100 days in office, the Red-Green government had to accept a surprising defeat in the Hesse regional election, and the CDU victory caused the SPD-Green federal government to lose its majority in the second chamber of Parliament, which it needed to approve the dual nationality legislation (Green, 2000; Schmidtke, 2004).

In the post-9/11 climate, issues of migration have become more controversial and subject to fierce partisan wrangling in public and parliamentary debates. This became critical when the then SPD–Green coalition sought to introduce Germany's first immigration law in the early 2000s. What was originally designed as a decisive step towards a Canadian or Australian-style immigration policy ended up being watered down in party disputes and a prolonged process of re-negotiation in Germany's second chamber. In the end Germany adopted its first immigration law in 2005 that commits it to recruiting highly skilled migrants while erecting considerable barriers for potential migrants to qualify. Commentators have pointed to the underlying logic of protecting Germany from unwanted immigration and restricting access to permanent residence cards (the result is a meagre influx of a couple hundred skilled migrants every year).

The debate on Germany's first immigration law highlighted the similarities and differences in how this country's main parties defined their position regarding migration and integration. In terms of the overall orientation of the policy there was a considerable amount of agreement among the centre-left (SPD and Greens) and the centre-right (CDU-CSU and FDP). In light of Germany's serious demographic pressures, all parties were – in principle – in favour of an immigration law that selected newcomers primarily based on their professional qualifications and skills. A cross-party commission headed by CDU politician Rita Süssmuth recommended a gradual increase in immigration levels in order to meet labour-market needs. Yet, the fact that the actual immigration law proved to be far more restrictive and put far more emphasis on controlling immigration points to the differences between both political blocs. In particular the Christian Democratic parties also politicized immigration as a matter of cultural and national identity. In this respect they reflected and nurtured reservations about immigration in German society.

This second dimension of politicizing migration in public discourse and party politics became manifest in recent debates about multiculturalism in Germany. After the introduction of this half-hearted immigration law, the public and political debate in the national arena decisively shifted toward issues related to integration and the alleged threat of Islamic fundamentalism and cultural practices deemed unacceptable to German society. This is the background of the German Chancellor's recent statement about the 'utter failure' of multiculturalism in Germany.[8] Angela Merkel said that Germany was dependent on the influx of foreign workers but that the naïve endorsement of cultural and religious diversity proved to be a major threat to social peace and stability. The leader of the Bavarian Christian Social Union (CSU), Horst Seehofer, joined Merkel's refutation of 'multiculturalism' and went one step further by demanding restrictions on immigration from 'culturally alien' Arab countries or Turkey because they posed a greater challenge to successful integration and social peace.[9] The depiction of migrants and cultural diversity as a pertinent (security) threat strongly shapes public debate and limits policy options at the federal level.

This development has created new opportunities for sub-state levels of governance to establish themselves as significant actors in this field both with respect to the direction of the national debate on migration and policy development in the field. First, the national integration plan is designed to shift competence and responsibilities to regions and cities. With their competence in key areas of public policy, such as education, the German *Länder* are in a particularly privileged position to take on issues of integration. Indeed, the German *Länder* have been instrumental in pushing for and developing this national integration plan.

Second, at the national level, mainly due to the discursive practices of the conservative parties, the debate has become highly divisive and focused on the alleged implications of religious and cultural diversity. The latent populist undertone of this debate has left the SPD in a difficult position largely refraining from taking this issue on in its national campaigns. The divisive and partisan public debate on migration and integration at the national level has therefore discouraged the centre-left and 'diverted' their aspirations in this political arena to the sub-state regional level.

Bavaria: Christian Democratic hegemony and the temptation of populist politics

Party competition: Bavaria's conservative legacy and its aspiration for political autonomy

Bavaria is the *Land* in Germany with a long legacy of conservative hegemony and a related claim for regional autonomy. Over the past 60 years, Bavaria has been governed by the CSU, the 'sister party' of the CDU.[10] In particular under its charismatic leader Franz Josef Strauss (chairman of the CSU from 1961 until his death in 1988) the party regularly received over 55 per cent of the vote in state elections. It was only in the 2008 election in Bavaria that the CSU lost the absolute majority that it had enjoyed since 1962.

In terms of its position in the national party system, the CSU is in a unique position in Germany. At the federal level it forms a close alliance with the CDU, which does not stand for election in Bavaria. At the same time, however, it advocates the regional interests of Bavaria and has challenged the authority of the federal government on various occasions in the history of the Federal Republic of Germany (FRG). From the early years of the FRG, Bavaria has demanded a greater degree of political independence. In 1949, it was the representatives of the Bavarian regional Parliament (dominated by the CSU) that, along with the Communists, voted against the Basic Law (West Germany's Constitution). They demanded a greater form of political autonomy for Bavaria within the federal structure of the young state.

In terms of Germany's party politics, it is worth underlining that the CSU is structurally under the dual commitment of demonstrating loyalty to the CDU (in particular when in government) and of defending its distinct political identity as a conservative and regionalist party. Given its hegemonic position in Bavaria (Mintzel, 1999), the political appeal of the CSU is more strongly defined by how it relates to federal politics rather than the – non-competitive – centre-left opposition in its own region. The current political constellation illustrates this structural feature of post-war German politics well. On various issues, the CSU has challenged the CDU-led government under Angela Merkel as a kind of conservative corrective to the more centrist approach of the conservative-liberal government at the national level. This outspoken conservative political identity has been a driving force in sustaining strong pleas for Bavaria's special status within the German federation and for maximizing the region's political autonomy from the federal government. The protection of Bavaria's cultural and religious traditions (the strong position of the Catholic Church in particular outside of urban centres) partly defines this Land's distinctiveness vis-à-vis the rest of the country (see, Hepburn, 2008).

Yet, the most important fights are rarely over policies designed to protect an indigenous language (which, arguably, is more a dialect than a distinct language) or distinctive cultural institutions.[11] The focus of political disputes between the Bavarian-led regional and the federal government is rather on the reach of regional jurisdiction over key public policies (economy, education, and so on) and, most importantly, control over fiscal resources. Bavaria has seen a major turn in its economic fortunes in Germany. From being the backward, industrially deprived southern periphery of the West German state, it has morphed into the country's economic powerhouse. This has led to Bavaria becoming the biggest net contributor to the fiscal equalization scheme in the German federation. The notion of having to share the region's wealth (currently Bavaria accounts for roughly 50 per cent of all transfer payments totalling about 7.5 billion Euro) has nourished (and been exploited for) regionalist aspirations.[12]

Party polarization on migration

Migration has been an increasingly important topic in the CSU's political identity and regional party polarization. On the one hand, the CSU has been exposed to mounting pressure from the business community to hire foreign specialists to address labour-market shortages. On the other hand and with a view to competitive party politics, the agenda of migration and diversity resonates well with the CSU's emphasis on regional and religious identity as well as its fervent opposition to the 'modernist' agenda of the left. In a recent debate on the state of multiculturalism in Germany, CSU chairman Horst Seehofer fuelled the emotional debate by demanding a greater restriction on Muslim immigrants from Turkey and Arab countries by referring to them as 'difficult to integrate'. He positioned the CSU clearly as supporting a German dominant culture (*Leitkultur*)[13] and rejecting the 'failed' multicultural experiment. The Bavarian CSU has traditionally been the established party in German politics that quite openly seeks to benefit from employing anti-immigrant sentiments. In competitive party terms, this political stance has a variety of interwoven functions: it underlines the staunch conservative nature of this party, helps the CDU to develop its distinct political profile vis-à-vis its sister party as well as the SPD or FDP, and is meant to prevent a more right-wing political force from gaining ground.

Flirting with and containing right-wing, anti-immigrant mobilization

It is straightforward to argue that the widely uncontested hegemony of the conservative CSU in conjunction with Bavaria's deep commitment to its traditional, religious culture has nurtured an environment that is genuinely unsympathetic or unwelcoming to migrants. Bavaria's key public institutions are designed to protect what is considered the genuine cultural and religious identity of this southern Land. One intriguing example of this is the provision in the state constitution that commits institutions of education (most prominently schools) to protect 'the love for the native Bavaria'.[14] This cultural environment provides the context for a widely assimilationist approach to managing migration whose guiding principle is to protect Bavaria's regional identity and to portray foreign influences as a genuine threat to the integrity of the region's social fabric. In 2000, the CSU released its own position paper on immigration, concluding that 'Germany is not a classical country of migration and must not become one in the future'. The CSU endorsed the *Leitkultur* concept, and said foreigners living in Germany should share 'values rooted in Christianity, the Enlightenment and Humanism'.[15]

This regionalist legacy of Bavaria is also a key factor in how the CSU has positioned itself with respect to a relatively conservative and largely marginalized SPD on the one hand, and the latent and at times manifest possibility of a more extreme-right-wing party attracting electoral support on the other. Ironically, the region demanding the greatest degree of autonomy in Germany reflects most closely Germany's primordial tradition of nationhood and its inherent tendency to see foreigners as a threat to national identity. According to a study from 2003, Bavaria has one of the highest potential bases for extreme-right voters. On various occasions since the 1980s, the CSU has exploited the issue of 'foreigners' and immigrants for strategic political purposes. For example, during the general elections in 1987 and the Bavarian state elections in 1986, the centre-right sought to make this issue a crucial element in its aim to mobilize support. In particular, the campaign of the CSU in Bavaria was shaped by the deliberate attempt to evoke fears about the allegedly unrestrained influx of asylum-seekers by portraying the party as the legitimate guardian of 'German interests'. However, this political option proved to be a risky political strategy to embark on at the time. One politically upsetting lesson for the more conservative CSU was that this agenda had unintended consequences that proved to be rather ambivalent in terms of enhancing the party's attractiveness. As much as this issue was able to steer public emotions and mobilize the conservative, nationalistically minded clientele (Ingenhorst, 1997), it also involved the risk of strengthening the radical right and alienating the liberal fraction of the political centre.[16] As a matter of fact, the rise of the extreme-right anti-immigrant party *Republikaner* (REP) in the late 1980s can be directly linked to the efforts of the established conservative parties in Germany to give weight to an agenda highly critical, if not outright hostile, to immigrants and foreigners. It is indicative of party competition in this region that the REP had its base in Bavaria when it was formed in 1983 under the leadership of Franz Schönhuber. The peak of the REP's success was the European elections of 1989 in which it received 7.1 per cent of the vote nationwide (the strongest support was in Bavaria with 14.6 per cent of the vote).

It was not by accident that the leader of the REP, Franz Schöhnhuber, used to be a close collaborator of former CSU leader Franz Josef Strauss before establishing his own nationalistic and anti-immigrant organization. Although the REP and other right-wing parties have never been elected into the national Parliament they remain a constant threat in particular to the CSU. Its populist stance on many issues related to migration are also driven by the attempt to absorb potential supporters of the anti-foreigner right into their own camp. In this respect, it meant an incalculable risk to the more conservative wing of the CDU/CSU to play the anti-foreigner card. On the one hand, it needed to stay within the narrow margins of what the German public was willing to tolerate in terms of an openly hostile attitude toward non-nationals, and on the other hand it was keen on keeping those votes from the far-right partly encouraged by its own nationalistic, anti-immigrant agenda.

While pointing to this nationalistic undertone in Bavarian politics and policy-making towards migrants is widely accurate (Hoadley, 2003), it tends to overlook other, more economically based pressures that the CSU is exposed to in this respect. Over the past two decades, Bavaria has been transformed into Germany's economic powerhouse with a strong emphasis on manufacturing in the automobile and machinery sector. In this respect, it has witnessed an enormous modernization taking it from a backward, mainly rural region to one that houses some of Europe's most competitive industries. This transformation has also left its mark on how issues of migration and integration are tackled in this region. In particular the big car manufacturers (Mercedes Benz and Audi) have been outspoken about the need to 'be open to the world' and to endorse immigration as a necessary means for maintaining its international competitiveness. The result is an integration policy that, also compared to other *Länder*, is relatively robust with respect to educational resources (language training) and labour-market assistance. Furthermore, the modernizing effects also translate into strategic/electoral considerations. If it engages in a highly exclusionary, nativist rhetoric the CSU runs the risk of alienating the business community (economic rationale for attracting migrant workers, international image of Bavaria, and so on) and certain parts of civil society.

In Bavaria, the CSU's approach to immigration and integration is shaped by this tension between identity-driven concerns for the acclaimed distinctness and homogeneity of a regional culture and pragmatic concerns for the imperatives of modernization and economic development. The former tradition is susceptible to populist politics surrounding the symbolic exclusion of migrants, while the latter prescribes policy initiatives directed at successful socioeconomic inclusion. Both approaches can also coexist side by side, albeit tension-filled and with notable effects on each other.. Yet, the pendulum tends to swing towards more aggressive anti-immigrant rhetoric and symbolic exclusion whenever the CSU feels threatened in its dominant political role. This can be triggered by a reformist agenda perceived to be at odds with Bavarian identities and interests (from the centre-left as well as from the CDU-led centre-right) or growing regional opposition. The latest multiculturalism-bashing by Horst Seehofer is an illustration of this point: his outspoken stance in public discourse is meant to strengthen the political identity of the CSU as a staunchly conservative and simultaneously regionalist force in Germany whose electoral advantage has gradually eroded over the past decade.

NRW: a social-democratic laboratory for new approaches to managing migration

There are some remarkable differences between Bavaria and North Rhine Westphalia (NRW) with respect to party rivalry and how the issue of migration plays out in the regional context. Party competition in Germany's most populated Land does not show the dominance of one party and has seen alternating Christian Democratic and Social Democratic coalitions in government. Yet, given the long period of left-of-centre rule in the 1980s and 1990s, it is legitimate to speak of NRW as a state with a distinct social-democratic legacy. NRW is the traditional industrial heartland of Germany with a historically strong, albeit steadily declining coal and steel sector (a sector that attracted considerable numbers of immigrants before and after the Second World War). This state has seen a rapid and at times painful transformation of its industrial base with relatively high unemployment rates and considerable social tensions as a result.

During the years of the post-war 'economic miracle', NRW with its extensive manufacturing sector was one of the main regions for guest-worker immigration. In spite of the official end to the recruitment policy in 1974, newcomers continue to come to NRW, which is reflected in the fact that almost one quarter of the population has a migration background (first or second generation). Of its almost 18 million inhabitants, 2.5 million were born outside of Germany; about one-third of Germany's Turkish-born population lives in NRW. In NRW's major cities, the foreign-born population reaches around 20 per cent (about 10 per cent live in NRW as foreigners).

The pre- and post-war legacy of immigration and the socioeconomic challenges in 're-inventing' the region after the era of coal and steel production provide the rationale for endorsing migrants to a considerably greater degree and promoting their integration as compared to Bavaria (as well as the federal level). In party political terms, it is noticeable that the main parties have largely taken ownership of the migration and integration issues beyond strategic considerations in electoral competition.

NRW has been a pioneer in promoting its own integration policy. A proactive approach in this field was developed under social-democratic rule before 2005 and continued under the Christian Democratic Premier Minister Jürgen Rüttgers.[17] In this respect, NRW has taken advantage of a gradual empowerment of the regional and local levels within the German federal state structure with regard to integration policies (the 2004 Immigration Law – *Zuwanderungsgesetz* – leaves considerable legal space for a new form of collaboration between federal and regional levels; it is in this context that more and more funds have been made available to regional and local authorities). It is somewhat surprising to realize that it was a member of the CDU who became the first minister for integration at the regional level in 2005, namely NRW's Minister for Intergenerational Affairs, Family, Women and Integration (or *'Integrationsminister'* as he is known), Armin Laschet. In this respect, NRW has been a trendsetter for the introduction of similar ministries in other, often CDU-governed regions (Lower Saxony, Hesse, Schleswig-Holstein and Berlin). NRW also spearheaded the idea of a conference for 'integration ministers' at the regional level against considerable resistance from other *Länder*.[18] Reflecting on the process of launching and implementing such policies it is remarkable how – in stark contrast to the highly controversial and emotional debate in the national political arena – the CDU-led government and its 'integration minister' Laschet addressed the challenge of incorporating migrants more fully in widely pragmatic policy terms.[19]

Under his leadership and continued by the current Red-Green government, NRW has developed innovative approaches to promoting integration designed to attract and retain newcomers (one of the most prominent recent examples is a comprehensive programme for language training for pre-school children). The major thrust of the legislative initiatives in this field has been directed toward (equitable) access to the labour-market and educational opportunities. It is indicative of the overall orientation of NRW's integration policies that the *Integrationsminister* has traditionally been incorporated into the Ministry for Labour and Social Affairs. In legislative terms, the 2001 *Integrationsoffensive Nordrhein-Westfalen* (Integration Offensive NRW[20]) set the agenda for a comprehensive strategy for promoting the integration of newcomers, an initiative that in its design and scope was unique in Germany. At the time supported by all political parties in parliament the plan outlined how the task of successful integration needs to involve all sectors of society (from the labour-market and the educational sectors, to urban planning, civil society organizations, and the business community) and to be driven by the primary concern of equal opportunities (*Chancengleichheit*).

Most recently (2011), the new Red-Green government and its current Integration Minister Guntram Schneider in Düsseldorf have started the process of launching a new *Teilhabe und Integrationsgesetz* (Participation and Integration Law) whose goal is to give integration policies a more binding, legally enshrined character. The Land of NRW is the first to embark on such an ambitious legislative initiative and might well set the agenda for governments at various levels in Germany's federal system.

Framing migration as socioeconomic modernization across party lines

These initiatives reflect the way in which issues of migration and integration are politicized in this regional context. Compared to the national level, issues of immigration and integration follow a distinctly different logic of politicization and policy implementation. It is noteworthy that it is under the CDU government of Jürgen Rüttgers that a proactive integration policy has been developed and implemented based on a broad bipartisan consensus. At the regional level there is hardly any populist attempt to exploit the issue and rather a thorough commitment to developing pragmatic, problem-oriented approaches to the challenge of integration. Parliamentary debates in Düsseldorf on this issue follow a different discursive script to national ones; general debates on the allegedly threatening effects of foreign cultures (as articulated in the *Leitkultur*-debate or, more recently, the discussion sparked by Thilo Sarrazin' book[21]) are largely absent from the regional political arena. Such identity and culture-oriented issues and the exclusionary rhetoric often accompanying them were also widely missing from the last electoral campaign in NRW. In short, the discourse on immigrants is de-dramatized and rarely subject to exploitation as an emotional mobilizing device in competitive party politics. Instead, the political rhetoric used by regional authorities from the centre-right as well as the centre-left is strongly shaped by pragmatic concerns resulting primarily from day-today issues emanating from community concerns and a long-term strategy to perceive newcomers as an asset for the region's economic future.

What is also distinct about how the issue of integration is approached in NRW is the way that migrants themselves have become a strategic force in electoral politics and the political process at large. With the high density of migrants and their descendants living in this German state they have become a constituency targeted by major parties in their electoral aspirations. Once migrants are primarily perceived and addressed as potential voters, the rhetoric of populist demarcation and exclusion becomes increasingly difficult to justify (see Chapter 11 by Erk in this volume for a similar appeal to immigrant voters by Quebec parties). Beyond the inclusion into electoral politics, we find a pronounced degree of informally including migrants and their organizations into the political process. Even though it is difficult to stipulate what kind of impact migrant organizations have on this field of public policy, we argue that the local and regional level has generated some marked opportunities for community input and initiatives. Indeed, in our case studies we find a link between the pragmatic orientation and breadth of integration initiatives and the way in which community organizations have become more firmly embedded in institutional practices and accepted by the wider policy community.

Conclusions

We started this chapter with a reflection on how national politics and the politicization of migration have increasingly been shaped by right-wing, anti-foreigner actors or a populist backlash against multiculturalism. The prominence of these political groups is evidence of how migration-related issues have moved into the centre of party politics in many European countries. Regions are not immune to, nor are they per se vectors of, populist anti-immigrant rhetoric in party politics. In this respect, regions cannot simply be described as inherently promoting an exclusionary version of – parochial – nationhood or, as mirror image, proposing a 'post-nationalist', more progressive community open to endorsing diversity and a more inclusive mode of promoting migrant integration. In addition, regional politics does not merely mirror national politics. The regional arena often shows a distinct logic regarding how migration-related issues are employed in competitive party politics and policy-making.

We have identified a series of factors that have shaped the preferences of parties and policies at the regional level. The comparative perspective on two different national and four regional contexts allows us to identify the following dynamics in forming regional positions on migration. First, we note that the regions under investigation here show considerable variety with how issues of migration and integration are politicized and addressed in policy terms. These issues can be instrumental in reinforcing and linking (or undermining) traditional cleavages that shape competitive party politics. In the case of Bavaria and Lombardy, we have mutually reinforcing cleavages in terms of a territorial agenda based on identity claims and the traditional left-right divide. In Bavaria, the CSU has successfully linked its autonomy claims (territorial cleavage) with a more conservative agenda than what its federal sister party (CDU) pursues at the national level. The migration issue is politically instrumental in both respects: it resonates with the demand for protecting society's cultural and linguistic identity and is suitable for the conservative idea of cultural (national or regional) homogeneity as opposed to a (multicultural) agenda of endorsing diversity. Yet, what is restraining both the CSU and the LN from fully exploiting the populist symbolic exclusion of migrants is the fear of cultivating an openly anti-immigrant, extreme-right opposition and the commitment to supporting a modern, globally oriented regional economy.

Second, there is the economic reality between the 'have' and the 'have-not' regions. The economic discrepancies between different regions in the national context prove to be an important factor in our case studies. In Lombardy and Bavaria, two regions with relatively successful economies and no real regional labour shortage, migration is not perceived as contributing positively to economic development. Instead, migrants are prone to becoming part of a 'welfare chauvinism' at the regional level (that is, portrayed in terms of an alleged drain on resources). The idea of a hard-working region whose prosperity is threatened by poorer regions or migrants can become a powerful image in politics. In contrast, however, in NRW (and to a certain extend Emilia-Romagna) immigration is framed as an asset that is economically advantageous. It resonates with plans of improving economic performance – a policy device that finds strong resonance in both the centre-left and centre-right in regions that need to address economic decline and transformation.

Third, it appears that the territorial cleavage remains important. It is difficult to make a causal link between the strength of a regional identity (linguistic or cultural) and political attitudes toward migration. However, what we can observe in our cases is how a latent sense of cultural or linguistic distinctiveness and/or grievance can become an important ideational vector for justifying a more exclusionary stand vis-à-vis newcomers. Indeed, the case of Lombardy (and to a certain degree Bavaria) is intriguing because of how migration as a political issue was employed to give meaning to a regional identity that had historically not been meaningful, in the case of Lombardy or Northern Italy, or in the Bavarian context had been jeopardized by gradual processes of modernization and the resulting pressure for national linguistic-cultural homogenization.

Fourth, our findings indicate that the mode of politicizing migration-related issues in competitive party politics is also shaped by opportunities for migrants' political participation and advocacy (for a more thorough development of this aspect see Schmidtke and Zaslove, forthcoming). Regions seem to be more susceptible to allowing for the political inclusion of migrants and minorities. We cannot discuss the reasons for this distinctive feature of the regional political arena in any detail. Yet, we suggest that it is related to organizational structures of political advocacy at the regional, and in particular the local, level and the more pragmatic nature of policy-making at these levels of governance. In our cases of NRW and ER, there is strong evidence that the inclusion of migrant organizations into the process of public deliberation and decision-making has a notable effect on the mode of political discourse on migration (less disposed to populist exploitation) and its use in party politics (less polarizing as an issue).

Fifth and finally, we find that there is an ideological (left-right) cleavage that is articulated through the lens of identity politics. One dimension of the revival of the territorial cleavage – once diagnosed by Lipset and Rokkan as the residue of the pre-modern political constellation – is likely to be related to the strategic twinning of identity and regional autonomy concerns from a right-of-centre perspective. In particular in countries where national identity is relatively weak (Germany and Italy, albeit under different auspices, fall into this category) regions can successfully exploit the identity card and the discursive use of migrants as the contested 'Other'. With this agenda of depicting the own collective identity in tension or open conflict with migration-driven internal diversity, regional political parties can benefit from a divisive and emotional agenda in a wider political environment in which the ideological left-right divide has lost much of its previous constitutive power. It is this populist agenda that makes territorial claims 'modern' and a potent weapon in the arsenal of competitive party politics. The negative view of immigrants is a critical component in particular of the conservative party platform (at least in Europe). However, migration issues do not fully fit into the left-right divide; it tends to undermine its economically based logic of this divide and replace it with identity concerns that do not necessarily resonate with established views of the right or the left.

Regions have become important sites for defining political identities and the ideological positions of parties. Migration-related issues play an important role in this respect: while traditionally perceived to be incongruent with the logic of the left-right divide, questions of migration, integration and cultural diversity have taken a far more central role in electoral and party politics. The depolarization of the left-right ideological divide in the post-Cold War environment has left a political void that identity issues associated with migration have attempted to fill with some notable success. Regions can clearly become staging grounds for politically framing the issue and employing them in competitive party politics.

Notes

1. This section is based upon an analysis of the debates in the regional legislature relating to the Norme per l'integrazione sociale (2004), the regional government's packing and presentation of the Norme per l'integrazione sociale dei cittadini stranieri immigrati (2004), along with other policy documents regarding immigration and integration concerns. The regional legislature debates analysed consist of seatings from: 24 February 2004 (morning and afternoon session); 25 February (morning and afternoon session) 2004; 17 March 2004.

2. http://www.regione.lombardia.it/cs/Satellite?c=News&childpagename=Regi one%2FDetail&cid=1213425057348&pagename=RGNWrapper
3. (http://www.legalombarda.leganord.org/main/?page_id=8: accessed 7 June 2012)
4. For example, in the 2010 regional elections, the Lega Nord obtained more than 30 per cent of the vote in the provinces of Bergamo, Brescia, Como, Sondrio, and Lecco.
5. In the 2010 regional elections it obtained 17 per cent of the vote in Milan.
6. Where there has perhaps been more success is at the municipal level. For a good discussion see Ambrosini (2013).
7.. The CDU/CSU was able to gather more than five million signatures against the proposal (Koopmans and Statham, 1999).
8. See: http://www.guardian.co.uk/world/2010/oct/17/angela-merkel-german-multiculturalism-failed
9. See: http://www.spiegel.de/international/germany/the-world-from-berlin-merkel-s-rhetoric-in-integration-debate-is-inexcusable-a-723702.html
10. Both parties originated in the post-war re-organization of Germany's conservative parties. While being organizationally separate parties, the CDU-CSU appear as one faction in Parliament. The most important difference between both parties is the more socially conservative political orientation of the CSU and the fact that the CDU is a national and the CSU a regional party.
11. The notable exception is the decision of the Bavarian government in the mid-1990s to defy Germany's constitutional court and to permit crucifixes to be displayed in public schools.
12. In 2012, Bavaria filed a complaint with the country's Constitutional Court arguing that Bavaria is unjustifiably burdened by the redistribution of fiscal funds between 'have' and 'have-not' regions.
13. In the 2000s, Germany witnessed a debate on the nature of national identity in light of massive immigration. In October 2000, Christian Democratic Union parliamentary leader Friedrich Merz said in a session of the *Bundestag* that immigrants to German society should conform to a German *Leitkultur* or guiding, hegemonic culture.
14. Bayerische Landesverfassung cited in Bayerisches Staatsministerium (1993: 9; Art. 131).
15. See the Homepage of the CSU at www.csu.de.
16. The CDU/CSU realized how restricted the opportunities were to employ this agenda in a political culture shaped by the taboo on any kind of racism. For instance, when former CSU leader Edmund Stoiber spoke of the tendency of a racially mixed society (*'durchmischte und durchrasste Gesellschaft'*) the public outcry over using a language reminiscent of the Nazi period made him rescind his comments immediately.
17. Korte (2009) speaks of a 'pronounced integration culture' and a tradition of 'openness' characteristic of NRW.
18. With its regular integration conferences at the regional level, NRW has created considerable pressure for other Länder to follow suit. These conferences have by now developed into an important forum for policy coordination among Germany's Länder and with the federal government.
19. It should be mentioned though that Laschet's political course has been controversial within the CDU itself.

20. The document is available at http://www.landtag.nrw.de/portal/WWW/dokumentenarchiv/Dokument/MMD13–1345.pdf
21. In 2010–2011, a controversial book by the *Bundesbank* executive board member and former social-democratic Berlin state finance minister, Thilo Sarrazin (*Deutschland schafft sich ab*; 'Germany Does Away with Itself') sparked a heated debate about cultural and religious diversity in Germany.

References

Ambrosini, M. (2013) '"We are against a Multi-Ethnic Society"': Policies of Exclusion at the Urban Level in Italy', Ethnic and Racial Studies, 36(1), 136–155.

T. Bale (2003) 'Cinderella and Her Ugly Sisters: The Mainstream and Extreme Right in Europe's Bipolarizing Party Systems', *West European Politics*, 26(3): 67–90.

T. Bale, C. Green-Pedersen, A. Krouwel, K.R. Luther and N. Sitter (2010) 'If You Can't Beat Them, Join Them? Explaining Social Democratic Responses to the Challenge from the Populist Radical Right in Western Europe', *Political Studies*, 58(3): 410–426.

R. Biorcio (1997) *La Padania Promessa: La Storia, Le Idee e La Logica D'Azione Della Lega Nord*. (Milano: Il Saggiatore).

F. Campomori and T. Caponio (2013) '*Le politiche per gli immigrati. Istituzionalizzazione, programmazione, trasparenza*' in S Vassallo (ed.) *Il divario incolmabile. Rappresentanza politica e rendimento istituzionale nelle regioni italiane*. (Bologna: Il Mulino).

F. Campomori and T. Caponio (this volume) Migrant Reception Policies in a Multilevel System: Framing and Implementation Structures in the Italian Sub-states.

A. Cento Bull (2002) 'Verso uno Stato Federale? Proposte Alternative per La Revisione Costituzionale' in Bellucci, P. and Bull, M. (eds) *Politica in Italia: I Fatti dell'Anno e le Interpretazioni*. (Bologna: Il Mulino), 205–223.

M. Cotta and L. Verzichelli (2007) *Political Institutions in Italy*. (Oxford: Oxford University Press).

I. Diamanti (1995) *La Lega. Geografia, Storia, e Sociologia di un Nuovo Suggetto Politico*. (Roma: Donzelli).

I. Diamanti (2007) 'The Italian Center-Right and Center-Left: Between Parties and "the Party"', *West European Politics*, 30(4): 733–762.

I. Diamanti (2009) *Mappe dell'Italia Politica:* Bianco, Rosso, Verde, Azzurro e Tricolore. (Bologna: Il Mulino).

V. Errani (2010) 'Il Nostro Impegno per L'Emilia-Romagna: Intervento Programmatico del Presidente Vasco Errani', Regione Emilia-Romagna.

R. Formigoni (2012) 'Aprirsi e Innovare con Fiducia e Coraggio: Programma IX Legislatura', Regione Lombardia.

S. Green (2000) 'Beyond Ethnoculturalism? German Citizenship in the New Millennium', *German Politics*, 9(3): 105–124.

S. Hellman (1992) 'Italy' in M. Kesselman and Joel Krieger (eds) *European Politics in Transition*. (Lexington, M.A.: D.C. Heath and Company), 327–423.

E. Hepburn (2008) 'The Neglected Nation: The CSU and the Territorial Cleavage in Bavarian Party Politics', *German Politics*, 17(2): 184–202.

S. Hoadley (2003) 'Immigration, Refugee, Asylum, and Settlement Policies as Political Issues in Germany and Australia', National Europe Centre Paper, No. 81, University of Sydney.

E. Ivarsflaten (2006) 'Reputational Shields: Why Most Anti-Immigrant Parties Failed in Western Europe, 1980–2005.' Paper presented at Annual Meeting of the American Political Science Association, Philadelphia.

R. Koopmans and P. Statham (1999) 'Challenging the Liberal Nation-State? Postnationalism, Multiculturalism, and the Collective Claims Making of Migrants and Ethnic Minorities in Britain and Germany', *American Journal of Sociology*, 105(3): 652–696.

Lega Nord (2010) 'Linee Guida per la Stesura del Programma Elettorale per le Elezioni Regionali 2010'.

A. Mintzel (1999) *Die CSU-Hegemonie in Bayern: Strategie und Erfolg; Gewinner und Verlierer.* (Passau: Wiss.-Verl. Rothe).

C. Mudde (2007) *Populist Radical Right Parties in Europe.* (Cambridge: Cambridge University Press).

La Repubblica (2010) 'Corsi di arabo nelle scuole milanesi: La Lega: "Ma non apriamoli agli italiani"', 29 April.

La Repubblica (2009) 'La Lega offre panettone e spumante a chi firma contro moschee e minareti', 7 December (Milan edition). *La Repubblica* (2005) 'La Lega dice no a Simini sulla scuola islamica', 29 June.

O. Schmidtke (2001) 'Trans-National Migration: A Challenge to European Citizenship Regimes', *World Affairs*, 164(1): 3–16.

O. Schmidtke (2004) 'From Taboo to Strategic Tool in Politics: Immigrants and Immigration Policies in German Party Politics' in Reutter, W. (ed.) *Germany on the Road to Normalcy. Policies and Politics of the Red-Green Federal Government (1998–2002).* (Basingstoke: Palgrave Macmillan).

O. Schmidtke and Zaslove, A. (forthcoming) 'Multilevel Governance and the Politics and the Public Policy of Immigration in Germany and Italy'.

A. Wilson (2009) *Multi-Level Party Politics in Italy and Spain.* PhD Dissertation, European University Institute.

10
Regionalist Parties and Immigration in Belgium

Régis Dandoy

Introduction

In Belgium, immigration is an important policy issue that has been highly politicized. Immigration is not only present in extreme-right parties' discourses, but also in the electoral platforms of other parties, often articulated with issues such as the economy, education, and culture. This chapter demonstrates that, even if extreme-right parties are leading the debate on this issue, regionalist (and liberal) parties also significantly emphasize this issue. Not only do these parties pay more attention to this issue than other party families, but they are also less influenced by the strength of extreme-right parties. The position of the regionalist parties on immigration is more a question of ideology than party competition and is often combined with the parties' main political interests, that is, the decentralization issue and the linguistic conflict between Flemish and French-speaking parties.

This chapter relies on a qualitative and quantitative analysis of the content of party manifestos in Belgium. Electoral platforms of the main parties in the Belgian national/federal Parliament between 1977 and 2007 have been analysed, allowing us to position these parties on various policy issues, including immigration, and to compare their positions over time and across party families and regions.

This chapter is structured into five main sections. The first section briefly presents the main characteristics of the Belgian party systems and the challenges of analysing party positions on immigration. The second section discusses the role played by extreme-right parties in these issues and the expected position of the regionalist parties. The third section analyses the content of party manifestos, tests whether the extreme-right parties 'own' the issue of immigration and distinguishes between different types of immigration issues. The last two sections test the impact of party competition on party positions and whether ideology can explain why parties associate some policy issues with immigration.

Immigration in multilevel Belgium

For the students of stateless nationalist and regionalist parties and of immigration issues, Belgium is a fascinating case. It relies on a peculiar and fully regionalized party system, characterized by the presence of both strong extreme-right parties and strong regionalist parties. In addition, the competence on immigration policy remains at the federal (national) level despite recurrent demands to allocate it to the regional (or community) levels (see Chapter 4 by Adam and Jacobs for more details).

The Belgian party system presents one unique characteristic when compared to other federations: there are no federal (or statewide) parties. The Belgian electoral system is divided according to linguistic lines. Broadly speaking, Flemish parties do not address French-speaking voters and vice versa, even in the officially bilingual city of Brussels. Since the split of the three major statewide parties between 1968 and 1978 (the Christian Democrats, the socialists, and the liberals), not one statewide party has managed to win elections and to obtain seats in the federal Parliament. All of the political parties that were created after 1978 – primarily the extreme-right parties, green parties, and populist parties – are organized at the community level and explicitly represent the interests of only part of the Belgian population. Due to the split of the statewide parties and the creation of new parties in each linguistic community, the Belgian party system is highly fragmented; the effective number of parties in the federal Parliament was 8.42 after the elections of 2010.

As a result, it might be better to speak of two party systems – the Flemish and the French-speaking ones – rather than of one party system in Belgium. Even in the bilingual electoral constituency of BHV (this territory contains the Brussels municipalities as well as the municipalities of Halle and Vilvoorde, which are officially bilingual), parties are organized and compete along linguistic lines. Very few lists provide candidates from both language groups for the federal elections and bilingual lists are forbidden for the regional elections in Brussels.

Although the regional party systems within Belgium contain different parties, at the party family level, we may observe similar characteristics and structures. For example, after the federal elections of 2010 the

Flemish- and French-speaking party systems were composed of one Christian Democrat (*Christen-Democratisch & Vlaams* – CD&V in Flanders and *Centre Démocrate Humaniste* – CDH in French-speaking Belgium), one socialist (*Socialistische Partij Anders* – SP.A and *Parti Socialiste* – PS), one liberal (*Open Vlaamse Liberalen en Democraten* – Open VLD and *Mouvement Réformateur* – MR), one regionalist (*Nieuw-Vlaamse Alliantie* – N-VA and *Fédéralistes Démocrates Francophones* – FDF), one extreme-right (*Vlaams Belang* – VB and *Front National* – FN), one green (*Groen* and *Ecolo*), and one populist party (*Libertair, Direct, Democratisch* – LDD and *Parti Populaire* – PP).[1]

Probably the most important critique formulated against the academic analysis of party positions concerns the fact that it is difficult to compare party systems across countries as each country constitutes a different institutional, political, electoral and socioeconomic environment in which parties compete, directly influencing the content of the party manifestos. In Belgium, the political environment at the federal level is exactly the same for the Flemish and the French-speaking parties, allowing a robust comparison between these two party systems.

The analysis of party positions on immigration in Belgium is rather peculiar since one of the main Flemish parties, the *Vlaams Belang* (previously named *Vlaams Blok*), oscillates between being a regionalist party and an extreme-right party. Indeed, its birth is linked to the Flemish regionalist party (*Volksunie*), and one of its most prominent programmatic claims concerns decentralization and, ultimately, the independence of Flanders (Billiet and De Witte, 1995; De Winter and Dumont, 1999; Evans et al., 2001). But at the same time, many comparative studies based on the analysis of party manifestos have confirmed that this party belongs to the extreme-right party family and – together with the FN – can be labelled as anti-migrant party (Phalet and Krekels, 1998; Newman, 1997; Van der Brug, Fennema and Tillie, 2005: 537). Billiet and De Witte confirmed in their analysis of the 1991 party manifestos that 'one of the major issues of the programme of that party: negative attitudes towards immigrants' (1995: 193) and Maddens and Hajnal (2001) go even further when stating that the VB has to be considered as a single- or near single-issue party on the immigration issue in 1991 and 1995. Yet, previous studies have observed that, in its first years of existence, the extreme-right Flemish party largely emphasized the decentralization issue, and Coffé (2005) has demonstrated that this party made a clear choice in favour of immigration after 1987. Still, claims of Flemish independence remained one of the party's most prominent characteristics over the years (Walgrave, De Swert and Dandoy, 2002; see

Chapter 11 by Erk in this volume). *A contrario*, the analysis of regionalist parties in Belgium seldom includes the issue of immigration.

Overall, not only are the issues of decentralization and immigration linked in the case of the *Vlaams Belang* (VB), but the electoral fortunes of the parties alleged to be the owners of these two issues – the regionalist and extreme-right parties – seem to be linked to the evolution of the two Belgian party systems. Figure 10.1 shows the electoral results of the main regionalist and extreme-right parties in each party system over the years. The two party families clearly display opposite trends. While the regionalist parties gradually lost strength since 1974 (almost in a linear way in the case of the Flemish regionalist party until 2007), the extreme-right parties witnessed important electoral successes. In this framework,

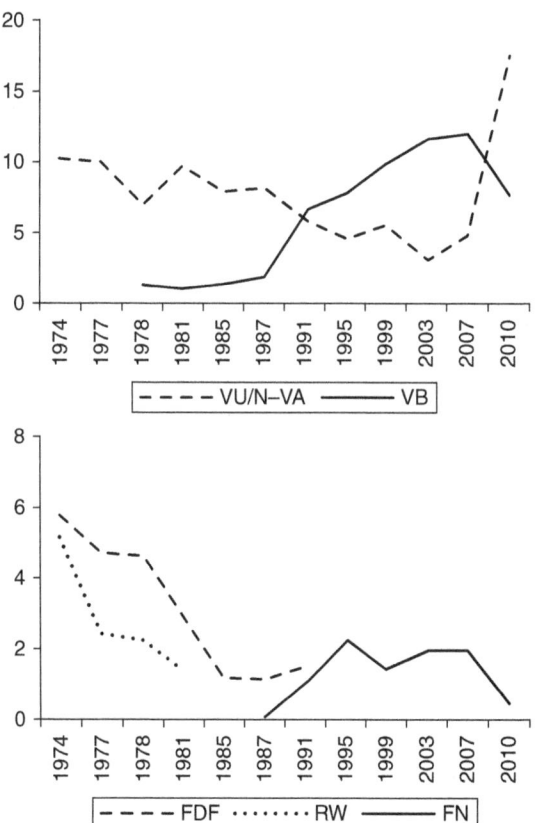

Figure 10.1 Electoral success of extreme-right and regionalist parties (1974–2010), in per cent

the analysis of party positions on the immigration issue, following these successes of the extreme-right parties, seems to be particularly relevant.

Immigration and party positions in Belgium

Extreme-right parties and immigration

Among the different issues that are addressed during electoral campaigns that allow us to distinguish between parties, immigration is often considered as a new issue since the 1980s and the early 1990s in several Western European countries (McElroy and Benoit, 2007: 21). The issue of immigration occupies a specific space in numerous analyses of the content of the party manifestos, either as a single-issue focus (see, for example, Van der Brug, Fennema and Tillie, 2005; Arzheimer and Carter, 2006) or as an issue among several other issues or policy domains. This is not only of interest to researchers focusing on immigration policies but also to those analysing (and explaining) electoral behaviour, party systems, and party competition. Indeed, the politicization of immigration has transformed politics in Western Europe, and it has been mainly linked to the emergence and success of extreme-right parties.

Extreme-right parties are considered as niche parties focusing mainly on the immigration issue (see, for example, Meguid, 2008). Guibernau (2010: 10) states that 'anti-immigrant sentiment and, in some instances, open hostility towards immigrants describe radical right-wing parties'. In addition, and in contrast to their mainstream competitors, extreme-right parties have been able to take up these new issues in a more pronounced and radical way, which has often translated into success (Spies and Franzmann, 2010).

The Belgian extreme-right cases have been widely covered, mainly in comparative terms (with the exception of Phalet and Krekels, 1998). These authors, as well as Newman (1997) and Van der Brug, Fennema and Tillie (2005) confirm through their analysis of the manifestos of the two extreme-right parties in Belgium[2] – VB and FN – that these parties can be labelled as anti-migrant parties. The presence of immigration issues in their manifestos is highly salient. In their quantitative analysis of the content of Flemish party manifestos between 1991 and 2004, Walgrave and De Swert (2004) observe that VB dedicated more attention to immigration and asylum issues than any other party.

However, even if these parties appear to be the 'owners' of the immigration issue, they also might own or be considerably strong on other issues. Maddens and Hajnal (2001) believe that since 1995, the VB has broadened its appeal by emphasizing or incorporating other policy issues including decentralization (see above), law-and-order and/or crime (Billiet and De Witte, 1995; Evans et al., 2001; Walgrave, De Swert and Dandoy, 2002; Delwit, 2002; Van der Brug and Fennema, 2003; Coffé, 2005; Ignazi, 2006; de Lange, 2007), national identity (Newman, 1997; Ignazi, 2006), family policy (Billiet and De Witte, 1995), morality (Billiet and De Witte, 1995; Ignazi, 2006), and anti-politics or anti-establishment issues (Billiet and De Witte, 1995; Walgrave, De Swert and Dandoy, 2002; Coffé, 2005; De Winter and Baudewyns, 2009).

In Flanders, the VB was created in 1978 by the merger of two small radical-nationalist movements that were disappointed by the policies of the Flemish regional party (VU). Originally, its ideology was primarily focused on decentralization issues, that is, more autonomy and even independence for the Flemish region. But gradually it developed other policy positions, among others an anti-immigrant position. In contrast, the French-speaking counterpart of the VB, the FN has no roots in a Walloon or French-speaking regionalist movement. The FN was basically created in 1985 as a 'sister party' to the eponymous French extreme-right party of Jean-Marie Le Pen. Since the very beginning, the ideology of this party was clearly directed against migrants, even though the first party manifesto was only drafted for the 1991 elections. The FN participated for the first time in the national elections in 1987.

Yet even if they 'own' the issue, extreme-right parties are not the only ones paying attention to the immigration issue. The literature argues that the positions of other parties on immigration are linked to the success of the extreme-right parties (Givens and Luedtke, 2005; Arzheimer and Carter, 2006; Meguid, 2008; Guibernau, 2010). Indeed, according to the party competition model, the electoral success of extreme-right parties has an impact on the positions of all of the other parties on the immigration issue. This assumption basically relies on the fact that the electoral success of extreme-right parties directly threatens the other political parties and that these parties may adapt their strategy in order to face the new electoral challenge. They may either increase (confrontational strategy) or decrease (dismissive strategy) their attention to the issue. Yet, some studies (see, for example, Klingemann, 1987; Petry and Landry, 2001; Katsanidou and Gemenis, 2010; Van der Brug, 2001) have demonstrated that the actual pattern of party competition is rather a mixed one. Party strategies display a mix of confrontational as well as dismissive characteristics. In addition, not all of the parties react in the same way to the emergence and electoral success of extreme-right parties, and certain parties are more likely to adapt their positions accordingly than others, mainly depending on their party family, their ideology, their initial position, or even their policy positions on other dimensions.

Regionalist parties and immigration

If scholars have often tried to link the effects of decentralization or federalism with the success of extreme-right parties (see, for example, Arzheimer and Carter, 2006; Spies and Franzmann, 2010), then the opposite relationship – that is, linking immigration issues with the success of regionalist parties – has been rarely done. Nonetheless, Hepburn (2009) links the regionalist parties with the issue of immigration, identifying economic, ideological, party competition, and statewide influences on the relationship between the two. She states that 'immigration has become a mobilising issue for stateless nationalist and regionalist parties, which have sought to protect and advance regional identities and interests' (Hepburn, 2011: 523).

There are three main regionalist parties in Belgium. Their most important electoral results were obtained in the early and mid-1970s and they participated in several national and regional governments. In Flanders, the Flemish regionalist party *Volksunie* (VU) was created in 1954 and demanded more autonomy for Flanders within a Belgian federal state. Later, the radicalization of the party's ideology led it to support the independence of Flanders. In 2001, the party was split into the N-VA and *Spirit*. The latter has been in an electoral alliance with the Socialists and Greens, while the former is nowadays considered the heir of the VU.

On the French-speaking side, both the Brussels and Walloon regions have witnessed the emergence of regionalist parties. In Brussels, the *Fédération des Démocrates Francophones* (previously *Front démocratique des Francophones*, FDF) was created in 1964 with the aim of defending the interests of the French-speaking population in and around Brussels against the Flemish majority. Between 1992 and 2011, the FDF created a long-lasting and stable electoral alliance with the French-speaking liberal party. In Wallonia, the *Rassemblement Wallon* (RW) was founded in 1968. The party's ideology was based on demands for the creation of a federal Belgium, and it basically disappeared from the national political arena in 1985 when this aim was soon to be achieved. Most of its former elites and members rallied towards the socialist or liberal parties.

Very few studies have empirically analysed regionalist party positions on immigration in the Belgian case. One exception is Coffé (2005), who observes the 'marriage' of Flemish nationalist-separatism and a strong position on immigration. Similarly, Hepburn (2011) observes that, among the Flemish parties that adapted their party positions on the immigration issue following the electoral fortunes of the Flemish extreme-right party, the left-wing regionalist party *Spirit* adopted a more inclusive pro-immigrant position. Concerning the right-wing N-VA, Pauwels (2011) confirms that, even if the Flemish extreme-right party remains the principal 'owner' of the immigration issue, that issue is also relevant to voters of the N-VA.

Immigration issue in party manifestos

Owning immigration

Inspired by the original work of Baumgartner and Jones (1993), the Belgian Agenda Setting Project[3] uses a slightly adapted version of their topical codebook to identify and track issue attention from 1970s onwards. Aimed at analysing the positions of the Belgian political parties, the Project set a systematic thematic coding of the content of the party manifestos. The codebook contains about 250 topic codes, organized by main topic categories. Party manifestos were coded per quasi-sentence, a procedure similarly used by the Comparative Manifesto Project (CMP). These coding procedures allow multiple coding for the same quasi-sentence, and various dummy variables were also added, allowing us to identify pledges, titles, references to other parties, and so on. Among the various coded issues, no less than eight subcategories directly deal with immigration issues.[4] This high number of immigration items contrast with previous studies that used approximated indicators (see, for example, Van der Brug, Fennema and Tillie, 2005; Arzheimer and Carter, 2006; Meguid, 2008).

I analyse the manifestos of all of the parties that were represented in at least three elections in the federal House of Representatives, which equals 13 parties: two Christian Democrats, two social democrats, two liberals, two greens, two extreme-right, and three regionalists. With the exception of the French-speaking *Parti Socialiste*, Ecolo, and *Front National*, all of the other parties changed their names within the observed period. In addition, several electoral alliances were formed, as well as some party splits, but the structure of the party system remained rather stable over time. The content of the manifestos of about 9 to 11 parties for each election year were coded. The data therefore comprises the content of exactly 100 party manifestos on about 250 different policy issues for over more than 30 years. About 250,000 quasi-sentences were coded, with an average of 2,435 per manifesto.

This data on Belgian party manifestos allows us to test different hypotheses concerning party positions on migration. The first hypothesis of this chapter concerned the extreme-right parties' ownership of the immigration issue. The data shows that the extreme-right parties are the leading parties when emphasizing immigration in their manifestos. Table 10.1 shows that the percentage of attention to that issue in their manifestos is significantly higher than any other party family, to a great extent confirming their 'ownership' of that issue (on average 8.79 per cent in the case of the Flemish extreme-right party VB and about 10 per cent in the case of its French-speaking counterpart FN). In addition, immigration occupies a much larger place in the Flemish manifestos than in the French-speaking ones. With the exception of the socialist party family, each Flemish party dedicates on average more attention to this issue than its French-speaking sister party. In both party systems, the manifestos of the liberal and the regionalist parties display a relatively high emphasis on immigration.

Table 10.1 Average attention to immigration in party manifestos (1981–2007)

Party family	Flemish parties		French-speaking parties	
Christian Democrat	CVP/CD&V	1.84%	PSC/CDH	1.62%
Socialist	SP/SP.A	1.11%	PS	2.36%
Liberal	PVV/Open VLD	4.16%	PRL/MR	2.61%
Regionalist	VU/N-VA	3.17%	FDF	2.89%
			RW	0.74%
Green	Agalev/Groen	2.13%	Ecolo	1.62%
Extreme-right	VB	8.79%	FN	10.11%
Weighted average[a]		2.97 %		1.96%

[a]Weighted by each party's electoral strength (in % of the total number of votes at the national level).

Nonetheless, when looking at specific elections, ownership of the immigration issue is not as clear-cut as expected. Table 10.2 displays the leading party emphasizing immigration in its manifesto per election year. If as expected the extreme-right parties dominate the immigration 'market' since their first measurement (in 1978 for VB and in 1991 for FN), it is not the case for each individual election. In 1995, the Flemish liberal party dedicated more attention to this issue (8.42 per cent) than the extreme-right party (5.32 per cent), as well as the regionalist N-VA in 2007 with 11.76 per cent (the VB follows with 8.15 per cent). On the French-speaking side of the linguistic border, it is surprisingly the green party that dedicates more attention to immigration in 2007 with 5.31 per cent (the FN with only 1.84 per cent).[5]

Table 10.2 Leading party emphasizing immigration in its manifestos (1977–2007)

Election year	Flemish parties		French-speaking parties	
1977	Regionalist	1.25%	–	–
1978	Extreme-right	8.98%	–	–
1981	Extreme-right	4.06%	Liberal	2.09%
1985	Extreme-right	9.95%	Regionalist	3.34%
1987	Extreme-right	8.37%	Regionalist	3.37%
1991	Extreme-right	13.61%	Extreme-right	13.38%
1995	Liberal	8.42%	Extreme-right	12.73%
1999	Extreme-right	9.58%	Extreme-right	14.29%
2003	Extreme-right	11.11%	Extreme-right	8.33%
2007	Regionalist	11.76%	Green	5.31%

Immigration control vs. migrant integration

Extreme-right parties do pay more attention to immigration issues than any other party, but can they be considered the owners of this issue? Policy positions regarding the immigration issue diverge not only in terms of salience (that is the degree of attention to the issue in manifestos) but also in terms of policy sectors of immigration. Givens and Luedtke (2005) identify two main types of immigration policy: immigration control and migrant integration.[6] Immigration control basically concerns policy areas around illegal immigration, political asylum/refugees, family reunification, and legal labour immigration/visas. As indicated by its name, migrant integration deals with citizenship and anti-discrimination aspects of integration. These two types of policy may be emphasized differently by different parties (or party families) according to their ideological profile (for example, immigration control may refer to the issue of law-and-order, while migrant integration may refer to the idea of multiculturalism) and to different patterns of party competition.

In the coding process, and in similarity to Givens and Luedtke (2005), I differentiate between the two types of position on immigration,[7] allowing us to explore whether the extreme-right parties own both policy types of immigration issues in their manifestos. One might expect that right-wing parties compete with the extreme-right party on the 'control' of immigration, while left-wing parties dedicate more attention to the 'integration' side of immigration. Table 10.3 demonstrates that extreme-right parties in Belgium own both types of immigration issues in both party systems. They clearly allocate more attention to these policy issues than any other party.

We also observe two additional elements. First, the Flemish parties allocate on average more attention to both types of policy immigration in their manifesto than the French-speaking parties. Second, if right-wing parties score better than left-wing parties concerning immigration control, we do not observe more attention to integration policies in the manifestos of the left-wing parties. On the contrary and, besides extreme-right parties, the greatest attention given to this type of policy issue is observed in the manifestos of the liberal party in Flanders (1.79 per cent), followed by the regionalists (1.43 per cent), and the regionalist FDF (0.81 per cent) in French-speaking Belgium.

Table 10.3 Average attention given to immigration control and integration in party manifestos (1981–2007)

	Flemish parties		French-speaking parties	
	Immigration control	Immigration integration	Immigration control	Immigration integration
Christian Democrat	0.90%	0.64%	0.49%	0.62%
Socialist	0.34%	0.67%	0.90%	1.01%
Liberal	1.76%	1.79%	1.05%	0.49%
Regionalist	1.33%	1.43%	0.57%	0.81%
			0.38%	0.03%
Green	1.03%	0.82%	0.50%	0.58%
Extreme-right	3.58%	4.05%	4.66%	1.44%

Regression model

In order to verify the ownership hypothesis of the extreme-right parties on immigration issues, I use a regression model based on panel data with party family dummies, as well as control variables: language, party size, and manifesto length. As discussed above, the distinctive characteristic of the Belgian electoral system is its scission according to linguistic lines. Since the split of the traditional political parties, manifestos are no longer released in both languages and are not even translated. In this framework language is an important variable as it allows us to distinguish Flemish from French-speaking parties.

Confirming the findings of Adam and Jacobs in Chapter 4, distinct patterns between Flemish and French-speaking parties are observed regarding the importance given to immigration (see Tables 10.1 and 10.3). Overall, the emphasis on the issue of immigration appears to be rather stable in the case of the French-speaking manifestos (around 2 per cent of attention), while the Flemish manifestos poorly emphasize that issue between 1977 and 1987, then increase their attention to above 5 per cent in 1991, 2003, and 2007. These trends confirm that the Flemish parties always dedicate on average more attention to this issue than the French-speaking parties. The greater emphasis observed since 1991 for the Flemish parties is mainly due to the high attention to immigration in the extreme-right party manifestos.

The size of each party is measured by its electoral strength and calculated as a percentage of the votes obtained in elections. Finally, I control for the length of the manifesto as previous empirical analyses with the same data (Dandoy, 2011) demonstrate that manifesto length matters when one wants to analyse its content. The content of a party manifesto is not similar in a small or a large manifesto. I therefore include a variable based on the number of coded quasi-sentences in each manifesto.

The results displayed in Table 10.4 confirm that the extreme-right parties in Belgium can indeed be considered as the 'owners' of the immigration issue. The observed coefficient is strong and positive, meaning that overall, the immigration category is larger by about 7.5 per cent in the manifestos of the extreme-right parties than in the green party manifestos (the latter having the lowest level of ownership).

This first model delivers additional results since another party family is significant: the liberal party family. Its coefficient is positive, meaning that the manifestos of these parties contain more references to immigration than other parties. The immigration category is larger by 2.2 per cent in the liberal manifestos than in the green party manifestos. A partial conclusion might be that the ownership of immigration by the Belgian extreme-right parties is not as clear as expected and that the liberal party family might compete with the extreme-right party on this issue. In addition, none of the control variables appear to be significant.

As indicated above, the two types of policies – immigration control and migrant integration – may be emphasized differently by different

Table 10.4 Immigration ownership model

		Immigration (all issues)	Immigration control	Immigrant integration
Party families	Christian Democrat	40.26033 (74.54952)	–	49.52739 (30.70797)
	Socialist	29.12886 (77.5253)	–14.01396 (26.16765)	64.72467 (33.73872)
	Liberal	220.8868* (96.45432)	79.7991 (40.8669)	100.2327* (39.38912)
	Regionalist	119.0173 (80.21754)	34.77617 (64.84999)	46.60756 (27.05031)
	Green	–	0.0636762 (43.60049)	–
	Extreme-right	753.167*** (105.7087)	326.1532*** (73.67298)	239.5033*** (40.9028)
Control variables	Language	43.26207 (56.74694)	23.88561 (33.32535)	93.87739*** (22.87821)
	Party size	–0.0478564 (0.070412)	0.0008787 (0.0463746)	–0.0626792* (0.0282253)
	Manifesto length	0.01067 (0.0098209)	0.0052323 (0.0057841)	0.0046643 (0.0041594)
	Constant	150.3468** (55.04835)	46.68964 (54.11669)	33.17691 (22.49077)
	N	100	100	100
	Groups	13	13	13
	R²	0.5383	0.3875	0.4802

Note: Prais-Winsten regression, heteroskedastic PCSE. *** $\rho < 0.001$; ** $\rho < 0.01$; * $\rho < 0.05$. Green party family dummy as reference category for the model including all issues and for the immigrant-integration model. Christian Democrat party family dummy as reference category for the immigration control model.

parties, according to their ideological profile and to different patterns of party competition. The division of the immigration policy domain into more specific policies will allow us to test whether extreme-right parties can be considered as the 'owners' of both policies.

The results indicate that extreme-right parties are the leading party when dealing with both types of immigration policies. These parties allocate significantly more attention to the issues of immigration control and migration integration than the socialist and Christian Democrat parties. Even if the liberal party dummy is significant in the model concerning migration integration, it does not mitigate the conclusions. When looking at more specific public policy proposals (on integration and control), the extreme-right parties can still be considered as the party family 'owning' the issue. Still, two control variables are significant in the ownership model concerning migrant integration: party size and language. Smaller parties dedicate more attention to migrant integration, as well as the Flemish parties. In the case of the latter, Flemish parties allocate about 1 per cent more attention to this policy issue than the French-speaking parties, independent of their party family.

Party competition

In a second model, I test the reaction of the Belgian parties to the emergence and electoral success of the extreme-right parties. Party competition on immigration is primarily determined by the electoral success of the extreme-right party in each party system. Two different indicators of the electoral strength of the extreme-right party are developed. The first one consists of its absolute electoral result (percentage of votes at the national level), while the second measures the electoral trends in the results of the extreme-right party since the last elections ($e_0 - e_{-1}$). These two measurements allow us to determine whether the extreme-right parties represent a (growing) electoral threat for the other parties in each party system.

Table 10.5 indicates that parties dedicated a larger share of their manifestos to the immigration issue when the extreme-right party was strong. An increase of 1 per cent in the size of the extreme-right party leads its competitors to increase their attention to the immigration issue in their manifestos by an additional 0.4 per cent. These results may appear modest, but when one thinks about the example of an extreme-right party that increases its vote share from 5 per cent to 15 per cent of the votes, this increase leads to an increase in the attention given to immigration in the other parties' manifestos by 4 per cent.

Surprisingly, the other two variables of party competition do not play a role in this model. Whether or not the extreme-right party wins or loses an election has no bearing on the attention given to that issue by its competitors. It is not an extreme-right party's ability to win elections that matters, it is its size. The larger the extreme-right party, the stronger the impact it will have on the emphasis on immigration in the other parties' electoral platforms. Concerning the variable of party defeat, we observe that this variable is positive but not significant. Whether a party loses the election does not have a significant impact on its emphasis on immigration in its manifesto. The explanatory power of the model reaches almost 50 per cent, meaning that about half of the variation of the preferences to emphasize immigration in party manifestos is explained by the variables. In sum, the emphasis on the issue of immigration in party manifestos is a consequence of extreme-right party size:

political parties will emphasize immigration when the extreme-right party is electorally successful.

Language appears to be significant but, surprisingly, negative. This means that the French-speaking parties dedicate more attention to immigration than their Flemish counterparts. It is likely that, *ceteris paribus*, some of the attention to immigration in the French-speaking manifestos is not grasped by the extreme-right party size variable, probably because the French-speaking party system witnessed the absence of an extreme-right party in 1981 and 1985.

The model also confirms that different processes are at stake, depending on the party family. The mainstream right-wing (the liberals) and the regionalist parties dedicate more attention to immigration than parties

Table 10.5 Party competition models

		Immigration (all issues)	Immigration control	Immigrant integration
Party competition	Party defeat	0.0152457	0.0431679	−0.0393346
		(0.0878238)	(0.0525374)	(0.036382)
	Extreme-right party size	0.4262207***	0.232475***	0.1477901***
		(0.0705177)	(0.0444094)	(0.0288892)
	Extreme-right party success	0.1237562	0.0492648	0.0668616
		(0.1933918)	(0.1227892)	(0.0802966)
Party families	Christian Democrat	−27.65324	−6.127386	–
		(68.34842)	(31.64432)	
	Socialist	−31.39506	−17.7121	22.47279
		(73.33536)	(37.81988)	(19.22406)
	Liberal	152.3261*	64.37312	69.13854**
		(73.70205)	(37.16406)	(25.6625)
	Regionalist	122.1166*	36.66459	72.68411*
		(63.56518)	(39.95194)	(29.66295)
	Green	–	–	23.43901
				(28.73248)
Control variables	Language	−186.56**	−79.01712*	−45.03119
		(58.75801)	(33.01889)	(25.12233)
	Party size	0.0417032	0.0182641	0.0206502
		(0.0540144)	(0.0289523)	(0.0249133)
	Manifesto length	−0.0046272	−0.0039668	0.0001801
		(0.0086843)	(0.0051041)	(0.0036072)
Model summary	Constant	105.5896*	26.27659	1.570213
		(50.55027)	(22.55996)	(31.66811)
	N	86	86	86
	Groups	11	11	11
	R^2	0.4918	0.4183	0.4565

Note: Prais-Winsten regression, heteroskedastic PCSE. *** $p < 0.001$; ** $p < 0.01$; * $p < 0.05$. The green party family used as a reference category, except for the immigration integration (Christian Democrat party family dummy as reference category).

from the reference party family[8] (by 1.52 per cent and 1.22 per cent respectively in the liberal and regionalist manifestos). But the most important element is that this attention is independent from the party competition variables around the extreme-right party, unlike the greater emphasis on immigration that was found in the manifestos of the Christian Democrat, socialist, and green parties in reaction to the size of the extreme-right.

Similarly, the models specifically concerning immigration control and migrant integration confirm previous findings regarding the patterns of party competition on immigration issues. The size of the extreme-right parties has a positive and significant impact on the amount of attention that the other parties dedicate to immigration in their manifestos. The stronger the extreme-right party, the larger will be the emphasis on both the control and integration policy issues. For both types of immigration policy, the liberal party family – as well as the regionalist party for the migrant integration policies – dedicate more attention to these issues in its manifestos than the reference party family.

Associating immigration with policy issues

In this section, I test Odmalm's (2012) hypothesis according to which parties assimilate immigration in policy issues where they have a strategic advantage. Odmalm considers immigration as an orthogonal issue and he argues that 'Parties need to assimilate – and frame – immigration so it corresponds to the position on the conflict dimension where they have a strategic advantage' (Odmalm, 2012: 3). In other words, parties play primarily to their strengths. Therefore, I test this hypothesis according to which a party's position on immigration corresponds to their ideological position (left vs. right and 'old' vs. 'new' politics) where they have a strategic advantage. In his analysis of UK manifestos, Odmalm links the immigration policy issue with other policy issues. For example, when dealing with immigration, the Labour Party focuses on economic and social aspects, the Liberal Democrats with human rights and labour-market concerns, while the Conservatives associate immigration with safeguarding the population from disease (immigrant health checks) and to maintaining sovereignty (Odmalm, 2012: 15).

In this chapter, I adopt the same perspective. Immigration is not only framed in correspondence with the party's position on the main cleavages, but the way in which immigration is framed corresponds to its position on other policy issues and, more particularly, on policy issues where the party has a strategic advantage. In the Belgian case – and in similarity to the UK case – this means that parties associate immigration with their classic left-right positioning and with their 'owned' policy issues.

The Belgian party manifestos have been coded according to a principle of multiple coding, which allows the coder to attribute a primary policy issue code to each quasi-sentence, as well as a second and third code. As a result, the data can test the co-occurrence of policy issues in manifestos alongside immigration. Tables 10.6 and 10.7 present the three main priorities of the Belgian parties aggregated for the 1977–2007 period. The results confirm Odmalm's hypothesis. Parties in Belgium discuss the immigration issue in relation to policy issues that are close to their 'owned' issues or issues where they have a strategic advantage. The green and mainstream parties (Christian Democrat, socialist, and liberal) do emphasize issues of democracy and rights. A qualitative analysis of the manifestos reveals that they primarily relate to the debate on the voting rights for migrants, a debate that has been very salient since the end of the 1990s. The French-speaking mainstream and green parties also emphasize issues related to international relations when discussing immigration. This is related to the importance of development aid in their manifestos as a way to deal with immigration. Social policy, housing, and education are also important issues when discussing immigration for the socialist, Christian Democrat, and green parties but also – and more surprisingly – for the liberal and regionalist parties.[9]

More interesting is the attention to law-and-order issues. As expected, this issue is associated with immigration in the manifestos of the extreme-right and liberal parties and, in the French-speaking case, in

Table 10.6 Most important policy domains associated with immigration: Flemish parties

Christian Democrat	Democracy and rights 17%	Education 14.4%	Community issues 11.8%
Socialist	Democracy and rights 17.2%	Education 16.2%	Social policy 16.2%
Liberal	Law-and-order 17.3%	Democracy and rights 14.9%	Education 13.8%
Regionalist	Community issues 21.1%	Housing 13.7%	Culture 12.6%
Green	Democracy and rights 20.8%	Social policy 17.6%	International relations 9.5%
Extreme-right	Law-and-order 38.4%	Democracy and rights 15.2%	Social policy 8.8%

Table 10.7 Most important policy domains associated with immigration: French-speaking parties

Christian Democrat	International relations 20.3%	Law-and-order 18.8%	Community issues 12.5%
Socialist	International relations 22.4%	Government and administration 17.5%	Democracy and rights 16.1%
Liberal	Democracy and rights 21.5%	Social policy 20%	Law-and-order 15.4%
Regionalist	Community issues 18.6%	Social policy 16.9%	Law-and-order 13.6%
Green	Democracy and rights 21.1%	Government and administration 15.5%	International relations 14.1%

Note: Figures for the extreme-right French-speaking party (FN) are not displayed because the N is not large enough.

the manifestos of the regionalist and Christian Democrat parties. In the case of the Flemish extreme-right party, it even concerns more than one-third of the items related to the immigration issue. Most of these references to law-and-order issues link the migrants with behaviour that (potentially) threatens public order and discusses the overrepresentation of migrants in crime statistics.

Finally, decentralization issues (that is, issues related to the linguistic tensions between the Flemish and French-speaking parties and to demands for more regional autonomy and a territorial state re-organization) are connected to immigration in the manifestos of the regionalist parties (21.1 per cent for the Flemish and 18.6 per cent for the French-speaking regionalist parties) and are also salient in the immigration sections of the manifestos of the Christian Democrat parties. These issues are not very salient in the case of the VB, confirming its ideological profile as an extreme-right party rather than a regionalist party.

Conclusion

This chapter sought to understand party positions in Belgium on the immigration issue and more particularly the positions of the regionalist parties. As in many other Western countries, immigration became an electorally salient issue with the rise of the extreme-right party, which focuses specifically on this issue and which has had a significant impact on the other parties' electoral platforms. Based on a quantitative and qualitative analysis of the party manifestos in Belgium during the last three decades, this chapter demonstrated that explaining the presence of immigration in those manifestos remains a complex issue. First, the extreme-right parties are identified as the 'owners' of the immigration issue. Interestingly, these parties allocate more attention to immigration than any other party in its two dimensions (immigration control and migrant integration). One does not observe that the issue of integration is particularly more salient in the left-wing party manifestos. Yet, this extreme-right ownership of immigration is not as clear as expected. Two other party families – the liberal and regionalist parties – also emphasize this issue significantly more than other parties. Furthermore, in 2007 and in election years where the extreme-right party did not compete, the regionalist parties are the parties that allocate the most attention to this issue.

Second, the results indicate that party competition has had a significant impact on the content of party manifestos, that is, Belgian parties tend to increase their attention to immigration when the extreme-right party is electorally strong. This is true for all party families, with again the exception of the liberal and regionalist parties. If it is naïve to believe that regionalists are not influenced by the electoral strength of the extreme-right party, the models show that independent party family effects are at stake here. Yet, the positions of the Belgian regionalist parties on immigration are partly explained by the fact that they are regionalist parties. In other words, independently of the success of the extreme-right party – so, on the basis of their own electoral success, their position in the government, or in the opposition, and the external environment – the regionalist parties will continue emphasizing immigration in their manifestos. In this regard, immigration can be viewed as an issue that belongs to the core identity – or ideology – of the regionalist parties. When distinguishing between types of immigration policies, regionalist parties react to the electoral success of the extreme-right parties regarding immigration control issues but they have their own separate policy agenda regarding integration issues that is not affected by extreme-right party attention to immigration. In sum, migrant integration is an issue that is specific to the regionalist parties' manifestos, independently of the evolution of the party system.

Third, political parties frame immigration in different ways, associating immigration issues with their preferred policy issues. The results confirm Odmalm's hypothesis but bring an additional element. Extreme-right and liberal (right-wing) parties do associate immigration with law-and-order issues, while the regionalist parties focus on the decentralization issues when dealing with immigration. In that sense, it explains earlier findings. Regionalist parties are fairly unreactive to the electoral success of the extreme-right parties, they have a distinct ideology on immigration and this ideology is closely connected to the parties' preferred issues, that is, decentralization and the linguistic conflict between Flemish and French-speaking parties.

In addition, the analyses of party manifestos on immigration reveal regional differences. Independently of the strength of extreme-right parties, French-speaking parties allocate less attention to immigration than Flemish parties. It is likely that different political cultures and attitudes regarding immigration exist in Flanders and in French-speaking Belgium, but these differences may also be partially explained by a different economic and demographic context in each region. Flanders is a good example of a flourishing economy that does not need to attract migrant workers, even though the region has an ageing population and fertility rates lower than in other regions. Concerning culture and language, an important share of migrants that arrive in Flanders speak French and not Dutch – for example, migrants from former French and Belgian colonies and, to a lesser extent, skilled workers coming to work for the European Union and other international organizations.

These findings call for further research. If immigration is indeed a core regionalist issue, then the analysis of immigration issues in the Belgian party systems must be re-framed. Given the fact that regionalist parties emerged in Belgium about two decades before the extreme-right parties,[10] one has to wonder whether the contamination hypothesis on immigration should not be reversed. Have regionalist (and probably also mainstream right-wing) parties and their electoral success influenced the position of the extreme-right parties on immigration? Further analysis is necessary to identify the party (or parties) that brought the new issue of immigration onto the political agenda before the emergence of the extreme-right parties.

Notes

1. Unlike the two other communities, the German-speaking community does not display a separate (and third) party system. Apart from the regionalist *ProDG* (and to a lesser extent *Vivant*), all parties present in this community are sub-regional branches of the French-speaking parties.
2. In their analysis of the Belgian case, Ignazi (2006) also included the UDRT while Meguid (2008) included Agir.
3. This project, under the direction of Prof. Stefaan Walgrave (University of Antwerp) for the Belgian case, is financed by the University of Antwerp and

the European Science Foundation (ESF) via the FWO. The coding management has been supervised by Jeroen Joly (University of Antwerp) and Régis Dandoy (University of Zurich).
4. Subcategories 201: Racial discrimination and discrimination against ethnic minorities; 900 : General (including combinations of subcategories); 929: Migration and Labour; 930: Migration and Integration ; 931: Refugees and Asylum-seekers; 932: Access to Nationality; 933: Illegal Migration and Deportations; 999 : Others. The only aspect of immigration that is not taken into account in these subcategories relates to the education of immigrants and asylum-seekers' children since it is part of a larger issue (Sub-category 603 – Education for less favoured persons).
5. The weak score of the French-speaking extreme-right party for the 2007 elections can be explained by a clear manifesto strategy to display immigration issues as 'censored' in the party manifesto, i.e., not displaying the manifesto chapter dedicated to the issues. As a result, I could not code the pledges and policy proposals on migration.
6. This distinction is even more relevant in the Belgian case since some aspects of the immigrant integration have been allocated to the regions and communities, while immigration control remains in the hands of the federal authority (see Chapter 4 by Adam and Jacobs for more details).
7. Leaving aside the general and the 'other immigration issues' category, I gathered the three categories 'Racial discrimination and discrimination against ethnic minorities' (item 0201), 'Migration and labour' (item 0929) and 'Migration and integration' (item 0930) in the 'Migrant integration policy' while the 'Migrant control' concerns the three categories of 'Refugees and Asylum-seekers' (item 0931), of 'Naturalisation' (item 0932) and 'Illegal migration and deportation' (item 0933).
8. In comparing across party families in the regression model, we have to determine which party family is the 'reference' family, i.e., the point of reference in order to understand the others. In this case, the reference party family is the green party family.
9. The Flemish extreme-right party (VB) also allocates 8.8 per cent of its immigration attention to social policies.
10. The Flemish regionalist party (VU) was founded in 1954 while the French-speaking FDF and the RW were founded in 1964 and 1968, respectively. Their most important electoral results were attained in the early and mid-1970s.

References

K. Arzheimer and E. Carter (2006) 'Political Opportunity Structures and Right-wing Extremist Party Success', *European Journal of Political Research*, 45: 419–443.
F.R. Baumgartner and B.D. Jones (1993) *Agendas and Instability in American Politics.* (Chicago: University of Chicago Press).
J. Billiet and H. De Witte (1995) 'Attitudinal Dispositions to Vote for a "New" Extreme Right-wing Party: The Case of the "Vlaams Blok"', *European Journal of Political Research*, 27: 181–202.

H. Coffé (2005) 'The Adaptation of the Extreme-right's Discourse: The Case of the Vlaams Blok', *Ethical Perspectives*, 12(2): 205–230.

S. de Lange (2007) 'A New Winning Formula? The Programmatic Appeal of the Radical Right', *Party Politics*, 13(4): 411–435.

R. Dandoy (2011) 'Explaining Manifesto Length: Empirical Evidence from Belgium (1977–2007)', *ECPR Joint Sessions of Workshop*, St Gallen, 12–17 April.

P. Delwit (2002) 'L'extrême-droite francophone: (non)positionnements institutionnels et implantations électorales', *Fédéralisme Régionalisme*, 2.

L. De Winter and P. Dumont (1999) 'Belgium: Party System(s) on the Eve to Disintegration?' in D. Broughton and M. Donovan (eds) *Changing Party Systems in Western Europe*. (London & New York: Pinter).

L. De Winter and P. Baudewyns (2009) 'Belgium: Towards the Breakdown of a Nation-State in the Heart of Europe?', *Nationalism and Ethnic Politics*, 15(3–4): 280–304.

J. A. Evans, K. Arzheimer, G. Baldini, T. Bjørklund, E. Carter, S. Fisher, G. Ivaldi and J. Evans (2001) 'Comparative Mapping of Extreme Right Electoral Dynamics: An Overview of Extreme Right Electorates and Party Success', *European Political Science*, 1(1).

T. Givens and A. Luedtke (2005) 'European Immigration Policies in Comparative Perspective: Issue Salience, Partisanship and Immigrant Rights', *Comparative European Politics*, 3: 1–22.

M. Guibernau (2010) 'Migration and the Rise of Radical Right', *Policy network paper*, March 2010.

E. Hepburn (2009) 'Regionalist Party Mobilisation on Immigration', *West European Politics*, 32(3): 514–535.

E. Hepburn (2011) '"Citizens of the Region": Party Conceptions of Regional Citizenship and Immigrant Integration', *European Journal of Political Research*, 50: 504–529.

P. Ignazi (2006) *Extreme Right Parties in Western Europe* (Oxford: Oxford University Press).

A. Katsanidou and K. Gemenis (2010) 'Why the Environment Might Not Be the Textbook Example of a Valence Issue', paper prepared for the 2010 *EPOP Conference*, University of Essex, 10–12 September.

H.-D. Klingemann (1987) 'Election Programmes in West Germany, 1949–1980: Explorations in the Nature of Political Controversy' in I. Budge, D. Robertson and D. Hearl (eds) *Ideology, Strategy and Party Change: Spatial Analyses of Post-war Election Programmes in 19 Democracies*. (Cambridge, Cambridge University Press).

B. Maddens and I. Hajnal (2001) 'Alternative Models of Issue Voting: The Case of the 1991 and 1995 Elections in Belgium', *European Journal of Political Research*, 39: 319–346.

G. McElroy and K. Benoit (2007) 'Party Groups and Policy Positions in the European Parliament', *Party Politics*, 13(1): 5–28.

B. M. Meguid (2008) *Party Competition between Unequals. Strategies and Electoral Fortunes in Western Europe*. (Cambridge: Cambridge University Press).

S. Newman (1997) 'Ideological Trends among Ethnoregional Parties in Post-industrial Democracies', *Nationalism and Ethnic Politics*, 3(1): 28–60.

P. Odmalm (2012) 'Party Competition and Positions on Immigration: Strategic Advantages and Spatial Locations', *Comparative European Politics*, 10(1): 1–22.

T. Pauwels (2011) 'Explaining the Strange Decline of the Populist Radical Right Vlaams Belang in Belgium: The Impact of Permanent Opposition', *Acta Politica*, 46(1): 40–62.

F. Pétry and R. Landry (2001) 'Estimating Interparty Policy Distances from Election Programmes in Quebec, 1970–89' in Laver Michael (ed.) *Estimating the Policy Positions of Political Actors*. (London & New York: Routledge).

K. Phalet and B. Krekels (1998) 'Immigration et Intégration' in M. Martiniello and M. Swyngedouw (eds) *Où va la Belgique? Les soubresauts d'une petite démocratie européenne*. (L'Harmattan, Paris).

D. Spies and S. Franzmann (2010) 'A Two-dimensional Approach to the Political Opportunity Structure of Extreme Right Parties in Western Europe', GK Soclife Working Paper, October 2010.

W. Van der Brug and M. Fenema (2003) 'Protest or Mainstream? How the European Anti-Immigrant Parties Developed into Two Separate Groups in 1999', *European Journal of Political Research*, 42: 55–76.

W. Van der Brug, M. Fennema and J. Tillie (2005) 'Why Some Anti-Immigrant Parties Fail and Others Succeed: A Two-Step Model of Aggregate Electoral Support', *Comparative Political Studies*, 38(5): 537–573.

W. Van der Brug (2001) 'Analysing Party Dynamics by Taking Partially Overlapping Snapshots' in Laver Michael (ed.) *Estimating the Policy Positions of Political Actors*. (London & New York: Routledge).

S. Walgrave, K. De Swert and R. Dandoy (2002) 'The Making of the (Issues of the) Vlaams Blok: Issue Ownership and Agenda Setting of Vlaams Blok Issues among Voters, in Party Manifestoes and in the Media (1991–2000)', paper presented to the *ECPR Joint Sessions*, Turin, 22–27 March.

S. Walgrave and K. De Swert (2004) 'The Making of the (Issues of the) Vlaams Blok', *Political Communication*, 21(4): 479–500.

11

FPTP Ain't All That Bad: Nationalist Parties, Immigrants, and Electoral Systems in Québec and Flanders

Jan Erk

Introduction

At the time of writing, the United States is recovering from one of its most divisive and bitter presidential elections. The contest between Barack Obama and Mitt Romney polarized the entire country into two camps, leading many observers to bemoan this state of affairs. This chapter offers a counter-intuitive view that goes against the grain in the scholarly literature as well as in popular perception. In this huge democracy of 300 million citizens, the election was divisive, true; but the polarization united the country from ocean to ocean – a phenomenon best captured by the German phrase *die Einheit der Zweiteilung* ('the unity of bifurcation'). Differences in race, ethnicity, religion, class, region, and demography all managed to merge around two nationwide camps who were offering different degrees of the same Whig ideology. Most pundits seem to believe that the Republican flirtation with the anti-immigrant sentiment originating from the right-wing of the party, which seems to have cost them centrist support, played a big role in Romney's defeat. While not being the sole reason for nationwide politics punishing extremist policy positions, this chapter calls for a second look at an electoral system that seems to have only a few friends left among political scientists. This is a call to evaluate the pluses and minuses of the first-past-the-post (majoritarian) electoral system in an even-handed way. The political context for the examination is a comparison of the nationalist parties in Québec and Flanders, their policy positions towards immigration, and the role their respective electoral systems (first-past-the-post in Québec and proportional representation in Flanders) might have played in their positioning on immigration. This fits in with the hypothesis on electoral systems that Eve Hepburn outlines in her framework in Chapter 3.

The French-speaking Canadian province of Québec and the Dutch-speaking Belgian region of Flanders have historically housed vibrant sub-state nationalist movements seeking self-rule. The *Parti Québécois* ('Party of Québec') in Québec/Canada and *Vlaams Blok* ('Flemish Bloc', now renamed *Vlaams Belang* 'Flemish Interest') in Flanders/Belgium are the two main contemporary sub-state nationalist parties committed to independence for their respective regions. In the last few decades, both regions have also faced growing immigration. While the nationalist goal of self-rule unites the agendas of these two parties, there is a clear difference in terms of their position on immigration. The Parti Québécois actively courts the immigrant vote, but opposition to immigration is a core policy of Vlaams Belang.

This chapter seeks to examine to what extent different electoral systems explain the different positions nationalist parties adopt towards immigration in Québec/Canada and Flanders/Belgium. The examination relies on a perspective that highlights how different political incentives arise from different electoral institutions. Accordingly, first-past-the-post voting in Québec creates incentives for the nationalists to broaden their voter base to include immigrants. In this majoritarian system based on single-member electoral districts, office-seeking parties naturally seek to maximize their votes. The proportional representation (PR) system in Flanders, on the other hand, puts a premium on retaining distinct political platforms that differentiate political parties from their competitors. Add to this the fact that such electoral systems tend to produce coalition governments. This system allows smaller parties with distinct ideological/ethnic/religious/linguistic agendas and a small fraction of the vote to still become part of the government by sticking to their core voters only. There are, thus, incentives for nationalist parties to strengthen their restricted appeal by excluding immigrants.

The chapter looks at the modern development of nationalist parties in both regions and how their positions on immigration diverge. The perspective that the chapter follows rests on the argument that electoral systems influence the policy positions of nationalist parties by affecting the incentives they face. In doing so, the chapter combines the literatures on party and electoral politics, sub-state nationalism, immigration, as well as Belgian and Canadian politics.[1] The author is aware that combining all this within a single chapter is a daunting challenge, but the expected return justifies the effort: By exposing the incentives for inclusiveness that majoritarian electoral systems carry and the potential for exclusiveness proportional systems might bring, the chapter's main goal is an even-handed reflection on electoral systems at a time when first-past-the-post voting has increasingly come under fire. The majoritarian electoral system has been criticized for the discrepancy between the percentage of votes and seats it creates, for the low level of representational accuracy that result from the 'wasted votes' which go to candidates who are not elected, for its bias against smaller parties and parties that lack territorial concentration, and for declining voter turnout. Proportional representation, on the other hand, has come to be seen almost as the cure for all these ills. In Canada, there are ongoing experiments with introducing proportionality into provincial electoral systems.[2] New Zealand went all the way and adopted proportionality in 1993. Yet, the examination of the role first-past-the-post has played in broadening Québec's nationalism base and its desire to incorporate the immigrant vote suggests that there is no need for undue haste in doing away with an electoral system without acknowledging some of its under-explored side-benefits.

Flanders/Belgium and Québec/Canada

Before focusing on the relationship between electoral systems and nationalist party positions, it is imperative that we outline the remarkable similarities between the cases. In both Canada and Belgium, recognition of diversity had started as a force of circumstances. Demographically, the French-Canadian community was too large and territorially concentrated to be assimilated by a thinly dispersed Anglophone population divided into old settlers in Nova Scotia and New Brunswick, Loyalists in Canada, and new settlers from the British Isles. Coupled with the American threat from the south, this practical difficulty in assimilation led to the first enfranchisement of Catholics in the British Empire and a federal system giving them self-rule. Like Canada, the multination characteristics of Belgium have historical roots. Similar to the French-Canadian community, Flemings were too numerous to be assimilated; so a similar demographic force of circumstances prevented the emergence of a linguistically homogenous new Belgian nation.

Due to these historical forces of circumstance, Belgium and Canada have both deviated from the one-nation-one-state principle and became multination federations; within these, Flanders and Québec both have nationalist movements that share similar historical grievances and a sense of cultural insecurity; as immigrant-receiving regions both have

witnessed the immigrants' tendency to assimilate into the culturally more dominant side (Anglophones in Canada, Francophones in
Belgium); and after decades of inward-looking isolationism, both regions
begat nationalist movements committed to independence.

Québec/Canada

By the end of the 1960s, Québec nationalism had permeated all shades
of political opinion within the Francophone population. There were new
political groups committed to Québec independence. Pierre Bourgault's
Rassemblement pour l'indépendence nationale RIN ('Rally for National
Independence') set up in 1960 and its offshoot *Parti Républicain du Québec*
('Québec Republican Party', est. 1962) represented left-wing nationalists.
Action Socialiste pour l'independence du Québec ('Socialist Action for the
Independence of Québec') was another such outfit further to the left.
Conservative Catholic nationalists were within the *Alliance Laurentienne*
('Laurentian Alliance', est. 1957), and centre-right nationalists within
Ralliement Nationale ('National Rally', est. 1964). However, on their own
none of these small groups had any chance of winning a seat. Former
Liberal cabinet minister René Lévesque's new nationalist *Mouvement
Souveraineté-Association* ('Movement for Sovereignty-Association', est.
1966) took the lead in trying to unite all these parties representing the
different colours of Québec nationalism. The result was the establishment of the Parti Québécois in 1970 which received 24 per cent of the
vote that very first year, consequently turning Québec politics into a
two-party competition between the nationalist Parti Québécois and the
pan-Canadian Québec Liberal Party (PLQ).

The Anglophone population fed by growing immigration was widely
seen by nationalists as a barrier to Québec's aspirations, particularly
the cosmopolitan island of Montreal with its prized 28 seats. French-
Canadian votes were simply not going to be enough, so nationalists
had to behave like any other office-seeking party and follow a twofold
strategy. The first initiative was to widen the definition of what it was
to be Québécois. The term 'French-Canadian' (*canadien français*) had
its roots in the 16th century French settlers, the *habitants*. Progressive
nationalists had been using the more inclusive *Québécois* referring to
all inhabitants of Québec – immigrants, Anglophones, and aborigi-
nals. From the 1970s onwards, the term became dominant as French-
Canadian was relegated to being a term denoting ethnic origins only.[3]

The second initiative was to tackle the question of the integration
of immigrants through government activism. The first sign of using
public policy to reverse the immigrant tendency to assimilate into the

Anglophone culture was in 1972. Previous legislation had given immigrant parents the right to choose the language of instruction for their children (Manzer, 1994). But the new Bill 22 made the French language alone the official language of Québec. Access to English-language schools now depended on the demonstration of a sufficient knowledge of English. That is, all immigrant groups with mother tongues other than English had to go to French-language schools (see also Chapter 5 by Iacovino in this volume). In 1977, Bill 22 was replaced by the more comprehensive Bill 101. This time the criterion determining access to English-language schools was not the child's proficiency in English – which could have been acquired in Canada – but the mother tongue of the parents. This new criterion was to be determined by whether or not the parents had received English-language education in Québec. The idea was to reserve English-language education to indigenous Anglophones only (Milner, 1986). Not surprisingly, Bill 101 came under attack from English-Canada. After a number of legal challenges, in 1988 the Supreme Court declared that Bill 101 violated the Canadian Charter or Rights and Freedoms. But using the 'notwithstanding clause' allowing legislatures to override certain portions of the Charter, the Québec government reinstated the legislation as the new Bill 178.

The successive language legislation managed at first to slow down the tendency of immigrant communities to adopt English and integrate into the Anglophone culture. With the new younger generation of Québécois with immigrant origins who had come of age under French-language education (the so-called 'children of Bill 101', *enfants de la loi 101*), the tendency of immigrants to adopt English began to decline (Castonguay, 1994: 142–143). Furthermore, many English-Canadians who could not adjust to the Québec government's new activism left the province, while the number of indigenous Anglophones with English-language proficiency increased (Rudin, 1993: 338–348; Guindon, 1988: 38–59). But despite the decline in the demographic tendency of immigrants to adopt English, Francophones were still likely to suffer from a lingering sense of cultural insecurity (Gidengil et al., 2004: 345–369; see also, Laczko, 1995). While the asymmetrical weakness of the French language in North America kept the sense of cultural threat alive, the division between immigrants and French-Canadians was no longer a main line of cleavage in Québec (Bolduc and Fortin, 1990: 54–77). The tensions between indigenous Anglophones and French-Canadians also started showing signs of abatement (Stevenson, 2003). In the last few decades, Québec has become more inclusive than it had historically been. A broader and more inclusive definition of being Québécois together with language legislation has managed to bring about a more heterogeneous self-image for Québec united by the French language and its territory (Kymlicka, 2001: 61–83). This change should not mean, however, that all supporters of Parti Québécois share this moderate frame of mind. On the night of the 1995 referendum on sovereignty, which nationalists narrowly lost with 49.42 per cent of the vote, the Québec Premier at the time, Jacques Parizeau, bitterly voiced a sentiment that some Parti Québécois voters had been privately contemplating: "It is true, it is true that basically we have been defeated, but by what? By money and the ethnic vote simply".[4] Parizeau's comment about money refers to the deep coffers of the federalist camp in the run-up to the vote and was a widely shared sentiment, but the comment on the 'ethnic vote' was a big liability for a party that needed all the votes that it could get.

Following the defeat of the referendum in 1995 and a change in leadership, the Parti Québécois government took a number of additional steps to reach out to the immigrant communities. A new Ministry of Citizenship was set up. French language as the medium of public life in Québec was put at the core of a new concept of citizenship (see Chapter 5 by Iacovino in this volume).[5] Emphasizing the role of language rather than ethnic roots was a way to continue expanding the boundaries of membership to Québécois who did not have French-Canadian ethnic origins (Gagnon and Iacovino, 2004: 360–388). According to Joseph Carens, the Québec Government's policies expect immigrants to adopt French as a language, but not French-Canadian history and culture as part of collective identity (Carens, 2000: 107–39; see also, Carens, 1995a). The Québec Government uses the term 'interculturalism' to distinguish its policies from the multiculturalism policies of the Canadian government (Gouvernement du Québec, 1990: 15). While recognizing ethnic, racial, religious, and cultural plurality, inclusion is to be attained through the use of French as the language of a common public space (Gouvernement du Québec, 1994: 11). To quote Joseph Carens: 'The central message seems clear. If you want to belong in Quebec, both feel that you belong and to have the rest of the population feel that you belong, you have to learn French and accept the central place of the French language in Quebec society' (Carens, 2000: 115; see also, Carens, 1995b).

Facing the threat of separatist Québec nationalism, the Canadian Government has also made the integration of immigrants a priority. In 1988, the Federal Government passed the Multiculturalism Act. The multicultural idea had been around since the late 1960s, but it had never been formalized into a federal policy. Some observers believe that multiculturalism in fact built on the policies and practices used in dealing with the French-English divide (Forbes, 1993: 78). Prime Minister Pierre-Elliot Trudeau endorsed multiculturalism in 1971, but specific legislation operationalizing the policy was late to follow. There is basically a consensus among political parties on immigration both within Québec and federally. It was a Liberal government that had endorsed multiculturalism in 1971, but a Conservative government passed the Multiculturalism Act.

In Québec, multiculturalism was initially seen as a way to dilute the dualism of the Canadian political system based on the 1867 French-English federal compact. Kenneth McRoberts believes that an inherent tension between dualism and multiculturalism exists (McRoberts, 2003: 103). Seen through this perspective, under multiculturalism Québécois were to become yet one minority group amongst many. According to Daniel Salée, this point of view persists, and many Québécois continue to believe that official multiculturalism trivializes Québec's claims for a distinct identity (Salée, 1995: 280). However, in the rest of the country, the 1988 Multiculturalism Act was welcomed as a reflection of a new Canadian society beyond the French-English duality.

The natural result of all of this was that immigrant communities benefited from the competition between the Canadian Government and Québec as both sides tried to win over the immigrants. According to Nathalie Lavoie and Pierre Serré: 'The existence of these two poles of language and identity inevitably leads to the emergence of a pull among the immigrants in Montréal upon which the two majority groups, French and English, compete to bring immigrants into their ranks'.[6] The electoral system allows these 'two poles of language and identity' to be reflected in the available political choices as well.

An important characteristic of the first-past-the-post Westminster system is its tendency to produce legislatures dominated by two big parties opposing one another (Duverger, 1954: 217).[7] In Québec, for a long time this opposition was reflected in the stand-off between the nationalist Parti Québécois (PQ) and the pro-federalist Quebec Liberal Party (PLQ). The Westminster system is based on the principle of parliamentary sovereignty which means that the party with the majority of seats forms the government while the only role the opposition can play is merely a government-in-waiting. This role tends to produce an adversarial parliamentary system; even the seating arrangements where opposition and government face each other with no room for shades of opinion in between underpins the confrontational zero-sum nature of political competition. Quite simply, one party ends up governing while the other sits until the next election and holds the government to account. It is in this system that parties following 'catch-all' strategies aiming for the median voter are generally rewarded with more seats. So the zero-sum competition the majoritarian system creates two big political parties that coexist with incentives for inclusiveness at the party level. While the electoral system encourages compromises within political blocks, it also brings in a more confrontational 'us versus them' type of politics. Since all parliamentary seats are up for grabs, the result is a competition to get the immigrant vote. According to the PQ's statute adopted on 5 June 2005:

> Everyone, independent of their social origins, their ancestry, or the time of their arrival in Québec, must be able to recognize and develop a sense of belonging to Québec based on their own references and experiences. The Québec nation is enriched by the diversity acquired in the last three decades...
>
> In order to maintain and increase international immigration to our territory, Parti Québécois intends to favour the retention of immigrants by measures of integration through work, the recognition of the attained learning and training, as well as by the development of a sense of belonging to the Québec nation (Parti Québécois 2005: sections 2.2.2. B and 4.2.2. B).[8]

However, it should be noted that the desire to bring in as many new recruits as possible coexists with reservations that a section of PQ voters hold towards immigration. Parizeau's referendum night outburst was an example of this. More recent examples have come from the PQ's rural heartland. The surreal 'code of conduct for immigrants' passed by the residents of the town of Hérouxville in 2007, which asks immigrants in their town not to stone adulterers or burn them alive and to refrain from the genital mutilation of women, has been an embarrassment to progressive Québec nationalists. The hearings held the following year by the Gérard Bouchard/Charles Taylor 'Consultation Commission on Accommodation Practices Related to Cultural Differences' in towns across rural Québec has exposed a noticeable anti-immigrant current as well. But these views representing a section of the party's members and supporters are not reflected in the party programme. The majoritarian system's pressures towards building pre-election political alliances capable of winning seats ensures that groups that might have reservations about the inclusion of immigrants are forced to accept the centrist line.[9] Students of electoral and party politics highlight this tendency of first-past-the-post electoral systems to produce broad alliances where various strands of opinion and interest tend to join forces.[10] Despite the similarities between Québéois and Flemish nationalist movements outlined in the beginning of this section, the picture in Flanders is quite different in terms of the positions of nationalist parties towards immigrants.

Flanders/Belgium

In the decades following the end of the Second World War, the tension between Flemings and Francophones was accentuated by the socio-economic transformation of Belgium. A country once characterized by Francophone economic domination over the numerically greater but rural and underdeveloped Flemings witnessed the rapid economic growth of the northern region of Flanders while Wallonia's traditional manufacturing industries faced decline. These changes gave resurgent Flemish nationalism an additional political clout. In 1954, a party explicitly committed to Flemish self-rule was set up. The party was initially called *Christelijke Vlaamse Volksunie* ('Christian Flemish People's Union'), but later changed its name to *Volksunie* ('People's Union'). Like Québécois nationalism, the driving force in Flemish nationalism was a desire to reverse the linguistic/cultural inequity. Flemings sought to redress the historical grievance by building an alternative nationalist project to that of the parent state while internally trying to stop and reverse the cultural imbalance between the two languages.

The 30 July 1963 law on education divided primary and secondary education into Francophone and Dutch language halves between Flanders and Wallonia. But the mainly Francophone Brussels region situated in Flanders was to remain a special case where education would be in French or Dutch depending on the mother tongue of the pupils. According to the law, the 'head of the family' would make a language declaration to establish the 'mother tongue'; however an important part of the law was that this declaration was subject to verification by officials. The underlying aim of this provision was to prevent parents from making a choice for the language of their children's education. This was a limitation on the old principle of the *liberté de père de famille* ('liberty of the father of the family') which had determined the language of education in the capital. At the insistence of Flemish leaders, the law was installed in order to prevent Brussels Flemings from sending their children to more prestigious Francophone schools. The 1962–1963 state reforms abolished the bilingual schools in Brussels. All of the schools which offered courses in both languages had to become unilingual. The language laws were initially designed to reverse the demographic trend of Brussels Flemings assimilating into the Francophone culture, but the growing number of newcomers found themselves subjected to the same pressures (see Chapter 4 by Adam and Jacobs in this volume). This pull between 'two poles of language and identity' shows remarkable parallels with Québec/Canada; and so does modern Flemish nationalism. Externally seeking further powers of self-rule and internally pursuing a project of cultural rejuvenation unite these two nationalist movements. But the Belgian party system's accompanying proportional representation did not come with similar pressures to build broad alliances.

Starting in the 1960s, nationalist positions in varying degrees found their way into the party programmes of mainstream Flemish parties. In the meantime, more radical elements within the Volksunie left the party and founded a hard-line nationalist party, the Vlaams Blok, in 1978. During the 1980s, the party carved a niche for itself on the right of the political spectrum by championing the causes of Flemish nationalism, anticommunism, anti-abortion, and pro-amnesty for Nazi collaborators. With the end of the Cold War, the party discovered immigration as a new issue that would set it apart from the other parties. In June 1992, the party published a 'Program of 70 Points' aiming to combat immigration:

> If we want to protect the distinctiveness of our nation, we must resolutely refuse the integration of non-European foreigners...The presence of many immigrants changes our lives, slowly but surely. The way streets look changes, the quality of education declines, criminality rises, unemployment increases...
>
> The repatriation [of immigrants] is to happen in an organized, supervised, and humane manner. Vlaams Blok foresees three different phases: the immediate repatriation of illegals, criminals and the unemployed; the repatriation of first generation foreigners; and the repatriation of second and third generation foreigners (Vlaams Blok, 1992: chapters II and X).[11]

In addition to the compulsory repatriation of all immigrants up to the third generation, the 70 Points also called for educational apartheid and a separate system of social security for immigrants that would cover the costs of their repatriation.

Under its older name, Vlaams Blok had received 24.2 per cent of the vote in the 13 June 2004 regional elections. With 32 deputies, the newly renamed Vlaams Belang was the largest single party in the Flemish parliament (although the party's support decreased in the June 2009 regional elections). One should also note that, while being the strongest, Vlaams Belang is not the only Flemish nationalist party.

In addition to a number of now defunct Flemish nationalist parties (such as the centrist *Volkunie* and left-liberal *Spirit*), Flemish nationalists of different colours have their own parties. Centre-right nationalists are within the *Nieuw-Vlaamse Alliantie* N-VA ('New Flemish Alliance') while left nationalists are within the ranks of *Vlaamse-Socialistiche Beweging* ('Flemish Socialist Movement'). This picture is inevitably related to the way the Belgian electoral system structures the political landscape. There is a premium for parties to establish distinct political platforms that target core constituencies and nurture long-term relationships with these groups. Furthermore, in a political landscape characterized by a multiplicity of parties (currently there are 13 parties represented in the Belgian Parliament), no party can govern on its own. This means that smaller parties with narrow agendas and a small percentage of the vote can be part of coalition governments. Thus, seeking office and maximizing votes do not necessarily mean the same thing.[12] Pippa Norris outlines the impact proportional systems have in the following way: 'In proportional electoral systems with low thresholds and large district magnitudes...parties and candidates can be returned to parliament by appealing to a far narrower segment of the population, which could be expected to exacerbate class, faith-based, or ethnic bonding strategies in plural societies' (Norris, 2004: 101). Donald Horowitz shares Norris' view: 'If many social groups are organized into separate parties, each of which can gain a small fraction of the total seats, the likelihood is that political differences will be magnified rather than compressed' (Horowitz, 2003: 121–122). Gary Cox's work on electoral systems shows how proportional systems create incentives for parties to pursue non-centrist policies (Cox, 1990: 903–935). Others have also drawn attention to the risks proportional representation presents for countries with ethnic or cultural divisions (Lardeyret, 2006: 88). According to Norris, the result is that social cleavages tend to become more politically salient in proportional electoral systems:

> Therefore, if electoral systems shape the electoral incentives for political actors to either reinforce their bonds with core homogeneous groups of supporters, or to dilute these linkages with bridging appeals to heterogeneous groups, and if parties have the strategic capacity to respond rationally to these electoral rewards, then cleavage voting should be stronger under proportional than majoritarian electoral systems (Norris, 2004: 101).

The result is that Belgium's electoral system not only represents the underlying cleavages within Belgian politics but it further fragments the electorate through what might be called a narcissism of minor differences. Coalition-building takes place after the election once parties which have managed to portion out narrow and clearly defined ideological appeals gain seats in the Parliament. In a first-past-the-post system, Flemish nationalists would not have been able to win a seat without a pre-election coalition within the ranks of one party and a centrist appeal.

The effects of proportional representation are underscored by the Belgian constitutional practice of formally fixing the number of seats per linguistic community. There is thus little incentive to win the loyalty of the immigrants within the battle for Brussels since Flemish and Francophone seats are fixed for the Capital Region. The Parliament of the Brussels-Capital Region has 89 seats, 17 of which are reserved for Flemings (Coffé, 2006: 99–107). These fixed seats remove the competitive characteristic that the majoritarian system produces in Canada.[13] Besides, voters choose between separate lists of Flemish and Francophone candidates anyway. The result is that, compared to Canada, Belgian political parties and the competing sub-state nationalist movements do not face the same degree of urgency to integrate the immigrant vote. Recent overtures towards the immigrant vote by smaller parties like the Flemish left-liberal *Spirit* and the Francophone post-Christian Democrat *CdH* have failed to bring in a decisive change in the parties' electoral performance. While the biggest Francophone party – the socialist PS – seems to have a better track record in attracting immigrants to its ranks, there has been opposition within the party itself towards the further incorporation of immigrants (Favell and Martiniello, 2003: 13).

Conclusion

Different electoral systems reward different political strategies. This, however, is not an automatic process. Instead, the impact is an indirect one in terms of providing different political incentives in two different institutional contexts. The majoritarian Westminster system is known to beget a confrontational winner-takes-all type of political competition, but high electoral stakes make it imperative to expand the voter base. The system encourages parties to cast a political net as wide as possible. Electoral pressures force parties to appeal to a broad range of political groups and a wide collection of diverse interests. Furthermore, this is an electoral system that tends to produce single-party governments. It is, therefore, only natural that office-seeking parties will seek to maximize their votes. As the composition of PQ demonstrates, constituencies of political parties in majoritarian systems tend to be more heterogeneous – since these are in many ways pre-election coalitions. In Belgium, on the other hand, coalitions are formed after elections among political parties with distinct ideological/ethnic/religious/linguistic agendas and a small fraction of the vote. The proportional system does not come with similar incentives rewarding 'catch-all' strategies aimed at the median voter. Together with the fixed number of seats between Flemings and Francophones, the perpetual big coalitions governing Belgium might initially appear as useful consociational devices for managing divided societies, but these also help seal off the immigrant vote.

The above comparison of the nationalist parties in Québec and Flanders, their policy positions towards immigration, and the role of their respective electoral systems relies on a perspective that highlights how different political incentives arise from different electoral institutions. The full story for each case is always a little more complex and contingent on a number of *sui generis* details of course. Eve Hepburn's work shows how the rise of the anti-immigrant *Action démocratique du Québec* (ADQ) in the early 2000s pushed the PQ to take a more hard-line stance on immigration and Québec citizenship (Hepburn, 2011). The presence of a Québec nationalist party to the right of PQ had threatened the party's catch-all left-centrism. But ADQ did not survive the first-past-the-post electoral environment in the long run however, and Québec nationalism has gone back to its pro-immigrant left-centrism. Régis Dandoy's work on Belgium shows how a similar dynamic also affects Belgian parties as they also have to change some of their positions in response to what other parties do (see Chapter 10 by Dandoy in this volume).

The aim of this chapter is therefore not to reduce everything under the sun to electoral systems. Rather, the aim is to call attention to an under-explored side-benefit of majoritarian electoral systems, despite their well-documented shortcomings. It is also imperative to note that the argument that this chapter rests on is not about the role of electoral systems and anti-immigrant parties only. It is about how different electoral systems come with different structural and long-term political incentives for political parties. First-past-the-post electoral systems tend to produce broad alliances where various strands of opinion and interest tend to join forces, while proportional electoral systems allow political parties with narrow agendas and a small percentage of the vote to become part of governments. While first-past-the-post voting creates centrist incentives for political parties – akin to pre-election coalitions – the proportional electoral systems further fragment the electorate. As a counter-factual thought exercise, just imagine what type of political parties would exist in the United States had there been a proportional system ...

Notes

1. According to Will Kymlicka, there is a dearth of work dealing with the relationship between immigrants and nationalist movements as these topics are discussed in isolation from one another (Kymlicka, 2001: 62); in addition to Kymlicka, an exception is Hepburn (2009). Work that combines nationalism, immigration, and electoral politics, on the other hand, is virtually non-existent.
2. For example, the province of Ontario recently explored the possibilities for electoral reform. The Ontario Citizens' Assembly on Electoral Reform, made up of 103 randomly selected Ontarians, released a report on 15 May 2007 proposing a new provincial electoral system based on mixed-member proportional representation. Ontarians, however, failed to endorse the new electoral system in a provincial referendum held on 10 October 2007; http://www.citizensassembly.gov.on.ca/. The chief electoral officer of Québec has also recently released a report proposing reforms to the provincial electoral system on 21 December 2007.
3. For a collection of views on the future of Québécois identity, see Venne (2000).
4. "C'est vrai, c'est vrai qu'on a été battus, au fond, par quoi? Par l'argent puis des votes ethniques, essentiellement" Jacques Parizeau, 30 October 1995.
5. For an earlier discussion of the relationship between immigration and French language as a medium for public life, see Caldwell (1988: 8).
6. "La présence de ces deux pôles linguistiques et identitaire crée inévitablement parmi les CIIRM [citoyens issus de l'immigration de la région montréalaise] un tiraillement sur lequel jouent les deux groupes majoritaires, français et anglais, pour attirer les immigrants au sein de leurs rangs", (Lavoie and Serré, 2002: 59).
7. For an overview of the relationship between majoritarian electoral systems and two-party systems, see Riker (1982: 752–766).
8. Translated from the original French by the author.
9. A similar logic can be observed in Donald Horowitz's stand advocating Westminster-type majoritarian electoral systems for ethnically divided societies due to the incentive these bring in terms of appealing to broader political alliances (see Horowitz, 1991).
10. For more on electoral systems and party politics, see Sartori (1976); and Mair (1990).
11. Translated from the original Dutch by the author.
12. For further discussion on the different objectives of political parties, see Müller and Strøm (1999: 101).

13. The practice of formally fixing the number of seats per linguistic community exists at the federal level as well. The Belgian lower House of Parliament, the Chamber of Representatives, is composed of 150 directly elected deputies. Of this 150, 91 are Flemings and 59 Francophones. The upper House of Parliament, the Senate, is composed of 71 members: 40 are directly elected, 25 of this 40 are Flemings, 15 are Francophones. There are four co-opted Francophone senators, and six Flemings. The Council of the French Community appoints 10 senators, another 10 are appointed by the Flemish executive, and one senator is appointed by the Council of the German-speaking community.

References

S.M. Arnopoulos and D. Clift (1980) 'English Business and French Nationalism' in Arnopoulos and Clift, *The English Fact in Québec* (Montréal: McGill-Queen's University Press).

M. Behiels (1987) 'Quebec: Social Transformation and Ideological Renewal, 1940–1976' in M. Behiels (ed.) *Quebec Since 1945: Selected Readings*. (Toronto: Copp Clark Pitman).

J.W. Berry, R. Kalin and D.M. Taylor (1976) *Multiculturalism and Ethnic Attitudes in Canada*. (Ottawa: Supply and Services Canada).

A. Blais and R. Nadeau (1984) 'L'appui au parti québécois: évolution de la clientèle de 1970 à 1981' in J. Crête (ed.) *Comportement électorale au Québec*. (Chicoutimi: Gaétan Morin).

D. Bolduc and P. Fortin (1990) 'Les francophones sont-ils plus "xénophobes" que les Anglophones au Québec? Une analyse quantitative exploratoire', *Canadian Ethnic Studies*, 22: 54–77.

A. Cairns (1991) 'Political Scientists and the Constitutional Crisis: The View From Outside Québec' in T.J. Courchene and A.E. Stewart (eds) *Essays on Canadian Public Policy*. (Kingston, ON: Queen's University).

G. Caldwell (1988) 'Immigration et la nécessité d'une culture publique commune', *L'Action Nationale*, 78.

J. Carens (1995a) 'Liberalism, Justice, and Political Community: Theoretical Perspectives on Quebec's Liberal Nationalism' in Carens (ed.) *Is Quebec Nationalism Just? Perspectives from Anglophone Canada*. (Montréal and Kingston: McGill-Queen's University Press).

J. Carens (1995b) 'Immigration, Political Community, and the Transformation of Identity' in Carens (ed.) *Is Quebec Nationalism Just?* (Montreal: McGill-Queen's University Press).

J. Carens (2000) 'Cultural Adaptation and the Integration of Immigrants: The Case of Québec' in Carens (ed.) *Culture, Citizenship and Community: A Contextual Exploration of Justice and Evenhandedness*. (Oxford: Oxford University Press).

C. Castonguay (1994) *L'assimilation linguistique: mesure et évolution*, dossier 41. (Sainte-Foy: Conseil de la langue française).

H. Coffé (2006) '"The Vulnerable Institutional Complexity": The 2004 Regional Elections in Brussels', *Regional and Federal Studies*, 16(1): 99–107.

G.W. Cox (1990) 'Centripetal and Centrifugal Incentives in Electoral Systems', *American Journal of Political Science*, 34(4): 903–935.

R. Cook (1966) 'The Meaning of Confederation' in R. Cook (ed.) *Canada and the French Canadian Question*. (Toronto: Macmillan).

R. Cook (1995) 'Au Diable avec le Goupillon et la Tuque: The Quiet Revolution and the New Nationalism' in R. Cook (ed.) *Canada, Québec and the Uses of Nationalism*, 2nd edn. (Toronto: McClelland and Stewart).

K. Deprez (1985) 'The Dutch Language in Flanders' in T. Hermans, L. Vos and L. Wils (eds) *The Flemish Movement, A Documentary History 1780–1990*. (London and Atlantic Highlands NJ, Athlone).

W. Dewachter (1992) *De duelistische identiteit van de Belgische maatschappij*. (Koninklijke Nederlandse Akademie van Wetenschappen, Amsterdam: Noord-Hollandsche).

Durham, the Earl of [1839] (1902) *The Report of the Earl of Durham Her Majesty's High Commissioner and Governor General of British North America*. (London: Methuen).

M. Duverger (1954) *Political Parties: Their Organization and Activity in the Modern State* (London: Methuen).

A. Favell and M. Martiniello (2003) 'Multi-national, Multi-cultural and Multi-leveled Brussels: National and Ethnic Politics in the "Capital of Europe"', *Transnational Communities Online Working Papers*, http://www.transcomm. ox.ac.uk/working_papers.htm, accessed 26 July 2006.

H.D. Forbes (1993) 'Canada: From Bilingualism to Multiculturalism', *Journal of Democracy*, 4(4): 69–84.

A.-G. Gagnon and R. Iacovino (2004) 'Interculturalism: Expanding the Boundaries of Citizenship' in A.-G. Gagnon (ed.) *Québec: State and Society*, 3rd edn. (Peterborough, ON: Broadview Press).

R. Gibbins (1987) 'Federal Societies, Institutions, and Politics' in H. Bakvis and W. Chandler (eds) *Federalism and the Role of the State*. (Toronto, Buffalo and London: University of Toronto Press).

E. Gidengil, A. Blais, R. Nadeau and N. Nevitte (2004) 'Language and Cultural Insecurity' in A.-G. Gagnon (ed.) *Québec: State and Society*, 3rd edn. (Peterborough, ON: Broadview Press).

Gouvernement du Québec (1990) *Au Québec pour bâtir ensemble. Énoncé de politique en matière d'immigration et d'intégration*. (Québec: Ministère des Communautés culturelles et de l'Immigration du Québec, Direction des communication).

Gouvernement du Québec, Conseil des relations interculturelles (1994) 'Culture publique commune et cohésion sociale: le contrat moral d'intégration des immigrants dans un Québec francophone, démocratique et pluraliste', in *Gérer la diversité dans un Québec francophone, démocratique et pluraliste: principes de fond et de procédure pour guider la recherche d'accommodements raisonnables*.

H. Guindon (1988) 'Two Cultures: An Essay on Nationalism, Class, and Ethnic Tension' in H. Guindon (ed.) *Quebec Society: Tradition, Modernity, and Nationhood*, (Toronto: Toronto University Press).

E. Hepburn (2009) 'Regionalist Party Mobilisation on Immigration', *West European Politics*, 32(3): 514–535.

E. Hepburn (2011) 'Citizens of the Region. Party Conceptions of Regional Citizenship and Immigrant Integration', *European Journal of Political Research*, 50(4): 504–529.

D.L. Horowitz (1991) *A Democratic South Africa? Constitutional Engineering in a Divided Society*. (Berkeley: University of California Press).

D.L. Horowitz (2003) 'Electoral Systems: A primer for Decision makers', *Journal of Democracy*, 14(4): 121–122.

Institut Bruxellois Statistique et d'Analyse IBSA (2005) *Indicateurs Statistiques de la Région de Bruxelles-Capitale, Tableaux*. (Brussels: Ministère de la Région de Bruxelles-Capitale).

W. Kymlicka (2001) 'Immigrant Integration and Minority Nationalism' in M. Keating and J. McGarry (eds) *Minority nationalism and the Changing International Order*. (Oxford: Oxford University Press).

N. Lacoste (1973) 'The Catholic Church in Québec: Adapting to Change' in D.C. Thomson (ed.) *Québec Society and Politics: Views from the Inside*. (McClelland and Stewart).

L.S. Laczko (1995) *Pluralism and Inequality in Québec*. (Toronto: Toronto University Press).

G. Lardeyret (2006) 'The Problem with PR' in L. Diamond and M. Platterner (eds) *Electoral Systems and Democracy*. (Baltimore: Johns Hopkins University Press).

N. Lavoie and P. Serré (2002) 'Du vote bloc au vote social: le cas des citoyens issus de l'immigration de Montréal, 1995–1996', *Canadian Journal of Political Science / Revue canadienne de science politique*, 35(1): 49–74.

P. Mair (ed.) (1990) *The West European Party System*. (Oxford: Oxford University Press).

R. Manzer (1994) *Public Schools and Political Ideas: Canadian Educational Policy in Historical Perspective*. (Toronto: University of Toronto Press).

M. Martiniello (2003) 'Belgium's Immigration Policy', *International Migration Review*, 37(1): 225–232.

K. McRae (1986) *Conflict and Compromise in Multilingual Societies: Belgium*. (Waterloo: Wilfrid Laurier University Press).

K. McRoberts (2003) 'Conceiving Diversity: Dualism, Multiculturalism, and Multinationalism' in F. Rocher and M. Smith (eds) *New Trends in Canadian Federalism*, 2nd edn. (Peterborough: Broadview).

H. Milner (1986) *The Long Road to Reform: Restructuring Public Education in Québec*. (Montréal: McGill-Queen's University Press).

W.C. Müller and K. Strøm (1999) *Policy, Office or Votes: How Parties in Western Europe make Difficult Decisions*. (Cambridge: Cambridge University Press).

P. Norris (2004) *Electoral Engineering: Voting Rules and Electoral Behavior*. (Cambridge: Cambridge University Press).

Parti Québécois (2005) *Un projet de pays: déclaration de principes, programme de pays, statut du Parti Québécois*, adopted on 5 June 2005.

W. Riker (1982) 'The Two-Party System and Duverger's Law: An Essay on the History of Political Science', *American Political Science Review*, 76: 752–766.

R. Rudin (1993) 'English Speaking Québec: The Emergence of a Disillusioned Minority' in A.-G. Gagnon (ed.) *Québec: State and Society*, 2nd edn. (Scarborough: Nelson).

D. Salée (1995) 'Identities in Conflict: The Aboriginal Question and the Politics of Recognition in Québec', *Ethnic and Racial Studies*, 18(2): 277–314.

G. Sartori (1976) *Parties and party Systems*. (Cambridge: Cambridge University Press).

R. Senelle with Edgard van de Velde and Emiel Clement (1999) *Kronieken van de Vlaamse Staatswording, Over de Identiteit van het Vlaming-Zijn*. (Lannoo: Tielt).

G. Stevenson (2003) 'English Speaking Québec: A Political History' in A.-G. Gagnon (ed.) *Québec: State and Society*, 3rd edn. (Peterborough: Broadview).

M. Venne (ed.) (2000) *Penser la nation québécoise*. (Montréal: Québec-Amérique).

Vlaams Blok (1992) *Immigratie: de Oplossingen. 70 voorstellen ter oplossing van het vreemdelingenprobleem*, adopted on 6 June 1992.

12
Immigration, Nationalism, and Politics in Scotland

Eve Hepburn and Michael Rosie

Introduction

Scotland has been vaunted for following a distinctive – and arguably progressive – path on policy issues within the United Kingdom (Bradbury and Mitchell, 2001; Keating, 2010). However, while key devolved policy issues such as education, healthcare, and environmental policy have received considerable attention (Paterson, 1997; Greer, 2005; McEwen, Bomberg and Swenden, 2010; Cairney, 2011), there is a notable research gap on reserved areas such as immigration. This is a key oversight given compelling evidence that Scotland is developing a distinctive approach to immigration, and in particular the social and political integration of migrants. Although immigration is reserved to Westminster, its impact on devolved policy issues has caused Scotland's parties to take a stance on this issue. Markedly, the positions of Scottish parties have diverged considerably from the UK party norm.

It is striking that while the 2010 UK election was characterized by an overwhelmingly hostile debate with parties vying to erect the most stringent barriers to immigration, the 2011 Scottish election exhibited a party consensus that immigration was a laudable, necessary, and positive thing for Scotland. Furthermore, while explicitly pan-UK nationalists – the British National Party (BNP) and the United Kingdom Independence Party (UKIP) – promulgate the most virulent anti-immigrant rhetoric, Scotland's governing Scottish National Party (SNP) adopts a very positive attitude towards immigrants. Indeed, the SNP is probably the most pro-immigrant of the major parties in the United Kingdom as a whole, confounding any assumption that minority nations, and in particular, minority nationalists, necessarily view immigration as a threat to their indigenous culture and traditions (see, Zapata-Barrero, 2007; Hepburn,

2011; Banting and Soroka, 2012. See also, Dandoy, Erk, Franco-Guillén and Zapata-Barrero and Schmidtke and Zaslove, in this volume). Instead, an elite discourse has been carefully created by Scotland's parties, especially the SNP and Scottish Labour, which presents immigrants as key players in an open, inclusive, and multicultural Scottish nation.

In line with the general aims of this collection, we seek to explore why immigration has been positively viewed by political parties in Scotland, in contrast to the more negative perception of immigrants at the UK level. In particular, we focus on the role of Scottish parties in creating a positive discourse about immigration through the concept of 'One Scotland'. This approach was initiated by the Labour-Liberal Democrat coalition in the first two sessions of the Scottish Parliament (1999–2007) and continued by the ruling SNP administration from 2007 onwards. Following from the conceptual framework set out by Hepburn in Chapter 3 of this volume, we explore four hypotheses for why immigration has been positively viewed in Scottish political circles. Two of these hypotheses concern socio-demographic factors and two correspond with political-economic factors.

> H1: Immigration is viewed positively by Scottish political parties because of low barriers to becoming a member of the nation.

Scholarship often refers to 'barriers' to national membership. These generally include birth, residence, and ancestry, but may also include language, accent, dress, and engagement in the national culture. Below we examine 'barriers' to becoming Scottish, in particular the absence of an additional language hurdle (present in sub-state nations such as Quebec and Catalonia). Furthermore, we explore Scottish identity as presenting low barriers for membership. We assume that this positively impacts parties' views of immigration, and the degree to which 'new Scots' can share/participate in the national culture.

> H2: Immigration is viewed positively by Scottish parties because of low levels of immigration and a demographic labour shortage.

High levels of immigration can often incite hostility, especially in countries with high population density. We examine the Scottish demographic situation, in particular the concerns of an ageing population and falling birth rates which have fuelled fears of Scotland falling below the symbolic 'five million' population mark.

H3: Immigration is viewed positively by Scottish parties because of low party polarization on immigration.

Next, we examine the extent to which Scottish politics is divided over immigration. Polarization tends to create a negative or unstable political climate on immigration. A strong anti-immigrant party may exacerbate polarization as mainstream parties 'accommodate' restrictions on immigration to prevent electoral outflanking from the right. Furthermore, the stance of nationalist parties, where they exist, on immigration may influence the position of other political parties. Relatedly, party polarization often results in high media interest on immigration, with commentary also becoming polarized on the issue, feeding back into party positioning.

H4: Immigration is viewed positively by Scottish political parties because of limited control over immigration policy.

Finally we examine whether greater control over immigration policy increases party polarization. Where aspects of immigration enter the remit of a regional assembly then parties must dedicate more time to developing policy. This may also lead to a greater variety of positions as parties produce technical and political details, from entry to integration. Furthermore, where regions have less control over immigration, then it is more likely to be associated with or subsumed under other 'regional' concerns such as economic development, education, or housing.

The remainder of this chapter explores how these hypotheses play out in Scotland. The chapter begins with an overview of the politics of immigration, comparing Scottish party rhetoric and positioning with that found at the UK level. It then explores each hypothesis with reference to the Scottish case. We include an analysis of Scotland's 'inclusive' national identity, the demographic situation, party positioning on immigration, and current devolved control over immigration. We then consider the relationship between immigration and nationalism in Scotland, in particular ethnic minority SNP support.

A Scottish approach to integration

In 2004, the Labour-Liberal Democrat Scottish Executive launched their 'Fresh Talent' initiative to address demographic trends in Scotland. The scheme promoted and encouraged inward migration and (with the agreement of the UK Home Office) extended the work permits of overseas graduates from Scottish Universities. In his foreword to *New Scots: Attracting Fresh Talent to Meet the Challenge of Growth* then First Minister Jack McConnell noted that:

> The single biggest challenge facing Scotland as we move further into the 21st century is our falling population. It is at its lowest level since the first half of the 20th century and is projected to fall below the symbolic 5 million in only five years' time. It is also getting older, with half the population over the age of 39 and the working age population projected to fall ... to below 3 million, by 2027. (Scottish Executive, 2004:1)

Scotland requires significant inward migration to maintain its standard of living and remain economically competitive. McConnell argued that this necessitated both 'a constant flow of fresh talent to flourish alongside our home-grown talent' and a welcoming political and social environment: 'Across the world, Scots enjoy a reputation for being warm, welcoming, friendly people. It is now time to extend that traditional Scottish welcome to the new Scots who will help our country grow' (Scottish Executive, 2004: 1). Notably the reaction of the opposition SNP was to 'unreservedly' support the proposals while calling for greater Scottish powers on immigration. Then SNP leader John Swinney welcomed that: 'The first minister has accepted for the very first time the need for a different approach to immigration north and south of the border' (BBC, 2004).

Party manifestos in 2005 demonstrated commitment to inward migration to improve Scotland's economic resilience. There was wide acceptance of the term 'New Scots', suggesting that those arriving in Scotland from elsewhere could stake some sort of claim to national belonging. The SNP committed to 'pursue an immigration policy that welcomes new Scots and encourages people to move back to Scotland' (SNP, 2005: 6). Scottish Labour argued much the same: 'Scotland needs fresh talent: to boost our population, but also to create a more diverse and dynamic economy. We will attract new people to live and work in Scotland and we want to attract Scots back home too.' This was tempered, however, by adherence to UK Labour's more stringent line on immigration, including fingerprinting, a 'crackdown on abuse', compulsory ID cards, and 'secure borders' (Scottish Labour, 2005: 52–3). Labour's coalition partners were on message, the Scottish Liberal Democrat manifesto arguing that: 'We will work with the Scottish Executive to ensure that decisions taken at Westminster help and do not hinder Scotland's drive to reverse population decline' (Scottish Liberal Democrats, 2005: 11).

Together these three parties comprised the core of Scottish political opinion, taking 74 per cent of the constituency votes in the 2003 Scottish election and 80 per cent of Scotland's votes in the 2005 UK election. The Scottish Conservatives, whose Manifesto pledged to 'bring immigration under control' (Scottish Conservatives, 2005: 2), was the only major party in Scotland not to encourage immigration into Scotland. Instead, and echoing their party's UK-wide policies, they argued that:

...we need to ensure that immigration is effectively managed, in the interests of all Britons, old and new. This Government has lost effective control of our borders. More than 150,000 people come to Britain every year, a population the size of Dundee...Our asylum system is in chaos...Britain has reached a turning-point. That is why a Conservative Government will bring immigration back under control. (Scottish Conservatives, 2005: 21)

The Conservative position here was, notably, on *Britain* rather than Scotland. Equally notably, Conservatism proved, yet again, a minority taste in Scotland with just 16 per cent of Scotland's 2005 vote and just one Scottish Westminster seat.

Fresh Talent built on earlier Scottish Executive initiatives, such as an Equalities agenda, hate crime legislation, and campaigns promoting 'One Scotland, Many Cultures'. Such progressive policies found a broad consensus of principle comprising the Labour-Liberal Democrats coalition and the SNP opposition. Smaller parties – Greens, Socialists, and independents – also encouraged increased immigration and a welcoming attitude towards 'New Scots'. Two key issues tempered these trends. Labour and, to a less marked extent the Liberal Democrats, have to reconcile their progressive positions in Scotland with an increasingly stringent position taken at Westminster. Secondly, the Scottish Conservatives, while rarely explicitly attacking progressive immigration policies, at best tolerate them. The Conservative Party's electoral marginality and, more so, that of the tiny parties to their right suggest that immigration is not key to Scotland's political agenda. This situation contrasts sharply with UK politics where immigration, asylum, nationality, and multiculturalism have proved bitter points of cleavage.

An inclusive national identity

There has been considerable attention to the place of national identities in contemporary Scotland. The ubiquity of Scottish identity – as compared to a gradually declining sense of Britishness – is a key social context for the continued salience of the 'Scottish Question' in UK constitutional politics. A now considerable body of research – in particular that centred around the University of Edinburgh's Institute of Governance – suggests that Scottishness primarily (though by no means exclusively) rests upon territorial or 'civic' markers, in particular where people were born and where they live (see, for example, Kiely et al., 2001, Kiely, Bechhofer and McCrone, 2005; Bond, 2006; Rosie and Bond, 2006). Scottish identification does not spring from the kinds of cultural or ethnic resources which mark out other sub-state nations. Unlike Wales, Catalunya, Québec, or Flanders, Scotland is not marked out 'linguistically' from the nations it shares its state with (see, Adam and Jacobs, Erk, and Arrighi de Casanova in this volume). Indeed few Scots, when asked, buttress claims to Scottishness through reference to their cultural background or ethnic authenticity. Rather, such claims draw upon the 'territorial' resources of birthplace and residence. As Smout (1994: 107) argues: 'Modern Scottish identity is much more firmly allied to a sense of place than to a sense of tribe – "I am a real Scot from Bathgate" has much more resonance than "I am a real Scot because my granny was a real Scot"'.

Emphasis on place and the institutions of everyday life means that Scottish identity has a more territorial than an ethnic basis. There is a very high likelihood that someone born, raised, and currently living in Scotland will not only self-identify as Scottish, but be accepted as Scottish by others. For McCrone (2001: 148): 'It is as if ... the Scots looked to see what was on offer, and have decided to travel light. No cultural icons need to be genuflected at, no correct representation needs to be observed'.

The extent of Scottish inclusivity can be tested in two ways. Firstly, to what degree do those who do not possess key markers (such as place of birth, upbringing, or ancestry) nevertheless claim identification with Scotland? Secondly, are such claims accepted or rejected by a broader public? On both questions the overall pattern is clear. Studies of ethnic minorities generally (Bond, 2011), and specifically on young Muslim men (Hopkins, 2007) and ethnic Pakistanis (Saeed, Blain and Forbes, 1999; Hussain and Miller, 2006), all suggest a widespread Scottish identification. Saeed, Blain and Forbes (1999: 835–836) suggest that Glaswegian Pakistani teenagers for example, are likely to assign themselves a plural identity such as 'Scottish Asian' or 'Scottish Muslim'. Hussain and Miller (2006: 147) find that the overwhelming majority of their sizeable ethnic Pakistani sample (91 per cent) assigned themselves some degree of Scottishness on a 'Moreno' scale, with around half

(49 per cent) being either 'Scottish not British' or 'More Scottish than British'. Hopkins (2007: 66) finds similar results amongst young Muslim men. Substantial evidence relating to Scotland's Catholics – long, and perhaps over-, associated with historic immigration from Ireland – show very high levels of Scottish identification, equal to the other major (ir) religious groups in Scotland (Rosie, 2004).

Scottish identification amongst those of Scotland's residents who were born in England is somewhat lower. Hussain and Miller (2006: 147) find that 53 per cent of their English-immigrant sample assigned themselves as Scottish to some degree though most of these gave equal or greater prominence to Britishness. In part this is because place of birth is a key marker – those born in England do not possess this marker, unlike members of other minority groups who were born in Scotland. An analysis by Rosie (2012) finds a high degree of Scottish identity among English-born people in Scotland who have at least one Scottish-born parent. Such migrants score much more highly on the Moreno scale than English-born migrants without any Scottish parentage (81 per cent of the first group claim *some* degree of Scottishness as compared to 51 per cent of the latter).

So much for the self-identification of particular groups: how are such claims received by the wider Scottish public? A series of questions in Scottish Social Attitudes Surveys propose a number of scenarios relating to markers of Scottishness (earlier results on these questions are explored in Kiely, Bechhofer and McCrone, 2005; Bond, 2006; Rosie and Bond, 2006; McCrone and Bechhofer, 2010). These scenarios measure responses to claims of Scottishness by permanent residents of Scotland, varying place of birth, parentage, and accent. The scenarios run first for a 'white person' and are then repeated for a 'non-white person'.

Table 12.1 reports the percentage who 'definitely' or 'probably' would accept such claims. The vast majority would accept a claim to Scottishness where the claimant is born in Scotland; and a smaller, but still large, majority would accept the claim of someone born in England but who had both Scottish parentage and accent (accent, here, operates as a proxy for where the claimant was raised). Over half would accept the claim of an English-born person with a Scottish accent, and around two-fifths would accept a claim by an English-born person resident in Scotland who had none of the markers.

These data suggest clear limits to inclusiveness in Scotland. Most people would not accept a claim to Scottishness from a resident of Scotland who was born in England and has neither a Scottish accent nor Scottish-born parents. Further, there appears to be a consistent 'ethnic-penalty' for

Table 12.1 Accepting claims of Scottishness

% accepting claim of:	White person	Non-white person
Resident in Scotland, born Scotland	99	87
Resident in Scotland, born England + Scottish accent + parents	80	72
Resident in Scotland, born England + Scottish accent	59	53
Resident in Scotland, born England	43	38

Source: Scottish Social Attitudes Survey, 2009.

non-white claims in each of the scenarios. Nevertheless, a majority of people would accept such claims where one or more marker is added, and even in the case of those born in England and with no 'markers' there is a large minority who would accept such claims. This finding suggests a strongly (though by no means exhaustively) civic basis for Scottishness, and a relatively low threshold to becoming Scottish. The notion of 'new Scots' resonates widely, then, among the Scottish public:

> The fact that place of birth was thought to be central to Scottishness to a greater extent than ethnicity provides at least some evidence to indicate that the kind of open, inclusive Scottish national identity favoured by Scotland's political classes is shared by a wider population. (Rosie and Bond, 2006: 156)

Finally, one can consider attempts to attract support from ethnic minority communities. While Labour in Scotland, as across the rest of Britain, has long been associated with such communities, others have also set out to win minority votes. The SNP has actively courted such support by creating affiliated organizations such as 'Asians for Independence' and 'New Scots for Independence'; by involving ethnic minority representatives in their organization; and by presenting ethnic minority candidates in elections. Scotland's first visible minority MSP, Bashir Ahmad, represented the SNP. Upon his death, warm tributes were paid across the political spectrum, with Alex Salmond describing Ahmad as 'the most patriotic of Scotsmen … a credit to both his faith and to his country' (BBC, 2009). Although minority ethnic groups comprise a tiny proportion of Scotland's electorate, they are 'of enormous moral significance for a party that wished to stress its "civic nationalist" credentials' (Hussain and Miller, 2006: 34). There is some evidence, too, that the SNP's approach has won them considerable benefit. Hussain and Miller (2006: 165) suggest that the SNP's vocal opposition to the Iraq War led to substantial electoral gains among Scotland's ethnic Pakistanis. It might be noted that, *contra* Erk's findings for Quebec and Flanders (in this volume), the electoral system does not appear to play any motivating role in the SNP's position.

The demographic crisis

Scotland's 2001 Census sparked concern over continued out-migration and a persistent decline in the number of births, fuelling fears of an ageing and shrinking population (for more details, see Chapter 6 by Arrighi de Casanova in this volume). In the early 2000s, demographic projections across the European Union highlighted population growth, whereas projections for Scotland predicted decline. Particularly striking in the Registrar General's *Annual Review* for 2001 (GROS, 2002) was that Scotland had experienced a natural decrease (numerically more deaths than births) for the past several years and that 2001 had seen the smallest number of births on record:

> The projected population decline by 2020...is higher than that currently projected for any other European country. Indeed, most countries (including other countries within the UK) are projected to increase in population over this period. The underlying difference is that in other countries assumptions about future levels of migration offset projected declines in natural change (births minus deaths). (GROS, 2002: 11)

Scotland's population worries, therefore, sprang less from declining fertility than from relative failure to attract and retain migrants. Unsurprisingly, therefore, 'Politicians in Scotland from most parts of the political spectrum are united in a desire to stimulate migration still further, particularly of highly qualified migrants.' (Bond, Charsley and Grundy, 2010: 485) The immediacy of the 'population crisis' eased in the intervening decade, with increasing births and greater in-migration (particularly from Accession 8 countries after 2004). These prompted a rise to a historic population high of 5.29 million in the Census of 2011. Current projections anticipate further growth: 'Longer term projections show the population peaking at 5.57 million in the mid 2040s' (GROS, 2011: 21).

Crucially, however, projections of an ageing population remain, as do concerns over increasing 'dependency ratios' and the likelihood that 'increases in the elderly population are likely to place a greater demand on health and social services' (GROS, 2011: 18). Attracting and retaining migrants, particularly young economically active migrants, remains crucial in addressing Scotland's demographic situation. The Registrar General noted: 'The recent increase in Scotland's population has been driven mostly by net in-migration' (GROS, 2011: 15). It is, then, unsurprising that Scotland's political consensus remains sympathetic to increased immigration and developing a welcoming environment by which skilled migrants can be retained.

Party competition on immigration

Immigration, therefore, has failed to become a key polarizing issue within a Scottish party system dominated by two cleavages: the divide on Scotland's constitutional future and the left-right cleavage (Hepburn, 2010). The absence of polarization on immigration sits in sharp contrast to party competition for the United Kingdom or (English) local elections. In the UK, party competition revolves primarily around the left-right axis but is also strongly influenced by 'new' conflict dimensions such as European integration and immigration (Odmalm, 2012). Immigration emerged as one of the key contentious issues in the 2010 UK election. In contrast, during the 2011 Scottish Parliamentary election, immigration was 'scarcely aired ... it is scarcely an issue here in Scotland as it is in much of England' (Massie, 2011). This section examines how Scottish parties compete over immigration, contrasting it to the UK situation. We look at three particularities: (1) the tendency of Scottish party competition to take place on the centre-left; (2) the weakness of anti-immigrant parties in Scotland; and (3) the positive stance of the main nationalist party – the SNP – towards immigration.

Scottish politics is dominated by the centre-left. The three largest parties in the Scottish Parliament: Labour, the SNP, and the Liberal Democrats compete on the left of the political spectrum, while the right is represented by the Conservatives. Tories have been deeply unpopular in Scotland since Margaret Thatcher's Premiership of 1979–1992 and have never recovered from losing all their representation in Scotland in the 1997 UK elections. While achieving better electoral results in the mixed-member system of the Scottish Parliament (as opposed to Westminster's majoritarian system), they remain of marginal influence. Perhaps more important than the left-right divide is the constitutional cleavage, highly polarizing parties on the 'national question' of Scotland's relationship within/towards the UK. Scotland's distinctive structure of party competition, in contrast with UK elections, has had an impact on the immigration question.

First, centre-left parties tend, broadly speaking, to be more favourably disposed towards immigration than centre-right parties. In Scotland, the main centre-left parties – Scottish Labour, the SNP, and Scottish Liberal Democrats – follow this tendency, with the Tories exhibiting a slightly less favourable position. These contrast sharply with the Scottish branches' UK counterparts – the Westminster-focussed Labour, Conservative, and Liberal Democrat parties – which have all in recent years adopted negative and restrictive policies and rhetoric on immigration.

At the UK level, Labour has shifted from an economically motivated liberalization of regulations in their 2001 UK manifesto, through a more 'managed' control of immigration in 2005 (Odmalm, 2012), to advocating a highly restrictive system, linking immigration to enforcement, control, and punishment (Labour, 2010). The Liberal Democrats advocated an approach based on human rights concerns in 2001 (Odmalm, 2012), but by 2010 were linking illegal immigrants with organized crime and advocating 'managing immigration' with a regional points-based system (Grayson, 2010; Liberal Democrats, 2010). Finally, the UK Conservative Party has been the most consistent in its passionate defence of stricter immigration controls (Conservative Party, 2010). Across the major parties the central message of the 2010 UK election was that immigration posed a threat to the British way of life, was linked to crime and security concerns, and that Britain was 'full-up' and immigration should be drastically reduced.

At the Scottish level, parties have refrained from casting immigration as a 'problem'; indeed, immigration has been widely perceived as the only robust way of tackling Scotland's economic and demographic concerns (see Hepburn 2009, 2011). Moreover, Scottish politicians emphasize humanitarian principles in welcoming foreigners to Scotland. Whenever there is a heated debate on immigration in the Scottish Parliament, it is usually to criticize the party or politician in question – be they Scottish or British – for not being humanitarian enough.

Immigrants, refugees, and asylum-seekers are generally portrayed by Scottish politicians as important contributors to Scotland, and significant effort is made to protect their human rights. A case in point is the debate surrounding the UK-controlled Dungavel Detention Centre which houses failed asylum-seekers. In 2008, the SNP issued a Scottish Parliamentary motion calling for an end to the detention of children at

Dungavel (Scottish Parliament, 2008), supported by various civic organizations and endorsed by the other political parties. The Scottish Liberal Democrats have, like the UK party, consistently stressed the humanitarian aspects of immigration and asylum. However, while the UK party moved to a more restrictive position in 2010, the Scottish party maintained a more positive approach. Scottish Labour supports a 'robust and fair' immigration policy that encourages diversity and attracts skilled workers from abroad. Former Labour First Minister Jack McConnell argued for a distinctive Scottish approach to immigration to deal with Scotland's skills shortage, which led to the Fresh Talent initiative. Scottish Labour also put forward a humanitarian approach to immigration, calling for the proper integration of asylum-seekers in Scotland and the humane and sensitive treatment of immigrants. There were strong multicultural undertones to Scottish Labour's approach, which involved a 'One Scotland' campaign that aimed to raise awareness of, and celebrate, Scotland's cultural diversity (Howard and Penrose, 2008). Labour's 2011 Scottish manifesto promised to 'tackle racial or religious prejudice, intolerance and discrimination, [and to] continue support for schemes that celebrate the diversity of Scotland's culture and its people' (Scottish Labour, 2011: 67). However, Scottish Labour's 2010 manifesto for the UK elections, identical to the UK party manifesto, marked a break from the previously humanitarian approach. Linking immigration with crime and security, they advocated an immigration system 'that promotes and protects British values' (Scottish Labour, 2010: 5–6). This may be an indication that Scottish Labour is converging with the broader UK party on immigration in both text and tone.

Finally, the Scottish Conservatives have adopted a less hostile approach to immigration than their UK counterparts. Their 2010 manifesto acknowledged that: 'Immigration has enriched our nation over the years and we want to attract the brightest and the best people who can make a real difference to our economic growth' (Scottish Conservatives, 2010: 20), though warning: 'But immigration today is too high and needs to be reduced'. However, the virulently anti-immigration language of some sections of the UK Conservatives is absent from Scottish Tory rhetoric. For example, after a rise in the Scottish population, the Tory Finance Spokesman noted that:

> traditionally people arriving in Scotland have been younger than the average age of the population, and that is important given we have an ageing demographic ... The majority of people who come to

Scotland want to make an economic and social contribution and it is important they continue to do so. (Scottish Conservatives, 2012)

In addition to the more pro-immigration approach of Scotland's branches of UK-wide parties, Scotland has escaped the development of anti-immigrant parties. The most explicitly anti-immigrant protagonist, the BNP, calls for 'an immediate halt to all further immigration, the immediate deportation of criminal and illegal immigrants, and the introduction of a system of voluntary resettlement' in order to halt the 'extinguishing of Britain and British identity under a tsunami of immigration' (BNP, 2012). The BNP began making electoral breakthroughs in some parts of England in the early 2000s but lost most of its seats in the 2012 English council elections. More recently the UK Independence Party has made advances while advocating the ending of both 'mass, uncontrolled immigration' and 'the active promotion of the doctrine of multiculturalism' (UKIP, 2013). There has been a resultant rush to the right on immigration with the main UK parties locked into a 'rhetorical arms race' over who can sound the toughest (Birrell, 2013). However, the extreme-right have consistently failed to make any impact in Scotland and are not seen as in any way representative of Scottish interests (Rosie, 2011).

While the UK's largest nationalist party is rabidly anti-immigrant, Scotland's largest nationalist party is notably pro-immigration. The SNP's civic and inclusive rhetoric has won over much of the ethnic minority vote in Scotland, in particular with the Muslim community. As discussed earlier, several studies have shown that Muslims in Scotland feel considerably more 'Scottish' than Muslims living in England feel 'English'. Some scholars argue that the smoother integration of minorities can in part be attributed to the positive stance of Scottish political elites towards immigration (Hussain and Miller, 2006).

The SNP articulate a strongly pro-immigration position, where immigrants constitute important members of the Scottish nation as well as contributors to Scottish economic and social well-being (SNP, 2003, 2011). The SNP emphasizes an inclusive Scottish nationality whereby 'citizenship will be established on the basis of residency or birth'. Here anyone living in Scotland – regardless of ethnic background – would qualify for citizenship (SNP, 1997: 7). Seeking to create a culturally diverse Scotland, the SNP also perceives immigration as a way of boosting the labour market and staving off demographic crisis. The SNP argues that Scotland's needs are distinctive (in particular, Scotland does not suffer from the level of over-crowding in some parts of England) and that immigration to Scotland should be significantly increased to address these specific economic, demographic, and community concerns.

In sum, party competition on immigration in Scotland takes a very different tone to that found in England. While UK parties have broadly linked immigration to insecurity and crime, Scottish parties focus on the economic, demographic, and humanitarian positives. Furthermore, while UK parties have portrayed immigration as a threat to British national culture, Scottish parties have broadly embraced the vision of a multicultural Scotland, where they have been 'united and consistent in proclaiming their vision of an "inclusive" Scotland' (Hussain and Miller, 2006: 27). (On civic nationalist impulses in Catalunya see Franco-Guillén and Zapata-Barrero in this volume).

Control over immigration policy

Immigration is a 'reserved' matter in the United Kingdom: policies concerning citizenship and residency are determined at Westminster. As one 'unit' within the UK, Scottish immigration is managed in accordance with UK immigration policy which, since 2008, has been based on a points-based system. Thus, the same visa categories, rules, and regulations for England, Wales, and Northern Ireland apply to Scotland. As a result Scotland's ability to advance its own immigration strategy ultimately depends on the extent to which it can influence UK-wide policy (see, Arrighi de Casanova, this volume).

The Scottish Parliament has sought to influence UK immigration policy with regard to three issues. The first is the inhumane detention of asylum children in Scotland, which crystallized around protests against the Dungavel Detention Centre. Both Labour-Liberal Democrat (1999–2007) and SNP administrations (2007) have called for the UK Home Office to end 'dawn raids' on asylum-seeker families and the detention of children. Scottish parties have argued that this position is justified because, although asylum is a reserved matter, the treatment of children is devolved. In response to Scottish lobbying, the UK Labour Government agreed to end the detention of young children at Dungavel. This was not implemented, however, and when the Conservative-Liberal coalition came to power in the UK in 2010 they too agreed to stop the practice. However children were still being detained in Dungavel in 2012 (Borland, 2012) and there are ongoing concerns over serious human rights abuses at the Centre (Briggs and McKay, 2012).

The second issue was the attempt to obtain some control over graduate immigration in Scotland. In 2004, the Labour-Liberal Democrat

Executive's Fresh Talent initiative was created to attract and retain skilled graduates (Skilling, 2007). Since 2007, the SNP Government has continued the initiative – although the UK-wide move to a migrant points system in 2008 removed the policy's teeth. However, the SNP views Fresh Talent as inadequate to address Scotland's migration needs and argues that Scotland should:

> take responsibility for immigration so that we can develop a system ... that more closely meets our needs. An 'earned citizenship' system ... would allow Scotland to attract high-skill immigrants who can add to the strength of our economy and help deliver growing prosperity for the whole nation. (SNP, 2010: 19)

This led to the third way in which the Scottish Government has sought to influence UK immigration policy. The SNP has argued for the full devolution of immigration policy to enable Scotland to address the particular skills, demographic needs, and labour shortages it faces. The SNP's proposed scheme allowed Scottish ministers to set population targets based on a points system that takes into consideration skills, age, and education (SNP, 2007). The SNP presented their citizenship policy as more open and inclusive than that of Westminster which it accused of operating 'discriminatory' citizenship rules (SNP, 2003). Less radically, Labour and the Liberal Democrats also argued for a Scotland-focussed approach to immigration. But rather than devolving powers, these parties advocated a regionally nuanced points system still controlled from London. The system would give applicants extra points if they moved to UK areas, such as Scotland, in need of increased population. Jim Murphy, former Labour Scottish Secretary, argued that Scotland should become 'a melting pot' by 'identifying the most talented workers for the Scottish economy' and rewarding them in a points system (Murphy, 2009). The Scottish Liberal Democrats argue for a similar system (Scottish Liberal Democrats, 2010).

However, a further scenario is possible: an immigration system controlled by an independent Scotland. The SNP Government will hold a referendum on independence in September 2014, and if successful, Scotland will gain all powers over Scottish residence and citizenship. Full control over immigration may well, of course, have a polarizing side-effect:

> the fact that immigration is a reserved matter might spare us to some extent from attempts to gain electoral advantage by pandering to

fears about migration ... in what can all too easily be constructed as a competition for scarce resources or limited services. (Shin, 2011)

Conclusion

Scotland bucks the European trend of political convergence towards restrictions on immigration. Lacking significant anti-immigrant parties, and bolstered by an elite party consensus, Scottish electoral competition revolves around a broadly centre-left, pro-immigration position. Spearheaded by the two largest parties in Scotland – Scottish Labour and the SNP – key political actors argue in favour of increased immigration. Their rationales have crystallized around several arguments, most notably demographic need (based on Scotland's ageing population), skilled-labour shortage, and humanitarian concerns (especially for refugees, asylum-seekers, and immigrant families with children). In addition, Scottish parties have engaged in, and been influenced by, the construction of a Scottish identity that is diverse and relatively inclusive of other cultures. As a result, and at least in theory, anyone may become part of the Scottish nation through living in, and contributing to, Scotland.

We have explored four hypotheses for why Scottish parties have adopted more positive and inclusive attitudes towards immigrants: an inclusive national identity, the demographic crisis, the lack of party polarization on immigration, and the lack of control over immigration policy. Each of these holds explanatory power. Scottish politicians frequently refer to the demographic crisis as a primary motivation for increasing levels of immigration. Furthermore, Scottish parties deploy arguments, in particular the construction of an inclusive and culturally diverse Scottish nation, to highlight Scotland's reliance on, and need for the positive integration of immigrants and minority ethnic groups.

Perhaps the most crucial explanatory factor, however, is that Scotland has hitherto escaped significant polarization on the issue of immigration. Scottish parties tend on the whole to be positive about increasing immigration to address Scotland's skills shortages and demographic needs. This is true for both 'regional parties' such as the SNP as well as regional branches of 'statewide parties' such as Scottish Labour and the Scottish Liberal Democrats. Both the latter have adopted positive approaches to immigration that diverge from their UK parent parties' increasingly restrictive and negative approaches. Scottish parties distinguish themselves from the United Kingdom, or more specifically England, through their support for a ('One Scotland') vision that welcomes and integrates incomers and emphasizes a humanitarian approach to asylum. This broadly consensual elite position is aided by the absence of significant far-right anti-immigrant parties. Furthermore, it is enhanced by the overwhelmingly positive rhetoric on immigration of the main nationalist party – the SNP – which embraces a vision of Scotland based on diversity, tolerance, and inclusiveness.

Finally, the Scottish Government's lack of legislative control of immigration policy has led to demands for a more Scotland-specific approach to immigration within the UK. Scottish parties base their arguments on the fact that Scotland has distinctive economic and demographic needs, and also that immigration overlaps with many *devolved* policy areas. In particular, immigration affects the provision of health, housing, education, and economic development, all controlled by the Scottish Parliament. As a result of Scotland's limited control over immigration policy, Scottish parties endorse demands for greater powers to encourage immigrants to live and work in Scotland, though while the SNP wants full Scottish control, Labour and the Liberal Democrats want a regionally attuned points system managed by Westminster. In any case, though, it appears that the general consensus on seeking a more Scottish-oriented immigration policy, in addition to the current lack of devolved control over immigration, has consistently subdued political polarization – in sharp contrast to the UK/English case.

References

K. Banting and S. Soroka (2012) 'Minority Nationalism and Immigrant Integration in Canada', *Nations and Nationalism*, 18: 156–176.

BBC (2004) 'Visa Move to Beat Population Drop', BBC News, 25 February.

BBC (2009) 'Scotland's First Muslim MSP Dies', BBC News, 06 February.

Birrell, Ian (2013) 'The Immigration Debate: Evidence-free and More Rancid than Ever', *The Guardian*, 25 March.

R. Bond (2006) 'Belonging and Becoming: National Identity and Exclusion', *Sociology*, 40(4): 609–626.

R. Bond (2011) 'The National Identities of Minorities in Scotland: Anticipating the 2011 Census', *Scottish Affairs*, 75: 1–24.

R. Bond, K. Charsley and S. Grundy (2010) 'An Audible Minority: Migration, Settlement and Identity among English Graduates in Scotland', *Journal of Ethnic and Migration Studies*, 36(3): 483–499.

B. Borland (2012) 'Coalition Reneges on Detention Camp Pledge to Children', *Sunday Express*, 26 February.

J. Bradbury and J. Mitchell (2001) 'Devolution: New Politics for Old?', *Parliamentary Affairs*, 54(2): 257–275.

B. Briggs and C. McKay (2012) 'UK "Illegally Detaining Victims of Torture" at Dungavel Immigration Removal Centre in Scotland', *Scotland On Sunday*, 30 September.

British National Party (2012) *Immigration*, www.bnp.org.uk/policies/immigration

P. Cairney (2011) *The Scottish Political System Since Devolution: From New Politics to the New Scottish Government*. (Exeter: Imprint Academic).

Conservative Party (2010) *Invitation to Join the Government of Britain*. (London: Conservative Party).

General Register Office for Scotland (2002) *Scotland's Population 2001: The Registrar General's Annual Review of Demographic Trends*. (Edinburgh: General Register Office for Scotland).

General Register Office for Scotland (2011) *Scotland's Population 2010: The Registrar General's Annual Review of Demographic Trends*. (Edinburgh: General Register Office for Scotland).

J. Grayson (2010) *Reflections on the Media, Immigration and the Election*, Institute of Race Relations. www.irr.org.uk/

S. Greer (2005) 'The Territorial Bases of Health Policy Making After Devolution,' *Regional and Federal Studies*, 15(4): 501–518.

E. Hepburn (2009) 'Regionalist Party Mobilisation on Immigration', *West European Politics*, 32(3): 514–535.

E. Hepburn (2010) 'Small Worlds in Canada and Europe: A Comparison of Regional Party Systems in Quebec, Bavaria and Scotland', *Regional & Federal Studies*, 20(4/5): 527–544.

E. Hepburn (2011) 'Citizens of the Region. Party Conceptions of Regional Citizenship and Immigrant Integration', *European Journal of Political Research*, 50(4): 504–529.

P. Hopkins (2007) '"Blue Squares", "Proper" Muslims and Transnational Networks: Narratives of National and Religious Identities amongst Young Muslim Men Living in Scotland', *Ethnicities*, 7(1): 61–81.

D. Howard and J. Penrose (2008) '"One Scotland, Many Cultures": The Mutual Constitution of Anti-racism and Place' in C. Bressey and C. Dwyer (eds) *New Geographies of Race and Racism*. (Ashgate, London).

A. Hussain and W. Miller (2006) *Multicultural Nationalism: Islamophobia, Anglophobia, and Devolution*. (Oxford: Oxford University Press).

M. Keating (2010) *The Government of Scotland: Public Policy Making after Devolution*. (Edinburgh: Edinburgh University Press).

R. Kiely, F. Bechhofer, R. Stewart and D. McCrone (2001) 'The Markers and Rules of Scottish National Identity', *Sociological Review*, 49(1): 33–55.

R. Kiely, F. Bechhofer and D. McCrone (2005) 'Birth, Blood and Belonging: Identity Claims in Post-devolution Scotland', *Sociological Review*, 53(1): 150–171.

Labour Party (2010) *A Future Fair for All*. (London: Labour Party).

Liberal Democrats (2010) *Change That Works For You*. (London: Liberal Democrats).

A. Massie (2011) 'The Arab Spring Provides a Unique Opportunity to Support Would-be Immigrants at Their Point of Departure', *Scotsman*, 18 April.

D. McCrone (2001) *Understanding Scotland: The Sociology of a Nation*. (London: Routledge).

D. McCrone and F. Bechhofer (2010) 'Claiming National Identity', *Ethnic and Racial Studies*, 33(6): 921–948.

N. McEwen, E. Bomberg and W. Swenden (2010) 'Pushing at Boundaries of Devolution: Energy and Climate Change Policy in Scotland', *Political Studies*

Association Specialist Group on British and Comparative Territorial Politics, University of Oxford, 07–08 January.

J. Murphy (2009) 'A Clear Solution to Demographic Woes', *Scotland On Sunday,* 26 July.

P. Odmalm (2012) 'Party Competition and Positions on Immigration: Strategic Advantages and Spatial Locations', *Comparative European Politics,* 10(1): 1–22.

L. Paterson (1997) 'Policy Making in Scottish Education: A Case of Pragmatic Nationalism' in M. Clark and P. Munn (eds) *Education in Scotland.* (London: Routledge).

M. Rosie (2004) *The Sectarian Myth in Scotland: Of Bitter Memory and Bigotry.* (Basingstoke: Palgrave Macmillan).

M. Rosie (2011) 'Aye Right? Scotland's Far Right Parties in 2011', *Scottish Affairs,* 76: 94–99.

M. Rosie (2012) 'Who Are You? National Identity and Contemporary Return Migrants in Scotland' in M. Varricchio (ed) *Back to Caledonia: Scottish Return Migration from the Sixteenth Century to the Present.* (Edinburgh: John Donald).

M. Rosie and R. Bond (2006) 'Routes into Scottishness' in C. Bromley et al. (eds) *Has Devolution Delivered?* (Edinburgh: Edinburgh University Press).

A. Saeed, N. Blain and D. Forbes (1999) 'New Ethnic and National Questions in Scotland: Post-British Identities among Glasgow Pakistani Teenagers', *Ethnic and Racial Studies,* 22(5): 821–844.

Scottish Conservatives (2005) *Are You Thinking What We're Thinking? It's Time for Action.* (Edinburgh: Scottish Conservatives).

Scottish Conservatives (2010) *Invitation to Join the Government of Britain.* (Edinburgh: Scottish Conservatives).

Scottish Conservatives (2012) *Scottish Conservative Reaction to Population Rise.* (press release), 31 May.

Scottish Executive (2004) *New Scots: Attracting Fresh Talent to Meet the Challenge of Growth.* (Edinburgh: Scottish Executive).

Scottish Labour (2005) *Scotland Forward Not Back.* (Glasgow: Scottish Labour).

Scottish Labour (2010) *A Future Fair for All.* (Glasgow: Scottish Labour).

Scottish Labour (2011) *Fighting for What Really Matters.* (Glasgow: Scottish Labour).

Scottish Liberal Democrats (2005) *The Real Alternative.* (Edinburgh: Scottish Liberal Democrats).

Scottish Liberal Democrats (2010) *Change That Works For You.* (Edinburgh: Scottish Liberal Democrats).

Scottish Parliament (2008) *Motion S3M-02043: Christina McKelvie, Central Scotland, Scottish National Party,* 03 June, www.scottish.parliament.uk

H. E. Shin (2011) 'Scottish Parliamentary Elections 2011: Is Migration a Matter Out of Place?' *Migration Pulse,* 26 April, www.migrantsrights.org.uk

P. Skilling (2007) 'New Scots: The Fresh Talent Initiative and Post-Devolution Immigration Policy', *Scottish Affairs,* 61: 101–120.

T. C. Smout (1994) 'Perspectives on the Scottish Identity,' *Scottish Affairs,* 6: 101–113.

SNP (1997) *Yes We Can Win the Best for Scotland.* (Edinburgh: SNP).

SNP (2003) *The Complete Case for a Better Scotland.* (Edinburgh: SNP).

SNP (2005) *If Scotland Matters To You, Make it Matter in May.* (Edinburgh: SNP).

SNP (2007) *It's Time for a Scottish Immigration Service.* (press release), 27 January.

SNP (2010) *Elect A Local Champion.* (Edinburgh: SNP).

SNP (2011) *Re-elect a Scottish Government Working for Scotland.* (Edinburgh: SNP).

UKIP (2013) *Immigration and Asylum: UKIP Policy*, www.ukip.org/

R. Zapata-Barrero (2007) 'Setting a Research Agenda on the Interaction Between Cultural Demands of Immigrants and Minority Nations', *Journal of Immigrant & Refugee Studies*, 5(4): 1–25.

13

Catalunya, terra d'acollida: Stateless Nationalist Party Discourses on Immigration in Catalonia

Núria Franco-Guillén and Ricard Zapata-Barrero

Introduction

In 1987, the *Generalitat*[1] launched the institutional campaign 'Som sis Milions' (*We are six million*). It was aimed at expressing the idea that there are no differences between being born in Catalonia or being an immigrant (*El País*, 2009). Today Catalonia has more than 7.5 million inhabitants and most of this increase is due to the arrival of immigrants from third world countries. Even if migration is not a new phenomenon in Catalonia, the diversity of origins and the rapid pace at which it has taken place during the last decades are new (Franco-Guillén, 2011). Furthermore, the management of immigration coincides with the rise of sub-state nationalist movements seeking to advance self-government and their own nation-building projects (Whithol de Wenden and Zapata-Barrero, 2011). This has been acknowledged by the different governments that have ruled the *Generalitat* since the beginning of the migratory process. Efforts have been made to manage what has been mostly described as 'a challenge'. From public policies to cross-sectional plans, including a National Agreement on Immigration (PNI, 2008) and a Law for the reception of immigrants, we can say that immigration has been monitored by the Catalan government since its very inception (for an overview see, Zapata-Barrero, 2012a). Furthermore, an awareness that certain discourses on immigration can lead to racist and xenophobic attitudes and thus threaten social cohesion has been present in many debates in the Catalan political arena. With the same conviction, most political parties have expressed the idea that defining an immigration policy is also deciding what kind of country Catalonia will be in the future. In this chapter we aim to explore this underlying idea, precisely through the examination of stateless nationalist and regionalist parties' (SNRP[2]) discourses on immigration. The starting concern of our focus is how elements of nationalism and national identity are reflected in the construction of a discourse on immigration. In particular, the objective is to explore SNRP discourses on immigration in Catalonia through the prism of one dimension of the territorial cleavage[3]: identity/culture. Our main argument is that SNRP with positive stances towards immigration tend to highlight the civic elements of the nation and downplay the ethnic ones. We start by presenting the theoretical framework, together with the methodology and justification of the case studies. Next, we move on to the contextualization of the Catalan case and present our results. In the conclusion, we attempt to explain the differences, but especially the similarities that have been found between the two cases (CiU and ERC), and how this framework can also be a useful analytical tool to study other cases.

Theoretical framework: linking nationalist debate with political discourse on immigration

Several authors have claimed that immigration poses specific challenges to minority nations (Kymlicka, 2001; Hepburn, 2009a) as it raises a double fear: one from internal 'minorization', and the other from external cultural dominance or assimilation into the supranational or state culture (Lipton, 2012). In sum, it alters the equilibrium of power relations in two ways. On the one hand, immigration impacts the *external* relationship between the sub-state units and the state level, and on the other hand it impacts the *internal* relationship between the sub-state unit of government and its associated societal culture (Zapata-Barrero, 2012b: 223). Immigration entails an additional pressure in the process of distinct nation-building for minority nations (Zapata-Barrero, 2009: 5) as immigrants tend to integrate into the majority nation. This can involve the minority nation becoming a minority within its own territory. In fact, the management of migratory flows can be a tool for the majority nation to undermine national diversity, and according to Catalan politicians (P13:0491 for ERC and P85:60 for CiU) this has already been used by the Spanish state. These specific challenges have led authors to open different lines of research using a wide range of approaches and disciplines, from normative questions that arise from the interaction of two types of collective rights and claims to the different policy responses and effects[4] of multiple diversity.[5] Indeed, as it is already assumed by the current literature, the way that immigration is approached sheds light on the society's self-understanding.

This premise has encouraged other scholars to explore how elements of nationalism have helped to construct public policy on immigration in Quebec and Flanders (Barker, 2010, 2012; Loobuyck and Jacobs, 2011; see also, Adam and Jacobs, Iacovino and Erk in this volume). Most contributions examining immigration and minority nations have equated the minority nation to 'regional' authorities as the main actors representing the nation. Political parties have hardly been taken into account, and when this has occurred (Banting and Soroka, 2012; Jacobs, 2011; Kymlicka, 2001), SNRPs have not been examined separately (with some exceptions – see, Hepburn, 2009a). However, SNRPs, in their capacity as agents that articulate and aggregate interests (Gunther and Diamond, 2001), also represent (or at least aim to represent) the (construction of the) nation, thus deserve special attention. As 'ethnic political entrepreneurs' (de Winter and Türsan, 1998), SNRPs play a central role in the re-construction of the regionalist 'imagined community' (Anderson, 1991) and its subsequent claims for changing the existing centre/periphery power arrangements. These parties highlight different components of sub-state identity in order to define the people as distinct and therefore pose the aforementioned claims. In this sense, immigration as a global phenomenon brings an important amount of diversity into communities, blurring to some extent the essence of nations depending on how they are defined by political actors. Hence, it poses a particular challenge to SNRPs in deciding whether or not, and how, to include non-nationals in their construction of a unified and distinct regional community (Hepburn, 2011). As a result, SNRPs can take a more inclusive or xenophobic approach, which has direct consequences on social cohesion.

In order to explore the nationalist dimension that can be found in SNRPs' discourses on immigration, we draw on the well-known ethnic/ civic distinction to classify these components. Most authors dealing with nationalism have departed from a classic distinction of these two main forms[6]. Despite the fact that Smith (1971) proposes a broader classification, the distinction between civic and ethnic nationalism is still today the most commonly used. In general, the civic form refers to the one characterized by using a subjective definition and insists on the free will of individuals in order to determine belonging. In contrast the ethnic form uses cultural, linguistic, religious, or ethnic criteria to determine a more objective membership (Lecours, 2000). This distinction has also been used to assert that ethnic nationalism is illiberal, while the civic one is more liberal (see, for example, Ignatieff, 1995). Some authors have noted that this is not always the case (Brubaker, 1999) and that the categorization is not suited to account for how elements of culture intersect in the two forms (Kymlicka, 1999). Furthermore, even if most minority nationalisms could be classified as ethnic, they are often more liberal than some statewide ones (Kymlicka, 2001; Hepburn, 2011; Loobuyck and Jacobs, 2011). Language is a critical element within this context. As Bauböck (2001:333) suggests, 'if a national linguistic minority were to become a minority within its own province, ... this demographic shift would undermine its power to claim regional autonomy'. Indeed, Erk and Koning (2009) have shown how language diversity influences institutional change and decentralization. Most literature using the civic-ethnic classification tends to include language within the ethnic elements of nationalism. However, as Taras (1998: 87) acknowledges, it is when languages are politicized that the struggle for national identity begins. He explores how language policies have sought to define or reinforce national identity in different cases such as Canada, Quebec, the former Soviet Republics, or the United States. This highlights the idea that language should be included within the analysis of nationalist discourses not on the side of ethnic discourse, but as a transversal element. As we will argue, the *way* language is introduced into the discourse is what distinguishes ethnic from civic nationalism.

With regards to immigration, it is true that the civic elements of the nation, and especially the voluntary dimension, make it easier for SNRP to include diversity within their discourses. By contrast, certain ethnic identifiers, such as religion or common ancestry, might make it more difficult to include diversity within the nation. Scholars dealing with immigration and minority nations have already found out how issues such as language play a central role in the Catalan or Quebec identity (Labelle, 2004; Gil Araujo, 2007; Blad and Couton, 2009; Chapter 11 by Erk in this volume), and not in others such as Scotland (Hepburn, 2011; Chapter 12 by Hepburn and Rosie, in this volume), and it is important to see how all of these elements are articulated. In this sense, ethnic elements have a potential for excluding newcomers[7], as immigrants cannot be born in the receiving society, and they can hardly change their religion or their skin colour. Hence, we might expect that the unwillingness of SNRPs to include or accept immigrants will advance an ethnic understanding of their nation. In contrast, civic elements will be more inclusive for newcomers, as fully participating in the nation will 'only' entail living within its territorial borders and respecting civic values. In sum, through the following hypotheses, we suggest that the SNRPs' stances on immigration determine the way their nationalist discourses are constructed.

In accordance with E. Hepburn's conceptual framework in Chapter 3 of this volume, we divide parties' stances on immigration into a dichotomy between positive and negative stances. In this sense, a 'positive stance' refers to those parties accepting immigration and describing it as an opportunity for social cohesion or even for nation-building. Neutral statements describing immigration as a fact or a reality are also included in this stance. In contrast, a 'negative stance' refers to parties which are clearly reluctant to accept the arrival of immigrants and describe it as a problem or threat to social cohesion and nation-building.

Hypothesis 1: SNRP with positive stances towards immigration tend to portray their nationalist discourse as civic

Alternative hypothesis: SNRP with negative stances towards immigration tend to portray their nationalist discourse as ethnic

Methodologically, we consider three main analytical dimensions or 'categories' of nationalist discourse: belonging, values, and the function of language. The first category refers to the arguments used by political parties to determine national belonging. Within a civic nationalist discourse, stress will be put on the subjective willingness of its members to become part of the nation. Thus, any person living within its territorial borders and willing to belong to the nation becomes socially considered as a member of the nation. In contrast, an ethnic nationalist discourse will propose objective elements that are beyond the person's will/ability to belong to the nation, such as common ancestry, history, religion, or blood ties. The second category is the group of **values** that are shared by the members of the nation and that are identified to be key to social cohesion. While, civic nationalism stresses the importance of democratic values, and concretely that of equality of opportunities as well as universal human rights, ethnic nationalism stresses the importance of maintaining traditions and customs and upholding traditional conservative values. Finally, as a third category, we propose the function of language. As we have suggested, disputing an assumption in the current debate on nationalism, we prefer to treat language transversally, across the civic/ethnic dichotomy. This is done by stressing its function within the integration process of immigrants. For instance, several authors have already noted how language, as a resource, can have the function of assuring equality of opportunities (Kymlicka and Patten, 2003). In this sense, it might well be that SNRP pose language as a matter of choice 'linked to occasions of social mobility, as a main source of motivation' (Zapata-Barrero, 2012b: 87). Concerning an ethnic nationalist discourse, language is an objective identity marker and a precondition to be accepted within the national community (Lind, in Taras, 1998). In this scenario, SNRPs would present knowledge of the language as necessary for being accepted into the national community and to be considered as integrated. Table 13.1 summarizes the analytical framework.

Table 13.1   Analytical framework to confirm the hypothesis

	Positive stance on immigration	Negative stance on immigration
Categories	Civic nationalist discourse	Ethnic nationalist discourse
Belonging	Stress the subjective willingness of the people to belong to a nation	Stress objective elements that are beyond the will/ability of the people
Values	Stress the importance of maintaining shared values relating to democracy (mainly equality of opportunities) and universal human rights, for social cohesion	Stress the importance of maintaining shared values relating to tradition, religion and customs for social cohesion
Function of Language	Social function of language. Language as a means to achieve equal opportunities. Instrumental dimension of language for social mobility	Language as an objective identity marker and as a precondition to be accepted in the national community

It is difficult to establish the direction of a causal relationship between civic/ethnic nationalism and positive/negative stances towards immigration as they most likely affect each other. Despite this endogeneity and both questions being a matter of political choice, we argue that, as any nation is a construction or 'imagined community', it provides both civic (especially in developed democracies) and ethnic elements throughout its history and political context. Therefore, to the SNRP, it becomes a matter of decision-making, of choosing which of these elements of nationalism to adopt[8] or dismiss, and thereby to make their nationalist discourses compatible with their stances towards immigration.

Case selection and methodology: SNRP in Catalonia

Selection of cases

The unit of analysis in this chapter is the discourse of SNRP. Following Massetti's (2009) definition, SNRP have four characteristics. First, they are self-contained political organizations that contest elections. Secondly, they field candidates only in a particular territory (region) of the state. Thirdly, the territorial limitation of their electoral activity is a consequence of their explicit objective of defending only the identities and interests of 'their' region. Fourthly, as stated by De Winter and Türsan (1998a: 204[9]), regionalist parties' core mission is to achieve/protect/enhance 'some kind of [territorial] self-government'. We agree that a party can be considered relevant when it is so in Sartori's terms[10] and when it survives at least one term of office. Two out of the six parties[11] represented in the Catalan Parliament accomplish the proposed criteria.

Table 13.2 Selection of cases and criteria

Criterion	Convergència i Unió (CiU[a])	Esquerra Republicana per Catalunya (ERC[b])
Ideological leaning	Left-Right: Centre-right Centre-periphery: autonomist[c]	Left-Right: Moderate left Centre-periphery: Secessionist
Party System relevance	Autonomous level: Two governing periods: 1980–2003 and 2010 to date. Coalition potential from 2003–2010. State level: Support to government formation (blackmail potential) in 1993 (PSOE) and 1996 (PP)	Autonomous level: Coalition potential from 2003–2010. Governing in the area of immigration from 2003 to 2010. State level: Moderate blackmail potential from 2008–2012.
Survival	Yes	Yes

[a]The CiU is in fact a stable coalition of two parties: CDC (Convergència Democràtica per Catalunya) and UDC (Unió Democràtica per Catalunya) Web pages: http://ciu.cat/index.php?idioma=EN CDC web page: http://www.convergencia.cat/index.php?idioma=EN UDC web page: http://www.unio.org/actualitat/index.asp (last accessed, September 2012)
[b]Web page: http://www.esquerra.cat/language/english
[c]Interestingly, while the CDC defines itself as 'sovereigntist' (referring to its autonomist goals), it contains some sectors that seek independence from Spain, ; the UDC rather defines itself as 'catalanist' and rejects independence. This only holds for the period of analysis. Currently, the CDC is embracing an apparently independentist position. This article was written before the anticipated elections in Catalonia on 25 November 2012, in which the president of the Generalitat and CDC, Artur Mas, has promised a Referendum for independence. One can assume that the CDC is currently an independentist party.

Period of analysis

The analysis covers three legislative periods from 1999–2010 as summarized in Table 13.3. We begin in 2000 because it is a crucial year for the beginning of the institutionalization of immigration in Spain and Catalonia. For the case of Catalonia, the levels of immigration started increasing in 1999 (2.33 per cent) until 2010, when it represented 15 per cent of the total population. As Zapata-Barrero (2003) notes, immigration emerged as an administrative and technical issue in the 1990s and as a political and social issue in 2000 (see also, Zapata-Barrero, 2012c, d).

Table 13.3 Period of analysis

Legislative period	Governing party(ies)	President
1999–2003	CiU	Jordi Pujol (CiU)
2003–2006	PSC, ERC, ICV	Pasqual Maragall (PSC)
2006–2010	PSC, ERC, ICV	José Montilla (PSC)

Sources of information

The analysis has been conducted through a Qualitative Document Analysis on the basis of primary sources of information. First, we have collected the manifestos and party programmes issued during the time period. Manifestos are definitive statements of positions and constitute the best-known documents produced by political parties (Cooke, 2000). Second, the main parliamentary debates have been taken into account. These often reflect in a deeper way the party stances in immigration, especially when debates on concrete conflicts emerge. Finally, semi-structured interviews have been carried out among party representatives (those in charge of immigration issues at the parliamentary and party levels) with the objective of confirming the findings. This information has been organized in a hermeneutic unit, consisting of 96 documents.[12]

Table 13.4 Sources of information

Type	Source
Primary	Party Manifestos (8)
	Party Political Programmes (8)
	Parliamentary Debates (74)
	Interview – Party Representatives (4)

Contextualization

As Hepburn noted in her conceptual chapter, SNRP discourses on immigration are more related to the centre-periphery cleavage rather than to the left-right axis. This cleavage includes not only identity but also the territorial and economic dimension where, as we will see, a distinct discourse also exists. In this section, we review this political context as well as the debates that were held during the period of analysis while we relate to some of the hypotheses suggested by Hepburn in her conceptual chapter.

Concerning the territorial dimension, the demographic importance of immigration in Catalonia was highlighted in most parliamentary discourses. In this sense, all politicians tended to highlight that Catalonia is a *Land of welcome* (Terra d'acollida[13]). This expression, which frequently appears in parliamentary debates and manifestos (P9: 09888), summarizes the idea that Catalonia is a land that has received immigrants throughout its history. Indeed, without immigration, the country would currently have around 2.5 million inhabitants, compared to the current 7.5 million.[14] This idea has been present during all the legislative periods, and contrasts with Hepburn's hypothesis, according to which we should expect a negative stance towards immigration. As it is developed in the following section, both the CiU and ERC have shown a rather positive stance towards immigration, frequently highlighting this aspect of 'Land of welcome'. A second issue that emerged and persisted across time is the relationship with the central government. Immigration belongs to the Spanish government as an exclusive competence,[15] although the *Generalitat* started designing public policy in the early 1990s (see Chapter 6 by Arrighi de Casanova in this volume). As a result, while the management of flows and naturalization has remained a competence of the central government, reception and integration policies have fallen into the hands of the autonomous government of Catalonia. In this context, debates took the form of general claims[16] and complaints about the lack of competences to manage immigration, and accusations that the central state had not used its competences to manage immigration efficiently. The CiU and especially the ERC have opposed the central government's policy-making on immigration. As J.M. Cleries (CiU) summarized in 2004:

> The Government of the State has failed to properly manage migration flows and border control, denying at the same time the right of Catalonia to intervene in these policies. The impediments … make the

existence of a Catalan own policy on immigration a political priority that has been continuously claimed by CiU. (P29:4100)

According to the interviewees, the relationship with the state was conflictive or tense, especially when the Spanish government (led by the Popular Party) started sending irregular migrants caught in Ceuta and Melilla to Catalonia (P13:0492). This was interpreted by both parties as a threat to Catalonia.

> ... the great majority was people sent from Madrid. All of them were illegals. It was the government of the PP who was sending them. And this has happened a lot of times. You can't say it is an official policy, because no one has dared to ... but it was an informal policy ... (P85: 60)

This aspect relates to the hypothesis according to which the level of control over immigration determines parties' stances on this issue. Although the answer is not clear-cut, as Catalonia holds *de facto* powers on immigration, both parties have revolved around this questions several times, highlighting a discontent with the Spanish government's way of managing immigration.

With regard to the economic dimension of the territorial cleavage, the objective of social cohesion has appeared in all of the debates on immigration. First, in order to prevent the rise of racism and xenophobia, all of the parties in the Catalan Parliament have agreed to an informal pact to avoid the use of immigration for electoral purposes. In this sense, the creation of the parliamentary Committee on Immigration in 1999 (P11) contained common references to racism and xenophobia by both the ERC and CiU. The agreement that immigration, with its potential of challenging social cohesion, cannot be treated in a populist way was commonly accepted by the parties over the years (P18: 1866). It is in this area where both the CiU and ERC, together with the rest of the left-wing political forces in the Catalan Parliament, have had more similar discourses. Second, in the realm of economic and social integration, the demographic deficit and the growth of the economy makes Catalonia – in the view of both political parties – an attractive country to potential newcomers. Both parties viewed the need to establish mechanisms of reception and integration of newcomers in the labour market from the very beginning of the period of analysis. The fight against illegal immigration was also seen as an important issue, but in this case, the ERC links it to its negative effects on the individual in question as irregular immigrants can only look for jobs in the black economy, which leads to an increased precariousness of labour conditions and therefore a challenge to social cohesion. Third, immigration has also been described as an opportunity for economic growth and development in the context of globalization. As the former president of the ERC, J. L. Carod-Rovira, stated in 2000: 'We have an enormous potential, splendid opportunities and we only have to take advantage ... the weight of the tourist sector, our condition as a country receiving foreigners, our internal diversity could allow us to enforce the Language industry' (P10:4013). However, after the economic crisis, the CiU revealed a concern for resources, suggesting that no more immigrants should be accepted as the labour market is currently unable to absorb them (P85:39).

Finally, with regard to the concrete debates held in the Catalan Parliament, during the first period of analysis (6th Legislative period, 1999–2003), the main debates on immigration related to the Law for the approval of measures to support Catalan returnees. The rest of the parliamentary debates dealt with questions related to socioeconomic issues, and the constitution of the first Parliamentary Committee on Immigration. We should also mention an initiative of the ERC to approve a Charter of Reception, which was refused by the Parliament. The 7th legislative period (2003–2006) did not include the approval of any immigration-related laws. However, the different questions held in the plenary sessions led to important debates such as the creation of the EBE (Educative Welcome Space), relations with the Spanish state, and the linguistic integration of immigrants. Special attention has been paid to debates on the approval of the new Statute of Autonomy (2006). Finally, the 8th Legislative period (2006–2010) was probably the most intense with regard to the debates on immigration. In addition to the approval of the Law on Reception, some questions related to the National Pact for Immigration (PNI) emerged. Finally, the economic crisis and integration shaped most of the questions posed in the plenary debates.

Testing the hypothesis: SNRP with positive stances towards immigration tend to portray their nationalist discourse as civic

General discourses on immigration in Catalonia

Immigration as a phenomenon has been mainly qualified as a 'challenge' by both the CiU and ERC, but also, and especially by the ERC, as an opportunity to construct a project and take advantage of diversity (P10:4013). In fact, immigration is presented in both parties' manifestos as a fact beyond the debate on whether it is desirable or not, and the discourses have been oriented towards its management, including illegal immigration. Rather than rejecting illegal immigrants, both parties have highlighted the need to manage several problems that this phenomenon raises, such as the black market economy. Furthermore, the ERC goes a step forward, urging the regularization of illegal immigrants (P9:07957). In sum, we consider the CiU and ERC to have had a rather positive stance towards immigration and that this has remained equal and consistent during all of the periods of study. In addition to the constant references to Catalonia as a *Land of Welcome*, the signature of the PNI (2008) by most political forces in the Catalan Parliament has helped to construct a shared discourse on immigration. It incorporates immigration as a part of the Catalan identity and history:

> Catalonia can be defined as a diverse society built largely through the settlement of persons from elsewhere. This process, produced in a global context and which has intensified in recent years, creates different needs, as well being a new opportunity to define the country that we will be in the future. (PNI, 2008: 15)

This shared discourse on immigration does not really start at, but culminates with the signature of the PNI. The consensus on different ideas, such as the image of Catalonia as having a history of immigration, the aforementioned agreement on not using immigration as an electoral tool, and the fact that both parties have been in charge of governing migration[17] have helped the convergence of these positions. This is similar to the party consensus on immigration, and its positive association with nationalism, in Scotland (see Chapter 12 by Hepburn and Rosie for more details). It should be noted that the generally positive position towards immigration is shared by most parties in the Catalan Parliament with the exception of the PPC (right-wing regional branch of the Spanish Popular Party), which again mirrors the situation in Scotland in which the right-wing Scottish Conservatives adopt a less enthusiastic approach. In this sense, both the PSC and ICV have also highlighted some of the arguments related to the history of Catalonia as a Land of welcome, although their discourse is generally more related to the left-right axis rather than the centre-periphery one.

This review of the Catalan parties' stances on immigration is in line with Hepburn's hypotheses related to party polarization. In this sense, despite the relative importance of the anti-immigrant party Plataforma per Catalunya at the local level,[18] its absence at the Catalan autonomic level, together with the fact that both the CiU and ERC have failed to develop a negative stance towards immigration, confirm Hepburn's hypotheses according to which these two factors lead to a positive stance among other parties (with the exception of the PP). With regards to party ideology, against the initial expectation, the CiU as a centre-right party has maintained a positive stance towards immigration. Hence, the hypothesis only holds for the ERC.

With regards to nationalist discourse, SNRP discourses on immigration reveal that a nationalist discourse on culture and identity appears in 69 per cent of the sample. Figure 13.1 shows the results for the three categories (belonging, values, and function of language) that have been explored.

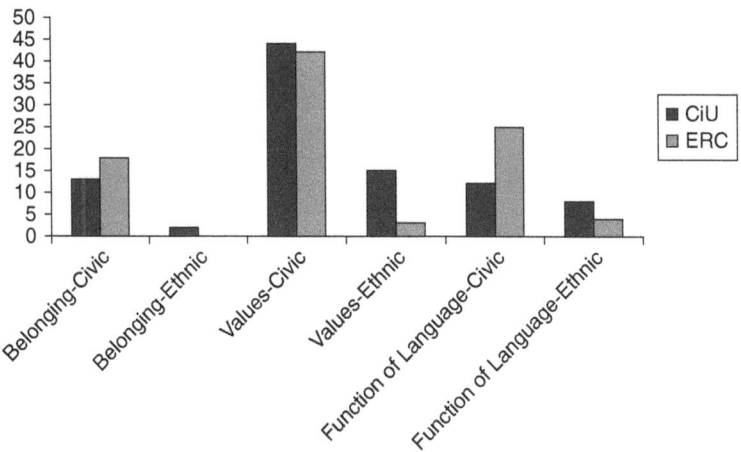

Figure 13.1   Civic and ethnic nationalist discourse on immigration (1999–2010)
Source: Own elaboration.

As we can see, there is a higher proportion of civic nationalist discourse both in the CiU and ERC, especially with regard to civic values. The figure also shows how the civic function of language is more significant within SNRP discourses than ethnic discourses. The CiU has a higher rate in the category of values, as the party has a special concern for the maintenance of traditions.

Belonging

The examination of Catalan SNRP discourses on immigration reveals a clear civic discourse with regard to belonging. Both parties have made references to the subjective willingness of the people to belong to the Catalan nation.

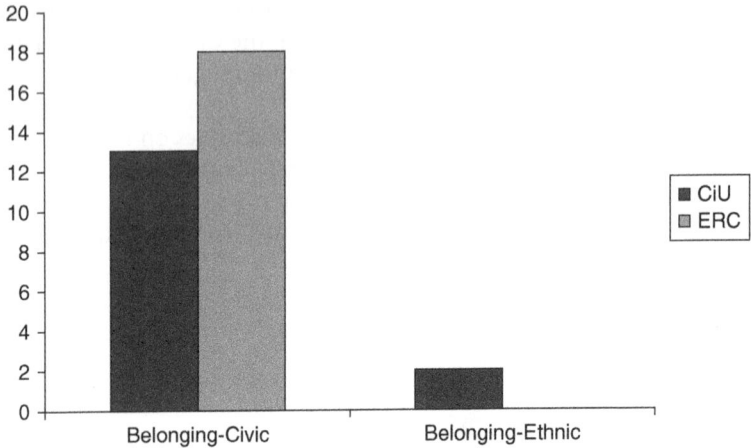

Figure 13.2 Civic and ethnic nationalist discourse on belonging (1999–2010)
Source: Own elaboration.

While in sum the CiU and ERC referred to a civic discourse on belonging 31 times, only two ethnic references were found for the CiU and none for the ERC. Most discourses were found in the third period of analysis (2006–2010), which is due to the elaboration of the Reception Law during this time.

Both the CiU (P21: 6235) and ERC (P40:0529) have largely repeated the sentence made famous by the first president of the Generalitat after the Francoist period, Jordi Pujol (CiU): 'És català qui viu i treballa a Catalunya i ho vol ser'.[19] This contains the essence of what has been defined as civic nationalism, expressing the voluntary incorporation of people to the nation, based on a concrete territory (Catalonia). This has been repeated in the majority of the SNRP discourses analysed. Moreover, interviewees have highlighted this subjective willingness to be part of the nation. For example, an ERC representative makes it clear 'when someone is living here, brings his children to school, chooses Catalonia as his place of residence, listen, then it's up to him to stop being an immigrant when he wants...when he voluntarily decides to be a part of the country' (P84:12). Finally, voluntariness has been highlighted by both parties in debates related to reception and integration where the

CiU (P102: 0915) and ERC had stressed the fact that all steps that an immigrant can take to become integrated depend exclusively on his or her willingness to do so. As an ERC representative mentioned during the Reception Law debate: 'It is about...a totally voluntary process. This is our model: voluntary ascription in a common space of society that invites, that asks new Catalans to integrate in the society' (P67: 2380). Finally, of the two references to ethnic nationalism, these were related to the reception of Catalan returnees, as these are considered by CiU as members of the nation as long as they have Catalan ancestors (P23: 1348). Although the ERC had a positive stance towards facilitating the return of descendants of Catalans abroad, its representative put an emphasis on the (unjust) circumstances of exile. No other objective conditions for belonging were found in the sample.

Values

References to values are the most prominent within SNRP discourses on immigration, appearing in 56 per cent of the documents analysed in this chapter. Most of the CiU and ERC nationalist discourses on the category of values were civic.

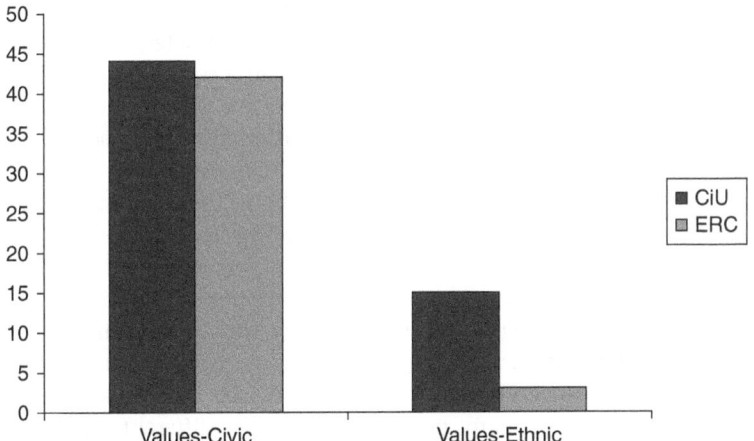

Figure 13.3 Civic and ethnic nationalist discourse on values (1999–2010)
Source: Own elaboration.

Both parties stressed the importance of maintaining civic values in order to secure social cohesion across the three legislative periods, although the CiU did make 25 per cent of the party's total discourse on values ethnic statements.

While it is clear that for both parties civic (common and shared) values are very important, in many cases, this concept remains vague. The CiU often speak about 'common traditions and civic values' (P67: 1979); the ERC uses forms such as 'values on liberties and rights', and most statements are reduced to these broad ideas. For example, a CiU deputy was calling on the integration of immigrants in these terms: '...also we have to facilitate their incorporation into a society with its own identity, and we are proud of it. Not only because it is a Catalan identity, but also because it is linked to peace, living together,[20] civicness and loving each other' (P29: 4554). In the few cases where both parties have been more concrete, civic values refer to democratic values, gender equality, equality of opportunities, living together, respect for universal rights, and laicism. This is clearly in line with the PNI which refers to respect for universal human rights in its section 'Integration into a common public culture'. Attention has been paid to religion, as the CiU, containing a Christian Democrat party, could have referred to Christianity as one of the main values.[21] Although the CiU recognizes the importance of the Catholic Church and its contribution to the cultural heritage in Catalonia, it does so while highlighting increasing religious diversity in Catalonia, hence proposing a defence of religious pluralism (see, manifestos 1999 and 2010) and a secular society.[22] In a similar vein, the ERC defends religious diversity with an emphasis of state laicism. With regards to the ethnic nationalist discourse, the CiU has sometimes put a special emphasis on the maintenance of Catalan traditions and costumes but without specifying the meaning of these traditions. For example, as a deputy put it during one debate:

> In the realm of culture, we have to remove our complexes for once and for all. Not everything is a matter of money, even if it is very important. Catalonia has forged a culture over centuries and we have to be able to defend and preserve it. It is true that we are a result of the mixture of many people coming from different places, and cultural origins. Nobody denies that. It is the reality. In this sense, our country is like a delta which is shaped by the sediments it receives. But it is the main river's current that feeds the delta and channels the different sediments. (P35:1109)

Other references in this category have tended to highlight those behaviours that are unacceptable in Catalan society. Without mentioning any immigrant or religious groups, both the CiU (P18: 2483) and the ERC (P68: 3456) have referred to gender equality and the unacceptability of using a burka in public buildings, the latter being based on arguments of liberal democracy and gender equality. This unacceptability is therefore justified through its incompatibility with certain civic values.

Function of language

The role of language is key to understanding the Catalan SNRP discourses on immigration, and most discourses related to nation-building. Indeed, it has been identified by both the ERC and CiU as the main identity marker of the Catalan nation. When speaking about reception, language courses are always included as part of the first right to be granted to newcomers. References to the function of language have been present in the three terms of office (especially in the second and third periods, 2003–2010). Overall, both the CiU and ERC have made efforts to portray language as a tool for ensuring the equality of opportunities.

As we can see from the Figure 13.4, a predominantly civic nationalist discourse has been articulated by the CiU and ERC during the three terms of office. In this direction, the ERC has put more effort into highlighting the role of the Catalan language in civic terms, though an ethnic nationalist discourse has also emerged within both parties.

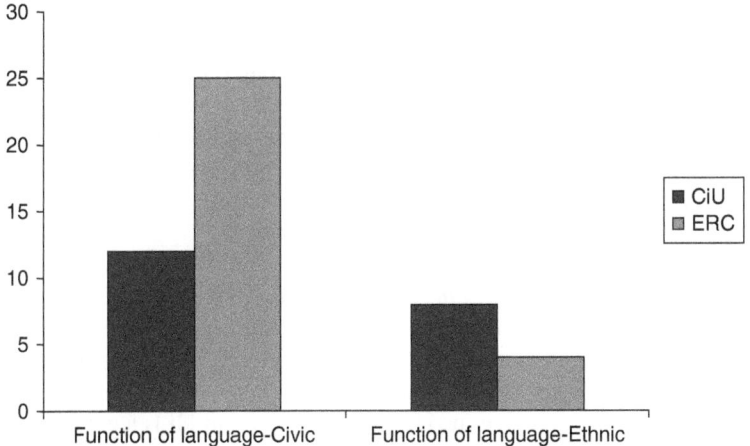

Figure 13.4 Civic and ethnic nationalist discourse on the Function of Language (1999–2010)

Source: Own elaboration.

The two SNRP parties stress the fact that newcomers must learn Catalan, given the language is a part of the country's identity. As suggested in the analytical framework, we expect both parties to link this need to learn Catalan to ensure equal opportunities. The CiU has put an emphasis on offering language courses to newcomers as a tool for ensuring that they have access to all available rights and resources, and as a first step for integration. The ERC goes a step further and puts special emphasis on promoting the learning of immigrants' languages of origin in order to respect diversity and not be a tool for 'negatively globalizing, pan-statist or pan-religious policies' (P9:11049). Its 2003 manifesto summarizes these two ideas:

> Knowing the language of the reception country is a basic right of immigrants, which must be guaranteed as other rights such as health or education are guaranteed. This is because knowing Catalan has a basic role in the integration process. ... learning Catalan not only an element of integration, but an unavoidable tool for ensuring equality of opportunities. At the same time, we also consider unavoidable the respect and reinforcement of teaching immigrants' languages of origin. (P9: 10907)

Despite this emphasis on language as the principal means for ensuring the equality of opportunities (civic discourse), Catalan has been portrayed not only as the main identity marker of the nation by the CiU and ERC, but also as a precondition for becoming incorporated into the society, which we identified as part of an ethnic discourse. This discourse has emerged in certain debates, such as the Reception Law (P67: 1801) and the failed proposal on a Charter of Reception in the first legislative period under study (P25: 4637). These ideas have always been surrounded by other civic aspects of the nation. The CiU's deputy on the debate on the Reception law exemplifies this idea:

> Catalonia is a *land of welcome* and this is a national characteristic. The proof is that we give in the innermost of our being, of our being as a country, that is our language and our culture, which is the country's *own* language. And you have not said it. You talk a lot of official languages, but ... there is also the *own* language and it is legally recognized. And therefore we do not want the Catalan language to be for a few. And those coming from outside ... – not you-, our language is also theirs, because we want them to be part of this People. We do not want ghettos, we want one community. Because you talk a lot about

individual liberties and each one is each one. Don't we have a right to be a community too? (P67:1801)

Although overall, both parties put their emphasis on learning Catalan as a basic tool for ensuring integration and equality of opportunities, it is true that the key role that language plays in the Catalan identity facilitates the emergence of traces of a rather ethnic discourse. In sum, learning Catalan is a right that enables immigrants to fully enjoy other rights and have access to equal opportunities, but to both parties it is also a duty.

Conclusion

In this chapter, we have analysed the Catalan SNRP nationalist discourses on immigration. We have hypothesized that those SNRP with a positive stance towards immigration tend to portray a civic nationalist discourse. We have divided this discourse into three main dimensions (belonging, values, and the role of language) and we have used it as a framework to explore all of the manifestos, programmes, and parliamentary debates produced from 1999 to 2010 by the CiU and ERC.

After identifying a positive stance towards immigration, we have shown how both parties have developed an overall civic nationalist discourse, thus confirming our hypothesis. This can be summarized as follows:

1. Subjective willingness is important to be considered a member of the Catalan society. In this sense, all parties share the belief that 'Anyone who lives and works in Catalonia, and wishes to be so, is Catalan' and that Catalonia is a land of welcome. These ideas have been present during all the periods of analysis, which explains the introductory paragraph of the National Agreement on Immigration.
2. At the level of social values, both the CiU and ERC believe that Catalonia's social cohesion is built on a set of shared values consisting of respect for pluralism and diversity, equality of opportunities, universal rights, and living together. These shared values collectively coincide with the CiU and ERC's open position towards immigration and the consensus achieved for the signature of the National Agreement and the approval of the Reception law, which at the same time corroborates Hepburn's hypothesis on party polarization. On some occasions the CiU has expressed a rather ethnic discourse on values; this is because the CiU gives a lot of importance to traditions and costumes.

3. Finally, language is the main identity marker in Catalonia where its knowledge is a right (and a duty) and a tool for ensuring equal access to rights and opportunities and therefore becoming fully integrated into the Catalan community. Less clearly than the two former categories, language lies between the purely civic and the purely ethnic nationalist discourses. In this sense, the fact that the Catalan language is the key identity marker of the Catalan nation makes the CiU (and the ERC in four cases) view it not only as a tool for ensuring equality of opportunities, but also as a requisite for becoming integrated in certain cases. Further research should explore the willingness of newcomers to learn the Catalan language in order to explore whether this affects the ERC and CiU's stances, as suggested in the conceptual chapter.

Despite the fact that some ethnic traces of the nationalist discourse (especially in the case of CiU) have been found for the last two categories, we have enough evidence to confirm our hypothesis according to which an SNRP with a positive stance towards immigration tends to articulate a civic nationalist discourse.

This chapter has sought to shed light not only on the Catalan case itself, but also the exploration of nationalist discourses in the context of immigration more generally. As we have seen, there are many elements that are important in the context of minority nations that might not be captured with a framework based exclusively on positive and negative stances. Therefore, we consider that this framework could be replicated in the context of other minority nations such as Quebec, Scotland, or Flanders, helping us to further explore the link between minority nations, immigration, and political parties.

Notes

1. Government of Catalonia
2. In line with E. Hepburn's (2009b) discussion, we use SNRP to refer to the party family which places stress on territorial power relations.
3. Although identity is the main objective, the analysis of the data reveal references to the other dimensions pointed out by Eve Hepburn in this volume, that is, territory and economy. We refer to them in another section.
4. See, among others, Kymlicka (2001), Bauböck (2001) Labelle et al. (2012) or Gagnon (2009).
5. Multiple diversity is proposed as a suitable terminology for contexts such as Spain (Zapata-Barrero, 2013).
6. Which became famous after the publication of Anthony Smith's *Theories of Nationalism* (1971), having as precedents Meinecke's distinction between *Staatsnation* and *Kulturnation,* and Kohn's work (Brubaker, 1999).

7. This was historically the case for the Basque Country and its main SNRP, the Partido Nacionalista Vasco (PNV), in its foundation (Conversi, 1997).
8. See Leith and Soule (2012: 149–50) for a reflection on this
9. Quoted in Massetti (2009).
10. According to Sartori (2005) a political party is party system relevant if it exhibits *blackmail potential* (the party's existence affects the party competition and the direction of the competition) or *coalition potential* (the party can be needed for a feasible coalition majority).
11. There are currently six political parties in the Catalan Parliament: Convergència i Unió (CiU), Partit dels Socialistes de Catalunya (PSC), Esquerra Republicana per Catalunya (ERC), Partit Popular de Catalunya (PPC) Iniciativa per Catalunya – Verds (ICV) and Solidaritat Catalana (SI). Only the CiU, ERC, and the SI respond to the definition of SNRP. However, the SI is a new party that emerged in the 2010, with only four deputies, no party system relevance, and a survival still to be proved. Given that, it is not included in the sample.
12. All quotations have been translated from Catalan to English by the authors. Hermeneutic Unit shall be facilitated upon request. Citations are done using the Primary document number and starting line. For example, a quotation in line 113 of the first document of the Hermeneutic unit is cited as follows: (P1:113).
13. 'Acollida' expresses a concept encompassing different aspects of welcome, reception and hosting.
14. Immigration has contributed 75 per cent to Catalonia's recent demographic growth, with the main countries of origin being Morocco (16 per cent), Romania (8 per cent) and Ecuador (6 per cent). For an overview of the demographic evolution of immigration in Catalonia, see Franco-Guillén (2011).
15. According to art. 149.1.2 of the Spanish Constitution, Immigration is a reserved matter to the Spanish government. The Constitutional Court's ruling on the Catalan Statute of Autonomy recognized the practice carried out by the Catalan Government, consisting in managing immigration through its devolved competences such as Education, Health and other social services.
16. Both the CiU and ERC have continuously posed claims for the decentralization of powers on immigration at all levels. In fact, even in the realm of naturalization, both SNRP agreed, through the signature of the PNI, that the average years for naturalization should decrease, suggesting at least the intention to influence the central government.
17. Both the CiU (since the early 1990s) and ERC (2003–10) interviewees have acknowledged that the fact of being in government forced the party to take in-depth reflections on immigration.
18. In the 2011 municipal elections, the party obtained modest results, involving coalition potential in important municipalities such as l'Hospitalet de Llobregat, the second most populated city next to Barcelona, el Vendrell, situated to the south of Barcelona, and Vic, geographically at the heart of Catalonia, and symbolically the first city that introduced PxC in its city council and where its leader holds a seat.
19. 'Anyone who lives and works in Catalonia, and wishes to be so, is Catalan'. This sentence was generated by the Assamblea Catalana, in 1971, taken from the texts of the socialist Rafael Campalans.

20. Living together is a translation of the concept 'convivència', whose meaning relates to peaceful coexistence.
21. Indeed, one of the main representatives of catholic conservative nationalism, Josep Torras i Bages, made famous the sentence « Catalunya serà cristiana, o no serà » (Catalonia will be Christian, or will not be).
22. In line with the discussion on the relationship between nationalist discourse and stances towards immigration, we see how an element such as the prominence of religion in CiU falls outside the discourse when tackling immigration.

Bibliography

B. Anderson (1991) *Imagined Communities: Reflections on the Origin and Spread of Nationalism*. (London: Verso).

F. Barker (2010) 'Learning to Be a Majority: Negotiating Immigration, Integration and National Membership in Quebec', *Political Science*, 62(1): 11–36.

F. Barker (2012) 'Immigration and Contested Nation Building: Explaining the Political Salience of Immigration in Multinational Societies', *GRITIM-UPF Working Paper Series*, 13.

R. Bauböck (2001) 'Cultural citizenship, Minority Rights, and Self-government' in T. A. Aleinikoff and D. Klusmeyer (eds) *Citizenship Today*. (Washington: Carnegie).

K. Banting and S. Soroka (2012) 'Minority Nationalism and Immigrant Integration in Canada', *Nations and Nationalism*, 18(1): 156–176.

C. Blad and P. Couton (2009) 'The Rise of an Intercultural Nation: Immigration, Diversity and Nationhood in Quebec', *Journal of Ethnic and Migration Studies*, 35(4): 645–667.

R. Brubaker (1996) *Nationalism Reframed: Nationhood and the National Question in the New Europe*. (Cambridge: Cambridge University Press).

J.H. Carens (1995) *Is Quebec nationalism just? Perspectives from Anglophone Canada* (Montreal, London : McGill-Queen's University Press).

D. Conversi (1997) *The Basques, the Catalans and Spain: Alternative Routes to Nationalist Mobilisation*. (London: Hurst & Co).

A.B. Cooke (2000) 'The Conservative Party and Its Manifestos: A Personal View' in I. D. Dale (ed.) *Conservative Party General Election Manifestos 1900–1997*. (London: Routledge).

L. De Winter and H. Türsan, H. (1998) 'A Comparative Analysis of Electoral, Office and Policy Success of Ethnoregionalist Parties' in L. de Winter and H. Türsan (eds) *Regionalist Parties in Western Europe*. (London: Routledge).

J. Erk and E. Koning (2010) 'New Structuralism and Institutional Change Federalism between Centralization and Decentralization' *Comparative and Political Studies*, 43: 353–378.

N. Franco-Guillén (2011) 'L'Immigration en Catalogne dans le contexte espagnol: l'évolution démographique et des politiques publiques', *Migrations Societés*, 23(134–135): 83–94

A.-G. Gagnon (2009) 'From *Laissez-Faire* to an Institutional Framework in Quebec' in R. Zapata-Barrero (ed.) *Immigration and Self-government in Minority Nations*. (Bruxelles: Peter Lang).

Generalitat de Catalunya (2008) *Un pacte per viure junts i juntes. Pacte Nacional per la immigracio.* (Barcelona: Generalitat de Catalunya).

S. Gil Araujo (2007) 'Discursos políticos sobre la nación en las políticas catalanas de integración de inmigrantes' in R. Zapata-Barrero and T. van Dijk (eds) *Discursos sobre la inmigración en España: los medios de comunicación, los parlamentos y las administraciones.* (Barcelona: CIDOB Foundation).

R. Gunther and L.J. Diamond (2001) *Political Parties and Democracy.* (Maryland: John Hopkins University Press).

E. Hepburn (2009a) 'Regionalist Party Mobilisation on Immigration', *West European Politics,* 32(3): 514–535.

E. Hepburn (2009b) 'Introduction: Re-conceptualizing Sub-state Mobilization', *Regional and Federal Studies,* 19(4): 477–499.

E. Hepburn (2011) 'Citizens of the Region? Party Conceptions of Regional Citizenship and Immigrant Integration', *European Journal of Political Research,* 50(4): 504–529.

M. Ignatieff (1995) *Blood and Belonging: Journeys into the New Nationalism.* (New York: Noonday Press).

W. Kymlicka (1999) 'Misunderstanding Nationalism' in R. Beiner (ed.) *Theorizing Nationalism.* (Albany: State University of New York Press).

W. Kymlicka (2001) *Politics in the Vernacular.* (Oxford: Oxford University Press).

W. Kymlicka and A. Patten (2003) *Language Rights and Political Theory.* (Oxford: OUP).

M. Labelle (2004) 'The Language of Race? Identity Options, and Belonging in the Quebec Context' in *Social Inequalities in Comparative Perspective* (Oxford: Blackwell Publishing Ltd).

M. Labelle, J. Couture and F. Remiggi (eds) (2012) *La communauté politique en question. Regards croisés sur l'immigration, la citoyenneté, la diversité et le pouvoir.* (Québec: Presses de l'Université du Québec).

A. Lecours, A. (2000) 'Ethnic and Civic Nationalism: Towards a New Dimension', *Space and Polity,* 4(2): 153–166.

M.S. Leith and D. Soule (2012) *Political Discourse and National Identity in Scotland.* (Edinburgh: Edinburgh University Press).

P. Loobuyck and D. Jacobs (2011) 'How to Understand the Peculiar Public Discourse on Immigration and Integration in Flanders?' in M. Huysseune (ed.) *Contemporary Centrifugal Regionalism: Comparing Flanders and Northern Italy.* (Brussels: Koninklijke Vlaamse Academie van Belgie voor Wetenschappen en Kunsten).

E. Massetti (2009) 'Explaining Regionalist Party Positioning in a Multi-dimensional Ideological Space: A Framework for Analysis', *Regional & Federal Studies,* 19(4): 501.

G. Sartori (2005) *Parties and Party Systems: A Framework for Analysis.* (Colchester: ECPR).

A.D. Smith (1971) *Theories of Nationalism.* (London: Duckworth).

R. Taras (1998) 'Nations and Language Building: Old Theories, Contemporary Cases', *Nationalism and Ethnic Politics,* 4(3): 79–101.

C. Whithol de Wenden and R. Zapata-Barrero (2011) 'Pourquoi la Catalogne intéresse-t-elle l'Europe ?', *Migrations Société,* 23(134–135): 49–55.

R. Zapata-Barrero (2003) 'The "Discovery" of Immigration in Spain. The Politicization of Immigration in the Case of El Ejido', *Journal of Internacional Migration and Integration,* 4, Autumn; 523–539.

R. Zapata-Barrero (ed.) (2009) *Immigration and Self-government of Minority Nations*. (Brussels: P.I.E. Peter Lang).

R. Zapata-Barrero (2012a) *Una ètica política mínima de la immigració a Catalunya*. *Cohesió, autogovern, llengua i frontera*. (Barcelona: Proteus).

R. Zapata-Barrero (2012b) 'La communauté politique en tant que fondement d'une théorie politique catalane de l'immigration. Enjeux clés' in M. Labelle, J. Couture and F. Remiggi (eds) *La communauté politique en question. Regards croisés sur l'immigration, la citoyenneté, la diversité et le pouvoir*. (Québec: PUQ).

R. Zapata-Barrero (2012c) 'Integration Immigration Governance Policies in Spain: A Practical Philosophy' in J. Frideres and M. Burstein (eds) *International Perspectives: Integration and Inclusion*. (Kingston-Montréal: McGill-Queen's University Press).

R. Zapata-Barrero (2012d) 'Catalan Autonomy-building Process in Immigration Policy: Conceptual, Institutional and Normative Dimensions' in A. Gagnon and M. Keating (eds) *Political Autonomy and Divided Societies. Imagining Democratic Alternatives in Complex Settings*. (Gordonsville, Virginia: Palgrave Macmillan).

R. Zapata-Barrero (2013) *Diversity Management in Spain: New Dimensions, New Challenges*. (Manchester: Manchester University Press).

Newspapers

(2009) 'Quien tiene ganas de luchar destaca rápido – Entrevista a Lluís Bassat', *El País – Extra Publicidad*, 18.

(2012) 'Catalunya garantirà l'atenció sanitària als sensepapers, malgrat el decret espanyol que ho prohibeix', *Ara*, 09/05/2012.

14
Conclusion: Exploring the Contours of a Theory of Immigration *in Multilevel States*

Ricard Zapata-Barrero and Eve Hepburn

This book explores the politics of immigration in multilevel states from two viewpoints: governance and political parties. Six multilevel countries have been examined in depth: Belgium (Flanders and Wallonia), Spain (Catalonia), Canada (Quebec), the United Kingdom (Scotland), Italy (Lombardy, Emilia-Romagna, Veneto and Calabria), Germany (Bavaria), together with the unitary state of the Netherlands and its two competing cities (Amsterdam and Rotterdam). In both the Governance and Political Parties Parts, the cases have drawn on a broad range of methodological approaches and perspectives on the relationship between territory and immigration.

Through each case study we can identify some common issues and challenges appearing in governance mechanisms and party competition, which can help us draw the first contours of a potential theory. Given the fact that the state of the art on this debate, which links the multilevel politics literature with immigration studies, is still in its infancy, the contours are necessarily exploratory. Let us first overview the main arguments developed in each Part before, secondly, identifying what we consider can be the premises of a theory. We will conclude by outlining some paths for further research.

Main issues in governance and political parties

Governance issues in multilevel settings are centred on the 'who governs?' question, since, as all of the case studies have shown, there is an essential tension in governance between 'who decides' (decision-making policy process) and 'who does' (implementation process). This picture is obviously complex and multifaceted, especially when the sub-state units are involved (or claim to be) in the decision-making process, and their policy preferences do not coincide with those of the central state. In this context, conflict may arise in most dimensions of immigration and integration policies: namely, key border issues such as access to the territory (admissions policy) and to membership (citizenship policies), and particular categories related to integration and accommodation of diversity on the grounds of linguistic, cultural, or economic interests. This complexity is multifaceted since it involves multiple directions of the multilevel interaction system: on the one hand, horizontal interactions among the same level of government (among local, among regional, and/or national/federal governments) and vertical ones between each sub-state government (be it regional/national or local) and central governments; on the other hand, internal interactions between one level of government and its own society.

Following this framework of analysis, some key foundational questions combining what Zapata-Barrero and Barker in Chapter 2 call the 'Structure and Policy' level of analysis have been addressed in the different case studies, which we shall briefly overview to highlight the main findings that can contribute to this exploratory theory.

Opening the Governance dimension, Chapter 4, written by Adam and Jacobs, outlines an important normative issue: in multilevel states, with a federal structure and multinational nature such as Belgium, two governance systems can work in parallel in different ways to interpret immigration challenges to their own society, and as a result two different policy focuses (and philosophies) can coexist. This seems to be unique with regard to other multinational states such as Canada, the United Kingdom, or Spain. The Belgian case study shows that the absence of horizontal and/or vertical intergovernmental cooperation in a structure of governance hinders the emergence of shared immigration policies. This in part affects the democratic dimension signalled at the end of the interpretive framework proposed by Zapata-Barrero and Barker in Chapter 2, since each side of the linguistic border also differentiates immigrants' rights within the Belgian state. The only minimum shared policy is access to citizenship. This lack of coordination weakens policy efficiency. The authors also highlight an important factor in need of further research: how the Europeanization of integration policies might alter the centrifugal tendencies of immigration governance in Belgium. In general, the tendency is that Europeanization stimulates regional policy convergence, bringing the party positions of the Francophone and Flemish sides closer together.

The authors conclude that Europe might thus constitute a centripetal force in multilevel states.

Chapter 5, written by Iacovino, makes visible the fragmentation of the governance regime in multilevel states through an analysis of the competing national projects in Canada and Quebec. The author shows very clearly how there can be competing host societies employing the tools of social and political integration in their respective national projects basically centred on language. This tension, again, challenges citizenship boundaries, mainly when there is an asymmetry in terms of the powers to drive integration policies. Another interesting contribution of Iacovino's analysis centres on the role of ideology, which he identifies as a driver of centralized markers of citizenship. Ideology then plays a functional role in drawing policy priorities in selection and settlement in multilevel states with competing national projects.

The comparative study of Arrighi de Casanova between Catalonia and Scotland in Chapter 6 gives light to new dimensions, especially in the case of multinational states where there is central government reluctance to share sovereignty on essential issues such as admissions policies (the question of how many and who enters) and citizenship acquisition. It corroborates a core assumption of the heuristic model on governance in multilevel states proposed in Chapter 2: the question of 'who governs' is likely to be particularly salient in a multinational context in which access to the territory and membership boundaries are essentially contested as a result of the ongoing dynamics of rival nation-building projects. This absence of policy transfer is also particularly evident when both 'national-questions' were hardly touched upon during the parliamentary debates that preceded major constitutional reforms, which included the formal distribution of immigration powers (1998 for the UK and Scotland; 1978 for Spain and Catalonia). Beyond political arguments, there are also economic ones which play, in Arrighi's view, an essential role in the blame-avoidance/credit-claiming discursive strategies, since nationalist elites have to convince their constituencies that further political autonomy does not undermine their economic prospects.

Caponio and Campomori's Chapter 7 gives us again renewed evidence that one of the main governance challenges in multilevel states, such as Italy this time, is the complex patchwork of centre-periphery/state-society relations with different policy frames which directly contradict the principle of coherence that is supposed to normatively inspire the governance of immigration in multilevel settings. This complexity is even more evident when we add local governments to the multilevel governance framework. Regions not only have different rhetoric and policy discourses, stemming from the political ideologies of governing parties, but they also leave local-level horizontal governance considerable room to manoeuvre, with the result that local reception policies can vary across municipalities and territories in the same region. This lack of coherence is coupled with the weakness of the coordination principle. Another interesting input is that this fragmentation and incoherence among regions and cities leaves room for nurturing the rhetoric of anti-immigrant political parties. The full argument is quite suggestive: with structural and policy governance incoherencies, fragmentation in reception policies can freely drive exclusionary practices with the support of the electorate which channels these contradictions in negative terms towards immigrants. The challenge of migrant integration, and of the changing attitudes of the electorate, is most keenly felt in this case.

Finally, to close the Governance Part, Scholten's findings in Chapter 8 show that multilevel governance is not an exclusive issue in decentralized states, but can also frame the immigration agenda of unitary states such as the Netherlands. Here we go from sub-state regional and/or national territories to the local level. The analyses of Rotterdam and Amsterdam show that local policies have sometimes taken very different turns compared to the higher levels of territorial governance. Responding to local (political, policy problem) circumstances, they develop their own migrant integration policies that do not necessarily accord with national policies. Just as there are no national-state models of integration there also does not seem to be one local model of integration. Scholten's chapter also reveals horizontal fragmentation of policy responsibilities and policy dynamics over time. Central models assume consistent and coherent national policy discourses and coordination mechanisms, but reality shows that the institutional responsibility for migrant integration has been fragmented between sectoral departments and contested over time. Finally, it remains an empirical question of whether the multilevel dynamics of migrant integration policy-making entails effective forms of multilevel governance. Decoupling and policy conflicts seem to have been much more characteristic of national-local policy relations than effective forms of multilevel governance.

The next Part on *Political Parties* considers the role of agency in the politics of immigration in multilevel states. In particular, it addresses key issues relating to how parties at multiple levels – in particular at the central-state and sub-state-regional levels – position themselves on the immigration dimension. It relates to the Governance Part in an important way; political parties form governments at each level, thereby becoming the main actors designing and implementing immigration policies. The position of political parties on immigration therefore shapes the policy programmes of government, whereby party approaches to immigration are affected by internal dimensions – such as their ideology, including their stance on socioeconomic (left-right) issues, and their conceptualization of the nation/multilevel state – as well as external dimensions – such as the dynamics of the party or electoral system or special structural characteristics of the territorial unit in question.

We can therefore identify several issues that may influence party positioning on immigration in multilevel states at the regional and central-state level. These variables were presented in Hepburn's conceptual framework in Chapter 3, which included hypotheses on (1) demography, (2) economy, (3) language/culture, (4) party ideology (in left-right terms), (5) electoral system, (6) degree of party polarization on immigration, and (7) degree of control over immigration policy at the regional/ state level. Let us now consider how these hypotheses have been verified – or falsified – in the case studies to see whether we can detect some general trends.

Opening the discussion on Political Parties, Chapter 9, written by Schmidtke and Zaslove, offers a rich and compelling analysis of the politicization of migration at both the regional and state levels in Italy and Germany. Their findings offer a resounding confirmation that the regional politics of immigration diverges not only from the state level, but also that there is significant variation between regions of the same state on this issue. For example, party approaches to immigration in Catholic conservative Bavaria are as different to those of post-industrial, multicultural North Rhine Westphalia as 'white' Lombard approaches are to those of 'red' Emilia-Romagna. In their careful analysis of regional heterogeneity, Schmidtke and Zaslove address four of the hypotheses laid out in the conceptual framework of Chapter 3. First, their findings demonstrate that the 'economy' hypothesis holds some weight in Italy and Germany: in the rich regions of Lombardy and Bavaria, immigrants tend to be viewed as a drain on resources, while they are viewed more positively as economic assets in the less wealthy regions of NRW and ER. Second, the cases reveal that culture/language may be employed as a 'barrier' to immigration, evident in the party platforms of the Lega Nord and the Bavarian CSU. Third, party polarization on immigration plays an important role, with the unenthusiastic stance of the two aforementioned 'regionalist' parties creating a negative political climate on immigration. Finally, left-right ideology is seen to play a role to some extent as centre-left parties in Italy and Germany tend to be more tolerant of, or enthusiastic about, immigration than their centre-right rivals. However, centre-right regionalist parties like the CSU must refrain from an all-out anti-immigrant approach for fear of alienating the important business community.

Chapter 10 by Dandoy makes an important theoretical contribution to the literature, by challenging the assumption that immigration is an exclusively 'national' issue that is associated with extreme-right parties. Instead, Dandoy marshals a wealth of evidence – both quantitative and qualitative – to reveal how parties in Belgium rate the importance of immigration in their respective regions. In doing so, he considers three hypotheses on party stances on immigration. First, he argues that confrontational politics is key in Belgium, whereby extreme-right parties at the regional level (*Vlaams Belang* and *Front National*) have had a huge impact on other party positions, leading to significant polarization. But it is not the only factor: the economic context also plays a role, whereby Flanders is an example of a flourishing economy where there is a strong politics of anti-immigration, while poorer Wallonia is not as polarized. Finally, analysis of the Belgian parties reveals few left-right differences on immigration. Overall, the parties have common positions (emphasizing democracy and rights), though the right-wing parties tend to emphasize law-and-order issues while left-wing parties tend to emphasize social policy issues. Therefore ideology is not a key determinant of immigration positions in Belgium. The paper also demonstrates that immigration is not exclusively 'owned' by the extreme-right; instead, this issue is prevalent in the discourse of the mainstream liberal party family, as well as the regionalist party family. But while liberals respond to the extreme-right in a reactionary form of politics, Dandoy demonstrates that the regionalist party family has *always* had a stake in migration issues, independent of other party positions, and indeed, this mobilization on immigration even *preceded* the rise of the extreme-right.

Erk's Chapter 11 considers the Belgian case from a different angle in a qualitative comparison with Quebec. His primary focus is on how regional electoral systems have shaped the positioning of regionalist parties on immigration. Erk thus tests the hypothesis that first-past-the-post (majoritarian or FPTP) systems encourage parties to view immigration in a more positive light than proportional representation (PR) systems. His analysis of the oft-forgotten advantages of the FPTP system is an important contribution to the literature. In Quebec, the FPTP system has encouraged parties to steer a middle course on immigration to attract the largest number of votes and thereby ward off extreme party polarization, while the PR system in Flanders has encouraged the growth of more exclusive parties which could afford to adopt anti-immigrant positions without undermining their electoral chances. However, the electoral system is not the only issue that has affected party positioning: cultural identity has also been of great significance. But while Quebec nationalists, in keeping with the need to appeal to voters across the political system, have portrayed language as a vehicle for the integration of newcomers (in similarity to the Catalans – see below); in Flanders, nationalists have adopted a populist discourse that appeals to their core voters, whereby Flemish is perceived as under threat by immigrants learning French.

Moving on to another 'stateless nation', Hepburn and Rosie in Chapter 12 examine why parties in Scotland have – in contrast to their UK counterparts – adopted such positive positions on immigration. They test four of the hypotheses presented in Chapter 3 – focussing on demography, culture/identity, party polarization, and policy control – all of which they find have some explanatory power in this case. The perceived 'demographic crisis' has led Scottish parties to highlight the need for higher levels of immigration; the low barriers to becoming Scottish (including the emphasis on residency and lack of a strong indigenous language – unlike Quebec, Flanders or Catalonia) has encouraged parties to support an inclusive 'One Scotland' conception of the nation; the lack of anti-immigrant parties and the overwhelmingly pro-immigration approach of the SNP has nullified party polarization on this issue; and Scotland's lack of policy control over immigration have made it less of a 'hot potato' than in UK politics. These factors have led to an elite political consensus that immigration is an unconditionally positive thing for Scotland, placing it in serious tension with their more sceptical UK counterparts.

Finally, to round up the Political Parties Part, Chapter 13 by Franco-Guillén and Zapata-Barrero explores the relationship between civic nationalism and political discourse on immigration in Catalonia. As in Scotland, a consensus exists on immigration between the main political parties in Catalonia. This is reflected in particular in the stances of the two leading nationalist parties, CiU and ERC, which have advanced a more civic conceptualization of the Catalan nation that is reflected in their positive stance towards immigrants. This party consensus helps underpin Catalonia's self-understanding as a 'Land of Welcome' and has ensured that the success of anti-immigrant parties is kept to a low. This finding corroborates the hypotheses set out in the conceptual framework of Chapter 3 that immigration is viewed more positively by parties if the predominant SNRP(s) are in favour of immigration and if there are low levels of party polarization on immigration. Furthermore, this case highlights the key role that language has played in party discourse. However, rather than viewing immigration as a threat to the Catalan language, parties have perceived the language as a vehicle for the integration and equality of immigrants in Catalan society, and have applauded the willingness of newcomers to learn the language – thereby verifying the language/culture hypothesis. Finally, the authors consider the importance of left-right ideology in determining immigration positions. But while the right-wing PPC confirms this hypothesis in its negative stance towards immigration, the pro-immigration position of the centre-right regionalist CiU demonstrates that ideology is not a reliable causal factor.

Drawing the contours for an exploratory theory of multilevel immigration: governance and political parties in perspective

What are the key drivers of a theory of multilevel immigration politics? As we have shown in the overview of the main findings, several arguments have appeared in this book which can help shape the first contours of an exploratory theory. Let us infer eight contours based on the Governance and Political Parties frameworks:

1. *Identifying the main political cleavages:* Perhaps one of the most basic premises is the fact that immigration politics in multilevel states can nurture the permanent challenge between centre and periphery. In other words, the deployment of immigration politics into a multilevel structure of governance can contribute to shaping the centre-periphery cleavage. This is an even more powerful argument in those multilevel states with multinational realities such as the United Kingdom, Spain, Quebec, and even Belgium. Competing host societies can drive the fragmentation of the governance system, and then the divided societies can compete for attracting immigrants to their own national projects. This has happened, for instance, in settings where linguistic competences are important such as Quebec and Catalonia. This centre-periphery tension challenges citizenship boundaries and makes visible the ideology behind citizenship membership projects. This is why in these multinational states identity tensions prevail over efficiency issues, with the latter being much more appropriate as policy drivers in nationally homogeneous multilevel states.

2. *Identifying the main explanatory factors driving centrifugal/centripetal forces:* Immigration policy can become a dependent variable for explaining multilevel dynamics towards more centralization (centripetal force) or decentralization (centrifugal force) when other external variables intervene. We can then argue, as a second premise, that immigration can take centrifugal or centripetal directions in divided societies, which is conditioned by external factors. As some contributors have shown (for instance Adam and Jacobs in Chapter 4), at least two external factors have been identified, such as the Europeanization of immigration policies, which play a clear centripetal force; or national identity-building processes of sub-state territories, which plays a centrifugal force. Other external factors are less clear, such as the economic interest of sub-states which can be either a centripetal or a centrifugal factor, depending on other factors such as the economic situation of the whole country.

3. *Understanding the cohabitation of different (and most of the time, incoherent) immigration policies, but also its effects from a democratic point of view:* As some contributors have argued (in particular Schmidtke and Zaslove in Chapter 9), sub-state politics do not merely mirror national politics. They often show a distinct logic regarding how migration-related issues are employed in competitive party politics and policy-making. Different philosophies are then possible in multilevel governance, but then some democratic challenges arise since immigrants in the same territorial state and jurisdiction can have different systems of rights, which is at odds with the concept of freedom of mobility within the same territory. In this framework, some contributions have shown that different policy frames can contradict the principle of coherence, both vertically and horizontally, mainly from a local perspective. The lack of coherence is coupled with the weakness of the coordination principle together with fragmentation, and this can nurture both an anti-immigrant rhetoric and negative public opinion towards immigrants and governments.

4. *Crossing borders into multilevel and multinational states: territory and belonging:* There are several dimensions at play related to border issues (understood in a broad sense, both in terms of territory and full citizenship). As some contributors have shown, we use a framework of shared sovereignty and competing host societies. It is difficult to manage border issues in a way that reflects the diversity of multinational states, since admissions policies are generally in the hands of the central state acting as a single homogeneous nation. The answer to the basic question of *who enters* the territory and *how many*

is monopolized by the central state alone. This unitary authority also extends to the management of renewals, temporary and permanent immigrant work and residence permits, and even the language of documents. Finally, there is also the codification of individuals' rights and duties in terms of *citizenship*. The citizenship code can present a conceptual challenge, since in a multinational state it needs to break the equation of 'one citizenship with one nation'. Here the notion of *multiple citizenship* assumes a practical meaning, which needs to be discussed in the debate about multinational states. In any case, competing host societies can drive fragmentation of the governance system, whereby divided societies compete to attract immigrants into their own national projects.

5. *Understanding the multilevel competitive party context of immigration:* In multilevel states, parties must compete in several electoral systems at different levels – state, regional, local – that have different dynamics and characteristics. Like any issue of electoral salience, immigration is refracted in different ways in different territorial systems according to the political culture of that unit and the dynamics of party competition. Importantly, party polarization has emerged as the most important variable determining party positions on immigration at any territorial level, having been positively tested in all of the case studies. In particular, the existence of extreme-right parties and stateless nationalist and regionalist parties on any territorial level – two party families that, as Dandoy demonstrates, clearly have a 'stake' in the immigration issue – can have an important 'contagion' effect on the immigration positions of other parties and sway the general discourse on immigration in a positive or negative fashion. There are therefore multiple territorial contexts in which immigration is debated in multilevel states, and there is significant evidence – especially in multinational states – that sub-state regional competition differs from statewide party competition. Furthermore, party competition is closely tied to the electoral system, whereby PR systems are more likely to encourage (though not in all cases; see Hepburn/Rosie on Scotland for a counter-example) less consensus and a more fragmented approach to immigration in the party system, and rewarding anti-immigrant positions.

6. *Exploring the importance of dominant and minority languages, cultures, and identities in party positions and policies on immigration.* While in homogenous nation-states such as Japan, one only has to consider the effect of one language, culture, and identity on the immigration positions on political parties, in multilevel (and especially multinational)

states it is necessary to take into account the dominant statewide *and* minority national/regional cultures. For immigration is viewed through different prisms in different cultures, especially when the minority culture/language is seen to be under threat by the majority. However, this is only one story. It was shown in this collection that language can be perceived as a vehicle for, as well as a barrier to, migrant integration by political parties at different levels. This was particularly true in the cases of Catalonia and Quebec, whereby there was a general consensus amongst parties that the minority Catalan and French languages should be used to encourage the positive integration of newcomers (though there are differences in the extent to which SNRPs in these two cases believe this should be a voluntary or mandatory process) and whereby linguistic competence can ensure the equality of opportunities, rather than simply blaming immigrants for bolstering the dominant Spanish/Canadian culture if they choose to integrate into the dominant language and culture.

7. *Identifying the role that a party's ideology or 'worldview' plays in shaping its approach to immigration:* The stance of a political party towards immigration is clearly influenced by its broader 'worldview', through which its responses to different policy challenges are filtered. This includes both the left-right ideological position of a party, as well as its territorial perspective. With regard to the former, the socioeconomic positions of parties often do correlate with a particular stance on immigration, with centre-left parties tending to link it more with social policy concerns, and centre-right parties focussing more on law-and-order issues (as revealed by party manifestos in Dandoy's chapter). However, it is more difficult to prove that centre-left parties are, on the whole, more positive about immigration than centre-right parties – as numerous cases have demonstrated (such as the pro-immigrant CiU in Catalonia and Christian Democrats in NRW or the shift of the Labour Party towards a more critical stance in the UK). Therefore, immigration does not map neatly onto the left-right divide; instead we must analyse all aspects of the party's worldview to explain its position on immigration (such as the conservative Bavarian CSU's reluctance to espouse full-out anti-immigrant rhetoric for fear of upsetting its international business investors). One important, and often under-studied, aspect of a party's worldview and attitude towards immigration is its conceptionalization of the nation. Indeed, nationalism is often understood as an ideology in its own right, which shapes a nationalist movement's position on other policy issues. Thus, a party's position on immigration is strongly affected by

its attitude towards the nation – be it a homogenous or plural self-understanding, otherwise known as a 'civic or ethnic' conceptualization of the nation, as argued in Franco-Guillén and Zapata-Barrero's chapter – leading to more or less tolerance of ethnic diversity.

8. *Understanding regional innovation and the tensions and divergence between regional and statewide parties on immigration matters.* In the multilevel governance literature, scholars have tended to perceive only a 'top-down' impact of politics and policies, that is, from the (European level to the) state level to the regional level, and so on. However, this collection has revealed that these impacts are not unidimensional: rather, there is clearly bottom-up regional party innovation on immigration, which has affected statewide party politics. This was clearly evident in the Schmidtke/Zaslove and Hepburn/Rosie chapters, whereby parties at the regional level in Northern Italy, Emilia-Romagna, Bavaria, NRW, and Scotland have not only chosen individual approaches to immigration, but have influenced statewide party positions. Indeed, regional branches of statewide parties, as well as SNRPs, often pursue more open, progressive and pragmatic approaches to immigration than statewide parties, who are more likely to link immigration to security concerns. This underlines an important factor affecting party positions: how the party itself is internally organized. Regional branches of statewide parties have often departed from their 'parent' parties to pursue a distinct immigration approach at the regional/sub-state nation level. However, when they are unable to carve out their own niche within the general party structure, this acts as a serious constraint on the self-positioning of parties on immigration at the regional level, who are unable to portray themselves as parties standing up for 'territorial interests'. This can be a significant electoral hindrance if they face competition from a stateless nationalist or regionalist party (SNRP), which claims to 'exclusively' represent the interests of the region – including on issues relating to the all-important demographic/ethnic make-up of the nation.

Paths for further research

The findings of this chapter legitimize further inquiry into the dynamics of migrant integration policies and party competition dynamics in multilevel settings. Let us draw the first premises that can help to drive pathways for further research.

Firstly, the entrance of the politics of immigration into multilevel governance shows there is a distinction that we have to take into account, since it implies different ways to react to the necessary policy transfer process. There are two multilevel governance regimes: multinational and multi-territorial. The first presents a higher degree of complexity and conflict since immigration policy is basically developed with the added value of being an identity policy and lies at the heart of national sovereignty (decisions taken and also questions posed can differ among two national projects, relating to two competing host societies). The difference between multinational and mononational states is then meaningful.

Secondly, immigration politics can have different effects when they take place in consolidated and less-consolidated multilevel states, or those that are still in the process of being defined by their decentralized structure, such as in Spain. Some countries such as the United States, Australia, or Canada have been shaped by taking immigrants into account. In some cases, immigration policies have come later but have been incorporated into a consolidated and already-existing federal/multilevel structure without any multinational dimension (such as Germany), or even with a multinational structure, but with a strict division of territory along language lines such as in Switzerland and Belgium. So Spain/Catalonia and the United Kingdom/Scotland are multilevel states where the entrance of immigration politics coincides with the historical process of defining its multilevel governance structure and nation-building project.

Thirdly, there are several pathways for further enquiry on the party politics of immigration in multilevel states. These include (a) exploring the extent to which SNRPs have made immigration a core issue and their subsequent impact on other party stances, (b) unpacking the relationship/tensions between regional branches and their statewide 'parent' parties on the question of immigration, (c) examining how a party's worldview affects its position on immigration at different territorial levels, and (d) exploring the ways in which political parties seek to appeal to, and engage with, immigrant communities in different regional/national contexts. On the latter point in particular, there remains an open question of whether political parties at the regional level are more active in incorporating immigrants into their activities than at the national level – given the alleged proximity of regional parties to 'the people'. Addressing these issues would greatly enhance our understanding of whether the multilevel governance of immigration policies and party politics may or may not provide stronger underpinnings for the creation of more representative, participatory and inclusive democracies.

Index

Printed and bound by CPI Group (UK) Ltd, Croydon, CR0 4YY